ICONS OF CRIME FIGHTING

ICONS OF CRIME FIGHTING

Relentless Pursuers Of Justice

VOLUME 2

Edited by Jeffrey B. Bumgarner

Greenwood Icons

GREENWOOD PRESS
Westport, Connecticut · London

Library of Congress Cataloging-in-Publication Data

Icons of crime fighting : relentless pursuers of justice / edited by Jeffrey Bumgarner.
    p. cm.
    Includes bibliographical references and index.
    ISBN-13: 978-0-313-34129-8 ((set) : alk. paper)
    ISBN-13: 978-0-313-34130-4 ((vol. 1) : alk. paper)
    ISBN-13: 978-0-313-34131-1 ((vol. 2) : alk. paper)
    1. Law enforcement—United States—History. 2. Crime prevention—United
States—History. 3. Criminal investigation—United States—History. 4. Criminal
justice, Administration of—United States—History. 5. Personality and history. I.
Bumgarner, Jeffrey B.
    HV8138.I36   2008
    363.2092′273—dc22   2008018447

British Library Cataloguing in Publication Data is available.

Library of Congress Catalog Card Number: 2008018447
ISBN-13: 978-0-313-34129-8 (set)
        978-0-313-34130-4 (vol. 1)
        978-0-313-34131-1 (vol. 2)

First published in 2008

Greenwood Press, 88 Post Road West, Westport, CT 06881
An imprint of Greenwood Publishing Group, Inc.
www.greenwood.com

Printed in the United States of America

The paper used in this book complies with the
Permanent Paper Standard issued by the National
Information Standards Organization (Z39.48–1984).

10   9   8   7   6   5   4   3   2   1

Icons of Crime Fighting is dedicated to all the individuals who have made it their life's work to fight crime and injustice in the United States and elsewhere. While this publication recounts the service of many individuals who are well known for this fight and are deserving of accolades, there are countless more men and women who work visibly in their own communities or behind the scenes in all realms of the criminal justice system—as police officers, federal agents, prosecutors, victims' advocates, social workers, etc. They too are deserving of tribute. This book set is for them.

Contents

Volume 2

Photos

Sculptured bust portrait of James Butler "Wild Bill" Hickock, atop tombstone (page 1), Deadwood, SD. © 2008 Chaiba.

Dodge City Peace Commission, 1882 (page 2). From left to right, members are shown as follows. Back row: W. H. Harris, Luke Short and Bat Masterson. Front row: Charles Bassett, Wyatt Earp, F. McClain and Neil Brown. Courtesy AP Images.

Allan Pinkerton of Antietam (page 27), MD, 1884. Courtesy of the Library of Congress.

Hon. James Francis Miller of Texas (page 57), ca. 1875. Courtesy of the Library of Congress.

Captain Samuel Hamilton Walker (page 58), ca. 1846. Courtesy of the Library of Congress.

August Vollmer (page 83), 1929. © Corbis/Bettmann.

J. Edgar Hoover (page 117), 1969. Courtesy of the Library of Congress.

Special prosecutor Thomas E. Dewey (page 143), holds up his right hand as he is sworn in by Supreme Court Justice Philip J. McCook in New York City, 1935. Courtesy AP Images.

Robert Kennedy (page 167), appearing before the Platform Committee, 1964. Courtesy of the Library of Congress.

Jim Garrison (page 197), who stands 6-foot-6, towers over assistants James Alcock, right, and Andrew "Moo Moo" Sciambra as they huddle prior to the trial of Clay Shaw, Jan. 16, 1969. Courtesy AP Images.

Sheriff Buford Pusser of Tennessee (page 235), shortly before he was killed in a suspicious car crash, 1998. © Getty Images.

From the 1971 film "The French Connection", directed by William Friedkin. Shown from left: Sonny Grosso as Det. Phil Klein, Eddie Egan as Lt. Walter Simonson (page 257). Courtesy of Photofest.

Washington Post writers Carl Bernstein, left, and Robert Woodward (page 291), who pressed the Watergate investigation, are photographed in Washington, D.C., May 7, 1973. Courtesy AP Images.

New York City detective Frank Serpico (page 319), with beard, sits in front of his attorney, Ramsey Clark, at the Knapp Commission's investigation of alleged police corruption at a hearing in New York, 1971. Courtesy AP Images/Jim Wells.

Joe Pistone (page 343), the American F.B.I agent upon whom the film 'Donnie Brasco' was based, 1997. © Fotos International/Getty Images.

Deputy District Attorneys Aaron Stovitz (left) and Vincent Bugliosi (page 371), display an aerial photograph of the home of Leno and Rosemary LaBianca. Courtesy of Photofest.

The death of the prime suspect in the kidnapping and murder of 6-year-old Adam Walsh (page 421), shown in this 1981 file photo, doesn't close the still-unsolved case. Police believed Ottis Elwood Toole killed Adam, who disappeared from outside a Hollywood, Florida shopping mall in 1981. Courtesy AP Images.

John Douglas working in his Virginia office (page 437), 2002. Larry Stone Photography.

Maricopa County Sheriff Joe Arpaio (page 463), speaks during a news conference in Avondale, AZ. The conference was held May 10, 2006, to kick off the beginning of the sheriffs' departments efforts to find illegal immigrants. Courtesy AP Images/Roy Dabner.

Former police Detective Mark Fuhrman (page 493), shown testifying at the O. J. Simpson trial, March 10, 1995. Courtesy AP Images/John McCoy.

U.S. Attorney Rudolph Giuliani (page 521), talks to media in New York City, Dec. 13, 1984. Courtesy AP Images/Debbie Hodgson.

Radio talk show personality and Guardian Angels founder Curtis Sliwa, center (page 553), enters Manhattan federal court in New York surrounded by other Guardian Angel members, Feb. 27, 2006. Courtesy AP Images/Louis Lanzano.

Forensic scientist Dr. Henry C. Lee (page 577), shows the court a cotton swab similar to the one he used to collect evidence from the crime scene at music producer Phil Spector's home, during Spector's murder trial for the murder of actress Lana Clarkson, 2007. Courtesy AP Images/Paul Buck, Pool.

Dr. Bill Bass (page 605), carefully cleans a skull before examining it in his laboratory at the at the University of Tennessee in Knoxville. Courtesy of the University of Tennessee.

Series Foreword

Worshipped and cursed. Loved and loathed. Obsessed about the world over. What does it take to become an icon? Regardless of subject, culture, or era, the requisite qualifications are the same: (1) challenge the status quo, (2) influence millions, and (3) impact history.

Using these criteria, Greenwood Press introduces a new reference format and approach to popular culture. Spanning a wide range of subjects, volumes in the Greenwood Icons series provide students and general readers a port of entry into the most fascinating and influential topics of the day. Every two-volume title offers an in-depth look at approximately 24 iconic figures, each of which captures the essence of a broad subject. These icons typically embody a group of values, elicit strong reactions, reflect the essence of a particular time and place, and link different traditions and periods. Among those featured are artists and activists, superheroes and spies, inventors and athletes—the legends and mythmakers of entire generations. Yet icons can also come from unexpected places: as the heroine who transcends the pages of a novel or as the revolutionary idea that shatters our previously held beliefs. Whether people, places, or things, such icons serve as a bridge between the past and the present, the canonical and the contemporary. By focusing on icons central to popular culture, this series encourages students to appreciate cultural diversity and critically analyze issues of enduring significance.

Most importantly, these books are as entertaining as they are provocative. Is Disneyland a more influential icon of the American West than Las Vegas? How do ghosts and ghouls reflect our collective psyche? Is Barry Bonds an inspiring or deplorable icon of baseball? Designed to foster debate, the series serves as a unique resource that is ideal for paper writing or report purposes. Insightful, in-depth entries provide far more information than conventional reference articles but are less intimidating and more accessible than a book-length biography. The most revered and reviled icons of American and world history are brought to life with related sidebars, timelines, fact boxes, and quotations. Authoritative entries are accompanied by bibliographies, making these titles an ideal starting point for further research. Spanning a wide range of popular topics, including business, literature, civil rights, politics, music, and more, books in the Greenwood Icons series provide fresh insights for the student and popular reader into the power and influence of icons, a topic of as vital interest today as in any previous era.

Preface

Americans have always been fascinated by the social problem of crime and society's response to it. This fascination is easily diagnosed by the number of murder mysteries that have been published over the ages, the fictional and nonfictional police television shows peppered throughout the network and cable channels, and the innumerable cinematic productions that focus on police officers, detectives, and federal agents marching through adversity to make the case and thwart the violent criminal villain.

Indeed, much of what Americans and others around the world know about crime fighting has been learned through these mediums. This often results in an incomplete, and in many cases, inaccurate, understanding of crime fighting and crime fighters. Criminal investigators and prosecutors are in wide agreement, for example, that securing a conviction in certain types of criminal cases has been hampered by popular television. The so-called "CSI effect" has resulted in many juries harboring an expectation that there will be significant scientific evidence in every serious case to link an alleged offender to the crime, just as on television. The fact is that most crimes continue to be solved through old-fashioned police work, eyewitness accounts, solid suspect interviews, and other circumstantial evidence. Most cases do not involve definitive forensic evidence, and certainly most cases are not resolved in the span of a sixty-minute television show (where none of the cops take notes, suspects' rights are marginalized, search warrants materialize out of thin air, and the offenders always seem willing to talk to the police in custody without an attorney).

In *Icons of Crime Fighting*, and in keeping with America's fascination with criminal justice and criminal investigation, readers are introduced to different individuals and organizations that have made significant contributions to general or particular realms of fighting crime. However, an emphasis is placed on historical accuracy and an accounting of how criminals are actually countered and thwarted. Most of the twenty-two chapters in this two-volume set relate to individuals who are noteworthy for their crime-fighting efforts and accomplishments. A few of the chapters relate to organizations that are regarded for their respective contributions to fighting crime. All of the individuals and organizations are "iconic" in the sense that people are aware of them, certainly in criminal justice circles, but also in popular culture. Their notoriety in popular culture, however, does not diminish their serious and significant professional contributions to the areas in which they operate or operated.

The two-volume set starts off with a historical chapter: "Gunfighters: U.S. Marshals of the Old West." This chapter explores the history of America's oldest federal law enforcement agency and profiles famed federal lawmen from the nineteenth century, including Wyatt Earp, Bat Masterson, and Pat Garrett. Chapter 2 continues with a nineteenth-century American historical theme by profiling Allan Pinkerton, America's most famous nonfictional private eye. Indeed, it was Pinkerton and his National Detective Agency that coined the term "private eye" to begin with. Rounding off the discussion of law enforcement in the American West and Southwest during the 1800s is Chapter 3, which focuses on the famed Texas Rangers. Texas lawmen from this organization such as W. J. McDonald (for whom the expression "one riot, one ranger" was coined) and Frank Hamer (who tracked down Bonnie and Clyde) are introduced.

Chapters 4, 5, and 6 bring readers forward into the early twentieth century. Chapter 4 profiles the life and career of August Vollmer, the most significant of police reformers. Vollmer was an early twentieth-century police chief who is credited with many innovations and approaches to crime fighting and police professionalization that are still in place today. Chapter 5 is concerned with the famous FBI director, the late J. Edgar Hoover. There is no law enforcement leader, past or present, who possesses a legacy that can rival Hoover's. This chapter also necessarily delves into the history of the Federal Bureau of Investigation, which by itself readers will find to be inherently interesting. Chapter 6 explores the career of one of New York City's most famous prosecutors, Thomas Dewey. His crime-fighting career was at its zenith during the 1930s—an accomplished career that would propel him eventually to become governor of New York and the Republican presidential candidate in 1948. Although he has been immortalized in the famous photo of President Truman holding up a *Chicago Daily Tribune* newspaper with the erroneous headline "Dewey Beats Truman" in 1948, his efforts at fighting organized crime and mobsters such as Dutch Schultz and Lucky Luciano were among his most significant accomplishments.

Beginning with Chapter 7, *Icons of Crime Fighting* shifts to more recent history, particularly the last half of the twentieth century through the present day. Chapter 7 is devoted to Robert Kennedy. Although well known as President John F. Kennedy's brother and attorney general, his service as an attorney for the U.S. Senate in the 1950s really marks the beginning of his crime-fighting career. In that capacity, he investigated the influence of organized crime in the labor unions as well as the infiltration of communists in American public service. Of course, his life tragically ended when he was assassinated as a presidential candidate in 1968. Speaking of the Kennedys, Chapter 8 examines the career and crusade of famed prosecutor Jim Garrison. He was a very well-known district attorney in New Orleans during the 1960s and 1970s, but Garrison became iconic when he prosecuted Louisiana businessman Clay Shaw as a conspirator in the John F. Kennedy assassination. Shaw was found "not guilty" by a jury after less than an hour of deliberation. Nonetheless, the case raised enough doubt about President Kennedy's death to warrant an Oliver Stone film (*JFK*) on the matter, with Kevin Costner playing the lead role—that of Jim Garrison.

Garrison isn't the only iconic individual profiled in this book about whom movies were made. Chapter 9 examines the life of Buford Pusser, the three-term sheriff of McNairy County, Tennessee, in the 1960s. His fight against the criminal element in his county inspired the movie *Walking Tall*. Pusser survived an assassination attempt in 1967, but his wife was killed in the attack. The resolve Pusser possessed to continue the fight for justice in the wake of this tragedy is truly an inspiration. Chapter 10 profiles two crime fighters: Eddie Egan and Sonnie Grosso. These two New York City police detectives were partners in the 1960s and conducted one of the most famous drug-trafficking investigations in American history. The international drug-trafficking scheme they investigated is famously known as the French Connection because of the fact that the drugs came into the United States through France. Egan and Grosso were the inspiration for the characters Jimmy "Popeye" Doyle and Sonny Russo, played by Gene Hackman and Roy Scheider, respectively, in the 1971 movie *The French Connection*.

The movies keep on rolling in Chapter 11. Here, readers will learn about the story of Bob Woodward and Carl Bernstein. The movie *All the President's Men* highlights the significance of their fight for justice in the political realm. These two *Washington Post* reporters investigated the 1972 burglary of the Democratic National Committee's office at the Watergate Hotel in Washington, D.C. Their efforts (and others') ultimately resulted in the convictions on conspiracy and perjury charges of several high-ranking government officials connected to President Richard Nixon. President Nixon eventually resigned over the scandal.

Chapter 12, which begins Volume 2, also deals with an individual associated with a fight against government corruption—Frank Serpico. Serpico was instrumental in fighting corruption in the New York City Police Department (NYPD) during the 1960s. He exposed widespread criminal activity among NYPD officers, including routine acceptance of gratuities and kickbacks, as well as acts of bribery and extortion. Al Pacino starred in the title role of the 1973 movie *Serpico*.

Interestingly, Al Pacino also starred in a movie about the icon profiled in Chapter 13, the 1997 film *Donnie Brasco*. Joe Pistone, aka "Donnie Brasco," was an FBI agent who went deep undercover to infiltrate the New

York Mafia. His six-year undercover effort resulted in more than one hundred convictions of members of organized crime. Pacino does not star as Pistone in the movie, but rather as a mobster befriended and investigated by Pistone. Johnny Depp plays Pistone in the movie.

Chapter 14 is the most exhaustive chapter in the book and profiles the life of famed prosecutor Vincent Bugliosi. Chapter author Ed Schauer interviewed Bugliosi extensively in preparing the chapter and brings a unique perspective on this influential and contemporary crime fighter. Bugliosi is mostly known for his successful prosecution of Charles Manson and Manson's associates. Later, he wrote *Helter Skelter,* a book chronicling Manson's crimes. Chapter 15 explores another contemporary crime fighter in the public eye: John Walsh. Walsh is best known for hosting Fox television's longrunning show *America's Most Wanted.* He is a tireless victims' advocate. Sadly, personal tragedy propelled him into his life's work. In 1981, Walsh's own 6-year-old son was abducted and murdered by a child predator. He has crusaded against child predators and for victims' rights ever since.

In Chapter 16, readers have the opportunity to learn about a group of individuals that has captured the imagination of America and Hollywood for many years: the profilers of the FBI. The chapter explores the history of profiling as a criminal investigative technique and delves into the FBI's early effort to develop profiling as a viable tool. Famous FBI profilers such as Greg McCrary, John Douglas, Robert Ressler, and Roy Hazlewood are introduced. These individuals, along with the FBI's Behavior Analysis Unit, inspired several popular movies and books, such as Thomas Harris' *Silence of the Lambs.*

Chapter 17 deals with another contemporary icon, the current and longserving sheriff of Maricopa County, Arizona, Joe Arpaio. Some have labeled him "America's Toughest Sheriff." He is famous for housing county prisoners in tents and subjecting them to unconventional forms of punishment. The chapter goes further to explore the efficacy of these alternate forms of punishment. The author of this chapter also had an opportunity to interview Arpaio personally and secure his unique perspective on his service as sheriff.

Although Joe Arpaio is controversial in many quarters, Chapter 18 deals with probably the most controversial individual profiled in *Icons of Crime Fighting*: Mark Fuhrman. Detective Fuhrman first received national attention as one of the investigating officers of the O. J. Simpson case. His denial of using the "n" word, which later proved to be false, impeached the credibility of the entire investigating team. However, his stature as an investigator has been resurrected after privately investigating the 1975 murder of Martha Moxley. His investigation resulted in renewed official interest in the case and the conviction in 2002 of Michael Skakel, who is a relative of the Kennedy family. He has similarly investigated and written about several other high-profile crimes.

Chapter 19 explores the career of Rudy Giuliani. Most recently, he was a presidential candidate in the Republican Party who dropped out of the race after the 2008 Florida primary. However, his career before that included many high notes and accomplishments as a crime fighter. Giuliani was the mayor of New York City from 1994 to 2001. He was affectionately dubbed "America's mayor" after his handling of the tragedy on 9/11. He presided over a sharp decline in violent crime in the city and was very supportive of aggressive police tactics. He also served as a U.S. attorney and is well known for his fight against organized crime in that capacity.

Another New York City icon is the subject of Chapter 20, Curtis Sliwa and the Guardian Angels. Sliwa is the founder of the Guardian Angels, a worldwide crime prevention organization that relies on citizen patrols. The chapter explores Sliwa's efforts in crime prevention as well as the issue of vigilantism and citizen crime prevention efforts generally.

Icons of Crime Fighting ends with its final two chapters devoted to iconic forensic scientists. Chapter 21 profiles Dr. Henry Lee, who is perhaps the world's most famous forensic scientist. He has consulted on hundreds of murder and sexual assault investigations, including many high-profile cases. He is affiliated with the University of New Haven, Connecticut, which is home to one of the most renowned forensic science degree programs in the world. Chapter 22 examines the career of Dr. Bill Bass. Dr. Bass, a professor at the University of Tennessee, is renowned for founding the "Body Farm," which is an outdoor forensic laboratory where donated dead bodies are permitted to decay. As a forensic anthropologist, Dr. Bass has consulted on numerous homicide investigations involving decomposed human remains. Both Dr. Lee and Dr. Bass are counted among the most famous and highly regarded criminal investigative scientists in the world.

It is hoped that readers of *Icons of Crime Fighting: Relentless Pursuers of Justice* will find the profiles of individuals and agencies contained therein to be interesting and informative. Certainly the chapters can serve as a springboard for further research into their respective and associated crime-fighting topics. In fact, each chapter ends with a Further Reading list, and there is an extensive Selected Bibliography at the end of Volume 2 to aid further exploration and study. Ultimately, my desire and the desire of the various chapter authors is that readers will be edified and inspired by the stories of dedication and professionalism relating to the many crime-fighting icons, past and present, who serve or have served to protect society from those who would perpetrate evil.

Jeffrey B. Bumgarner, Ph.D.
Minnesota State University, Mankato

AP Images/Jim Wells

Francisco Vincent Serpico

Morris A. Taylor

Police officers represent perhaps the most visible incarnation of governmental power. They have considerable authority and "we the people" have delegated to them nearly unfettered *discretionary power* for the purpose of protecting and serving the public in an efficient, effective, and equitable manner. In fact, discretionary power is absolutely essential for police if they are to be successful in accomplishing their goals. Nevertheless, as noted by John Emmerich Edward Dalberg (Lord Acton) in a letter to Bishop Mandel Creighton in 1887, "power tends to corrupt, and absolute power corrupts absolutely. Great men are almost always bad men, even when they exercise influence and not authority: still more when you super-add the tendency or the certainty of corruption by authority" (Dalberg 1972). Unfortunately this is too often the case in many police departments in the United States. On the one hand, police frequently accomplish great things but on the other, they have sometimes abused their power and breached the public's trust. In these later instances they are indeed "bad men." Concomitantly, police corruption and unethical behavior among these types of officers in the United States has always been a major concern of citizens, civil libertarians, scholars, police administrators, and reformers. Yet the idea of "guarding the guardians" and the emergence of a police officer *whistle blower* is particularly problematic in large, complex police organizations wherein the police essentially police themselves and where tight and protective organizational cultures often impede external oversight.

FRANCISCO VINCENT SERPICO

In the history of policing in the United States, there have been few people within police organizations who have addressed corruption issues directly. One person who did was Francisco Vincent Serpico, a major crime-fighting icon in the battle against police crime, repression, and corruption. Serpico, generally referred to as Frank Serpico, was a New York City police officer. It is noteworthy that he fought his battle against corruption in the largest and arguably at that time, one of the most dishonest and criminally tainted police departments in the United States. During Serpico's tenure in this highly bureaucratized, close-knit department, there were slightly more than 38,000 officers (Rummel 1974). Yet in a very real sense, Serpico nearly singlehandedly took on the corrupt NYPD, displaying uncompromising courage and tenacity in an effort to expose corruption and rebuild public trust. In Serpico's view, the notion of a "crooked cop" was an oxymoron: "You are either a cop or a crook" (Rummel 1974). Yet even from the inception of Frank Serpico's career, he was confronted with egregious acts of corruption and unethical police behavior. Although at times he was discouraged in his battle against dishonesty and criminality, Serpico remained undaunted and was instrumental in elucidating widespread police malfeasance within the New York City Police Department.

Serpico was born April 14, 1936, in Brooklyn, New York, to Vincenzo and Maria Giovanna Serpico. At the age of eighteen he enlisted in the U.S.

Army, serving for two years in Korea. He later joined the New York City Police Department on September 11, 1959, and began his tour of duty as a uniformed patrol officer in the 81st Precinct on the March 5, 1960 at the age of twenty-three. He was later transferred to the Bureau of Criminal Identification for two years, but was soon reassigned as a plainclothes officer in Brooklyn and the Bronx where he was assigned to target vice and racketeering. Even though Serpico had already observed corruption within the police department, it was here that he was first exposed to pervasive corruption and significant police abuse of power. Now, for perhaps the first time in his career, he realized that corruption within the NYPD was far worse than he had imagined and that the level of criminality was systemic.

In 1967, Serpico attempted to address these corrupt practices and began to provide credible evidence of such, but it was largely ignored until he and another police officer named David Durk began to go public. By 1970, Serpico exposed intractable criminal police practices and began to speak publicly about kickbacks, bribery, and other corrupt acts of fellow officers. This was unheard of within police cultures wherein the "code of silence" has always been honored and preserved and whistle-blowing is eschewed. As a result, both Serpico and Durk received numerous threats to their lives after they testified against a former police colleague. Serpico was always concerned that his fellow officers had knowledge of his secret meetings with police investigators and was forced to trust few, if any, of his fellow officers.

On April 25, 1970, *The New York Times* published a front-page story validating Serpico's allegations of police corruption within the NYPD. Shortly thereafter, Mayor John V. Lindsey appointed a five-member panel charged with investigating police corruption. The panel, chaired by Percy Whitman Knapp, became known as the Knapp Commission. Knapp was an accomplished and well-respected Wall Street attorney who once worked for New York District Attorney John Dewey during his crusade to address organized crime in New York. He had considerable experience investigating corruption starting as early as 1953–1954 as special counsel investigating waterfront corruption. In fact, Knapp would later blame New York Mayor John Lindsey as part of the problem with corrupt police officers in New York City. Although he cited no criminal issues with Lindsey, he suggested that Mayor Lindsey had not taken a proactive stand against corruption despite strong evidence that it existed.

During this time Serpico was becoming increasingly more unsettled by the continued egregious corruption and lack of attention paid to it by both the NYPD Internal Affairs Division and various political leaders. He was also keenly aware of the fact that many officers were becoming increasingly more uncomfortable with his actions, when all of this appeared to reach a dramatic climax on the night of February 7, 1971, at approximately 10:42 P.M. On this night, Serpico was assigned to a stakeout at 778 Driggs Avenue located in Brooklyn, New York, in an attempt to make a heroin arrest. He was assisted by three officers, two of whom, Gary Roteman and Arthur Ceasre, remained in a parked car in front of the apartment building with a third officer, Paul Halley, stationed on foot in front of the building. Serpico, feeling very uneasy about this situation, began to have serious reservations about this "routine arrest." In fact, he had become so frustrated with the department that he started to throw his badge and gun as far away as possible and just disappear. Yet, being a good cop, he proceeded up the fire escape and visually surveyed the area. He then proceeded out of the fire escape door, walked down some steps, and observed a heroin buy in progress. He listened for a password and followed two individuals out of the building. The two were immediately arrested by officers Roteman and Ceasre and placed in the unmarked car occupied by officer Halley. Officer Roteman instructed Serpico to attempt to make a fake drug purchase to gain entry into the third floor apartment where drugs were suspected of being sold. Both officers Roteman and Ceasre, along with Serpico, proceeded to the third floor landing of the apartment building. Serpico, who spoke Spanish, was armed with a .38 caliber revolver when he knocked on the door. When the door opened a few inches, it was still partially secured by a chain. Serpico then suddenly pushed hard on the door, snapping the chain. He was able to wedge a part of his body into the apartment while the dealers inside were trying to close it. At this point, he called for help from the two officers assisting him but they did not respond.

All of a sudden, Serpico was shot point blank in the face with a .22 LR handgun. The bullet penetrated his cheek just below the eye and eventually became lodged at the top of his jaw. He subsequently lost his balance, fell to the floor, and began bleeding profusely. While all of this was happening, there was never a call placed for a code 10–13 (officer in distress needing assistance) indicating that an officer had been shot. Instead, Serpico was saved by an elderly Hispanic man residing in one of the apartments adjacent to the suspects', who called for emergency services, reporting that a man had been shot. He then stayed with Serpico until the ambulance arrived, but a police squad car arrived before the ambulance and transported him to Greenpoint Hospital. The officers were unaware at the time that they were transporting Frank Serpico. As a result of the shooting, Serpico's auditory nerve was severed, leaving him permanently deaf in his left ear. He continues to suffer from chronic pain from bullet fragments lodged in his brain.

Yet in spite of all of these events Serpico remained focused on publicly addressing police misconduct. On May 10, 1971, Frank Serpico testified at the departmental trial of an NYPD lieutenant who had been accused of accepting bribes from gamblers. In October and December of 1971 he testified before the Knapp Commission, becoming the first police officer in the history of the United States to testify openly about pervasive police corruption within his or her department. This type of whistle-blowing was thought to be nearly impossible within most police organizations, and for the New

York City Police Department, many of its officers viewed his testimony as unconscionable.

The Knapp Commission's preliminary report was issued on August 15, 1972, and its final report on December 27, 1972. The final report found widespread evidence of corruption within the New York City Police Department. As a result of its investigation it made the following recommendations:

- Commanders should be held accountable for their subordinates
- Commanders should file periodic reports on key areas that would breed corruption
- Field offices of the Internal Affairs Division should be created at all precincts
- Undercover informants should be placed in all precincts
- Improve screening and make selection methods standard
- A change in police attitudes

Additionally, the Knapp Commission on Police Corruption identified and focused on two specific types of corrupt police officers: (1) "grass eaters" and (2) "meat eaters." These classifications referred to petty corruption stemming from peer pressure (eating grass) and premeditated, aggressive major corruption (eating meat). The grass eater connotation describes those officers who "accept gratuities and solicit five, ten, twenty dollar payments from contractors, tow-truck operators, gamblers, and the like but do not peruse corruption payments" (Knapp Commission 1972). However, the idea of grass eating was activities participated in by a considerable number of officers, which were learned from other officers or from emulating the very criminal element, which they often investigated. In fact, the commission discerned that grass eating was even used by NYPD officers to prove their loyalty to and among their fellow officers. This type of loyalty often led to jobs on the side. Hence, the commission reasoned that a way of preventing this type of behavior was to remove the corrupt veteran officers, essentially eliminating the basis for officers to learn how to eat grass.

The meat eaters, on the other hand, consisted of officers who spent considerable cerebral energy looking for criminal opportunities for financial gain. For example, it was quite common to shake down drug dealers, pimps, and others for money that was part of financially lucrative criminal activity. They often justified it by suggesting that these dregs of society somehow deserved what they got when they decided to participate in these types of behaviors.

Numerous newspaper articles chronicling corrupt activities were published in *The New York Times* (1970–1972) as indicated by the headlines below:

Graft Paid to Police Here Said to Run into Millions; Survey Links Payoffs to Gambling and Narcotics; Some on Force Accuse Officials of Failure to Act;

Graft Payments to Policemen Here Are Reported to Run into the Millions Annually; Some Members of Force Say Officials Fail to Act. April 25, 1970.

Mayor's Committee Investigating Police Corruption Here Meets Tomorrow to Determine Procedures. April 26, 1970

Panel on Police May Be Replaced; Mayor Is Expected to Name a Larger Unit on Graft That Excludes Lear. May 9, 1970.

Lindsay Appoints Corruption Unit; Subpoena Power Asked for 2d Panel to Study Police. May 22, 1970.

Knapp Says Laws Spur Police Graft; Lindsay Appointee Explains Objectives of Inquiry. June 7, 1970.

41 Policemen Are Subpoenaed By Knapp Unit in Betting Inquiry. February 17, 1971.

Perjury Laid to 2 in Police Inquiry; Patrolmen in Meat Incident Are First to Be Accused in Knapp Investigation; Perjury Charged to 2 Policemen In Knapp Inquiry on Corruption. June 9, 1971.

Knapp Says Mayor Shares Blame for Corrupt Police; Knapp Faults Lindsay on Corruption of Police. July 2, 1971.

Knapp Unit Tells of Police Bribery as Hearings Open; Reports "Extensive" Problem in Corruption Here; Tape Evidence Is Presented; Details of Vice Graft; 2 Patrolmen and a Lawyer Linked to Payoffs to Help an East Side Madam; Knapp Panel Tells of Police Bribery as Hearings Begin Here. October 19, 1971.

Patrolman Says "All But 2" of Colleagues Got Bribes; Numbers Runner Tells the Knapp Panel That He Paid Off a Detective Monthly with Money from Social Security. October 23, 1971. Knapp Unit's Head Defends Legality of Investigation; Public Attention Is Essential in Combating Corruption; Lawyer Tells Critics "Hogan Backs Hearings But Roberts Scores Actions"; Police Bid Businessmen End Giving of Gratuities; Knapp Commission Chairman Defends Legality of Investigation. October 24, 1971.

Knapp Urges a Permanent Body on Police Corruption to Succeed His Panel. October 25, 1971.

Knapp Witness to Tell of Lindsay Officials' Apathy; Witness Will Tell Knapp Panel Lindsay Officials Ignored Graft. October 30, 1971.

Leary Agrees to Be Knapp Witness. December 14, 1971.

Serpico's Lonely Journey to Knapp Witness Stand. December 15, 1971.

Phillips, a Knapp Witness, Indicted in Two Murders; Phillips, Knapp Witness, Is Indicted. March 21, 1972.

Knapp Nominated as Federal Judge; Head of Police Inquiry Unit One of Four Named Here. June 16, 1972.

Knapp Panel's Recommendation a Touchy Problem for Mayor and Governor. August 27, 1972.

Knapp Panel Says Walsh and Others Ignored Tips by U.S. on Police Crimes; Kriegel Is Scored. December 1972.

These types of articles were nearly a daily occurrence in *The New York Times*. Needless to say, public trust of the NYPD was severely damaged, and Frank Serpico was by now a marked man.

Although the Knapp Commission's findings were significant, its efficacy had been impeded by several factors. When the commission was first formed it was given only six months to complete its investigation and findings and to make appropriate reform recommendations, and it appeared that the commission was going to run out of money before it could ever complete its tasks. The investigation would have ended at this point but for intervention by the U.S. Department of Justice, which provided a $215,000 grant enabling the commission to continue its efforts as part of a federally sponsored law enforcement program.

Also during this time the Knapp Commission was in a real fight for survival because its legality was now being challenged in court by none other than rank-and-file NYPD officers. A lawsuit filed by the Patrolman's Benevolent Association charged that the commission had violated a New York City charter provision that prohibited any police review board that lacked a majority of members of the department on it. It even charged that the investigation could result in "great expense, harassment, and inconvenience" (Mass 1973) to police officers. This was illuminated further when two deputy inspectors and their captains, who had been ordered to respond to questions concerning their personal finances, brought a later action against the commission. All five individuals lamented that to respond to the commission about their personal finances was tantamount to compelling them to waive their constitutional rights "against self-incrimination." Various police personnel filed similar lawsuits against the commission's subpoena power, but all of those actions were eventually invalidated and thrown out.

As a result of Serpico's activities he was awarded a gold shield by the police commissioner, promoted to detective, and ultimately received the New York City Police Department's highest honor—the Medal of Honor. But according to Serpico, he received it not for battling corruption but as he put it, he "was stupid enough to have been shot in the face." (Mass 1973). He then retired one month after receiving this award after twelve years of service. After his retirement he traveled and studied in Europe for a decade and recuperated from being shot. Several newspaper articles were written documenting the events of his heroism, culminating in a 1973 movie staring Al Pacino and a book written by Peter Maas. There have also been several news documentaries about his experiences that have helped expand discussions about police corruption and unethical behavior.

The events of Serpico's shooting are still being debated today. Was he set up by a person or persons within the NYPD? Why was no "10–13" ever issued? And what about the various officers supposedly assisting him on the drug bust? Yet arguably one of his biggest contributions could be that he reminds us of the cautionary words of Dalberg concerning power and how unchecked power may lead to insidious abuses. But police corruption and unethical behavior within many police departments in the United States has been and continues to be a major area of concern. However, in spite of

Serpico's significant contribution in fighting police corruption, little has changed since he left the New York City Police Department.

POLICE CORRUPTION

Corruption and unethical behavior by police officers has a long and undistinguished history in the United States generally and New York City particularly. Hence, numerous reform measures have proved to be only marginally effective before, during, and after the experiences of Frank Serpico. In fact, according to Serpico, "nothing has changed."

A major impediment to police reform has been the strong organizational cultures that sanction officers who speak out against police criminality, and many police departments have long been bastions of police crime and repression. Concomitantly, police corruption has led to U.S. Department of Justice lawsuits being filed against departments whose officers commit constitutional torts, resulting in the issuance of consent decrees.

Yet even when litigation has taken place, many departments continue to struggle with reform in spite of the law and new knowledge and insight gained through research. Various reasons are cited for this that transcend organizational culture and seem to be a function of the nature of the police work. First, police officers have significant amounts of discretion and considerable autonomy in carrying out their jobs. Second, this combined with the very closed nature of most police organizations provides a breeding ground of sorts for police malfeasance. Finally, officers often work varied shifts, and much of their work is done with little close supervision. In a very real sense they are sometimes out of sight and out of mind until a major event occurs that attracts widespread media attention. Thus, it is very difficult to provide proper oversight given their autonomy and considerable close-knit organizational relationships. This is particularly difficult in very large departments such as New York City, and was a real dilemma for Frank Serpico because of the scope of corruption that permeated nearly all aspects of the NYPD, encompassing various precincts and specialized units.

Although Serpico was the first police officer in the history of the United States to testify *formally* on police corruption, the NYPD has a long history of being mired in police misconduct. In the early part of the 1870s the idea of corruption and politics was inextricably linked under the auspices of Tammany Hall—a political machine power supported largely by Irish immigrants who infiltrated the New York City Police Department. During this time the acceptance of bribes by police department leaders from local businessmen was the rule rather than the exception. Police often looked the other way concerning illegal liquor sales and other types of criminality. Officers also supervised polling places at the behest of political figures and would simply ignore ballot box stuffing and/or acts of fraud. By 1894 the

Lexow Committee was established to investigate police corruption. The committee ultimately made reform recommendations that included the idea of making the police department adopt a civil service system.

However the NYPD seems to have cycles of corruption spanning twenty-year intervals. Although the events surrounding Serpico emerged from the late 1960s through the early 1970s, allegations of corruption surfaced again in 1992 after six NYPD officers were arrested on drug charges by the Suffolk County Police Department. What was puzzling was the length of time involved before their corruption was ultimately uncovered. The Mollen Commission's final report published in July 1994 found pervasive corruption within the highest-crime precincts in the city.

Notwithstanding Serpico's testimony and the Knapp Commission conclusions on corruption, some of the Mollen Commission's findings were unprecedented in the department's more recent history. For example, it was determined that groups of officers actually were protecting and assisting drug traffickers while simultaneously conducting unlawful searches and seizures. There were widespread instances of perjury and falsifying of official records. In some cases there was evidence of direct involvement in robberies and narcotics trafficking. Part of the problem, according to the commission, was that top police officials simply failed to monitor officers' behavior and as a practical matter, ignored it. Concomitantly, the Internal Affairs Division seemed to work at minimizing the level of corruption rather than aggressively investigating and exposing it. In fact, a former police officer Kevin Hembury, testifying before the Mollen Commission, validated this notion when he learned, while in the police academy and when serving in the 73rd Precinct, the "us against them" mindset, the concept of the "blue wall of silence," and that "cops never rat on other cops, that ratting on corrupt cops is worse than corruption itself." (Armao and Cornefield 1993) Hembury quickly learned that there was money to be made and power to be had if officers were willing to deal in drugs and corruption. Commission members were awestruck when Hembury testified that, "no commanding officer ever asked how he and his colleagues were spending their days...or how well they were serving the residents they were supposed to protect" (Armao and Cornefield 1993) (Note: Armano and Cornefield were chief counsel and deputy chief counsel, respectively, to the Mollen Commission.).

This kind of police criminality has implications for communities. No police department can accomplish their mission without the support of the people whom they serve. When citizens lose confidence in their local police because of issues of malfeasance and brutality, the police department's efficacy is often destroyed. It has been suggested that "when the police are subjects of complaints, the process of law enforcement begins to break down" (Decker and Wagner 1989). This was evident during Serpico's tenure and is still evident today in many police departments across the United States.

Law Enforcement Code of Ethics

Given the widespread corruption of the New York Police Department and other departments around the country during the 1960s and 1970s, as is evident from the Frank Serpico story, it would be easy to conclude mistakenly that law enforcement as a profession was entirely unconcerned about its ethical obligations and responsibilities. However, the profession was aware of these responsibilities. In 1957, the International Association of Chiefs of Police adopted the following Code of Ethics at its 64th Annual Convention. The code was strongly worded and very intolerant of police graft and corruption—both minor and major. This particular Code of Ethics is still widely proclaimed by today by the law enforcement agencies around the country:

"As a law enforcement officer, my fundamental duty is to serve the community; to safeguard lives and property; to protect the innocent against deception, the weak against oppression or intimidation and the peaceful against violence or disorder; and to respect the constitutional rights of all to liberty, equality and justice.

"I will keep my private life unsullied as an example to all and will behave in a manner that does not bring discredit to me or to my agency. I will maintain courageous calm in the face of danger, scorn or ridicule; develop self-restraint; and be constantly mindful of the welfare of others. Honest in thought and deed both in my personal and official life, I will be exemplary in obeying the law and the regulations of my department. Whatever I see or hear of a confidential nature or that is confided to me in my official capacity will be kept ever secret unless revelation is necessary in the performance of my duty.

"I will never act officiously or permit personal feelings, prejudices, political beliefs, aspirations, animosities or friendships to influence my decisions. With no compromise for crime and with relentless prosecution of criminals, I will enforce the law courteously and appropriately without fear or favor, malice or ill will, never employing unnecessary force or violence and never accepting gratuities.

"I recognize the badge of my office as a symbol of public faith, and I accept it as a public trust to be held so long as I am true to the ethics of police service. I will never engage in acts of corruption or bribery, nor will I condone such acts by other police officers. I will cooperate with all legally authorized agencies and their representatives in the pursuit of justice.

"I know that I alone am responsible for my own standard of professional performance and will take every reasonable opportunity to enhance and improve my level of knowledge and competence.

POLICE ETHICS

The idea of ethics is perhaps one of the most complex and least understood areas of social and philosophical inquiry. Many believe they know intuitively what it means to be ethical. However, within complex organizational settings the notion of what constitutes ethical behavior is not always so clear when there exist juxtapositions of sometimes incompatible value systems.

> *"I will constantly strive to achieve these objectives and ideals, dedicating myself before God to my chosen profession ... law enforcement."*
>
> Source: http://www.theiacp.org.

Van Wart provides guidance in understanding the nature and extent to which value systems may influence ethical or nonethical behavior within an organizational setting. He argues that "values are the foundations of ethical systems" and that "values determine what is right and wrong," (1998) and, he identifies five major sources of values: (1) individual values, (2) professional values, (3) organizational values, (4) legal values, and (5) public interest values. According to Van Wart, these values convey at least five questions that must be considered when analyzing ethical dilemmas:

1. What is the legal thing to do?
2. What is best for the organization?
3. What is best for the public at large?
4. What best meets professional standards?
5. What is an appropriate role for me to play and to what extent should my interests influence the decision-making process?

Yet arguably, police officers' personal value systems affect many of their decision-making actions because of the large amounts of discretion they wield and the conditions under which they work, most notably tremendous autonomy with limited supervision or oversight. In addition, officers' behaviors have often tended to reflect their understanding of community-based norms wherein they justify unethical and corrupt acts as necessary to accomplish their goals and community expectations. However, the idea of an "ethical system" as noted by Van Wart is somewhat problematic, depending on the scope, purpose, and strength of the various cultures of a particular organization.

The battles fought by Frank Serpico and others raise serious questions about police ethics and values and its implications for efficient, effective, and accountable law enforcement. In terms of accountability and oversight, police organizations typically provide a form of self-regulation wherein fellow officers investigate potentially corrupt activities of their colleagues. This has been largely ineffective and problematic in large complex police organizations with strong cohesive cultures and where the code of silence is predominant.

Stoddard suggests that officers often become socialized to what he refers to as "blue-coat crime," wherein he contends that some role ambivalence is unavoidable among police, given the nature of our democracy. He argues that officers charged with protecting and serving the public are at a stark disadvantage and thus must sometimes violate the law to accomplish their goals of service and protection. One problem associated with this type of reasoning is that over time, illegal or corrupt activities become routine; activities thought to be minor begin to escalate and become an informal police norm. Stoddard's blue codes are described below:

Mooching: Accepting free coffee, cigarettes, meals, liquor, groceries, or other items, justified as compensation either for being in an underpaid profession or for future acts of favoritism the donor may receive.

Bribery: The receipt of cash or a "gift" in exchange for past or future assistance in avoidance of prosecution, such as a claim that the officer is unable to make a positive identification of a criminal, an officer's agreement to be in the wrong place at a time when a crime is to occur, or any other action that may be excused as carelessness but not offered as proof of deliberate miscarriage of justice. Distinguished from mooching by the higher value of the gift and by the mutual understanding in regard to services to be performed upon the acceptance of the gift.

Chiseling: Demanding price discounts, free admission to places of entertainment whether in connection with police duty or not, and the like.

Extortion: A demand for placement of an advertisement in a police magazine or purchase of tickets to a police function; the practice of holding a "street court" where minor traffic tickets can be avoided by the payment of cash "bail" to the arresting officer, with no receipt given.

Shopping: Picking up small items such as candy bars, gum, and cigarettes at a store where the door has been left accidentally unlocked at the close of business hours.

Shakedown: The practice of appropriating expensive items for personal use during an investigation of a break-in, burglary, or unlocked door, and attributing their loss to criminal activity. Distinguished from shopping by the value of the items taken and the ease with which former ownership may be determined if the officer is caught in the act of procurement.

Premeditated theft: Planned burglary, involving the use of tools, keys, or other devices to force entry, or any prearranged plan to acquire property unlawfully. Distinguished from *shakedown* only by the previous arrangement made in regard to the theft, not by the value of the items taken.

Favoritism: The practice of issuing license tabs, window stickers, or courtesy cards that exempt users from arrest or citation for traffic offenses (sometimes extended to spouses, families, and friends of recipients).

Perjury: Lying to provide an alibi for fellow officers apprehended in unlawful activity approved by the "code."

Prejudice: Treatment of minority groups in a manner less than impartial, neutral, and objective, especially members of groups who are unlikely to have "influence" in city hall that might cause the arresting officer trouble. (Stoddard 1992)

These kinds of improper police activities taint police credibility and present confounding problems for ethical officers attempting to do their jobs. But early in many officers' careers they are exposed to heavy-handed pressure to conform to the existing culture. In fact, prior research emerged from socialization theories of the 1960s where it was suggested that belief systems and values are shaped by the occupational and organizational experiences as opposed to learned behavior. Yet Kappeler et al. contends that "recruit and probationary officers are profoundly affected by their training and socialization" (Kappeler et al. 1998).

However, attempting to measure the level of integrity within police organizations is problematic for reformers and researchers attempting to shed light on these issues. Attempting to study corruption within police organizations is fraught with methodological problems and is challenging when attempting to apply quantitative techniques. Reasons vary for this, but in many instances corrupt activities are never reported or even recorded by the police agency. Rather, a police department's data on corruption typically may be classified as "anticorruption activity" as opposed to any measured level of corruption.

However, police corruption takes various forms and police behavior has been construed differently among various agencies. For example, the issue of gratuities has not always been a *major* concern of some police agencies. The idea of the "freebie" or police discount was in some jurisdictions simply common practice that was part of the overall police tradition and culture. Some merchants actively counted on providing gratuities with the idea of having a more visible police presence. As a practical matter this could lead to differential provision of police services. The merchant that provides freebies or police discounts arguably may have a more visible police presence than those who do not. In the view of some merchants, especially those anchored in high-crime areas, the idea of having a more visible police presence is very important to their actual and perceived sense of security. Merchants not providing gratuities and not having the same type of police presence could be victims of differential policing, thereby possibly putting them at risk of increased criminality.

Further, it has been argued that acceptance of gratuities is the first step down a slippery path toward corruption, and it has been suggested that gratuities never be accepted or if they are, they should be clearly minimal and that the officer must be aware of the possible consequences of such acceptance. Nevertheless, Fedberg posits that there is little empirical evidence that suggests that the acceptance of gratuities will ultimately lead to corruption. In fact, he posits that the "slippery slope" analysis is not founded in logic and is

> unrealistic, somewhat hypocritical, and insulting to a police officer's intelligence. They are unrealistic because the great majority of gratuities, such as free coffee, half priced meals, and other discounts come from basically honest merchants who attach no strings or expectations to the offering. (Fedburg 1985, 268).

Although Fedburg's insights may have common-sense application, the idea of a "freebie" may have much more invidious and economic implications. First and foremost police officers are public sector workers and thus are agents of the sovereign; they work at the behest of the citizens they serve. As agents of the sovereign, their actions "have the force of law and the coercive power of the government behind them." Consequently, a much higher ethical standard and calling is warranted if the public trust is not to be breached. Still, as noted in Table 1 from Ruiz and Bono (2004, 44–54), there are real economic costs associated with the acceptance of gratuities.

It should be noted that the gratuities in Table 1 were calculated using a fifty-week work year and eight-hour shifts from 7:00 A.M. to 3:00 P.M. The calculations for coffee and soda assumed two breaks per eight-hour shift; although, based on the author's experience as a former police officer in the department studied, they were probably considerably higher. According to Ruiz, "it was commonly held that there was no need to pay for something when it could be obtained for free; hence, it was the practice to wait until the shift began before having breakfast. Doughnuts were a natural with the morning coffee and three could easily be consumed" (Ruiz and Bono 2004).

Ruiz and Bono (2004, 52) further demonstrate how gratuities relate to officer income, as shown in Table 2.

Table 1
List of Common Gratuities

Gratuities	Cost	Frequency	Annual Cost
Coffee/Soda	$1.00	$1.00 × 494	$494.00
Doughnuts	3@ .60 = 1.80	$1.80 × 247	$444.60
Lunch	$6.00	$6.00 × 247	$1,482.00
Cigarettes	$3.85	$3.85 × 10 = $38.50×52	$2,002.00
Alcohol	4@ $6.00 = $24.00	$24.00 × 104	$2,496.00
Laundry	3/p @ $11.75	$11.75 × 50	$587.50
	5/s @ $7.50	$ 7.50 × 50	$375.00
Movie Theater	$8.00 × 2 = $16.00	$16.00 × 52	$832.00

Total Annual Gratuities: $8,713.10

From Ruiz and Bono (2004, 52).

Table 2
Gratuities as a Portion of an Officer's Annual Salary

Total annual gratuities	$8,713.10
Tax and benefits on total @ 30 percent	$2,613.93
Total gratuity gross income	$11,327.03
National police officer salary	$34,556.00
Percentage of annual salary	33 percent
Weekly gratuity take	$217.83
Monthly gratuity take	$943.92

From Ruiz and Bono (2004, 52).

Ruiz and Bono go further by identifying and conceptualizing the nature of gratuities as incipient corrupters and economic corrupters. They argue that incipient corrupters are analogous to what the Drug Enforcement Administration has done with respect to marijuana being a gateway drug. They suggest the acceptance of police gratuities could also be viewed as a gateway of sorts to higher levels of police corruption. With respect to economic corruption, Riuz reasons from the perspective of a former practitioner:

> We argue that because of the frequency and, over time, magnitude of gratuities received, personal feelings, friendship, and indebtedness develops between police officers and the givers of gratuities. We cannot imagine how a police officer could accept gratuities from merchants and their employees that amount to thousands of dollars annually without personal feelings, friendships, and indebtedness to them being established. It was the experience of the ex-practitioner author that merchants who gave gratuities were quick to remind him of their generosity when stopped for a traffic violation or other minor infractions of the law. At the very least they expected to be given special consideration when calling for service. Police officers who claim otherwise are either less than honest or fortunate enough to work in cities with loving philanthropists. (Ruiz and Bono 2004, 46)

Although these observations may or may not be typical in other jurisdictions, it should be noted that Ruiz was a former member of the New Orleans Police Department. The salary level for New Orleans officers was quite low, and according to the author, "in fact, had it not been for gratuities in the way of food and cigarettes," it essentially would have been difficult to make ends meet.

Interestingly, the New Orleans Police Department has a history of corruption and police misconduct. In fact, between 1992 and 1996, forty police officers of the New Orleans Police Department had been arrested for auto theft, bank robbery, and numerous other illegal and criminal acts. Furthermore, another 200 officers ultimately were fired or reprimanded or chose to retire because of their involvement in various illegal or criminal acts. And more recently during the events of Hurricane Katrina, the entire nation observed police corruption, criminality, and abuse of authority in a time of crisis when citizens needed their police more than ever.

Yet gratuities remain the most prevalent form of police corruption. In fact, one survey found that about half of all police departments had any written policy that mentioned free meals—but not all those policies prohibited the practice of gratuity acceptance. For example, in another survey conducted in Reno, Nevada, it was found that of those business merchants and others who offered free gifts such as coffee or meals, nearly 33 percent specifically denoted that they wanted special treatment or favors in return for the gratuity provided. This latter survey seems to validate, to some degree, Ruiz and Bono's concern with respect to the quid pro quo established between officers and merchants when gratuities are given. This is the reason why some have argued that police officers should never be allowed to accept gratuities under any circumstance because it leads down a slippery path to further corruption.

Although Ruiz suggests that low salaries within the New Orleans Police Department may have been an incentive for the acceptance of gratuities in some cases, all officers understand that police work traditionally has been a lower-paying job in many departments. There has been much progress in raising police officers' salaries across the country, but compensation still varies substantially by jurisdiction.

Consider, however, the current starting salary for a NYPD probationary patrolman, which by nearly all accounts is very low at $25,100. Once the officer completes his or her academy training, the salary increases to $32,700 and continues to increase each year to a maximum (after $5^1/2$ years of service) of $59,588. Of course these salaries do not include average overtime and night shift differential, holiday pay, or uniform allowances. Thus on average an officer will probably earn around $77,000 per year after six years.

These types of salary and working condition issues are common in many police departments in general and in the public sector in particular, and new recruits are well aware of them prior to joining their respective police agencies. Thus, although it could be argued that these factors may be an issue affecting police ethics and corruption, they are surely are not root causes of it. Ethical behavior for law enforcement officers should be something they possess long before they decide to become officers.

Serpico was frequently challenged with the same types of issues in his dealing with the New York City Police Department in the latter 1960s to early 1970s, as well as others continuing into the 1990s. However, one is challenged to consider when officers actually begin to head down the unethical "slippery slope." As noted by Thompson, the idea of ethics training may even have implications within the police academy training process when he points out that

Ethics training may help to shape the officers' perception of right and wrong behavior. However, one officer recently described his police academy ethics training as several hours on where to obtain free or half price meals and product discounts, and how to obtain a free apartment or live without paying for utilities. The remainder of the block of instruction included how to maximize off-duty employment and how to get out of traffic tickets. Early in the indoctrination into policing, some officers receive the message that they are above the law. (Thompson 2001)

These types of observations lend credence to Van Wart's elements for analyzing ethical dilemmas in terms of what the law requires, the organization's best interest, the public interest, meeting professional standards, and the role played by each officer and his/her personal interest. Among these various interests, officers' personal value systems seemed to predominate. This was certainly the case during Serpico's trials and tribulations when numerous corrupt officers were involved in a myriad of not only unethical but also criminal activities. And in many of these instances, when the evidence of corruption was clear and convincing, upper management simply looked the other way.

Given the increasingly dynamic and complex society today in the United States, combined with increased demands on police, the need for administrators to manage ethics and address corruption more effectively is critical. O'Malley argued three critical factors for the ongoing ethical issues in law enforcement: (1) a growing level of temptation emerging from the illicit drug trade market, (2) the decentralization of police organizations, and (3) "the potential compromising nature of the police organizational culture" (O'Malley 1997). In short, officers tend to be confronted with more temptations and opportunity for wrongdoing. The illegal drug industry appears to be a major factor wherein unscrupulous officers can make enormous amounts of money and profits within very short time frames. In some cases the amounts of money an officer could make by dealing in drug trafficking would more than triple his salary.

The idea of decentralization inherent in the philosophy of community-oriented policing may be influencing police ethics because it requires officers to work as partners with community members. The historical quasi-military models of policing have been supplanted by a more open, flat structure where control of officer behavior has become more challenging. According to Kane, some neighborhoods may influence police officers' deviant behavior when there exist high poverty levels, high population turnover, and high levels of racial diversity with low levels of informal social control. He contends that because police officers work in socially disorganized neighborhoods and are thus subject to essentially the same types of community maladies that lead to increases in criminality amongst residents, these factors may also explain police misconduct.

Unfortunately the scope of police corruption extends to numerous areas such as gratuities, bribes, theft and burglary, police brutality, and homicide, and given the nature of police work and the problems confronting the various communities in the United States, the idea of control becomes even more daunting. This is especially the case considering the advent of terrorism and the additional burdens of planning for eventual disasters such as Hurricane Katrina and others. Additionally, it is sometimes difficult to ascertain exactly what citizens actually want from their police, including their behavior in certain areas. In fact, some surveys have shown that only about 5 percent of people approached by a police officer for a bribe ever report the activity.

Perhaps the most egregious police corruption observed recently has been within the Los Angeles Police Department, associated with the Rampart Division. From 1998 through 1999 numerous Los Angeles Police officers were found to be engaging in "hard core" criminality. Many of these officers in the Rampart CRASH (Community Resources Against Street Hoodlums) unit, an elite unit focusing on gang activity, ultimately were found to be attacking gang members and then falsely accusing them of committing crimes, which they had not. Further investigation found that officers routinely punched, brutalized, and choked individuals simply to invoke fear and generally to intimidate them. In one instance an officer in the Rampart Division beat a hand-cuffed suspect after he was brought in for questioning. The suspect was beaten so badly in the chest and stomach that he began to vomit blood. When he was finally released, he went to a local hospital for treatment and later notified LAPD officials of his severe injuries. The suspect was eventually awarded $231,000 in a civil law suit. In another case an officer, with the assistance of his girlfriend, robbed a Los Angeles branch of Bank of America of $722,000. He was later arrested and convicted of bank robbery. There was widespread activity of planting drugs on suspects just to effect arrests, which was confounded further when corrupt supervisors (sergeants) in the Rampart Division actually provided awards for the nefarious criminal acts and even gave an award for shooting an innocent unarmed person. These types of malevolent activities clearly tend to taint the overall image of a police agency and go beyond the pale of acceptable police practices.

In many respects the sensational police corruption scandals of the LAPD demonstrate how strong cultures can have devastating effects on police behavior. To their credit the Los Angeles Police Department's own criticism of its police evaluation system is elucidating: "Our personnel evaluations have little or no credibility at any level in the organization." (LAPD 2000). That was very important because it was produced and delivered by the LAPD's internal Board of Inquiry report on the activities stemming from Rampart in 2000. Alarmingly, it highlighted numerous failures within the more than thirty policies designed to ensure integrity, but it concluded that the systems in place had not worked as designed. Strong cultures within police organizations following a traditional notion of policing combined with the idea of a "potentially compromising nature of the police organizational culture," (LAPD 2000) further add to the problem of corruption and control.

Even police performance evaluations are suspect when completed by supervisory personnel. For example, in the New York City Police Department Officer Michael Dowd who served in the 75th Precinct had received numerous excellent evaluations. As noted by his supervisor, Dowd "has excellent street knowledge, relates well with his peers and is empathetic to the community, and could easily become a role model for others to emulate" (Mollen Commission 1994). But Officer Dowd was arguably one of the most corrupt police officers in the history of the NYPD. He was involved with drug sales or other activities, and he ultimately was convicted on several criminal charges. In fact, a major television news documentary hosted by Barbara Walters with commentary by Frank Serpico highlighted corruption during Serpico's career and the events surrounding the activity of Michael Dowd.

Even with the innovation of community-oriented policing, new technologies designed to enhance efficiency and professionalism, some police cultures have appeared to change little since Frank Serpico's tour of duty as an NYPD officer. Thus, police corruption remains a constant problem. In many regards police agencies seem to focus largely on little more than controlling space and have not changed significantly during the last forty years.

CONCLUSION

The legacy of Frank Serpico will be an integral part of police reform for years to come. In fact, he is not only an icon of crime fighting but in many respects has been, and remains, the conscience of many police reformers and those interested in ensuring that our police are not corrupt and that future generations of officers live up to their oath of office and their promise to "protect and serve." Part of this is due to increased standards for police, including higher education and advanced training. Yet even today at the dawn of the twenty-first century, Frank Serpico is still not convinced that much has been done to address this vitally important issue. Indeed recent newspaper articles appearing in *The New York Times* seem to validate his concerns:

Ex-Police Chief Breaks Ranks, Testifying Against His Men. Vol. 148, Issue 51481, p. B1, Op, 1c. April 3, 1999.

Panel Monitoring Police Corruption Is Revived. Vol. 152 Issue 52575, p. B4, Op. August 14, 2003.

3 Are Assigned to Desk Duty in Police-Corruption Inquiry. Vol. 153 Issue 52758, p. B1-B6, 2p, 1c. February 13, 2004.

Former Officer in Newark Pleads Guilty to Corruption. Vol. 154 Issue
52982, p. B1-B2, Op, 1c. September 24, 2004.

Detective Fired in Aftermath of New York Police Inquiry. Vol. 154 Issue
52982, p. B1-B4, Op. September 24, 2004.

Time, and Time Served. Late Editions (East Coast). p. 14.1 February 25, 2007.

Board Calls Police Department Lax on Cases of Misconduct. p. B. 2. Late
Edition (East Coast). August 4, 2007.

Interestingly, even the mention of Serpico's name in some police circles
yields both disgust and admiration among the various officers. Some still
view him as the consummate rat because he broke the code of silence, but
others consider him a hero in his own right who has inspired us to look
closely at the type and quality of law enforcement a free and democratic society deserves. But ethics will remain important to the field of policing not
only in the United States but in many parts of our global community as
police departments and others attempt to come to grips with the reality of
failing to do so and the challenges that must be overcome. Yet policing in
the twenty-first century in the America faces unprecedented challenges in an
era of terrorism, asymmetrical war, and where large urban police department budgets are challenged to do more with less. The continued influx of
drugs, gang violence, immigration issues, and the general feeling of mistrust
between police and some of the communities they serve provides fertile
ground for increased police temptation, which may lead to corruption.

Even with the advent of community-oriented policing, in some communities nothing has changed and the old system, wherein the "code of silence"
was traditionally invoked, is still viable. Undeniably, the police subculture is
still very strong and has not been amenable to significant change in almost
forty years. In fact, during Serpico's tenure, Westley found that police officers
in general took little issue with covering for their colleagues' criminality.
Astonishingly, as recently as 2000 it was found that 52.4 percent of police
officers believed it was common practice and not particularly unusual to
ignore misconduct by fellow officers. Further, 39 percent of officers believed
officers would not even report severe or significant police criminality and misconduct. In the final analysis, Serpico's admonitions are still accurate to some
degree when he posits that "nothing has changed" (Village Voice 1999).

FURTHER READING

Armao, Joseph P., and Leslie U. Cornefeld. 1993. Why good cops turn rotten. *New
York Times* November 1: A-12.

Barker, T. and Robert W. Wells. 1982. Police administrators: Attitudes toward the
definition and control of police deviance. *Law Enforcement Bulletin* 11.

Buenker, John D. 2004. A battle for the soul of New York: Tammany Hall, police
corruption, vice, and Reverend Charles Parkhurst's crusade against them,
1892–1895. *American Historical Review* 109 (4): 246–47.

Bittner, E. 1971. *The Functions of the Police in Modern Society*. Washington, D.C.: U.S. Government Printing Office.

Brown, M. K. 1981. *Working the Street: Police Discretion and the Dilemmas of Reform*. New York: Russell Sage Foundation Press.

Bureau of Justice Statistics. 2002. Police Departments in Large Cities: 1999–2000. *National Criminal Justice* May 175703.

Coleman, Stephen. 2005. Conflict of interest and police: An unavoidable problem. *Criminal Justice Ethics* 24 (2): 3–11.

Conditt, John H., Jr. 2001. Institutional integrity. *FBI Law Enforcement Bulletin* 70 (11): 18–22.

Conti, Norman, and James Nolan III. 2005. Policing the platonic cave: Ethics and efficacy in police training. *Policing and Society* 15 (2): 166–86.

Crank, J., Dan Flaherty, and Andrew D. Giacomazzi. 2007. The noble cause: An empirical assessment. *Journal of Criminal Justice* 35 (1): 103–116.

Dalberg, John E. E. 1887. Lord Acton, Letter to Mandell Creighton, April 5. In Acton, *Essays on Freedom and Power*, ed. Gertrude Himmelfarb, 335–36, 1972.

Davis, M. 2003. Rank has no privilege. *Criminal Justice Ethics* 22 (2).

Decker, S., and Allen Wagner. 1989. *Critical Issues in Policing: Contemporary Readings*, ed. Roger G. Dunham and Geoffrey P. Alpert. Prospect Heights, IL: Waveland Press.

Del Pozo, B. 2005. One dogma of police ethics: Gratuities and the "Democratic ethos" of policing. *Criminal Justice Ethics* 24 (2, Summer/Fall).

Dewan, Shaila, and Brenda Goodman. 2007. Prosecutors say corruption in Atlanta police department is widespread. *The New York Times* (Late Editions, East Coast). April 27. P. A18.

Fedburg, M. 1985. Gratuities, corruption, and the democratic ethos of policing: The case of the free cup of coffee. In *Moral Issues in Police Work*, ed. F. Elliston and M. Feldburg, 267–76. Totowa, NJ: Rowman & Littlefield.

Goldstein, H. 1975. *Police Corruption: A Perspective on Its Nature and Control*. Washington, D.C.: Police Foundation.

Grant, J. Kevin. 2002. Ethics in law enforcement. *FBI Law Enforcement Bulletin* 71 (12) 11–14.

Harris, R. N. 1973. *The Police Academy: An Inside View*. New York: John Wiley & Sons.

Harrison, Bob. 1999. Noble cause corruption and the police ethic. *FBI Law Enforcement Bulletin* 68 (8).

Herbert, Steve. 1997. *Policing Space: Territoriality and the Los Angeles Police Department*. The University of Minnesota Press.

Huberts, Leo W., J. C., Terry Lamboo, and Maurice Punch. 2003. Police integrity in the Netherlands and the United States: Awareness and alertness. *Police Practice & Research* 4(3).

Ivkovic, Sanja Kutnjak. 2003. To serve and collect: Measuring police corruption. *Journal of Criminal Law & Criminology* 93 (2/3): 593–649.

Ivkovic, Sanja Kutnjak. 2004. Evaluating the seriousness of police misconduct: A cross-cultural comparison of police officer and citizen views. *International Criminal Justice Review* (Georgia State University). 14:25–48.

Johnson, Roberta A. 2005. Whistle blowing and the police. *Rutgers Journal of Law and Urban Policy* 3(1): 74–83.

Johnson, Terrance A., and Raymond W. Cox III. 2004/05. Police ethics: Organizational implications. *Public Integrity* 7(Winter 1).

Kahan, D. M. 2005. Reciprocity, collective action, and community policing. *California Law Review* 90 (5): 1513.

Kane, R. 2002. The social ecology of police misconduct. *Criminology* 40 (4).

Kania, Richard. 1982. Should we tell the police to say 'yes' to gratuities?" *Criminal Justice Ethics* 7 (2): 37–49.

Kappeler, V. K., R. D. Sluder, and G. P. Alpert. 1998. *Forces of Deviance: Understanding the Dark Side of Policing.* Prospect Heights, IL: Waveland Press.

Kelling, G. L., and R. B. Kliesmet. 1972. Resistance to the professionalization of the police. *The Law Officer* September 16–22.

Kingshott, Brian F., Kathleen Bailey, and Suzanne E. Wolfe. 2004. Police culture, ethics, and entitlement theory. *Criminal Justice Studies* 17 (2): 187–202.

Klockars, C., S. K. Ivkovich, Willam E. Harver, and Maria R. Haberfeld. 2000. The measure of police integrity. *National Institute of Justice Research in Brief.* May.

Knapp Commission. 1972. *Commission to Investigate Allegations of Police Corruption and the City's Anti-Corruption Procedures.* New York: George Braziller.

Lexow Committee. 1895. Committee Report Official Title: *Report of the Special Committee Appointed to Investigate the Police Department of the City of New York.* January 18.

Los Angeles Police Department. 2000. *Board of Inquiry into the Rampart Area Corruption Incident* (Los Angeles: LAPD March. Executive Summary, p. 7; Chapter 10, "Police Integrity Systems."

Lundman, R. J. 1980. *Police Behavior: A Sociological Perspective.* New York: Oxford University Press.

Lyman, M. D. 1999. *The Police: An Introduction.* Upper Saddle River, NJ: Prentice Hall.

Maas, Peter. *Serpico.* 1973. New York: Bantam Books.

McCormack, R. 1987. An update. In *Managing Police Corruption: International Perspectives,* ed. R. H. Ward and R. McCormack, Chicago: Office of International Criminal Justice.

Miller, Eric J. 2006. Role-based policing: Restraining police conduct "outside the legitimate investigative sphere." *California Law Review* 94 (May, 3).

Mollen Commission. 1994. *The City of New York Commission to Investigate Allegations of Corruption and the Anti-Corruption Procedures of the Police Department: Commission Report.* New York, NY.

Morton, J. 1993. *Bent Coppers: A Survey of Police Corruption.* London: Little, Brown, and Company.

Murano, Vincent. 1990. *Cop Hunter.* New York: Simon & Schuster.

Newburn, T. 2003. Understanding and Preventing Police Corruption: Lessons from the Literature. Police Research Series Paper 110, Policing and Reducing Crime Unit; Research, Development and Statistics Directorate, London, UK.

New York Police Department Official Website. 2007. http://www.nyc.gov./html/nypd (accessed August 14, 2007).

O'Malley, Timothy J. 1997. Managing for ethics. *FBI Law Enforcement Bulletin*, 97 (4): 20–25.

PBS *Frontline*. L.A.P.D. Blues: The Scandal: Rampart Scandal Timeline. http://www.pbs.org/wgbh/pages/frontline/shows/lapd/scandal/cron.html (accessed August 14, 2007).

Perry, Frank L. 2001. Repairing broken windows. *FBI Law Enforcement Bulletin*, Feb 70 (2): 23–26.

Punch, M. 1985. *Conduct Unbecoming: The Social Construction of Police Deviance and Control.* New York: Methuen.

Rosenbloom, David H., and Robert S. Kravchuck. 2005. *Public Administration: Understanding Management, Politics, and Law in the Public Sector.* New York: McGraw-Hill Companies.

Rothwell, Gary R. and Norman J. Baldwin. 2007. Ethical climate theory, whistle-blowing, and the code of silence in police agencies in the state of Georgia. *Journal of Business Ethics Dordrecht* 70 (4).

Ruiz, Jim, and Christine Bono. 2004/2005. At what price a "freebie"? The real cost of police gratuities. *Criminal Justice Ethics* 23 (1, Winter/Spring): 44–54.

Rummel, David. 1994. The Tarnished Shield: When Good Cops Go Bad [video recording]; New York: ABC News; Princeton, NJ Films for the Humanities, Host: Barbara Walters, Publisher Number: FFH 5298 Films for the Humanities.

Senate Committee. 1895. *Report and Proceedings of the Senate Committee Appointed to Investigate the Police Department of the City of New York.* Vol. III: Transmitted to the Legislature January 18, 1895.

Sherman, L. W. 1974. The sociology and the social reform of the American police: 1950–1973. *Journal of Police Science and Administration* II (2): 255–62.

Sherman, L. W. 1985. Becoming bent: moral careers of corrupt policemen. In *Moral Issues in Police Work,* ed. F. Elliston and M. Feldberg, 250–67. Totowa, NJ; Rowman & Littlefield.

Sigler, Robert, and Timothy Dees. 1988. Public perception of petty corruption in law enforcement. *Journal of Police Science and Administration* Vol. 14.

Skolnick, Jerome H., and James J. Fyfe. 1993. *Above the Law: Police and the Excessive Use of Force.* New York: Free Press.

Smothers, Ronald, and Jason George. 2004. Former officer in Newark pleads guilty to corruption. *The New York Times*, 154 (52982): B1-B2, Op, 1c. September 24.

Stephens, Norman. 2006. Ethics do not begin when you pin on the badge. *FBI Law Enforcement Bulletin* 75 (11): 22–23.

Stoddard, E. R. 1968. The informal "code" of police deviancy: A group approach to blue-coat crime. *Journal of Criminal Law, Criminology and Police Science* 59:210–13.

Sykes, Gary. 1985. The functional nature of police reform: The "myth" of controlling the police. *Justice Quarterly* 2:52–65.

Taylor, Morris A. 2000. Quasi Theory, Organizational Change, and the Seduction of Raw Data. Ph.D. Dissertation, Saint Louis University.

Thatvideosite. 2005. New Orleans police looting store during Katrina. http://thatvideosite.com/video/6#CDB87 (accessed August 14, 2007).

Thompson, D. 2001. Above the law? *Law and Order* 49 (1).

United States vs. City of Pittsburg. (W.D. Pa., 1977).

USDOJ Official Website. 2007. U.S. Department of Justice civil rights division special litigation section. http://www.usdoj.gov/.webloc (accessed August 14, 2007).

Van Wart, Montgomery. 1998. *Changing Public Sector Values.* New York: Garland Publishing.

Vartabedian, Ralph, Richard A Serrano, and Richard Marosi. 2006. The long, crooked line: Rise in bribery tests integrity of U.S. border. *Los Angeles Times* Main News, National Desk, Part A, August 23.

The Village Voice. 1999. Serpico: 'Nothing has changed' cops in danger from other cops. www.villagevoice.com/news#CDD95 (accessed August 15, 2007).

Weisburd, David, and Rosann Greenspan. 2000. *Police Attitudes toward Abuse of Authority: Findings from a National Study.* Washington, D.C.: National Institute of Justice.

Westley, W. 1970. *Violence and the Police.* Cambridge, MA: MIT Press.

Westmarland, Louis. 2005. Police ethics and integrity: Breaking the blue cope of silence. *Policing and Society* 15 (2): 145–65.

Joseph Pistone, AKA "Donnie Brasco"

John Dombrink

JOSEPH PISTONE'S UNDERCOVER CAREER—THE VIEW FROM THIRTY YEARS OUT

Looking back through the horrific lens of the events of September 11, 2001, and the challenges posed to the U.S. law enforcement and intelligence communities since that day, it seems quaint to consider the exploits of one FBI agent, Joseph Pistone, who successfully infiltrated a New York City organized crime group in the 1970s, stayed undercover for six years, and eventually testified in 100 trials and the successful prosecution of scores of racketeers. In a country now concerned with the shadowy and elusive patterns and grouping of terrorists—a phenomenon that concerned other countries might have worried about, but not the United States in 1978: the territorial-bound "wiseguys," with their local social clubs and pre-cell phone, pre-e-mail aversion to being caught in an incriminating conversation in a wiretap or bug, seem farther away than thirty years.

Federal Bureau of Investigation (FBI) Fact Sheet: Organized Crime

About Organized Crime

When you think of organized crime, you probably picture the Italian and Sicilian Mafioso of television and the silver screen. But in recent years, the face of organized crime has changed, and the threat is broader and more complex than ever.

Today, organized crime includes:

- Russian mobsters who fled to the United States in the wake of the Soviet Union's collapse;
- Groups from African countries like Nigeria that engage in drug trafficking and financial scams;
- Chinese Tongs, Japanese Boryokudan, and other Asian crime rings; and
- Enterprises based in Eastern European nations like Hungary and Romania.

All of these groups have a presence in the United States or are targeting our citizens from afar—using the Internet and other technologies of our global age. More and more, they are literally becoming partners in crime, realizing they have more to gain from cooperating than competing.

The Impact of Organized Crime

It isn't easily measured, but we know it's significant. Organized crime rings manipulate and monopolize financial markets, traditional institutions like labor unions, and legitimate industries like construction and trash hauling. They bring drugs into our cities and raise the level of violence in our communities by buying off corrupt officials and using graft, extortion, intimidation, and murder to maintain their operations. Their underground businesses—including prostitution and human trafficking—sow misery nationally and globally. They also con us out of millions each year through various stock frauds and financial scams.

The economic impact alone is staggering: it's estimated that global organized crime reaps illegal profits of around $1 trillion per year.

Fighting Organized Crime

To combat the ongoing threat posed by these groups, we have a long-established—yet constantly evolving—organized crime program dedicated to eliminating the criminal enterprises that pose the greatest threat to America.

Dismantling and disrupting major international and national organized criminal enterprises is a long-standing area of FBI expertise. We have the experience and training to target criminal enterprises, the broad statutory jurisdictions to bring down entire organizations rather than just individuals, and a presence throughout the nation and the world.

Our Organized Crime Program is based on the following framework:

- Employing a methodology that yields maximum impact with our limited resources;
- Pursuing targets that have direct ties to significant national and international criminal enterprises and systematically dismantling those enterprises;
- Remaining flexible enough to pursue regional organized crime groups conducting significant racketeering activity; and
- Ensuring that our targets are permanently dismantled or significantly disrupted.

We are also reaching out globally. Partners all over the world help us track down criminals and provide critical information during investigations. We even have agents working side-by-side with colleagues in Italy, Hungary, and elsewhere.

How We're Organized to Combat Organized Crime

The Organized Crime Section at FBI Headquarters is divided into three units, devoted to La Cosa Nostra, Italian organized crime and racketeering; Eurasian/Middle Eastern organized crime; and Asian and African criminal enterprises.

(continued)

Our headquarters is tasked with the overall coordination and support of all organized crime investigations. Each of our 56 field offices investigates criminal enterprises within its own territory and relies on headquarters for additional support and help.

We also participate in joint task forces with other federal, state, and local law enforcement agencies. These task forces allow us to pool resources of various agencies, taking advantage of the efficiencies of each of these agencies to combat organized crime.

The following are among our recent successes:

- In fiscal 2005, we had 651 pending investigations related to Italian organized crime and labor racketeering alone. We had another 468 cases related to Asian and African criminal enterprises, plus investigations into groups affiliated with other parts of the globe.

- In the same year, nearly 1,500 individuals affiliated with organized crime were arrested and 824 were convicted.

- Of the roughly 1,000 "made" members of Italian organized crime groups in the United States, more than 200 are in jail.

Source: http://www.fbi.gov/hq/cid/orgcrime/aboutcs.htm/.

The view from 2008, however, shouldn't diminish the accomplishments of Pistone, who achieved what no federal law enforcement officer—indeed, no officer of any level—had done in twentieth-century American policing. He was able to successfully act as an undercover operative within traditional organized crime circles in New York for six years, eventually providing testimony and evidence against scores of racketeers, at the time when the federal government was making inroads into the policing of racketeers.

THE PISTONE CAREER

Joseph Pistone was born in 1939 and joined the FBI a few years after graduating from William Paterson College in New Jersey in 1965. He worked briefly as a teacher, then was with Naval Intelligence, and passed the entry test and joined the FBI in 1969.

His first FBI years were spent in Florida, where he occasionally worked as an undercover operative—as police in some sections of local and federal police departments did in the course of their duties. From there, he worked in Virginia and worked some truck hijackings, a staple of the racketeering world in certain circles. Such hijackings (or "driveaways," in which the trucker was complicit with the theft) also connected the racketeers to their working-class neighbors, as they sold the stolen merchandise or "swag" at steep discounts out of the back of bars or out of the trunks of cars. Pistone notes:

> I had an undercover assignment up and down the East Coast with a theft ring that stole high-end automobiles, trucks, a couple airplanes. I was using the name Donald Brasco at that time. When I came off that assignment, I had a supervisor…and we had this idea for an undercover operation that would infiltrate fences that were dealing with the mafia in stolen goods. (Diehl 2006, 17)

At the time Pistone entered his undercover role, it was common for local and federal police—in particular drug police—to use "buy-and-bust" techniques, in which the police posed as illegal drug purchasers or sellers and were exposed to violence in the main.

One of the reasons Pistone has given for his ability to be so bravely effective is that he came from a similar background and milieu as the racketeers he was infiltrating:

> I grew up in a neighborhood in Paterson, New Jersey, which is basically a suburb of New York City…you could get your complete wardrobe in a neighborhood bar: shoes, pants, shirts, even underwear and socks. The suit I wore my first day to the FBI was swag. (Pistone and Brandt 2004).

Pistone has gained justifiable notice for his six years undercover among New York racketeers, who are variously referred to as "the Mob," "wiseguys" (his preferred usage), "La Cosa Nostra" (LCN), or traditional organized crime. In a sentence, he explains: "I had the goal of gathering sufficient evidence to establish a RICO charge against the Bonnano family, as well as the other New York Mafia families by association" (Pistone and Brandt 2007).

But at the start, he didn't necessarily envision the impact he would have. The assignment was supposed to be for six months. Only at the nine-month mark did a bartender introduce him to some of the people he was hanging around and trying to meet.

As Pistone recollects, he began his stint in New York as Donnie Brasco with the same expectations of a short-term endeavor as his previous work had been:

> On the day in September 1976 that I left the New York FBI office to start my 6-month undercover role, our main goal was not with the intention of infiltrating the Mafia, nor did we have any idea that it would result in my being undercover for all those years. (Diehl 2006, 16).

Posing as a jewel thief, Pistone set in motion an evolving relationship with members of the New York City-based Bonnano crime organization:

> I chose a jewel thief because you need a legend that's non-violent. As an undercover FBI agent, you can't be saying you're going to break someone's

legs or shoot someone. A jewel thief is a profession where you can say you operate alone, which is key. You can come in with some jewelry and diamonds and say, "I did a score last night," using stuff confiscated by U.S. Customs or whatever.

His entree into the group was "Lefty Guns" Ruggiero, and this cover provided enough of a "back story" for Pistone to hang around and eventually insinuate himself into the local crime group:

> ... the whole idea about being a thief is to earn money illegally. I had the ability, they thought, to earn them money. I would bring around the precious gems. Plus, I had a skill that not many of them had, which was picking locks, burglar alarms, safes. That's a skill they needed and I had from my years in Naval Intelligence and taking different FBI courses.

Mike Newell's film *Donnie Brasco* necessarily makes "Lefty" an approachable figure, largely through the portrayal by renowned actor Al Pacino, which a *New York Times* movie reviewer lauded for bringing "color" and "pathos" to the role. Pistone says Lefty was a "stone-cold killer"—but Pacino plays him with great empathy.

Many times investigative agencies worry about their undercover operatives being "captured" by the perspective of their subjects, or "going native" and becoming less useful as operatives of their agency. Although Newell's film hints at the difficulties for Pistone and his family, with his unexplained absences and conflicts as he inhabits his undercover persona, Pistone himself assured the Congress that he held no such romantic visions of those he hung out with:

> I think it is important to observe that law enforcement's success in our operation should once and for all destroy the romantic illusion about the Mafia. Organized crime is neither invincible nor honorable. Combined with the series of publicized prosecutions in New York and elsewhere that the Subcommittee is reviewing in its hearings, law enforcement has shown that this secret society called the Mafia is no longer so secretive. Its ranks can be penetrated, its meetings recorded, and its hierarchy indicted, convicted, and all sent to jail. (Pistone 1988)

Although the federal effort against organized crime could conceivably have succeeded without the fruits of Pistone's undercover work, relying primarily instead on the products of wiretaps and bugs, there also was a synergy from the undercover work and the other forms of surveillance and evidence gathering that succeeded in crippling these racketeers. As Pistone writes in a recent book: "At one time there were twenty-six wires and bugs up and running that were based on reasonable cause taken from intelligence reports of mine from the field" (Pistone and Brandt 2007).

> Pistone's testimony was an indispensable element in cases made against the Bonnano crime family, the international Pizza Connection case, and the

path-breaking case against the group of the heads of the New York organized-crime families, known as the Commission Case: "...my testimony in over ten trials and even more grand juries throughout the United States...resulted in more than 200 indictments and over 100 convictions of members of organized crime across the country." (Jacobs 1994)

It wasn't always easy to implement these novel strategies. FBI agent Jules Bonavolonta, who had a central role in organized-crime law enforcement, writes about how difficult it was to overcome FBI bureaucracy and intransigence.

Bonavolonta also praises Pistone, in this assessment:

I can honestly say that to this day, he's still the most successful undercover agent we've ever had. Including the fact that he walked out of it with his head screwed on straight. You see a lot of problems undercover agents encounter. But he's a very level-headed guy and he used his experience to benefit other undercover agents. A lot of them still call him and ask for advice. (Span 1997).

Pistone also worked with notable prosecutors of this emerging area of organized crime control: Rudolph Giuliani (later to be New York City Mayor and 2008 Republican presidential hopeful), Louis Freeh (later the Director of the FBI), and Michael Chertoff (later to be the Secretary of the Federal Department of Homeland Security).

Pistone's coauthor Charles Brandt pays tribute to the character of his friend and coauthor, when he writes at the beginning of a 2007 book exploring untold stories and the ramifications of the "Donnie Brasco" career. To him, Pistone had "...no rulebook to follow" and exhibited "...prolonged heroism, tactical brilliance, and pure mental toughness..." (Pistone and Brandt 2007, 10).

In fact, Pistone succeeded to the extent that he was being considered for elevation into the ranks of the "made" gangsters, when the FBI ended his undercover career. He has also lived with an apparent contract out for his murder because his revelations and testimony led to the jailing (and death in some instances) of many who he worked with.

While the global situation of today might make the accomplishment of Pistone seem from a simpler time, one comparison is apt. The likelihood today of an FBI agent penetrating Al Qaeda and shaking hands with a leading Al Qaeda operative clearly seems remote. To many, that was how impenetrable the pre-1970s traditional organized-crime groups were in the United States, having been built on decades of experience in keeping the legal apparatus from knowing much of their activities. In that context, Joseph Pistone's accomplishments, as well as his eventual reports to us back from the "field" as an anthropologist of wiseguys, are notable.

ORGANIZED CRIME AND THE FAILURE OF POLICING STRATEGIES BEFORE PISTONE'S ERA

The years that Joe Pistone spent undercover coincided with a dramatic change in the approach of American federal police and prosecutors toward organized criminal enterprises and leaders, a situation in stark contrast to the ineffectiveness that had so characterized even the best-intentioned efforts before. Even as Pistone was in his first year of being undercover, the General Accounting Office (GAO) released a report that questioned the effectiveness of American organized-crime control. The GAO reported in 1977 that federal organized-crime prosecutors were "...not achieving a planned and coordinated, multiagency effort against organized crime" (GAO 1989).

Law professor James B. Jacobs, the author of three comprehensive books on the prosecution of organized crime in the 1980s and beyond, looked back on the period and told one writer: "...as late as the late 1970s/the early 80s, organized crime was as strong as it ever was in the United States" (Adler 2007). In 1908, there were few federal crimes: bankruptcy fraud, antitrust crime, neutrality violations, and peonage/compulsory servitude. Now there are 271 federal crimes.

The primary agency for federal efforts against organized crime has been the FBI, which, in 1991, had 22,000 employees, of which 10,000 were special agents (smaller than the police force of New York City).

There were many good reasons for "federalizing" this function throughout the twentieth century, given the interstate nature of many organized crimes. However, for various reasons, the FBI did not choose to make organized crime a targeted federal priority. Some analysts suggest this was because of Hoover's fear of the potentially corruptive influence of organized crime on FBI agents. Others, such as Summers, argue that personal attributes of FBI Director Hoover made him susceptible to organized-crime influence.

It was Robert Kennedy who brought federal focus to control organized crime in the federal arena, often battling with Hoover, who was putatively under his control.

Ever since Kennedy's tenure as attorney general (1961–1964), there has been increased federal interest in and responsibility for organized-crime policing and prosecution. Fresh from his pursuit of Teamster leader Jimmy Hoffa as counsel of the McClellan Rackets Committee in the Senate, Kennedy made organized-crime prosecution one of his top priorities.

When Professor Robert Blakey moved from the Organized Crime and Racketeering section of the Justice Department, where he had been a prosecutor under Kennedy and the newly energized war on organized crime, he eventually ended up as a counsel in the U.S. Senate. With Kennedy departed from office in the wake of his brother's assassination, Blakey became the key drafter of the legislation that would radically change the ability of government to sanction organized criminals: the Racketeer Influenced Corrupt Organizations, or RICO, statute part of the Organized Crime Control Act of 1970. There was also a general shift from what has been termed an "attrition strategy" against organized crime, to an "enterprise strategy," which focused on the destruction of organizations and their leadership, as well as their assets and profit bases. Blakey's contribution to the 1967 organized-crime report of the President's Commission on Organized Crime and to the use of asset forfeiture and other emerging strategies shaped this shift in strategy over these crucial decades, even while the federal effort against organized crime was criticized for lacking coherence and effectiveness. At the same time, these strategies have taken advantage of changes in the organized-crime groups themselves that make them more vulnerable to organized-crime control, even as their interests have become more diversified.

Goldstock has credited this "synergistic effect of the sociological and law enforcement changes"—increased aggressiveness of law enforcement, and the disenchantment of organized criminals—for the decline, when he testified before a U.S. Senate Committee in 1988:

> By the late 1970s, for many family members, traditional values had been replaced by simple cost-benefit analysis. When faced with prosecution, forfeiture and incarceration, they chose instead to cooperate with law enforcement. They testified not only before Senate Committees…but at trials as well. By the mid-1980s, some were even willing to wear concealable recorders to gather evidence against their colleagues. (Goldstock 1988, 675)

Goldstock further described the "mob yuppies," who…sought quick monetary rewards but were unwilling to take time to develop the skills and undertake the responsibilities of their predecessors" (674).

This transformation included many organized criminals' being willing to break the sacred code of *omerta*—secrecy—and testify for the government to prevent long prison sentences, an unheard-of event in the heyday of traditional organized crime. Salvatore Gravano's testimony against Gambino family crime boss John Gotti was the highest example—an underboss testifying against the most powerful boss of New York's crime families.

Ironically, even as this development gave police and prosecutors the upper hand in effectively sanctioning the once elusive traditional organized criminals, a similar street code against "snitching" or cooperating with authorities has come to trouble police in their efforts to build leads on common crime, gang crime, and drug crime in urban American high-crime areas. The "stop-snitching" campaign by street criminals has frustrated prosecutors who depend on victim and witness information and testimony to successfully sanction criminals.

Goldstock described the synergy of aggressive law enforcement with new legal weapons and with this new mobster:

> The increased aggressiveness of law enforcement, using modern substantive and procedural law in a sophisticated way, has created new leverage against potential witnesses. And mob figures, disenchanted with the organizations of which they were a part, choose to cooperate more and more frequently. (Goldstock 1988, 675)

The strategies that the FBI deployed in sending Pistone undercover—using surveillance information and the newly devised RICO statute to implicate many racketeer bosses—were developing as he entered his undercover assignment. In the previous decade, they had been found wanting, as a national commission on crime explained in 1967.

THE 1967 REPORT ON ORGANIZED CRIME

The opening paragraphs of the Task Force on Organized Crime report of the 1967 President's Commission on Law Enforcement and the Administration of Justice begins:

> Organized crime is a society that seeks to operate outside the control of the American people and their government. It involves thousands of criminals, working within structures as complex as those of any large corporation, subject to laws more rigidly enforced than those of legitimate governments. Its actions are not impulsive but rather the result of intricate conspiracies, carried on over many years and aimed at gaining control over whole fields of activity in order to amass huge profits. (President's Commission 1967, 1)

In addition to listing the traditional illegal activities in which organized crime takes part—gambling, loan-sharking, narcotics, and other forms of vice—the Task Force Report emphasized the activities of organized crime in legitimate business and in labor unions. "Here," the report states, "it employs illegitimate methods—monopolization, terrorism, extortion, tax evasion—to drive out or control lawful ownership and leadership and to exact profits from the public"

In defining the world of private and violent economic and social power that organized crime occupies, the Task Force Report continued:

> What organized crime wants is money and power. What makes it different from law-abiding organizations and individuals with those same objectives is that the ethical and moral standards the criminals adhere to, the laws and regulations they obey, the procedures they use are private and secret ones that they devise themselves, change when they see fit, and administer summarily and invisibly...It is organized crime's accumulation of money, not the

individual transactions by which the money is accumulated, that has a great and threatening impact on America...The purpose of organized crime is not competition with visible, legal government but nullification of it. When organized crime places an official in public office, it nullifies the political process. When it bribes a police official, it nullifies law enforcement. (1–2)

In discussing the role of law enforcement, the Task Force Report stated, "Investigation and prosecution of organized criminal groups in the twentieth century has seldom proceeded on a continuous, institutionalized basis," and "Law enforcement's way of fighting organized crime has been primitive compared to organized crime's way of operating." (10–16) (The Report then listed a number of ways in which those two statements were borne out: difficulties in obtaining proof, lack of resources, lack of coordination, failure to develop strategic intelligence, failure to use available sanctions, and the lack of public and political commitment.

The 1967 Task Force Report on Organized Crime of the President's Commission on Law Enforcement and the Administration of Justice summarized the state of organized crime and the state of law enforcement's strategies and successes against it at a time when the federal government had committed to organized-crime control as a major focus of the Justice Department. Many who had either served in investigative or prosecutorial capacities or analyzed organized crime, or both, were frustrated with the government's inability to make inroads against criminals who were well known for their exploits. Far more than the 1950s Kefauver Committee in the U.S. Senate, the 1967 Task Force Report set out to frame a range of responses and strategies that would be implemented and have a direct effect on controlling organized crime, rather than merely identifying it and railing at its presence and power.

FAILURE OF TRADITIONAL STRATEGIES

Before the shift in federal prosecution strategy, the government waged a war of attrition—in effect, removing one member of an organized crime family at a time, while that member is replaced, and the organization functions relatively undisturbed.

The GAO, an auditing arm of the federal government, found that the average sentence for convicted organized criminals was two years, when it issued a 1977 report. Further, it found that the government's strategy against organized criminals was not very well organized. From that assessment to the state of organized crime policing in 1997 is a giant leap.

Taken as a group, the new strategies and laws involved represent a wholesale shift in the focus of government efforts against organized criminals and drug traffickers, a development that has put traditional organized criminal groups and drug entrepreneurs on the run. Early prosecutorial efforts to control organized crime centered around what has been termed an "attrition" strategy. This involved an approach that sought to control organized crime through the prosecution and incarceration of key figures in organized criminal enterprises. As described by two organized crime scholars in the 1970s:

> The most commonly employed strategy is that of attrition, in which individual suspects are apprehended and prosecuted for specific alleged crimes under due process of law. The main approach has been and continues to be the apprehension of a person who is violating (or has violated) the law by means of penalties calculated to remove him from society and, using his confinement as an example, to deter others from similar activities." (Smith and Salerno 1970, 101–11)

The attrition strategy, however, underestimated the flexibility of organized crime leadership and so had little impact on the organizational structure. Many of those concerned with organized crime control were frustrated by the ability of criminal groups to absorb personnel losses or disruptions, especially insofar as these organizations were designed to reduce risk and avoid detection of activity of their most important members. The strategy, in fact, may have aided the criminal succession process without damaging the organizations themselves by removing aged leaders. The shortcomings of the attrition strategy caused law enforcement officials to recognize that organized criminal groups were resilient and readily able to replace convicted members, with only the slightest disruption of their ongoing enterprises. This frustration was clearly articulated by former deputy U.S. Attorney General Irvin B. Nathan:

> ...[w]e have learned that the incarceration of individual criminals, even those of the highest rank, is generally not sufficient to immobilize or even to reduce the incentive of entrenched criminal organizations. As long as immense criminal profits remain available as operating capital, a convicted criminal's compatriots will be able to keep the organization functioning, and the prisoner himself may be able to resume business upon or even before his release. (GAO 1981)

The problem of resilient criminal leadership has been compounded by the impingement of organized crime onto white-collar criminal activities, the growing sophistication of organized criminals, and the inability of federal law enforcement agencies to sanction targeted organized criminal entrepreneurs in a meaningful way.

To offset the limitations of the attrition strategy, federal law enforcement officials added an "enterprise" strategy in the mid-1970s, aimed at upsetting the financial stability of criminal groups, rather than punishing replaceable members. In testimony before the U.S. Senate in 1979, Justice Department

Criminal Division Chief Philip Heymann answered charges from a 1977 GAO report accusing the Justice Department of having no strategy against organized crime. Heymann explained that in 1977 intensive planning for this strategy shift took place. Another Justice Department official, Mark Richard, explained how that process unfolded:

> There was a growing frustration that was being experienced at the grass roots level of addressing the vice area. A general feeling that notwithstanding a variety of successful prosecutive actions in the area, that the impact on the total scheme of things was relatively minor, that we were not directing our resources adequately, focusing them in any meaningful fashion. A general consensus arose, if you will, throughout the organization, that a hard look was required and from a variety of sources you saw suggestions coming to the surface to where best we could utilize our resources, how we should [utilize resources] make maximum impact on these organizations and in this fashion we arrived at the position we are in now. (GAO 1981)

CHANGES IN THE FBI: FROM A FOCUS ON THE "QUANTITY" OF CASES TO A FOCUS ON THE "QUALITY" OF CASES

Organized crime, one of seven sections in the Criminal Investigative Division, has 80 percent of the bureau's agents. Former chief of that division William Baker said: "...If there's a key to all the cases we are working out of these programs, it's the criminal enterprise." After the change in the directorship of the FBI, with the passing of J. Edgar Hoover, a leadership philosophy emerged that emphasized the development of more "quality" cases in complex areas such as organized crime. This shift was done with the realization that such cases might take much longer, even years to develop. This change was in marked contrast to Hoover's earlier emphasis on the quantity of cases handled, one that may have been suited to isolated events such as bank robberies, but not to systemic and complex crimes and organizations such as organized crime groups.

Former high-ranking FBI official Oliver (Buck) Revell said about the FBI changes after Hoover's death, "...We shed almost entirely our methodologies and our almost obsessive concern with subversion. We established national priorities: organized crime, foreign counter intelligence, and white-collar crime. Perhaps the most important thing internally was we deemphasized statistics" (Wilson 1978).

As former FBI director Louis Freeh, who was the lead federal prosecutor in some of the 1980s "Pizza Connection" organized-crime cases in New York City, writes: "Clearly, the Bureau was giving American taxpayers their money's worth. In truth, the numbers were a lot of sound and fury signifying very little" (Freeh 2005).

RICO: ATTACKING THE CRIMINAL ENTERPRISE

RICO (Racketeer Influenced Corrupt Organization) has been hailed as one of the most prominent weapons against organized crime in recent decades. It has also been critiqued as an overexpansion of government authority and an unnecessary addition to the weapons available to prosecutors.

Part of the Organized Crime Control Act of 1970, RICO, with its novel conspiracy provisions and lengthy sentence allowances, has allowed federal prosecutors to reverse their long period of frustration and send many of the leaders of America's traditional organized crime families to prison for many years.

The broad reach of RICO has relieved the government of the previous limited focus on individual specific crimes, allowing a broader perspective encompassing patterns of criminal activity. This provides a prosecutorial weapon that reflects the organizational and expansive diverse character of organized crime.

HOW RICO WORKS

RICO incorporates by reference more than two dozen federal and state predicate crimes under the umbrella concept of "racketeering activity." These predicate crimes are state felonies that range from the more violent such as murder, extortion, arson, and kidnapping, to some less violent federal crimes such as embezzlement, gambling, mail fraud, wire fraud, and security fraud. Racketeering activity is defined as the committing of two instances of one or more of the designated offenses within a ten-year period. RICO specifically outlaws four types of racketeering activity by any person, persons, or organization:

1. Using income derived from a pattern of racketeering activity to acquire an interest in an enterprise [18 U.S.C. Ss 1962(a)]
2. Acquiring or maintaining an interest in an enterprise through a pattern of racketeering activity [18 U.S.C. Ss 1962(b)]
3. Conducting the affairs of an enterprise through a pattern of racketeering activity [18 U.S.C. Ss 1962(c)]
4. Conspiring to commit any of these offenses [18 U.S.C. Ss 1962(d)]

Penalties include both fines and enhanced sentencing. That means defendants can be sentenced for engaging in racketeering activity, plus the penalties associated with the predicate crimes that constituted the pattern of racketeering. In addition, assets associated with the racketeering activity are subject to forfeiture upon criminal conviction.

The way RICO works is this: It must be proved that the defendant (either an individual or organization) has committed two separate acts from a list of state and federal predicate crimes. The two acts have to be separate and form a pattern within a ten-year period. These acts must also be in furtherance of a criminal enterprise.

A criminal enterprise "includes any individual partnership, corporation, association or other legal entity, and any union or group of individuals associated in fact although not a legal entity" [18 U.S.C. Ss 1961(4)]. This concept has generally been liberally construed by the courts. One of the early problematic issues involved with this concept was whether it can be applied to an enterprise engaged in wholly illegitimate activities or restricted only to involvement in legitimate enterprises. The Supreme Court did not settle this issue until 1981 when it held that enterprises included both legitimate and illegitimate enterprises (*U.S. v. Turkette*, 101 S.Ct. 2524).

In an entertaining wiretap, federal authorities captured conversations between Boston's leading organized-crime figures discussing the applicability of RICO to their wholly illegitimate enterprises, as they followed the path of Turkette through the Supreme Court process:

> What are they gonna do with shylocking? What are they gonna do with numbers? What are they gonna do with horses? What are they gonna do with marijuana? What are they gonna do with junk? It says if they don't prove a legitimate business was infiltrated, we're off the hook. We can do anything we want. I wouldn't be in a legitimate business for all the money in the world. The law says that whoever infiltrates legitimate business in interstate commerce shall be susceptible to this. Our argument is, we're illegitimate business." (Goode 1988)

RICO requires two or more predicate offenses within a ten-year period. There has been some dispute concerning the extent to which the acts have to be related or whether they can be isolated events. One court has interpreted the statute as containing an implicit requirement that the prosecutor prove the two acts are interrelated in some manner and are not isolated events.

One of the major innovations of RICO concerns the doctrine of conspiracy. Under prior law, prosecution for conspiring to engage in organized criminal activity required a single agreement or common objective among defendants concerning a specific crime. For example, the prosecutor must show that defendants agreed to commit a specific crime such as arson, selling narcotics, or obstructing justice. This is often difficult to show, with the highly diverse criminal pursuits by unrelated individuals that is typical of organized criminal activity.

This traditional approach does not attack the organizational structure of organized crime and cannot be used to tie in a number of different individuals all engaged in different aspects of organized criminal activity. RICO allows the prosecutor to focus on the organizational nature of the criminal activity in establishing a conspiracy. Instead of establishing a series of separate conspiracies between different individuals agreeing to commit different crimes, under RICO a conspiracy is established by proving that

> [e]ach agreed to participate, directly or indirectly, in the affairs of the enterprise by committing two or more predicate crimes. Under the statute, it is irrelevant that each defendant participated in the enterprise's affairs through different, even unrelated crimes, so long as we may reasonably infer that each crime was intended to further the enterprise's affairs. (Kadish, Schulhofer, and Paulsen 1983)

RICO can be applied to both those who participate directly and indirectly, as well as those who are peripherally involved. In the words of a former assistant attorney general,

> RICO's concept of a racketeering "enterprise" to which heavy penalties are attached, begins to address the central problems of organized crime that an "enterprise" gives the continuity needed to conduct and maintain the activities on which organized crime depends. (GAO 1981)

Along with the criminal forfeiture provisions of that law and other laws, as well as the civil asset forfeiture laws, the Bank Secrecy Act—which is the primary law against money laundering, and the Continuing Criminal Enterprise statute (the drug kingpin statute)—these laws have been prominent in the shift of the prosecution of organized crime and corruption from one that focuses on crimes against individuals to taking the profit out of organized crime.

The record from the legislative consideration of the Organized Crime Control Act of 1970 shows that RICO was created and imbued with a stronger mission than are many similar pieces of federal legislation: it was encouraged to be "liberally construed" to "effectuate its remedial purpose." In drafting the statute, the Senate Judiciary Committee specifically stated the purpose of RICO was

> the elimination of the infiltration of organized crime and racketeering into legitimate organizations operating in interstate commerce by the fashioning of new criminal and civil remedies and investigative procedures. (Senate Judiciary Committee Report 1969, 76)

The RICO statute can be used criminally, against traditional organized crime figures, as well as against corrupt public officials or white-collar criminals—Michael Millken and securities law infractions, and Savings and Loan fraud crimes. It can also be used civilly, both by the government and by private parties—thus the term "private attorney general"—to compensate public and private victims of organized criminal activity through the civil courts. This unique component of RICO has been the center of a vociferous debate in legislative and legal circles ever since its passage and growth in its use.

By far the biggest story of the decade was the unparalleled success of federal prosecutors against organized crime family leaders throughout the nation, using RICO and other federal criminal laws. As former FBI Director William Sessions testified before Congress:

> Prior investigations had resulted in the incarceration of large numbers of high-level and influential LCN members. These investigations, as yet, had not significantly disrupted the all-pervasive control and influence which the LCN exerted over legitimate business and industries, and within the labor movement.
>
> Therefore, a strategy was formulated and developed to implement an attack upon the LCN family as a criminal enterprise, utilizing the RICO statute to prosecute the hierarchy, members, and associates of an LCN Family for all the predicate criminal violations in which they were allegedly involved. (Sessions 1988)

The year 1988 was a good year to take stock of the successes of the federal government's organized crime control. It was a good year to mark the changes, but also from a long view to look across the twenty-five years since the federal government had penetrated enough to produce a cooperating witness in the person of Joseph Valachi.

In many ways, selecting 1988 as a silver anniversary was too self-congratulatory, suggesting that there had been a continuous growth in presence and prosecutorial success since 1963. In fact, after Valachi, there had been a lot of focus, buildup, and planning, but it would be years—until about the time of Pistone's undercover efforts—before the fruits of those efforts would appear.

On the one hand, someone arguing for the linear growth from Valachi to 1988 would point to moments like the publication of the organized crime report of the President's Commission on the Administration of Justice. One of the products of that committee was the Organized Crime Control Act, which was introduced in 1969 and eventually passed as the Organized Crime Control Act of 1970, with the Racketeer Influenced Corrupt Organizations statute passed as part of that. The cases that Pistone contributed to began with his undercover assignment in 1976 and were a symbol of RICO's reach.

The second school of thought would emphasize the slow start, the small successes, and the discontinuities in this period. One primary source of reluctance was the weak commitment of FBI Director J. Edgar Hoover during this period.

As political scientist James Q. Wilson has argued, it took the death of Hoover to bring a shift in FBI case-making priorities from the quantity of cases it solved to the quality of criminal cases. This was an advantage in certain types of investigations that required more time to work and didn't produce the immediate barrage of statistics that Hoover liked to trumpet in Congressional hearings as proof of his Bureau's efficacy. It also typified FBI advances in cases involving white-collar crimes and public corruption, which, along with organized crime, formed the basis of an FBI refocused effort in the 1980s, with an accompanying focus on proactive policing that represented a change in the culture of the Bureau.

FBI Director Clarence Kelley, who served from 1973 to 1979, was credited with causing this shift in the Bureau's investigative priorities and operations, away from an excessive focus on the number of cases solved held out by Hoover.

To former prosecutor Goldstock, RICO was the prosecutorial weapon that brought together a set of other unfolding investigative techniques in a synergy that would effectively work against the targeted organized criminals:

> Well, RICO was part of a whole host of tools that came together to give government the edge in the fight. Before that there was really nothing directed at organized crime. We used the same tools of conspiracy that we had used for small groups of people engaged in individual criminal activities. But syndicated criminal activity was different and there were a variety of conspiracies occurring at the same time, hierarchies within the family, and so RICO allowed you to target the entire group, the family, rather than individuals. And when used with electronic surveillance and witness protection and use immunity, it provided a whole way of rethinking about how you attacked organized crime. (Adler 2007)

These concepts were combined with a variety of weapons, or dormant weapons, that the new philosophy and personnel breathed life into. For example, the growing effectiveness of the federal witness protection program offered an option for those witnesses who figured that testifying for the government was the best alternative, but feared reprisals after they did.

Vertical prosecution also grew, a concept in which local or federal police were joined in the early stages or throughout key investigations, to ensure that they proceeded in a way that would maximize the strength of the evidence they eventually collected for trial.

To Robert Blakey, who worked as hard as anyone to spread the knowledge of the statute's provisions and attractiveness for use in organized crime cases, it was a long and ultimately successful endeavor:

> I thought that the statute would become law and it would be used both by prosecutors and private litigators. It didn't work that way. And it never works that way—getting law enforcement to rethink what they do and to take risks by starting to do something new is an extremely difficult task. It requires changing the most rigid thing in the world, the mind of a prosecutor. (Adler 2007)

PISTONE AS ANTHROPOLOGIST—BEING AND SEEING INSIDE THE MOB

The period of Pistone's undercover work also increasingly produced transcripts from authorized bugs and wiretaps that provide a good look inside the racketeering world, but Pistone paints a world through its everyday-ness, going where researchers haven't (beyond Francis Ianni and Elizabeth Reuss-Ianni in their heralded 1972 study). Like an anthropologist visiting an unusual culture, Pistone's observations on the ordinariness of the wiseguy life are valuable, and we can decide the extent to which they are colored by his commitment to the policing of his newfound "friends."

As he says,

> One thing I will never forget from my 6 years with them is the daily grind of trying to make a "score" that they face from the time they wake up in the morning to the time they go to sleep at night. This is not the romantic life of "The Godfather" or television drama but, rather, is a life of treachery, violence, and, ironically, boredom.

Pistone's *Donnie Brasco* (and the subsequent movie) offer a palpable sense of the rhythm and feel of the "wiseguy life."

> To Lefty and all the rest of the people I met in the Mob, what they do is legitimate. They do not view themselves as morally reprehensible, they do not think of themselves as being criminals. Coming from a subculture where crime is acceptable, where their elders, friends, and neighbors view criminal behavior as normal, as even honorable, these men would take issue with being called criminals or gangsters. To this subculture, cooperating with the Government is morally reprehensible and criminal. That is why it is so significant when Government agents successfully convince a wiseguy or an associate to become a Government witness.

To organized crime chronicler Selwyn Raab, Pistone's observations demystify the myths concocted by novelists and moviemakers about a benevolent, roguish side to the Mafia. "As witnessed by Pistone, daily life for the rank-and-file mobster is as dreary as toiling on an assembly line. Most of their time is devoted to endless scheming for a share of someone else's illicit plunder and bickering over advancement. Gangster life consists mainly of looking for the score, making the weekly 'earn,' and kicking money 'upstairs'" (Raab 1988). In this way, Raab's observations of Pistone's reportage fit nicely with the work of economist Peter Reuter and colleagues and sociologist Sudhir Alladi Venkatesh, who stress the "blue-collarness" of street drug sales—no get-rich-quick schemes in their view.

In his book, *Donnie Brasco*—and especially illuminated by the Mike Newell film *Donnie Brasco*, Pistone captures his "sponsor" Lefty Ruggiero as explaining at different times what the allure of the gangster world is for those who live in it: "When you're a wiseguy, you can steal, you can cheat, you can lie, you can kill people—and it's all legitimate" (Pistone and Brandt 2004).

Pistone's stories, while fashioned for the eventual prosecution of those he hung around with, provide insight into the "working personality" of the racketeer:

> The wiseguy does not see himself as a criminal or even a bad person; he sees himself as a businessman, a shrewd hustler, one step ahead of ordinary suckers. The wiseguy lives by a vastly different set of rules than those observed by regular people, rules that were fashioned by their criminal forefathers and proven to work by generations of mobsters before them. Wiseguys exist in a bizarre parallel universe, a world where avarice and violence and corruption are the norm, and where the routines that most ordinary people hold dear—working good jobs, being with family, living an honest life—are seen as the curse of the weak and the stupid. (Pistone and Brandt 2004)

ETHICAL ISSUES OF UNDERCOVER

The year that Joe Pistone went undercover with the New York racketeers, national attention was being shone upon the activities of the FBI and the CIA in intelligence gathering and special operations both internally and abroad. With the resignation of President Richard Nixon in 1974 following the revelations of his administration's abuse of power and investigative efforts, Americans were far more conscious of the excesses of governmental power and the necessity for accountability and the specific setting of limits. In what has been referred to as a "post-Watergate morality" (referring to the Nixon reelection campaign's break-in at the National Democratic Headquarters), a U.S. committee headed by Senator Frank Church probed the actions of the CIA. The U.S. Senate Select Committee to Study Governmental Operations with Respect to Intelligence Activities, and its confirmation that the FBI had also engaged in surveillance and disruptive efforts against dissident political groups, through the COINTELPRO program, also caused many to wonder whether the FBI had been reckless in its surveillance of Americans, ironically during the same years that it had shied away from intensively policing American racketeers.

The Church Committee concluded:

> The intelligence community has employed surreptitious collection techniques— mail opening, surreptitious entries, informants, and "traditional" and highly sophisticated forms of electronic surveillance—to achieve its overly broad intelligence targeting and collection objectives. Although there are circumstances where these techniques, if properly controlled, are legal and appropriate, the Committee finds that their very nature makes them a threat to the personal privacy and Constitutionally protected activities of both the targets and of persons who communicate with or associate with the targets. The dangers inherent in the use of these techniques have been compounded by the lack of

adequate standards limiting their use and by the absence of review by neutral authorities outside the intelligence agencies. As a consequence, these techniques have collected enormous amounts of personal and political information serving no legitimate governmental interest. (Select Committee to Study Governmental Operations 1976)

Issues of civil liberties had already been foremost in many of the discussions of the use of state power against the organized criminal. The issue of whether Attorney General Robert Kennedy had been justified in using bugs against selected organized crime targets certainly foreshadowed today's discussion of The Patriot Act and FISA wiretaps.

The Pistone case exemplifies a number of ethical considerations that were much discussed in the era of Pistone's work. One of the expressed bases was Director Hoover's reluctance to use undercover operatives within the FBI for policing of organized crime (this didn't deter him from using the technique in anticommunist "red squads," however).

One writer, detailing the analysis of noted sociologist Gary Marx on the rise and use of surveillance during this period notes:

The most obvious change is the tremendous growth of covert and undercover operations by local and federal law enforcement agencies during the last decade: in 1977, for example, the FBI appropriated $1 million for 53 undercover operations. Seven years later, the bureau alone spent more than $12 million for nearly 400 such operations. A major impetus for the increase in undercover operations is the growth of white-collar crime and the need for law enforcement agencies to become more aggressive in anticipating, rather than just reacting to, crime. (Gelbspan 1988)

The writer further quotes from Marx, who had written:

Undercover work grows easily out of an emphasis on planning, prevention and productivity. It offers a means of actively pursuing crime through direct involvement and police initiative. It fits with the notion of the modern police officer prevailing via intelligence, skill and finesse, rather than brute force and coercion. (Gelbspan 1988)

Elsewhere, Marx had reflected on the unintended social and psychological costs that undercover work can have for its practitioners.

Also during Pistone's time undercover, the experience in FBI political corruption undercover operations, including members of Congress and the selling of influence in New Jersey casino licensing, also led to consideration on the limits and ethics of undercover operations, as explored in Gerald Caplan's *ABSCAM Ethics*. Ironically, it was one racketeer's reading of a story highlighting the ABSCAM boat used by the FBI, which also was borrowed for use by Pistone with his counterparts, that nearly blew Pistone's cover. One distinct product of the attention and the hearings to surveillance and undercover activities was the promulgation of new guidelines to control such activity.

CONCLUSION: THE "TWILIGHT OF THE MOB" AND THE RISE OF OTHER THREATS

Joseph Pistone's undercover work is justifiably celebrated for its contribution to the efforts at that time to dismantle the reach and strength of organized crime in America. The convictions and sentencing of the Commission members—heads of New York crime families convicted for their roles in coordinating and adjudicating New York's traditional organized crime business and interrelationships—was a highlight in 1987. Anthony Salerno, Carmine Persico, and Anthony Corallo, bosses of three families, were sentenced to 100 years. The head of the Bonnano family was sentenced to twelve years that year for his part in a labor racketeering conspiracy, and the Pizza Connection trial resulted in the conviction of eighteen others and the indictment of more than 100 in Italy.

In 1988, FBI Director Webster reported that since 1981, nineteen bosses, thirteen underbosses, and forty-three capos had been convicted. The GAO estimated that there were 2,500 indictments of Cosa Nostra members and associates between 1983 and 1986 alone. Jacobs lists the traditional organized crime bosses convicted between 1981 and 1992, and the list includes organized crime leaders in New York City (eight leaders), New Orleans, Denver, Chicago, Kansas City, Los Angeles, Boston, Philadelphia, Cleveland, St. Louis, Buffalo, Providence, and Newark.

With the successes of the FBI, the Justice Department, and other agencies against traditional organized crime adding up, the challenges then turned to the emerging groups, for whom the successes of the 1980s would serve as models, even as the law enforcement intelligence and expertise were being constructed. The FBI and aligned agencies were not as able to deploy equal numbers of agents in the same capacity or with the same success as Pistone had, and there was always an additional tension: agents or employees with the linguistic and cultural skills that would make them suitable for undercover work were also coveted for their use in counter-intelligence (or foreign counter-intelligence) work.

The racketeers whom Joe Pistone targeted in the 1970s were homebodies who rarely left the comfortable confines of their neighborhood. They were replaced increasingly as the century went on with global criminals in a fluid, rapid, borderless, and electronic world in which certain criminals thrived.

At the time of his retirement, shortly before September 11, 2001, FBI Director Louis Freeh spoke proudly of the efforts during his time as director to make the FBI into a more effective organization with precisely these international aspects in mind:

We have more than doubled the FBI's overseas presence—now in 44 critical foreign locations—in order to enhance cooperation with our foreign counterparts. These measures already have proven invaluable in the international fight against terrorism, organized crime, cyber-crimes, and trans-national crimes in the Information Age. (Freeh 2006)

By 2007, the significant successes of the FBI and federal prosecutors against traditional organized crime in the United States would serve as a model for work against other challenges, such as terrorism and global crime. The current FBI emphasizes this in their Web page:

How is the FBI fighting organized crime, particularly international organized crime? The FBI uses a variety of laws, asset forfeiture statutes, and sophisticated investigative techniques in its domestic and international cases. The criminal and civil provisions of the Racketeer Influenced and Corrupt Organizations (RICO) statute are particularly suited to dismantle criminal organizations. These investigations frequently utilize undercover operations, court-authorized electronic surveillance, informants and cooperating witnesses, and consensual monitoring. Many of these are conducted with foreign and domestic police agencies. The FBI operates under an organized crime/drug strategy that focuses its investigations on major international, national, and regional groups that control large segments of the illegal activities. (FBI 2007)

Current FBI Director Robert Mueller elaborated on this, with specific detail for organized crime, in testimony before a Congressional committee in 2007:

Trans-national organized crime continues to evolve with advances in globalization and technology. We are also actively investigating Eurasian, Albanian, Asian, and African organized criminal syndicates. Between 2001 and 2007, for example, pending Eurasian organized crime cases increased by 65 percent and an average of 160 individuals were indicted per year between 2002 and 2006. We are working with the Italian National Police to combat Sicilian Mafia activity in Italy and in the United States, in a partnership known as the Pantheon Project. The FBI-Hungarian National Police Organized Crime Task Force has been up and running for more than six years, working to dismantle organized crime groups, with FBI agents permanently stationed in Budapest to work with their Hungarian counterparts. The Albanian Organized Crime Task Force will commence operations this fall, with partial funding from the Department of Defense. (Mueller 2007)

At the same time, the national discussion of the Patriot Act and its intrusiveness and role of government, the issue of American detention of foreign nationals suspected of terrorism links at Guantanamo Bay without court hearings, a range of debates about the appropriateness of torture, as well as the classification of "waterboarding" and other interrogation techniques as torture (or not) reflects a world far changed from the 1976 world of racketeers on street corners.

The FBI still utilizes undercover agents, and Joe Pistone has helped train them at the FBI Academy in Quantico, Virginia. He writes nonfiction accounts and observations based on his undercover years, as recently as 2007, and even pens "Donnie Brasco" mystery novels. What he told a reporter last year about the nature of his contribution as "Donnie Brasco" captures the nature of this specialized area of policing in the 1980s: "I really feel that what we did in those six years—me and all the others who worked on the case—was the beginning of the breaking of the Mafia's stronghold on the American public" (Diehl 2006). As Jacobs and others have noted, this was precisely the context of Pistone's work and career.

ACKNOWLEDGMENT

I thank James W. Meeker and John Song, researchers and coauthors with me on various aspects of the policing of organized crime in the traditional (Meeker) and nontraditional (Song) settings.

FURTHER READING

Adler, Margot. 2007. Organized Crime in the 21st Century, Radio Transcript, Justice Talking, National Public Radio, January 1.

Anderson, Elijah. 2000. *Code of the Street: Decency, Violence, and the Moral Life of the Inner City.* New York: W. W. Norton.

Blakey, G. Robert, Ronald Goldstock, and Charles Rogovin. 1978. *Racket Bureaus: Investigation and Prosecution of Organized Crime.* Washington, D.C.: National Institute of Law Enforcement.

Blumenthal, Ralph. 1988. *Last Days of the Sicilians At War With the Mafia: The F.B.I. Assault on the Pizza Connection.* New York: Times Books.

Bonavolonta, Jules, and Brian Duffy. 1996. *The Good Guys: How We Turned the FBI 'Round and Finally Broke the Mob.* New York: Simon & Schuster.

Caplan, Gerald M., ed. 1983. *Abscam Ethics: Moral Issues and Deception in Law Enforcement.* Cambridge, MA: Ballinger.

Diehl, Christine S. 2006. *WP* has a "sit-down" with Joe Pistone/Donnie Brasco. *WP, The Magazine of William Paterson University.* Winter:16–20.

Dombrink, John, and James W. Meeker. 1986. Beyond "buy and bust": Nontraditional sanctions in federal drug law enforcement. *Contemporary Drug Problems: A Law Quarterly* 13, (4, Winter), 711–40.

Dombrink, John, and James W. Meeker. 1993. Organized crime in the "Twilight of the Mob": Groups, enterprise, and legal innovation from 1967–1992. In *The President's Crime Commission: 25 Years Later,* ed. John A. Conley, Cincinnati: Anderson Publishing Company.

Dombrink, John, and John Huey-Long Song. 1994. Of twilights and dawns: The challenges of policing emerging organized crime. In *Handbook of Organized*

Crime in the United States, ed. Robert J. Kelly, et al., 415–30. Westport, CT: Greenwood Publishing Group.

Federal Bureau of Investigation. 2007. Frequently Asked Questions. http://www. Fbi.gov/faq.

Freeh, Louis J. 2005. *My FBI: Bringing Down the Mafia, Investigating Bill Clinton, and Fighting the War on Terror*. New York: St. Martin's Press.

Gelbspan, Ross. 1988. Undercover work: A necessary evil? *Boston Globe*, Nov. 26.

Geller, William A., and Norval Morris. 1992. Relations between federal and local police. In *Modern Policing. Crime and Justice*, Volume 15, ed. Michael Tonry and Norval Morris. Chicago: University of Chicago Press.

General Accounting Office. 1977. *War on Organized Crime Faltering—Federal Strike Forces Not Getting the Job Done*. Washington, D.C.: United States General Accounting Office, GGD-77-17, March 17.

General Accounting Office. 1981. *Stronger Federal Effort Needed in Fight Against Organized Crime*. Washington, D.C.: United States General Accounting Office, GGD-82-2, December 7.

General Accounting Office. 1989. *Issue Regarding Strikes Forces*. Washington, D.C.: United States General Accounting Office, GGD-89-67, April 3.

Giuliani, Rudolph. 1986. Interview with United States Attorney, Southern District of New York, New York City, March 28.

Goldfarb, Ronald. 1995. *Perfect Villains, Imperfect Heroes: Robert F. Kennedy's War Against Organized Crime*. New York: Random House.

Goldstock, Ronald. 1988. Testimony of Director, State of New York Organized Crime Task Force, U.S. Senate, Permanent Subcommittee on Investigations, Committee on Governmental Affairs, 100th Congress, April 21. Printed in committee report, S. HRG. 100-906, *Organized Crime: 25 Years After Valachi.*

Goode, James. 1988. *Wiretap: Listening In on America's Mafia*. New York: Simon & Schuster. http://stopsnitchin.com. 2007.

Ianni, Francis J. and Elizabeth Reuss-Ianni. 1972. *A Family Business: Kinship and Social Control in Organized Crime*. New York: Russell Sage Foundation.

Jacobs, James B., with Christopher Panarella and Jay Worthington. 1994. *Busting the Mob: United States v. Cosa Nostra*. New York: New York University Press.

Jacobs, James B., with Coleen Friel and Robert Radick. 1999. *Gotham Unbound: How New York City Was Liberated from the Grip of Organized Crime*. New York: New York University Press.

Jacobs, James B. 2006. *Mobsters, Unions, and Feds: The Mafia and the American Labor Movement*. New York: New York University Press.

Jacobs, James B. and Lauryn P. Gouldin. 1999. Cosa Nostra: The final chapter? In *Crime and Justice,* Vol. 25, ed. Michael Tonry, 129–89. Chicago: University of Chicago Press.

Kadish, Sanford H., Stephen J. Schulhofer, and Monrad G. Paulsen. 1983. *Criminal Law and Its Processes: Cases and Materials*. 3rd ed. Boston: Little, Brown Publishers.

Kahn, Jeremy. 2007. The story of a snitch. *The Atlantic* April: 79–92.

Kallstrom, James K. 1997. Statement of FBI Assistant Director James K. Kallstrom Concerning the "Second Notice of Capacity," Washington, D.C.: Federal Bureau of Investigation, FBI National Press Office, January 14.

Kelly, Robert J. 1999. *The Upperworld and the Underworld: Case Studies of Racketeering and Business Infiltrations in the United States.* New York: Kluwer Academic/Plenum.

Lehmann-Haupt, Christopher. 1996. Corralling the brutes and boobs of the Mob, Review of Jules Bonavolonta and Brian Duffy, *The Good Guys. New York Times*, February 8.

Maas, Peter. 1997. *Underboss: Sammy the Bull Gravano's Story of Life in the Mafia.* New York: HarperCollins.

Marx, Gary T. 1988. *Undercover: Police Surveillance in America.* Berkeley: University of California Press.

Marx, Gary T. 1995. Recent developments in undercover policing. In *Punishment and Social Control: Essays in Honor of Sheldon Messinger,* ed. Thomas G. Blomberg and Stanley Cohen. New York: Aldyne de Gruyter.

Maslin, Janet. 1997. Donnie Brasco: Al Pacino as gangster, a guy who's not wise. *New York Times*, February 28.

Moore, Mark. 1977. *Buy and Bust.* Lexington, MA: D.C. Heath.

Mueller, Robert S. 2007. Testimony of FBI Director, U.S. Congress, House of Representatives, Committee on the Judiciary, July 26.

Navasky, Victor S. 1971. *Kennedy Justice.* New York: Atheneum.

New York State Organized Crime Task Force. 1990. *Corruption and Racketeering in the New York City Construction Industry.* New York: New York University Press.

Pistone, Joseph. 1988. Testimony of Joseph D. Pistone, Former Special Agent, Federal Bureau of Investigation, before the U.S. Senate, Permanent Subcommittee on Investigations, Committee on Governmental Affairs, 100th Congress, April 21. Printed in committee report, S. HRG. 100-906, *Organized Crime: 25 Years After Valachi.*

Pistone, Joseph D. with Richard Woodley. 1987. *Donnie Brasco: My Undercover Life in the Mafia.* New York: NAL Books.

Pistone, Joseph D. and Charles Brandt. 2004. *The Way of the Wiseguy: True Stories from the FBI's Most Famous Undercover Agent.* Philadelphia: Running Press.

Pistone, Joe, and Charles Brandt. 2007. *Donnie Brasco: Unfinished Business.* Philadelphia: Running Press.

President's Commission on Law Enforcement and Administration of Justice. Task Force on Organized Crime, 1967. *Task Force Report: Organized Crime.* Washington: U.S. Government Printing Office.

Raab, Selwyn. 1988. Donnie Brasco: My undercover life in the Mafia. Book Reviews. *Washington Monthly*, June.

Rachal, Patricia. 1982. *Federal Narcotics Enforcement: Reorganization and Reform.* Boston: Auburn House Publishing.

Reuter, Peter H., Robert MacCoun, Patrick Murphy, Allan Abrahamse, and B. Simon. 1990. *Money From Crime: A Study of the Economics of Drug Dealing in Washington, D.C.* Santa Monica, CA: RAND Corporation.

Rhodes, Robert P. 1984. *Organized Crime: Crime Control vs. Civil Liberties.* New York: Random House.

Schlesinger, Arthur M., Jr. 1978. *Robert Kennedy and His Times.* Boston: Houghton Mifflin.

Select Committee to Study Governmental Operations. 1976. Intelligence Activities and the Rights of Americans, Book II of the Final Report of the Select Committee to Study Governmental Operations with Respect to Intelligence Activities, U.S. Senate, April 26.

Sessions, William. 1988. Testimony of Director, Federal Bureau of Investigation, before the U.S. Senate, Permanent Subcommittee on Investigations, Committee on Governmental Affairs, 100th Congress, April 21. Printed in committee report, S. HRG. 100-906, *Organized Crime: 25 Years After Valachi.*

Shelley, Louise. 2002. The nexus of organized international criminals and terrorism. *International Annals of Criminology* 20 (1/2): 85–92.

Smith, Dwight C., Jr., and Ralph F. Salerno. 1970. The use of strategies in organized crime control. *The Journal of Criminal Law, Criminology, and Police Science* 61 (1, March): 101–11.

Span, Paula. 1997. The FBI's veiled threat: Joseph Pistone spent six years inside the Mafia and lived to tell the tale. *Washington Post*, February 28.

Summers, Anthony. 1993. *Official and Confidential: The Secret Life of J. Edgar Hoover.* New York: Pocket Books.

Sykes, Gresham M., and David Matza. 1957. Techniques of neutralization: A theory of delinquency. *American Sociological Review* 22:664–70.

Taylor, Francis X. 2004. A Global Perspective on Terrorism and Organized Crime, Presentation by Ambassador Francis X. Taylor, Assistant Secretary for Diplomatic Security and Director, Office of Foreign Missions, Keynote Speech to the International Conference on Asian Organized Crime and Terrorism, Honolulu, April 12.

Theoharis, Athan. 1978. *Spying on Americans: Political Surveillance from Hoover to the Huston Plan.* Philadelphia: Temple University Press.

U.S. Senate Select Committee to Study Governmental Operations with Respect to Intelligence Activities. 1976. Final Report. Washington: D.C.: United States Senate, April 26.

Venkatesh, Sudhir Alladi. 2006. *Off the Books: The Underground Economy of the Urban Poor.* Cambridge, MA: Harvard University Press.

Wilson, James Q. 1978. *The Investigators: Managing FBI and Narcotics Agents.* New York: Basic Books.

Courtesy of Photofest

Vincent T. Bugliosi: Justice Purist—The Prosecutor with a Heart

Edward J. Schauer

Vincent T. Bugliosi is considered by citizens, scholars, and criminal justice professionals alike to be the world's foremost criminal trial prosecutor. Working out of the Los Angeles District Attorney's office as a deputy district attorney, he won 105 of the 106 felony trials that he prosecuted. His prosecution record is even more amazing when his murder trials are considered: He successfully prosecuted all twenty-one of his murder cases. Finally, never has one of Bugliosi's cases been reversed upon appeal. Starling Lawrence, the person whom Vince personalizes as "my editor," exclaims, "Vincent Bugliosi should be on any knowledgeable person's short list of the great lawyers in America, but as a *prosecutor* he stands alone, in a class by himself" (Bugliosi 1996a, 11).

Vincent Bugliosi is known for trying difficult cases that represented major uphill battles, three of which are chronicled in his true-crime murder mystery books. For example, Vince reports in his book *Helter Skelter,* that when the Tate/LaBianca trial was assigned to him, the Manson case was not yet solved; therefore, it fell upon him to lead the investigation in this complex case regarding those bizarre, bloody, and complex murders.

Whether serving as a prosecutor in criminal trials, as the leading author in the true-crime murder mystery literary genre, or as a murder trial defense attorney, Vincent Bugliosi puts his whole being into the challenge. He is dedicated, focused, and precise—an advanced workaholic. Vince is never without a major project; he lives his professional life with a list of projects in various stages of completion and of planning, so that his mind is never idle. For example, after he successfully defended Jennifer Jenkins in her trial for the Palmyra murders, after February 1986, he simultaneously selectively practiced law, worked on a book on the drug problem, and was working on an in-depth book on the Kennedy assassination.

Bugliosi's courtroom style is expansive, theatrical, and thorough. He is almost obsessed with his determined and exquisite preparation. His bravery is amazing: He remained dogged throughout the prosecution of the Manson family in the face of his observation that the judge, all the witnesses, all the lawyers, and others associated with the trial were afraid for their lives.

How does Vince Bugliosi view himself? He perceives himself to be primarily a criminal trial prosecutor, and only secondarily an author. When I mentioned that he is listed on the Web as an author and asked about his public speaking, he replied that he seldom speaks publicly. I asked how highly he would rank his public speaking. Vince answered, "I'm first and foremost a prosecutor; second, an author; and third, a public speaker. But the public speaking is way down the list." (Schauer 2007c). Even when in private practice he defended Jenkins in the Palmyra murder trial, Vince thought of himself as a prosecutor: In determining how best to go about defending her, he concluded that he was best at trial prosecuting. So he determined to prosecute Buck Walker aggressively for the murders as his defense technique.

THE FINAL SUMMATION: KEY OF TRIAL SUCCESS

Much preparation, both before and during the trial, for the final summation is the foundation of Vincent Bugliosi's success in the prosecution of his criminal cases. "I write everything down. It is all there on the yellow pad." (Schauer 2007c). He does not turn the page until he covers everything on that page in court. He has studied his notes well enough that he looks at the page and remembers everything on that page. He usually does not have to look at that page again until he has covered that material in court and it is time to turn the page.

Vince states, "I have 90 percent of the trial choreographed before the trial begins: All is on the yellow pad." He knows the strengths of his case, as well as the weaknesses of the defense. He knows the law relating to the case because he has done his homework before the trial begins. He repeats, "All is on the yellow pad." (Schauer 2007c).

Bugliosi has called his yellow pad "my security blanket." (Bugliosi 1996a, 189). He also uses the yellow pad to lead in murder investigations. He considers it to be of highest importance to have carefully written and thoroughly studied notes covering all segments of the trial. These notes must contain case law required, direct examination planned, cross-examination predicted, objections anticipated, and final summation. "In a complex trial involving many witnesses and thousands of pages of transcript, to discuss the highlights and nuances of the case and draw the necessary inferences, in the most telling sequence, always seeking simplicity and clarity of expression, requires an enormous amount of written preparation." (151).

Vince Bugliosi views the final summation as the choreography or blueprint in planning and directing the criminal trial. He explains:

> Usually, the very first thing I think about when I get on a case and begin to learn the facts is: *What* am I going to argue, and *how* can I best make the argument to obtain a favorable verdict? In other words, I work backward from my summation, the exact reverse of what is normally recommended. Since final summation has to be based on the evidence at the trial, virtually all of my questions at the trial, and most of my tactics and techniques, are aimed at enabling me to make arguments I've already determined I want to make. In fact, before the first witness at a trial has even been called, I've usually prepared my summation to the jury. As soon as I learn the strengths and weaknesses of my case I begin to work on how I'm going to argue these strengths and what I'm going to say in response to the opposition's attacks on the weaknesses. Getting an early start on my summation, and continuing to expand and modify it during the trial, gives me ample time to develop arguments and articulations. (148–149)

In essence, Vince uses the written notes early on to try the case against himself; then he determines how the evidence will be presented, how he will deal with the defense motions he expects, how he will preempt the defense by bringing out the weaknesses in his own case, how he will cross-examine the defense witnesses, and finally, how he will communicate the logic and law of the trial to the jury in his final arguments. He continues, "I realize I have almost an obsession about the preparation of a final summation. For instance, in the Manson case, I put in several hundred hours working on my opening and closing arguments." (149).

Bugliosi feels that the critical goal of the final summation is to communicate clearly to the jury—to make bridges between the law in the judge's instructions with the facts of the case in hand. The step-by-step logic of the state's case must be understood by the jury so that they can make informed decisions, and it is the prosecuting attorney's task to clearly explain to the jury the logical connections between evidence brought by the state which prove the defendant's guilt. Vince explains, "With almost any jury, you have to spoon-feed them. That's what I do. I never take a chance on assuming a jury is going to see something important without my help. So many times in life things are only obvious once they are pointed out." (139).

One of the issues that must be clearly explained to the jury is the issue of reasonable doubt. Most citizens confound this issue with the interpretation of beyond the shadow of a doubt. Citizens also confuse the state of being declared *not guilty* by the court with being *innocent*; and common communication from courts, including statements from the U.S. Supreme Court, further confuse this issue for the jurors. Bugliosi feels so strongly about this that he apparently always includes a clarification in his final summation to the jury. His expanded explanation was published under the title, "Not Guilty and Innocent—The Problem Children of Reasonable Doubt."

In terms of doubt, Vince explains that even the most minute doubt must be answered in the final summation because it may lead to losing the case back in the jury room, where the tiny doubt may grow to be of larger significance. Also, the prosecutor should point out weaknesses in the state's case whether they were mentioned by the defense or not, because the jury may have caught those weaknesses and may feel that the state is hiding evidence. "Therefore cover all points." (Bugliosi 1978, 331, 341).

Since he strongly believes that the final argument is the most important part of the trial, Bugliosi puts hundreds of hours into his final arguments. He states, "Final argument is nothing more than a speech, and I know of no great speech in history that was not carefully prepared before it was delivered." (Bugliosi 1996a, 151).

Vincent Bugliosi has been challenged for his insistence on a carefully written, rewritten, contemplated, and committed-to-memory final summation, on the grounds that summations should be extemporaneous in nature for fluidity and freshness of presentation. Vince argues, "It's simply not possible to powerfully articulate a great number of points, one immediately following another, extemporaneously. There *is* a best way to make a point, and to find it takes time and sweat on the yellow pad." (151). He continues:

> The one advantage in arguing extemporaneously is to be able to talk to the jury eye to eye, with the candor of spontaneity. But if a trial lawyer is willing to put in the hours, he can have such a grasp of his written or outlined argument that, *like an actor on a stage* whose lines flow naturally, he can deliver it to the jury giving the appearance of spontaneity. If I've had adequate time to prepare, I only have to glance at my notes sparingly. I can look at one word on a page, and the whole page is vivid in my mind. (151)

Probably his most convincing argument for his ability to marry spontaneity and carefully prepared notes is found in his rhetorical question, "Is instant improvisation and flexibility the domain only of those who are unprepared?" (151).

BACKGROUND AND PERSONAL: BUGLIOSI THE MAN

Much is known about the professional life of Vincent Bugliosi, the deputy district attorney who determinedly fought crime through his vigorous prosecution of criminals in the trial court, the author who writes books about true murder mysteries. But who is Vincent Bugliosi behind the scenes? How did he become the superior trial lawyer? Where does his strength of character originate? Who is his support group?

So dedicated to his practice of law and his authoring of books, Vince offers little help in the attempt to discover what makes him tick, what energizes and motivates him. For example, in *Helter Skelter,* he stresses his professional career almost exclusively, offering little insight into his background or family life, when in 1974 he states:

> A conventional biographical sketch would probably have read more or less as follows: Vincent T. Bugliosi, age thirty-five, Deputy District Attorney, Los Angeles, California. Born Hibbing, Minnesota. Graduate Hollywood High School. Attended the University of Miami on a tennis scholarship, B.A. and B.B.A. degrees. Deciding on the practice of law, attended UCLA, LL.B. degree, president graduating class 1964. Joined the Los Angeles County District Attorney's Office same year. Has tried a number of highly publicized murder cases—Floyd-Milton, Perveler-Cromwell, etc.—obtaining convictions in all. Has tried 104 felony jury trials, losing only one. In addition to his duties as deputy DA, Bugliosi is a professor of criminal law at Beverly School of Law, Los Angeles. Served as technical consultant and edited the scripts of two pilot films for Jack Webb's TV series "The D.A." Series star Robert Conrad patterned his part after the young prosecutor. Married. Two children. (Bugliosi 1974, 157)

PROCESS OF ELIMINATION: OF WORDS AND TENNIS BALLS

Bugliosi states that he became a lawyer through the process of elimination. He did not wish to take advantage of people, so sales were out. He simply does not like to impose on people. He does not care much for math, so that further limited his career choices. Finally, he does not like blood, so that factor closed the door for him on considering the practice of medicine as a profession.

On the other hand, Vince Bugliosi is big on words. As a youth, he used to study the dictionary. He was eager to learn the meaning of words. He liked big words in order to impress people and to confuse them. Later he became sensitive to the fact that words are to be used for communication and that if you are using words with abstract meanings or words of uncommon usage, you are not communicating. So he modified his usage of words in order to improve his communication with others.

When he graduated from college, Bugliosi was still unsure what profession he should begin to prepare himself for. Others, whom he respected, suggested that he should go to law school and that his love of words would be a good fit for his practicing law.

While in law school, Vince Bugliosi found himself gravitating more and more toward the practice of criminal law because he was so intent upon the centrality of justice. The appeal of the criminal law for him was the trial: An arena of action, an environment in which he could use his beloved words. He says he became a DA because "I wanted to prosecute the guilty. I wanted to prosecute, because the DA has more control of justice than the defense does." (Schauer 2007c).

Bugliosi believes that the defense attorney defends mostly guilty people; he has to take the cases that will be prosecuted and thus has little choice in the matter. He explains that the justice system pretty well weeds out those who are innocent in a series of steps of elimination, so that when a case comes to trial, 99 of 100 are guilty. Bugliosi is pleased that he sees more liberals today wanting to become prosecutors, because they have some control of who they will not charge and prosecute as well as in who they will.

Did Bugliosi have heroes in his childhood, those to whom he looked up, those whose lives and characteristics he aspired to emulate? When asked, he said that he did not consider anyone to be his hero as he was growing up: He was impressed, however, with two commonly acknowledged sports heroes. He was impressed with Joe D'Maggio, the Yankee Clipper, the American hero, for his perfection and his flawlessness in athletic performance. He was also impressed with Rocky Marciano, the only world champion boxer to complete his career undefeated, not for his style, but for his persistence. "He was a slugger!" Bugliosi exclaimed. (Schauer 2007c).

When asked how he became the best known prosecutor in the world, Bugliosi replied:

> Well, I had this wall; there was this wall, and I kept hitting tennis balls against it. I practiced, and practiced, and practiced hitting tennis balls against the wall again and again; and I never made a point against that wall. Well, I kept hitting balls against that wall until I became the Minnesota High School Tennis Champion. That got me into college on a full tennis scholarship. (Schauer 2007c)

Bugliosi went on to explain that the average kid can play all sports with the exception of tennis. Tennis is not a natural thing. He has played tennis with Jim Brown over the years; and while Jim Brown is noted for his superior football playing skills, Bugliosi hints that Jim will never be a superior tennis player.

So, love of words and devotion to tennis led Vincent Bugliosi into a successful college career. Love of words and determination led him to complete law school. Thirst for justice led him into criminal law. Love of words and logical deduction, a need for action, and determination led him to become a trial lawyer. And finally, a wish to prosecute guilty people and the desire to have some choice in charging and prosecuting, placed him in the Los Angeles district attorney's office.

IMMIGRANT PARENTS: NATIONAL PERSPECTIVE

In addition to tennis and a love of words, what more can be said of the background and support that factor into the person known as Vincent T. Bugliosi? Although he was born in Hibbing, Minnesota, in 1934, of parents who immigrated to the United States from Italy, Vince never did view himself as being *Italian American*. Bugliosi believes that his perspective on nationality stems from the fact that there were hundreds of Italians living in the town of Hibbing during his youth—all of whom thought of themselves simply as *Americans*.

Life for the new Italian immigrants was strenuous. Bugliosi's dad worked hard to feed his family of seven, first as an owner of a grocery store and then as a railroad conductor.

IN THE BACKGROUND: GAIL

The reader of Vincent Bugliosi's books may notice a mysterious figure in the background, a person of whom one catches glimpses now and then, but is never seen in the limelight. This person, by the name of Gail, enters the reader's consciousness first when her name is mentioned on the dedication pages of several of Bugliosi's books or when it is mentioned that she sits in to hear his final summations.

This biographer wondered about Gail and pondered her part in Vince's life; fortunately in a recent attempt to phone Vince, Gail answered and proved willing to answer questions. Vincent T. Bugliosi and Gail Talluto married in 1956, just after Bugliosi graduated from the University of Miami Florida. They have two children, Wendy and Vince Jr.

They met and married in Miami. Gail laughed, then said, "I'm a high school dropout: I quit school to marry Vince. I was seventeen years old at the time." (Schauer 2007b). Bugliosi finished college but did not go directly to law school. He was in the Reserves, so they spent some time at Ft. Benning, Georgia, and then at Ft. Riley, Kansas, before moving to California to begin law school. Bugliosi graduated from the University of California at Los Angeles (president of his graduating class) with his L.L.B. in 1964 and immediately went to work for the Los Angeles district attorney's office.

When asked whether she serves regularly as a sounding board for Bugliosi in his professional work, Gail exclaimed, "Yes, I've gotten to be a pretty good sounding board in fifty-one years!" As I continued to question her part in Bugliosi's professional success, she laughingly replied, "Ha, ha, I thought up the names of most of his books. He probably doesn't want that fact to be known." (Schauer 2007b). Later, Bugliosi admitted the same but said that Gail had named "all" of his books, rather than "most" of them as she had claimed.

I said, "Vince looks like a one-man show; but I suspect that the reason he is able to carry that off is because he is a part of a team, a team which includes Gail."

"Yes, Vince is certainly part of a team!" Gail replied thoughtfully.

Vincent Bugliosi mentions Gail in his true-crime murder mystery books: Gail is mentioned as always being supportive of him and his work. He lauds her as being his stability, his normalcy—she who brings him back to the world of reality. Ah, Gail!

Gail proofreads all his books and manuscripts. Bugliosi debates with her whether to defend a particular client and again to decide whether to pursue a risky trial tactic. Gail helps him answer his phone messages and mail and sends documents in the mail for him. Gail went down to the court to pay his fine for his using his trial tactic of calculated indignation and the resultant finding by the judge of his direct contempt of court, because Bugliosi did not have $50.00 with him.

On the other hand, Bugliosi writes about his feeling that he neglects Gail. Gail is alone yet another Friday night. Bugliosi works through the Christmas recess. Bugliosi works in his yellow pad until 2 A.M. on Christmas Eve. Bugliosi's mind is elsewhere during a family Thanksgiving meal at his sister's house.

When I asked whether Gail felt neglected by Bugliosi, she answered, "No! Well, sometimes just a little bit. I might have felt more neglected if I had not created a life outside of my life with Vince. I have many friends. I might feel deprived if I did not have my friends." (Schauer 2007b).

I interjected, "Well, you married Vince when you were quite young; you had time to get used to his ways—even developed along with him."

Gail replied, "Yes, I was programmed young; so I've never felt that I was deprived." (Schauer 2007b).

On another note, without prior introduction, Vincent Bugliosi is difficult to contact by phone or by mail. His private practice consists of a mail drop (which he may only check once every three months) and an answering service. When Starling Lawrence, Bugliosi's editor with W. W. Norton, was asked if he would say that Vince lives a reclusive existence, Lawrence replied, "Yes, that's fair enough. He works extraordinarily hard at what he does, and doesn't have much time for amusements. How else would one master and argue the *entire* case of the Kennedy assassination?" (Schauer 2007a).

Gail agrees with Starling Lawrence that Bugliosi lives a reclusive life, mainly because he is so dedicated to his work. "Oh," she continued, "we do go out most Saturday nights—we call it a *date*. We usually go out to eat and to a movie. And once in a while we go out into the desert for a couple of days (no further than four hours from home)—usually out toward Palm Springs. But Bugliosi usually carries his work along." (Schauer 2007a).

Examples of Bugliosi's reclusive lifestyle, or thinking, are illustrated in the two following examples: First, one of the reasons Bugliosi gave in explaining why he usually turns down opportunities to appear on TV is that he is so busy with his work. He is so driven to keep busy that he even forgets to pick up his mail—sometimes for three months. Sometimes his phone is turned off because he has not gone to get his mail for three months.

Second, once when Johnny Carson invited Bugliosi over to play tennis in June or July after publication of one of his books, he asked for a rain check because he felt he was too busy. He kept putting Carson off—asking for three or four more rain checks—until March, seven or eight months later, when they finally had lunch together and played tennis.

In *Helter Skelter*, Bugliosi details the mortal danger the courtroom actors faced. I mentioned the Tate/LaBianca case to Gail, emphasizing the fact that their lives were in danger at that time and mentioned the possibility that others might have it in for Vince and try to get back at him. I asked, "Do you still look over your shoulders?" Gail replied,

> No, not really. During the Manson trial we had a police officer living in our home with us; and someone picked up Vince and drove him to work, and another brought him home. I worried some because I had two small children. But we no longer think about that much. (Schauer 2007b)

Following Vincent Bugliosi's lead, I called Vince on June 9, 2007, prepared with a list of fifteen questions to ask him that I had written in longhand on (of course) a yellow legal pad. His newest book, which Vince refers to as "The Kennedy Book," (Bugliosi 2007) hit the stands at the end of May. Currently in the midst of appearing on talk shows and book signings to advertise *Reclaiming History: The Assassination of President John F. Kennedy* and dealing with Tom Hanks who intends to produce a ten-hour television mini-series for HBO on the book, Vince said he only had time to respond to one question.

I asked, "Can you tell me more about this special person Gail? Would we know the same Vincent T. Bugliosi if there were no Gail?" I also mentioned Gail's statement that Vince was part of a team with her.

Vince answered, "Gail represents strength to me; she is an anchor." Bugliosi, while totally illustrious in the trial court and a superior researcher and writer when working in his study, feels confused when confronted with the cares of everyday, normal life. He is simply not sure what to do. He continued in that vein, "In normal life Gail's feet are firmly planted. She allows me freedom so I can do my work and don't have to worry about anything. I can focus entirely on my work. Gail has enabled me to be stronger in professional life." (Schauer 2007c).

UNIQUE INSIGHT

Throughout his career, Vincent Bugliosi has regularly been the first to state an insight, and others have responded by saying that now that they have been enlightened the fact seems obvious. Vince, in his self-deprecating way, states:

> I don't think I'm a genius, or that I'm very bright. I do seem to have the ability to see things in my public life that other people don't see. I am not sure why. I see things in a very pristine condition without taking into consideration how I'm supposed to see them—how others have interpreted the situation before me and told me how I'm supposed to see them. (Schauer 2007c)

In *Outrage*, Bugliosi argued that in the Orenthal James (O.J.) Simpson trial, the public (including the actors and the participants in the trial) saw what they wanted to see or what they expected to see, and their eyes were blinded by American sports-hero worship. Bugliosi was able to review the evidence and then very quickly separate the wheat from the chaff. To this superior trial prosecutor, the smoke and the mirrors set aside, it was obvious that no one except Simpson could be guilty of the double murders.

ASPIRES TO PRODUCE MASTERPIECES

Whether in prosecuting criminals, in writing books, or in critiquing legal or political policies or actions, Vincent Bugliosi attempts to produce his best possible product. Vince has stated that his philosophy of writing a book or of trying a murder case is that he always aspires to produce a masterpiece. One of his criticisms in fact in the Simpson trial was that the prosecution had so many deputy DAs involved that the state's case was segmented and disjointed. Bugliosi wrote, "Whenever I prosecuted a murder case, I always at least aspired to a masterpiece. Whether I achieved it or not is another story. But you cannot have a prosecutorial masterpiece with so many hands in the pot." (Bugliosi 2006a, 45).

I asked Bugliosi's book editor, probably the person who knows him best professionally, "If you were to write a character reference for Vince Bugliosi, what would you list as his major virtues? Another way to ask this is, 'What are the things you can count on when dealing with Vince?'"

Starling Lawrence responded, "I would say that Vince can be depended on to do exactly what he says he is going to do, in any situation, and to do an absolutely thorough job of it, perhaps ruthlessly thorough. That is the secret of his success both in the courtroom and on the page." (Schauer 2007a). Thus we may conclude that Vince Bugliosi is ruthlessly thorough in his pursuit of each of his masterpieces, whether murder trials or the Kennedy book.

AESTHETICS AND ART

In the course of our first discussion, on March 5, 2007, Vincent Bugliosi claimed to be "unaesthetic: Totally." He does appreciate, however, the great writers of fiction and loves a good murder mystery. That is why he had no interest in the Simpson case: There was no mystery. His editor, Starling Lawrence, hounded Bugliosi until he agreed to write *Outrage*, his critique of the Simpson trial.

He mostly reads the things he has to read. An exception he gave was that he had read Hemingway's *The Old Man and the Sea*, but he quickly followed with the explanation, "But that was partially because I was, at that time writing *And the Sea Will Tell*.

Bugliosi does appreciate some music, he says, because music offers some objective standards for taste. He enjoys and is attempting to collect the jazz and Latin American music from all the greatest singers and musicians. He asked, "Say Ed, did you know that I have published an album of Latin American music?" (Schauer 2007c). Next to tennis, Bugliosi considers his main hobby to be his collecting of music from the great artists worldwide. "With the recent compilation CD he produced, *Greatest Latin Love Songs of the Century*, which the incomparable Chilean, Lucho Gatica—whom many believe to be the greatest singer of boleros Latin America has ever produced—calls 'the best album of Latin love songs I have ever heard,' Bugliosi seems to be launching yet another career." (Bugliosi 2006a, 1).

In our second discussion on April 14, 2007, Bugliosi once again spoke of his lack of interest in art when he stated, "I don't have an aesthetic bone in my body." When he was in France with his family at the Louvre, he noticed that the eyes of the Mona Lisa followed him wherever he walked and stood. He asked, "Do all paintings do that?"

Bugliosi did acknowledge that a couple of his values possibly approach aesthetics: Symmetry and logic mean much to him. "I am big on symmetry and order," he offered.

I challenged Bugliosi on the low artistic/aesthetic assessment he gives himself. First, I mentioned his artistry in acting—reminding that in his books he did speak of being like an actor on a stage in presenting his final summations in trials and that cross-examination is drama in which the best techniques used are those of the theatrical dramatists. I also reminded Bugliosi that he himself writes of the choreography of and dramaturgy in the courtroom and of his explanation that trial law is an interweaving of science, logic, and art. I also mentioned his esthetic spirit and his applied art in writing orderly and artistic prose—some of which approaches the poetry of free verse as he uses his beloved words to communicate clearly. Bugliosi replied that I had opened his mind: He had never thought of himself and his products in that way before.

PHILOSOPHY

Professional

While Vince Bugliosi has stated powerfully his personal philosophy of the components of professionalism through his words and actions, one short definition that he uses to honor a fellow trial lawyer serves to summarize his definition. Vince states, "It is said that the principal element that distinguishes a profession from a business is that in a profession, one's primary obligation is to those he serves, not to himself." (Bugliosi 1991a, 206). He goes on to explain that when so defined, Leonard Weinglass is of a dying breed.

Agnosticism

Bugliosi is skeptical about religion. He openly and honestly states his doubts and his struggles of faith and religion. He volunteers, "[I]n my own little mind, I, for one, can't be sure at all there's a God." In a *Playboy* magazine interview, he responded to the question of whether he believed in God by replying, "If we were in court I'd object on the ground that the question assumes a fact not in evidence." He continues, "I don't disbelieve in him either. I'm an agnostic. In other words, although I'm actually from a little town in northern Minnesota, Hibbing, I'm from Missouri on the God issue." (Bugliosi 1996a, 247–248).

When I told Gail that what I appreciate most about Vince's statement of agnosticism in *Outrage* is his complete honesty—admitting that he just does not know—Gail leapt to his defense: "But he doesn't say that he doesn't believe in God either. In fact, he is more quick to criticize those who say that they don't believe in God. It is just that Vince requires proof for everything he believes." She said later, "Sometimes I think that when Vince sees a baby, or a puppy—a sunset or a flower—he begins to think that there must be a God." (Schauer 2007b).

UBIQUITY OF HUMAN INCOMPETENCE AND MEDIOCRITY

Vince Bugliosi believes that the twins, incompetence and mediocrity, are so common in the experience of everyday life, that thinking people ought to expect to encounter the pair regularly. He introduced the book *Outrage* with this thought, "Incompetence is rampant in our society, from presidents on down. It is everywhere. In fact, it is so prevalent and so bad that the only adjective I've ever been able to come up with in the lexicon that adequately describes it is 'staggering.'" (Bugliosi 1996a, 32). He commonly observes the twins in ordinary life's experiences (with grocery store clerk and plumber), in the courtroom (with judge, prosecution, and defense attorneys), and in the media (in local, national, or international decision making, reporting, and broadcasting personnel).

Nonmaterialistic

Vince Bugliosi has no desire for material things. What he desires most is peace of mind. He has no desire to own anything. Music and books are the only material things he values. He has no desire for sculpture or art.

Back in his early twenties he wanted money, but he lost interest in accumulating money. In his private practice, he has been offered blank checks as encouragement to defend people. He has turned those cases down—pushed back those blank checks. Other attorneys accepted those cases, and in so doing, gained notoriety. But Vince rejected the offers because he either knew the person he was to defend was guilty or he was not convinced of the person's innocence.

On the other hand, Bugliosi hopes that his Kennedy book will produce lots of money: Not that he wishes the money for his own personal use, but he would like to have a considerable amount of money to give to the poor.

A visible example of his nonmaterialistic nature can be found in the old, dilapidated car that he drove until recently. His wife, Gail, urged him to get a new car because he is a professional person. She did not want people to think less of him due to the condition of his car. He was, on the other hand, perfectly happy with the old car.

NOT ARROGANT: THOUGH SOME HAVE SAID

On April 14, 2007, Bugliosi was asked, "Vince, your detractors say that you are pompous, full of yourself, egoistic, conceited; how do you see yourself in reply to these charges?" Vince replied, "Concerning ego, I am arrogant on a professional level. Privately, I view myself as 'common'—not special at all. Also, I have no ego as a writer; only as a prosecutor."

Self-Deprecation

Bugliosi, whether in communication with the jury in his final summation or in private conversation, commonly employs self-deprecating humor. Even when asked about his strengths, he replied, "One of my greatest strengths, if I have any strengths, is that I know my limitations. For example, it is difficult to find many Americans who have fewer opinions than I do: I will not venture an opinion without sufficient evidence, without knowledge." (Schauer 2007c).

Common in his writing, and common in private and public communications, are Bugliosi's statements to the effect that he does not feel that he is of above normal intelligence. He says, "I don't think I'm very bright." The ubiquity of the statement begs its purpose: This biographer postulates that Vince uses the *I'm not so smart* statement to emphasize the importance of determination, hard work, and long hours in the pursuit of success.

Private Life

Totally unpretentious, Vince Bugliosi is dedicated to the proposition that "Every one has human dignity: I treat all people as such." When people call, he or his wife always gets back to them. He returns their calls because "It's a thing of respect: I respect them."

Vince is not arrogant, though such some have called him so: He is happy with "a cup of coffee in Boise for a buck." In fact, when people ask for his autograph, he asks, " 'Why do you want my autograph!' I'm shocked. Then it happens again that someone wants my autograph, and I'm shocked all over again."

"My thinking is very literal," Vince explains. "If directions are given and 95 percent of the people in a room get up and leave, I am still sitting there—confused." (Schauer 2007c).

Writing

Bugliosi explains, "My abilities in writing are clarity of expression and the ability to use sarcasm, neither of which I feel qualifies me to be called 'a great writer.'" He continues, "My ability is seeing things as extremely obvious that no one else has seen. I see things in pristine clarity, without preconceptions." (Schauer 2007c).

Prosecution

Bugliosi states that he is more arrogant professionally: "Sloth and incompetence bothers me." He is intolerant of, and gets angry about, incompetence. Why? "Because, incompetence is not benign!" he exclaims.

"I'd work out of court if this fellow didn't get a fair trial because of incompetence on his lawyer's part." He sees it as a dual obligation—to give a person a fair trial.

He will approach the bench to guide the defense so that the defendant gets a fair trial. He is not worried about the outcome of the trial, because he knows that he will get in his evidence. He helps the defense attorney put on a fair trial.

At the bench, he has told the judge and the defense attorney, "While I have plenty of admissible evidence to meet the state's burden of proof, if the defense continues the present line of examination, the door will be opened for me to bring in even more damaging evidence—evidence which I can not bring in at this moment. So I would urge the defense to change the line of direct examination." (Schauer 2007a).

Starling Lawrence puts a fitting quietus to Vince Bulgiosi's detractors when he responds to their attacks:

> I have never had the privilege of being present in the courtroom with Vince, only an active bystander to the arguments in the books. I can see how his sense of himself and of the validity of his case would give the impression of an outsized ego—pompous is simply not an appropriate criticism—but you might as well criticize a tiger for eating rabbits or sheep: Vince is simply doing, and doing very well, what any prosecutor is supposed to do. Much of the criticism could be described as sour grapes. He has both a sense of fairness in his arguments—however sarcastic and dismissive they sometimes seem—and a sense of courtesy, even in the courtroom, as a glance at the YouTube segments of the docutrial of Lee Harvey Oswald in London will demonstrate to the impartial observer. I have never seen him be impolite to people he meets, or heard of his being high-handed with members of a jury. (Schauer 2007a)

PROSECUTION: OBSESSION WITH JUSTICE

Vincent T. Bugliosi must be listed very high in the rankings of *Icons of Crime Fighting* on the basis of his superlative career record of successful criminal prosecutions alone. But in addition to his trial record, he continues as a crime fighter by making his trial tactics, his interpretation and application of the law, and his philosophy of the characteristics and action required of the successful criminal trial lawyer available to legal professionals, students of law, and true-crime murder mystery aficionados alike. Vince's writings alone would qualify him for inclusion in any serious list of the superior crime fighters of America, whether they fought crime in time past or whether they are currently fighting crime.

Total Dedication to Justice

Vince Bugliosi insists that justice is done: The trial for him is not primarily about which side wins, but rather that the guilty are convicted and punished and that the innocent go free. Vince powerfully stated his strong feelings about justice in *Outrage* when he reacted to the lavish celebration party thrown by a defense lawyer at the close of the Orenthal James Simpson trial. "Picture Simpson with his sharp knife viciously stabbing Nicole and Ron to death, while imagining the festive party-goers dining on the best food, laughing and enjoying themselves. It's so goddamn obscene there are no words for it." (Bugliosi 1996a, 54).

Bugliosi was able to speak so powerfully because he did his homework: He found that the Simpson prosecutors possessed a great deal of strong evidence pointing toward Simpson's guilt and no evidence whatsoever that pointed to the guilt of anyone else. Justice had not been served; the defense was smearing their win in the face of the American courts and citizens, and the enormity of it all left Vince incredibly angry.

In *Till Death Us Do Part*, Bugliosi argued against the defense's motion that their client requested a court trial, in which the case is heard and decided solely by the judge. Vince felt that the defendant had a much better chance to receive justice in a jury trial, in which a jury of citizens hears the case and determines guilt. Feeling so strongly that justice must be served, Vince (the prosecutor) argued against the defense motion in behalf of the accused murderer in order to ensure a fair trial for her.

In *Helter Skelter*, Vince helped the defense by calling the defense lawyers to give them knowledge that he was able to impeach the testimony of one of the key defense witnesses. In response, the defense chose not to call that witness and so saved effort, time, and possible harm to their case.

Belief in His Own Ability in the Trial Court

Bugliosi has intimate knowledge of the trial court and a strong belief in his own abilities as a prosecutor. This is not to say that he does not suffer from self-doubts now and again, but those self-doubts drive him to redouble his efforts to decipher evidence and to win cases. There is no doubt in his mind that had he been the prosecutor in the Simpson case, he would have convicted Simpson of the murders and could have gained the conviction with far less evidence than the actual prosecutors had available to them.

CRITIQUE OF JUDGES

Vincent Bugliosi feels that Americans rate judges far too highly. He explains that most judges begin as mediocre lawyers who are owed political favors. The illogic of the American public in their rating of judges is found in their very low ratings of lawyers and politicians, yet judges are both lawyers and politicians.

Bugliosi has identified three infirmities that are commonly found in trial judges: (1) They have little or no experience as trial lawyers. (2) They are pompous, capricious, or dictatorial during trials. And, (3) they show partiality to one side in a trial. It is a worst-case scenario when a trial judge is characterized by all three weaknesses. He considers it a pleasure to work with a judge who displays none of these flaws.

Bugliosi feels that a great injustice is done when a lawyer does not object to a judge's show of disrespect for that lawyer in court. If the judge shows disrespect to the lawyers during the trial, Vince feels that they must approach the judge in chambers to demand respect. Vince explains the process of putting the judge on notice concerning disrespect in *Outrage* and explains how he dealt with Judge King for his demeaning tone and rudeness in dealing with the defense during the Palmyra murder trials.

CRITIQUE OF LAWYERS

High Praise

Vincent T. Bugliosi is quick to praise those trial lawyers who display the highest standards of professionalism, those who are characterized by great concern for justice and equity, and concern for powerless citizens and those who produce the most stirring, theatric, and consistent products in the trial court drama. Recently Vince wrote the following evaluation of top criminal trial lawyers:

> F. Lee Bailey, of course, has for years, along with San Francisco lawyer Melvin Belli, been the most famous of America's trial lawyers, and he and Edward Bennet Williams (now deceased) were considered by many to be the preeminent criminal defense attorneys in the land. Since his loss in the Hearst case, however, he hasn't maintained the stature he once enjoyed, and the cowboy lawyer from Wyoming, Gerry Spence, is now considered the premier criminal defense attorney in the country. (Bugliosi 1996a, 244).

Bugliosi had insisted before that "great trial lawyers are about as rare as fishermen who don't exaggerate." (52). His praise must therefore be taken as studied, heartfelt, and sincere.

In his books, Bugliosi highlights certain lawyers whom he obviously holds in high regard—some of whom he may have even studied to emulate: So highlighted are trial lawyers from the past like Samuel Leibowitz in *Lullaby and Goodnight* and Clarence Darrow in *And the Sea Will Tell*.

More contemporary lawyers who receive praise in Vince's books are Leonard Stein, David Golden, and Terry Callas in *And the Sea Will Tell* and Aaron Stovitz in *Helter Skelter*. Bugliosi gives Leonard Weinglass his highest praise as his cocounsel in *And the Sea Will Tell*.

Criticism

As stated previously, Vincent Bugliosi rates all the courtroom lawyers as incompetent in *Outrage*, including the trial judge. Earle Partington is damned by faint praise in *And the Sea will Tell*. The list could be extended, but due to the fact that Vince's expectation is that of finding mostly incompetent lawyers in the trial courts, we may simply conclude that incompetence in trial court lawyers is what he usually observes.

OBSERVATIONS ON JURIES

Although Bugliosi has had some bad experiences with juries, he has confidence in the jury system: He states that he views the jury system "as the most fundamental safeguard against tyranny we have in a very real sense, the American jury is all that stands between the accused and his loss of liberty." (Bugliosi 1996a, 287). He does, however, feel that juries are unpredictable and he feels less than adequate in jury selection. In fact, he feels that as a trial lawyer he is at his weakest in the jury selection process because he does not believe that he is a very good judge of character.

Bugliosi insists that the trial jury must understand that it is not to interpret a grand jury's indictment as evidence of a defendant's guilt. Trial juries tend to overrate the grand jury's indictment, and thus justice is not served. He feels that it is incumbent on the prosecutor to convey the information to the trial jury that the grand jury bases its indictment only at the *probable cause* level of proof.

PROSECUTOR AS INVESTIGATOR

Bugliosi feels that the district attorney should be actively involved and indeed lead in the investigation of a serious or difficult case. When the prosecutor leads the investigation, the evidence collected will prove much more effective in court because the evidence is then definitely gathered with the purpose of building a solid case. Again, here Bugliosi uses his yellow legal pad to write notes and to list questions to share with detectives. When he fills a page with questions, a meeting is called, and the questions are discussed. Investigative assignments result. After every interview, Bugliosi also converts his interview notes into tentative interrogation questions for future use, already preparing for the development of his final summation and his choreography of the trial.

Bugliosi found amazing incompetence in police departments and mediocre attitudes among detectives, some of which are chronicled in *Helter Skelter* and *Till Death Us Do Part*. These examples alone should convince district attorneys of their need to lead in the investigations of serious and complex crimes.

Opening Statements

Bugliosi usually waives opening statements. He feels that the jury may tire of his telling them the same thing over and over. Thus, he brings the state's evidence to the attention of the jury for the first time during direct and cross-examinations, and follows by clearly connecting the elements of evidence and the crime charged during his final summation.

Evidence

Bugliosi feels it is critical that the prosecution present all the relevant evidence it possesses. By failing to present all evidence the prosecution may have lost the state's case against Orenthal James Simpson. Vince states this as a vital and immutable rule of prosecution.

As a trial tactic, when Bugliosi believes that evidence harmful to the prosecution's case is held by the defense, he usually presents that evidence first—in essence, preempting the defense, stealing their thunder, as it were. It softens the blow against the prosecution's case and communicates to the jury that the prosecution has nothing to hide. One of his common trial practices, therefore, was to cross-examine his own witnesses during direct; this left little for the defense attorney to ask upon cross.

Persistence: Dedication to Hard Work

Whether in Vince Bugliosi's true-crime murder mystery books or in his crime-mystery novels, the reader is struck with the intensity with which the super trial lawyer must put him- or herself totally into winning the case. Vince portrays the trial as open warfare demanding great stamina on the part of the legal participants. He speaks of working 100 hours per week in preparation for and during the trial and the full attention that the prosecutor must give toward the painstaking building of the case—often constructed from the gleanings of mere pieces and tiny bits of information.

In a major murder case, as recorded in *Helter Skelter*, simply replying verbally and in writing to the hundreds of motions made by the defense becomes a voluminous and exhaustive task for the prosecution. In a close trial, winning may be founded simply upon the relative stamina of the adversaries.

Preparation may include insightful, though not necessarily less stressful or less time-intensive, tactics. For example, we find in *And the Sea Will Tell* that Vince and his cocounsel, Len Weinglass, intensely observed the entire Buck Walker murder trial in order to learn from it so that they could better defend Jennifer Jenkins for the Palmyra murders. Not the least of their discoveries was the evidence possessed by the prosecution and the manner in which the evidence was presented, the trial tactics of the prosecutors, and the necessity of dealing with a judge who was disrespectful of the defense lawyers.

Another time- and energy-expending, trial-winning ritual, which Bugliosi practiced religiously, was the night's study of that day's trial transcript. It was in the reading of the transcript that Vince found solutions to trial problems, and questions for the next day's cross-examinations became clear to him. During the trial, Bugliosi often worked through his lunch hour, through Christmas recess, into the wee hours of the morning on Christmas eve and attended family holiday dinners in body, but not in mind.

Motive and Intent

Vincent Bugliosi carefully distinguishes motive from intent—two terms that are often used interchangeably:

> Motive is the emotional urge which induces a person to say or do something. It is different from intent, for a person may intend to steal property or kill someone, and will be guilty of the theft or homicide irrespective of what his motive was (e.g., need, avarice, revenge, jealousy, etc.). While intent is an element of every serious crime, motive is never an element of the *corpus delicti* of any crime. Therefore the prosecution *never* has to prove motive.
>
> However, even though the prosecution doesn't have any legal burden to prove motive, it is always better if it can, because just as the presence of motive to commit a crime is circumstantial evidence of guilt, the absence of motive is perhaps even stronger circumstantial evidence of innocence. (Bugliosi 1996a, 167–168).

Bugliosi is convinced that the jury will expect the prosecution to show motive; therefore, although the prosecution has no legal burden to prove motive, it necessary for the prosecution to prove motive anyway—in order to satisfy the jury's expectations.

Cross-Examination

Vince Bugliosi believes that the best cross-examination techniques are those used by theatrical dramatists. In fact, he states that cross-examination *is* drama.

While most lawyers avoid the *why* question in cross-examination, for Bugliosi, asking "why?" is probably his main cross-examination technique. When he feels that a witness is lying, to expose the witness' prevarication, Vince says,

> I usually employ the following technique to block off the exits. First I elicit answers from the witness on preliminary matters, answers which, when totaled up, show he would be expected to take a certain course of action, or act in a certain way. The witness having committed himself by his answers, I then ask him what course he in fact took, and follow this up with the "why" question. If a witness is unable to justify or explain conduct of his which is incompatible with the behavior of a normal person under the same circumstances, the jury will usually conclude that his testimony is suspect. (229).

Bugliosi puts forth a great deal of effort preparing for cross-examination, feeling that it can be critical to winning a trial. For example, believing that

Charles Manson would take the witness stand in his defense, by the end of the trial, Vince had three notebooks of questions prepared to ask the defendant.

Interviewing and Preparing Witnesses

Bugliosi attempts to interview all witnesses, defense as well as prosecution. He states, "Interviewing the opposition witnesses is absolutely essential to effective cross-examination." (Bugliosi 1996a, 223). When it is possible, he interviews witnesses four or five times. He goes on to explain that the more often witnesses are asked to repeat their stories, the more likely those stories will illustrate contradictions and discrepancies. Some lawyers avoid this to guard against conflicting testimony. Vince sets this worry aside by simply saying that if there are conflicts in a witness' testimony, he wishes to know about it early in the trial process.

In his true-crime, murder mystery books, Bugliosi explains the great efforts he expends in the preparation of witnesses for trial. The witness who proved to be the greatest challenge for him in her preparation as a witness was the defendant in the Palmyra murder trial.

Reasonable Doubt—Not Guilty or Innocent?

Vincent Bugliosi feels strongly that juries must understand that they do not have to find the defendant innocent of a crime. A jury's charge is to simply determine whether the state proved guilt beyond a reasonable doubt. Yet, judge's directions to the jury, and language used by courts, including the Supreme Court of the United States, confuse the legal finding of *not guilty* with the concept of *innocence*. Based on his true-crime books, it may be assumed that Vince explained this distinction to each of the juries that heard his 106 felony trials. He also attempted to lead the trial judges in the cases that he prosecuted and defended to omit the commonly uttered error in their jury instructions: *A finding of guilt or innocence.*

So strongly has he felt about this legal distinction, that he has written a professional article titled "Not Guilty and Innocent—The Problem Children of Reasonable Doubt." Published in the *Criminal Justice Journal*, the article thoroughly discusses the issues of reasonable doubt in relationship to the struggles of juries for understanding in making their decisions.

Consciousness of Guilt/Innocence

Consciousness of guilt—statements and behaviors indicating guilt—can be held by the trial courts to be circumstantial evidence of guilt. Bugliosi argues that if behaviors indicating guilt can be entered into evidence, so too can behaviors indicating innocence. He has titled this principle, "con-sciousness of innocence." (Bugliosi 1996a, 239).

Objections

Objections can hurt a trial lawyer's case in the eyes of the jury. Vince Bugliosi always attempted to make as few objections as possible.

Death Penalty

Vince Bugliosi always found it difficult as a prosecutor to seek the death penalty. He actually once opposed the death penalty for a non-trigger man in a felony-murder trial. He feels so strongly about the death penalty that he included not only one, but two treatises on the death penalty in *Till Death Us Do Part*. He supports the death penalty for only the most serious and violent murders, although shallow or flippant motives for murder lean his support toward the death penalty.

Defending Guilty Persons

Vince Bugliosi has concluded that from the professional standpoint, it is easy to switch from prosecution to defense, but it is not easy from the emotional standpoint. In the courtroom he feels like an actor on a stage, and his intense preparation and theatrical performance tend to add up to winning a case. The courtroom wags over the years have repeated that Vince is frightening in the court trial—that he could convict innocent people. Likewise, it is probable that he could by defending them, get guilty people off. He has therefore concluded that he can not defend people whom he knows are guilty. He worries, "If I do defense and get a guilty person off, what if they do it again? I would feel responsible for letting another crime be committed! So, I've retreated into writing." (Schauer 2007c).

Bugliosi stated publicly before the trial that he would not have represented O. J. Simpson if he had been asked because he knew that Simpson was guilty of murdering his wife and her friend. Bugliosi believes that it is not legal ideology that drives trial lawyers to defend guilty people, but rather that in reality, most lawyers represent guilty people because there are many lawyers and all need work. He also hints, by stating that he has not taken signed checks with the denomination lines left blank, that some lawyers defend guilty persons for self-aggrandizement. He summarizes, "In a nutshell, although I have never been a law-and-order fanatic—in fact, I'm suspicious of those who are—I do believe that those who have committed serious crimes should be severely punished, and I do not want to be in a position of actively seeking to thwart this natural justice." (Bugliosi 1996a, 274–275; Schauer 2007c).

Bugliosi believes that having passed through the criminal justice screening process, the probability that the defendant in a criminal trial is guilty is about 99 percent. Therefore, most defense attorneys tend to earn their livings largely by defending guilty people. He will not defend a person whom he believes is guilty of a violent crime. He argues that he is simply not willing to put in his normal trial workweek of 100 hours to help a violent criminal escape justice. Thus, when he was asked to defend Jennifer Jenkins for the Palmyra murders (chronicled in *And the Sea Will Tell*), he felt that he had to be confident that she had not aided in the murders of Mac and Muff Graham. Even then, Bugliosi knew that he could never be 100 percent certain of her innocence. He continued to suffer doubts about her throughout the trial. The doubts led him to feeling that somehow his working so hard to win the case, if his client were indeed guilty, was incredibly obscene and vile.

In summary, the superlative professional career of Vincent T. Bugliosi identifies and emphasizes key trial issues. In a sense, his writings constitute a more complete and more intense education in criminal trial law than is received by most students in their law school experience.

AUTHOR: TRUE-CRIME MURDER MYSTERIES

"The only type of criminal case that really appeals to me is a true murder mystery, and the interest is in the mystery, not the murder." (Bugliosi 1996a, 16). So states Vincent T. Bugliosi in the introduction to *Outrage*, his criticism of the murder trial of Orenthal James Simpson.

Bugliosi is broadly read in the literature relating to his subject matter: In his writing he mentions Hemingway and quotes many authors, from humorist Will Rogers to trial lawyers F. Lee Bailey and Clarence Darrow, to old Chinese proverbs, and emphasizes his points by including statements from such novelists as Henry Roth, Gertrude Stein, and Mark Twain. While Bugliosi is best known for his nonfiction murder mystery books, he has written in other genres, including two fictional murder mysteries and several books of legal or political criticism, and he has authored several criminal law-related articles in journals and magazines.

What follows is a series of reviews of his murder mystery books, both nonfiction and fiction, organized in chronological order of their publication.

Helter Skelter: The True Story of the Manson Murders (1974)

Starling Lawrence, editor of Bugliosi's 1996 book, *Outrage: The Five Reasons Why O.J. Simpson Got Away With Murder*, observes that *Helter Skelter* is "the book that established him (Bugliosi) as the most celebrated true-crime author in America." (Bugliosi 1974). Written two years after his retirement from the Los Angeles County District Attorney's office, *Helter*

Skelter brought the professional legal career of Bugliosi to national attention and secured international recognition of him as a serious author and a top legal expert—thus he quickly became the best-known criminal prosecutor in the world.

Soon after it hit the bookstands, *Helter Skelter* was listed as a national best seller by the *New York Times*, the first of three nonfiction best sellers for Bugliosi. It won the Edgar Allan Poe Award for the best fact crime book of the year in 1975, given by the Mystery Writers of America. It also became a main selection of the Book of the Month Club. Bugliosi himself became the executive producer of the docudrama of *Helter Skelter* produced by CBS. *Helter Skelter* became a main selection of the Literary Guild and is probably the best selling true-crime book of all time.

In *Helter Skelter*, Bugliosi documents the Tate/LaBianca murder trials in which he served as the prosecutor. The Tate/LaBianca murders, which were perpetrated in August of 1969, just four years after the Watts riot, were the most publicized murders up to that time next to the assassination of President John F. Kennedy. The murders themselves rate as probably the most brutal and unprovoked mass murders recorded in American history. Adding to the gruesomeness and horror of the crimes is the fact that they were carried out willingly by young followers of the reclusive Charles Manson, a self-proclaimed leader and messiah, whose charisma drew youth who had broken with their families and who felt rejected by society.

Three major issues are juxtaposed in *Helter Skelter*: Bugliosi begins the book by introducing the victims and their murders. Second, the author guides the reader through the highly complex investigation, evidence gathering, and evidence interpretation that was necessary to tie the crimes to each other and to identify the murderers. Third, the personalities, actions, intents, and motives of the murderers are explored. These themes follow in logical sequence as first presented, but are increasingly intertwined as the author continues to explain his successful prosecution of members of the "Manson family." The book is written in the language of a district attorney; that is, it is totally unemotional except in certain cases when the author writes "asides."

In *Helter Skelter* the murders themselves, the investigation, the intense work and long hours of the prosecutor in building and trying the case, the courtroom drama, and the aftermath of the trial are presented in orderly sequence. Ever building upon groundwork laid, Bugliosi gives a step-by-step development of the case. He makes the reader aware of the missing pieces of evidence or seeming illogic, how the prosecutor works to find missing evidence or ponders what logical steps might help to explain the yet unsolved.

Aside from the three major issues mentioned above, Vincent Bugliosi shares information with the reader that was not reported by the media or mentioned during the Tate/LaBianca murder trial. For example, in *Helter*

Skelter the public first learns about revenge killings before, during, and after the trial; the fact that Bugliosi himself was assigned a twenty-four-hour police bodyguard throughout the trial; and that an attempt was made on the life of one of the prosecution witnesses. Part of the information shared in the book is simply (1) knowledge that the prosecutor chose not to enter as evidence in the trial, (2) evidence that may have been inadmissible as trial evidence for one reason or another, or (3) information that the media did not have or chose not to report. Other information contained in *Helter Skelter* was discovered and gathered by the author in the process of his research leading to the writing of the book; in essence, the product contains none of the expected and proverbial unturned stones.

Additional information first made public in *Helter Skelter*, however, was discovered due to the incredible mind and inquisitiveness of Bugliosi himself. First of all, Bugliosi is totally dedicated to the proposition that justice must be done and murderers must not go unpunished. Second, the author goes to great lengths to satisfy his intense innate curiosity. For example, Bugliosi simply was driven by his mind to understand the person, thinking, and socialization of his antagonist, Charles Manson. This intellectual quest led Bugliosi from the childhood, arrest, and prison records of Manson to inquiry into the ideologies of diverse cults; to the writings of Nietzsche; and finally, to the finding of striking similarities between the backgrounds, thinking, and leadership and recruitment styles of Charles Manson and Adolph Hitler.

In *Helter Skelter*, Bugliosi sets the standard for his subsequent true-crime mystery books, that which makes them resources of immense value to criminal justice and legal scholars, students, and practitioners. By detailed reviews of the backgrounds of key actors of the murder mystery and the subsequent trial; through careful explanation and emphasis of the legal issues and logic terminating in successful prosecution; and by making the reader a witness to the courtroom drama (suggested by the complete "Cast of Characters" that begins *Helter Skelter*) as it unfolds, the author communicates with a clarity and precision uncommon in both the true-crime mystery and in the legal literature.

As an example, Bugliosi explains how to anticipate the motions made by and the cross-examination questions of the defense, how to interview and prepare witnesses, how to anticipate and prevent legal pitfalls, how and why to prepare a clear and powerful final summation, how to deal with a biased or unprepared judge, how to communicate with clarity and precision to the jury, and how to explain the state's case as it is built logically—step by step and point by point. More complete citations and explanations are given in voluminous footnotes or endnotes and/or epilogue.

Helter Skelter: The True Story of the Manson Murders is the most universally recognized and the most acclaimed true-crime murder mystery of the twentieth century. Every serious student of crime must become personally and intimately familiar with the facts and criminal trial dramaturgy presented in the book. *Helter Skelter* should be made required reading in law schools and university criminal justice programs.

Till Death Us Do Part: A True Murder Mystery (1978)

Vincent T. Bugliosi introduces his second true-crime murder mystery, *Till Death Us Do Part* (*Till Death*), in a hard-hitting statement that gives the prospective reader a feeling for the mystery involved, in the following words found in the book's frontispiece:

> The Los Angeles Police Department detectives did not know on December 11, 1966, the night of the first murder, that they would soon be drawn into a long, exhaustive pursuit that would lead them from the scene of a modest working-class neighborhood, circuitously but ever steadily into the fast, sporty lifestyles of Southern California, Baja, and Nevada. Nor did they know that it would take a series of unsolved, attempted murders and finally a mysterious, terribly brutal second murder before the State of California would have what they believed to be sufficient evidence to commence a prosecution.
>
> The job of that prosecution fell to me. Never before or since as a criminal lawyer have I been involved in a case that raised so many disturbing doubts as to what had actually happened. (Bugliosi 1978)

In this trial, Bugliosi was forced to build the state's case based entirely on circumstantial evidence, with much of that evidence once or twice removed from the actual crimes. Elizabeth Peer, reviewer for *Newsweek*, wrote, "Neither murder would ever yield weapons, fingerprints or eyewitnesses; but dogged detective work knit the crimes together and a painstaking prosecutor constructed a probable-guilt scenario so persuasive that a California jury dealt out the death sentence based on circumstantial evidence alone—a rare courtroom feat." (Dear 1995, 51). The author creates, in *Till Death*, a work that intrigues and excites the reader's mind as a fictional Agatha Christie or Nero Wolfe murder mystery novel might. But in this volume, Bugliosi takes the reader beyond the typical fiction or nonfiction murder mystery tome and into the actual action and drama of the courtroom. He offers intimate introductions to both victims and murderers and paints a vivid picture of the intense work and attention to detail that goes into the thorough investigation and successful prosecution of a most difficult murder case.

The subject arrangement is in the logical order that was first presented by Vince Bugliosi in *Helter Skelter*. First, the human actors of the subject murder are introduced. The actual murders, the experiences of witnesses, and the characteristics and life's settings of the victims are intimately explained. The attributes, behaviors, and aspired lifestyles of the murderers follow.

Second, the author expands on the investigation. Bugliosi takes an active part in investigations once the Los Angeles district attorney's office assigns cases to him. These investigations are explained in detail, noting especially evidence needed and sought, strengths and weakness of that evidence, evidence lacking, and the intensity of the investigative process.

Third, the trial begins. Herein lies the artistry, brilliance, and public expertise of Vincent Bugliosi, and herein lies the precise courtroom techniques, attention to legal precedent, and choreography of the courtroom, which, although exciting to the casual reader, proves invaluable to students of law and criminal justice. But the author emphasizes that the trial is not won entirely through prior preparation and courtroom presentation; the trial for Bugliosi extends to evenings, nights, weekends, holidays, and even through the courtroom lunch hour.

For example, after a day in court, Bugliosi waits for a copy of that day's trial transcript. This he reads before retiring for the night in order to bolster his impressions of that trial day, and also to discover issues he might have missed that may help in his presentation of evidence, argument, or cross-examination on the following day.

During the trial, Bugliosi is concurrently leading investigations, seeking additional witnesses, preparing witnesses, doing trial-related legal research, and interviewing both prosecution and defense witnesses. Beyond these tasks, usually extending from before the trial begins, he continually works on upgrading and fine-tuning his final summation.

He uses his final summation to choreograph the trial. He continuously is revising the final summation throughout the trial, and he has it committed to memory before he presents his final argument. Bugliosi feels that summarizing the trial, emphasizing key evidence, and clearly explaining how the evidence is interrelated is of utmost importance for the jury's determinations. By having rewritten, updated, and rehearsed the final summation, he is able to be orderly and precise in his presentation while still being very able to be innovative and fresh as an actor on a stage.

Deviating somewhat from Vincent Bugliosi's other books, *Till Death* contains no footnotes and no epilogue. All of the materials commonly included in footnotes or epilogue are found embedded in the text. Many students of crime, the present author included, prefer this presentation style.

A more intimate look at the scene begins in Los Angeles, where citizens tend to believe that they can reach out to touch a fantasy, where no one feels like a nobody. Los Angeles is described as a city of created illusions and facades.

Then when the fire department is called to a fire in a working-class neighborhood, firemen find the murdered body of Henry Stockton, a humble stock clerk with few aspirations and no enemies. The police have difficulty contacting his wife Sandra, who is in another city with their four-year-old son, visiting a friend.

Motive for the murder eludes the investigators, and while the murder victim had a life insurance policy and insurance on the house, it did not seem possible that he would be murdered for his paltry net worth of less than $25,000.

Two years later, Judy Palliko, the newlywed wife of Alan Palliko, was brutally bludgeoned and shot to death as she sat in her car in the carport of their apartment complex. One of the investigators remembered questioning Alan Palliko in the course of the Henry Stockton murder investigation; he was known to have been close to Sandra Stockton at that time.

Both murders were well planned and executed: There were no witnesses; no real evidence was discovered (e.g., a gun, a club, or a fingerprint); and although circumstantial evidence existed to tie the two murders together and to implicate Alan Palliko and Sandra Stockton for the murders, all circumstantial evidence was rather distanced from the actual murders and crime scenes.

Vince Bugliosi had been out of law school and working for the Los Angeles District Attorney's office for just under four years when the Palliko/Stockton case was assigned to him for prosecution. He had prosecuted eleven murder cases before this trial, and although he was not inclined toward asking for the death penalty in murder trials, he sought the death penalty for both of the defendants in this trial. He had never seen murders as reprehensible as these: The murdering of spouses for relatively small sums of money so that the defendants could live the fast lifestyle of southern California.

The trial began with one of America's most accomplished trial lawyers, Melvin Belli, defending Sandra. Later, David Golden, an able attorney from Belli's office, took over her defense. Friends before, and friends after, Bugliosi and Golden clashed in the courtroom. At one point, Bugliosi apologized to Golden in the open court for a mis-statement that had been interpreted as a lack of respect.

Items of interest in the trial follow: The chief witness for the prosecution damaged his credibility early in the trial. Evidence for Judy Palliko's murder was dismally circumstantial. A key defense witness boldly lied to counter a major item of evidence for the prosecution. Bugliosi himself gambled on presenting an alternative murder theory late in the trial.

In explaining his final summation, the author expands on the importance of words for communicating to the jury. This is one of the major themes of Vincent Bugliosi's professional life—both as prosecuting attorney and as author of true-crime mysteries.

In chambers, the judge complimented Bugliosi on his final summation, comparing his performance to that of Clarence Darrow. Vince had to smile to himself: While he appreciated the judge's intended praise, he remembered that Darrow lost most of his cases. He hoped that the compliment was not a foreboding of the outcome of the present trial. The judge also suggested that someone should write a book about this trial.

After awaiting the decision of the jury—a period of great stress for all actors in a trial—Bugliosi was elated at the jury's verdicts. His only desire, after hearing the verdicts, was to go home to his family, whom he had greatly neglected during the course of this trial.

Till Death Us Do Part won the Edgar Allan Poe Award for the best true-crime book of the year. Mystery and unanswered questions are myriad within the pages of this masterpiece. Legal issues and concerns are noted and thoroughly discussed. This present author recommends *Till Death* as a book that must be read by the true-crime, true-murder mystery aficionado and as a great legal resource for the advanced student of law or criminal justice.

Shadow of Cain: A Novel (1981)

Shadow of Cain is an allegory of the worst-case scenario of that which may happen when a lawyer successfully defends a guilty person against the charge of premeditated murder. Considering this a serious professional and emotional issue, Vince Bugliosi has repeated his long-held beliefs and fears concerning the defense of guilty persons in each of his true-crime mystery books.

After leaving the Los Angeles District Attorney's office in 1972, going into private practice, and beginning to author books, Vince wrestled with the question of defending the guilty. He explains, "From the professional standpoint, it is easy to switch from prosecution to defense. But it is not easy from the emotional standpoint." He has explained further, "Most defense attorneys necessarily spend their careers defending guilty people." Finally, Vince bares to the world the horns of his ethical and legal dilemma: "If I do defense and get a guilty person off, what if they do it again? I would feel responsible for letting another crime be committed!" (Schauer 2007c).

In *Outrage: The Five Reasons Why O.J. Simpson Got Away With Murder*, Bugliosi strongly stated his opinion that most lawyers—prosecutors, judges, and defenders—are inept, and produce, at best, a mediocre legal product. If this common mediocrity among lawyers is contrasted with the author's dedication and skills (as explained both in print and proven by his legal track record), the likelihood of his successful defense of guilty people becomes apparent. Bugliosi emphasizes the contrast when he states, "I simply have no motivation whatsoever to knock myself out working a hundred hours a week, as I frequently do, trying to figure out a way to get some murderer off." (Bugliosi 1991a, 197).

In *Shadow of Cain*, Raymond Lomak commits premeditated multiple murders based on his ideological and socioeconomic ponderings (reminding the reader of multiple-murderer Charles Manson in *Helter Skelter*, 1974). Lomak, a hospital orderly, is identified by the type of shoes worn by his profession.

Arrested, prosecuted, tried, convicted, and sentenced to death, Ray Lomak is reprieved when the California death sentence statute is found to be unconstitutional. His sentence automatically reverts to a life sentence with possibility of parole in seven years. Again, the reader is reminded of the death sentences of Charles Manson in *Helter Skelter* and of the two murderers in *Till Death Us Do Part*, because those sentences were reduced to life with possibility of parole.

The reader may discover characteristics of Vince Bugliosi, himself, in not only one, but in two of the characters of this novel: The first is Ray Lomak's antagonist, Richard Pomerantz, the psychiatrist appointed by the parole board to oversee Lomak's parole. Pomerantz, discerning Lomak's murderous potential, fights a one-man battle to get Lomak back behind bars, and through his determination to terminate Lomak's parole, places his own life in imminent danger.

Lomak is once again arrested and tried for two murders. The prosecution's case rests entirely on circumstantial evidence, as have many of the premeditated murder cases that the author prosecuted. The reader may tend to recognize Vincent Bugliosi in the well-prepared, insightful, and animated trial lawyer who defends Lomak in this second murder trial.

California Board of Parole Press Release Regarding Charles Manson 11th Parole Request (for Immediate Release: May 23, 2007)

Parole Denied for Charles Manson

Corcoran, CA: The California Department of Corrections and Rehabilitation Board of Parole Hearings (BPH) today denied parole for convicted mass murderer Charles Manson during a hearing at Corcoran State Prison.

The denial was for five years, the maximum allowed by law. Manson did not appear before the panel and will be eligible for another hearing in 2012. The BPH decision marks the eleventh time that Manson has been denied parole since 1978.

In its denial, the BPH panel noted that Manson, 72 years old, "continues to pose an unreasonable danger to others and may still bring harm to anyone he would come in contact with."

Manson was convicted of seven counts of first degree murder as a result of separate incidents in an August 1969 crime spree in Los Angeles County, including the fatal stabbing of five people in the home of actress Sharon Tate and the murders the following day of Leno and Rosemary LaBianca.

Manson was initially sentenced to death. That sentence, as well as those of 107 other inmates, was modified in 1977 to life in prison with the possibility of parole after a 1972 ruling by the California Supreme Court that determined the state's death penalty statute at the time was unconstitutional.

Source: http://www.cdcr.ca.gov/.

Just as Lomak's hot-shot defense lawyer upstaged the prosecutor's final summation in *Shadow of Cain* and later in *And the Sea Will Tell*, Vincent Bugliosi used the same technique in his defense of Jennifer Jenkins. Bugliosi carefully studied the prosecutor's final summations presented in former trials to discover his presentation style, similes he used, and the prosecutor's logic in reviewing the trial evidence. Bugliosi then preempted the prosecutor's final summation—thus weakening its impact—by telling the jury what they should be expecting from the prosecution.

The reader knows that Ray Lomak is guilty of the two premeditated murders charged by the prosecution, but the defense is successful. Ray Lomak is found "not guilty;" and walks out of the court a free man. But the psychiatrist, Pomerantz, realizes Lomak's murderous potential; and he works to stop Lomak at all costs.

Shadow of Cain rivets the attention of the reader, causing one to wonder what may actually happen if a violent multiple murderer is successfully defended, acquitted by the trial court, and allowed to roam free. Is the defense lawyer to be held partially responsible for his brilliant defense? Is the district attorney to be held responsible for his mediocre prosecution? The thoughts, insight, and fears of Vincent T. Bugliosi are faithfully and clearly communicated to the reader through the allegory, *Shadow of Cain*.

Lullaby and Good Night: A Novel Inspired by the True Story of Vivian Gordon (1987)

This book is a novel that began as nonfiction. Vivian Gordon, the woman behind the story, was in the process of testifying before the Seabury Commission against Tammany Hall when she turned up dead. As the authors were researching the book, they realized that all of the court documents were missing. Suspicious? Yes, indeed. Tammany Hall at work? Quite possibly.

An Internet search on Benita Franklin Bischoff (aka Vivian Gordon) yields only the news of her death, very little on the scapegoat who "confessed" to her murder, and some short statements concerning Tammany Hall's reaction. Nothing is noted of her background except that she is called a racketeer, a procuress, and a blackmailer.

So, what to do? Make the story a murder mystery, use the little information you have, refine it with your best educated guess, and write a book. There are components of this story that are very well documented. The infamous Tammany Hall, the speakeasy culture, crooked cops and gangsters, and the call-girl lifestyle—all have been recorded for history. And so begins the story of Emily Stanton.

There are three areas of interest to the reviewer: The main character, Emily Stanton; Tammany Hall; and lawyer Samuel Leibowitz. Emily Stanton is at the same time a very nice girl and very believable, yet an unbelievably naïve, even stupid, woman. Many times, the reader felt like yelling, "No, don't go there!" as one does at the TV or a movie.

The story synopsis is that small-town Emily ran away from home (which included a cold prison-warden father, an ineffectual mother, and a convent school) and came to New York to be an actress. She met and married Warren Matthews and after being beaten and raped by him, she ran away from him, taking their six-year-old daughter with her. Matthews was heavily involved with Tammany Hall, a social club housed in a Georgian-style building that looked like many other New York gentlemen's clubs. Many of the members arriving and departing were transported in big, black chauffeur-driven luxury cars, wearing expensive clothes with flowers in lapels that proclaimed their power and wealth. However, most of these men rose from the working class of peasant-stock Irishmen who populated New York at that time. But no matter the lineage, Tammany Hall ran New York and was a political power to be reckoned with. City Hall and Tammany Hall were one and the same, and controlling elections was the corrupt and pervasive game. Tammany Hall was compared to a tiger devouring New York, and indeed, a flag was flown in Tammany Hall right beside the Stars and Stripes depicting this tiger.

The exclusive and secret rites; the Indian themed meetings; the initiations; the secret deals and contract negotiations; the alcohol, women, and money were all part of the make-up of Tammany Hall. Named after the Indian Chief Tamanend whose motto was, "Stand together and support each other and you will be a mountain," the Hall borrowed liberally from the Indian culture. Members became braves, elders were called sachems, and the meeting place was the wigwam. Chants using supposed Indian words and oaths of allegiance were required of new members.

City commissioners, judges, police officers, businessmen, lawyers—all made up Tammany Hall. At one point the reader eavesdrops on a conversation between Emily Stanton's husband, Warren Matthews, and a city commissioner. Matthews is bemoaning the fact that his wife had left him and taken their daughter. The commissioner assures Matthews that if he wanted his daughter back that badly, there was a way to make it happen. Curiously enough, Matthews felt reassured after this: Indeed not too many weeks later, Emily was framed for prostitution and sent to prison for two years. She was brutalized and traumatized in prison, Matthews divorced her and remarried, and she lost all contact with her little girl.

When Emily got out of prison, she had a hard time finding a job. No one would hire her because she had been in prison. After several futile tries at acting jobs, she finally became a call girl. Her only goal in life was to get her daughter back; therefore she needed money to hire a good lawyer. What so horrified her was that she had been innocent of the charge that sent her to prison, yet she had actually become what she was accused of being, a prostitute. One lesson she learned was how to make money, and she ended up a wealthy woman. She hired a lawyer, received visitation privileges, and finally was able to reestablish a relationship with her daughter.

At this point she planned her revenge. Emily testified before the Seabury Commission, which was investigating Tammany Hall and the corruption that was so rampant in New York. She was convinced that Matthews was behind her first visit to prison; she also wanted very badly to see the police officer who framed her punished. She foolishly went to Matthew's office and told him about this, and next thing you knew he was dead, and she framed for his murder. So, back to jail. This time, though, she had money and was able to get her friend to hire Sam Leibowitz to defend her.

Sam Leibowitz was the son of Romanian immigrants who worked hard and believed in education. He was known for successfully defending people arrested for murder; in fact, according to press reports, he never lost.

Leibowitz was a big man, well dressed. "Beneath his impeccable three-piece suit…was a big man with the soul of a fighter, everything held tightly in check for when the battle call sounded." So after talking to Emily and insisting that she tell him the whole, bare truth about her life and the murder of Matthews, he got to work, first doing his homework. He went himself to investigate Emily's alibi, he asked questions and saw her life. His acceptance of the case kept the headlines active.

Sam Leibowitz carefully studied and selected his jury. He wanted men of detail, men who would listen, intelligent men. He wanted them to understand and appreciate irony and sarcasm. He did everything in his power to weed out Tammany Hall men. When the trial started he told Emily to dress in such a way that she could evoke sympathy. The prosecutor (a hand-picked Tammany man) portrayed her as a jealous woman, a woman scorned, a failure at everything.

With his opening statement, Leibowitz established himself as the calm, authoritative wise man. He was cool and adult, reasonable and nonadversarial. He told the jury that at first he didn't want to take the case, that he was busy, and that it didn't look like a good case; but after meeting and talking to Emily, he was honored to represent her, to get her the fair trial that she wasn't given the last time she was in court. Then his demeanor changed and he was no longer the calm scholarly lawyer; he became the wolf, the hawk, never losing eye contact with the jury. "In one fell swoop, an innocent housewife is transformed into a prostitute. How's that for the magic of the magistrate's court!" He felt that he could prove that Emily did not kill her ex-husband. He was certain that someone in Tammany Hall, to protect Tammany Hall, killed him. He felt that the information Emily was bringing to the Seabury Commission was threatening enough to Tammany Hall to make them nervous.

Leibowitz strove to make the jury partners in his search for truth. He used rhetorical questions to open their thoughts to the possibility that Emily was innocent. He wanted to leave enough doubt that they would have to declare her not guilty. When Emily took the stand, he told her to be completely honest about her life and her work—better for them to bring it out in the open than for the prosecutor to reveal her secret life.

At one point during the trial, Leibowitz made the prosecution so uncomfortable that he (the prosecutor) called to the stand the police officer who had initially framed Emily. Leibowitz was able to point the finger of justice toward the officer by showing that he had the means, motive, and opportunity to kill Warren Matthews. One question of how the gun was planted in Emily's room was suggested by asking the officer about his ability to pick locks and the fact that he had worked for a locksmith for two summers as a teenager. Everyone was amazed at the depth that Leibowitz had probed while preparing for the trial. At his summation, Leibowitz pointed out enough facts to be able to suggest to the jury that there was at least a reasonable doubt as to Emily's guilt. He asked them for a verdict of not guilty.

In conclusion, first, in the casting of the main character, Emily Stanton, the reviewer is reminded of Jennifer Jenkins, whom Vincent Bugliosi was defending in her trial for the Palmyra murders as this book was being written. His struggles with preparing her as a witness and his wrestling to get her to become an active partner in her defense are recorded in *And the Sea Will Tell*.

Second, if only half of what we read here about Tammany Hall and this era in New York City are true (and there is no reason to believe that the descriptions have been embellished), then it is easy to see what motivated Vincent Bugliosi to write this critique. Of course today we are not surprised to see the same attitudes and behaviors being acted out in government at all levels: federal and state, large city or small town. After all, the politicians of today are the philosophical progeny of Tammany Hall.

And third, while it may be easy to see why the authors needed to write about the era, it may be even more obvious why Vince Bugliosi wanted to write about Sam Leibowitz. Rhetorically, how much of Sam Leibowitz is Vincent Bugliosi, and how much did Sam influence Vince? Their similarities are striking: Both possess controlled kinetic energy—always keeping a reserve ready to launch into conflict. Both see the trial as a battle. So too are each noted for taking on extremely difficult cases and for being unwilling to defend guilty persons, although Bugliosi was the more successful in this regard since it is a known fact that Leibowitz defended Al Capone. Their attention to detail and their extensive investigative work are also examples of their similarities.

In the courtroom, both Leibowitz and Bugliosi varied their presentations greatly for effect: Seeing themselves as actors on a stage, they whisper, they speak calmly, they shout, they make eye contact with the jury, to emphasize the purpose of the message and to insure communication. Both are concerned with educating the jury to both the facts of the case and to the intricacies of the law.

Lullaby and Good Night brings a message of history, human nature, and legal strife. Fascinating to read; it keeps the murder mystery aficionado riveted to the story, eager to turn the page. Best of all, as in many of Vincent Bugliosi's books, the mystery continues.

And the Sea Will Tell (1991)

Known primarily as a criminal trial prosecutor, and secondarily as an accomplished author of true-crime mystery books, Vince Bugliosi is found in the pages of *And the Sea* wearing an entirely new hat—that of murder trial defender. The book chronicles the knowledge and experiences of the author as he prepared for the trial and defended Jennifer Lynn Jenkins, who was accused of murdering a wealthy couple from California for the purpose of gaining possession of their immaculately maintained luxury yacht and the year's supply of food it contained. The alleged murders took place at the isolated Palmyra Atoll.

The Palmyra Atoll, an unincorporated territory of the United States, lies in the west-central Pacific Ocean. It is 1,000 miles southwest of Hawaii and lies far outside the regular ocean shipping lanes. Palmyra has no permanent inhabitants. Visitors to the island have over the years reported a feeling of sadness, of foreboding, while they were on Palmyra.

After a short introduction to Palmyra itself, the story begins with Mac and Muff Graham in San Diego, California, and Jennifer Jenkins and her ex-convict lover, Buck Walker, at Maalaea Bay on the island of Maui in Hawaii. The Grahams determined to sail to Palmyra, where they were sure they would have privacy for their planned lengthy stay at the atoll. They prepared their racy ketch, the *Sea Wind,* for the trip and stocked it with groceries and supplies to last the couple a year.

Unbeknownst to the Grahams, Jennifer Jenkins and Buck Walker also planned to sail to Palmyra in an old wooden sailboat, the *Iola,* with a fiberglass-patched hull, which Walker had worked on to make seaworthy. Jenkins and Walker were seeking escape from federal drug charges, and Walker wished to avoid imprisonment for federal parole violations. They planned to stay at Palmyra for an extended period and expected to exist by living off the land.

Having little sailing experience and with their poorly maintained and equipped sailboat, it took Jenkins and Walker far longer to make the trip to Palmyra than expected. When they arrived at the atoll, they found other visitors just preparing to leave. From those departing, Jennifer and Buck received a quick tour of the island, advice for subsisting on the island, and some desired food and supplies.

Expecting to find Palmyra deserted, Mac and Muff Graham were surprised to find the island inhabited. Jennifer Jenkins and Buck Walker greeted the Grahams when they arrived. Each couple was disappointed with having to share the tiny atoll with the other. Both couples had planned to remain on Palmyra Atoll for extended periods of time, while other travelers who stopped at the island tended to stay for only a few days rest.

In October of 1974, Jennifer Jenkins and Buck Walker sailed to Hawaii, not on their boat, the *Iola,* but in a painted-over and poorly disguised *Sea Wind*—Mac and Muff Graham's yacht. They explained that, while fishing, the Grahams had capsized their Zodiac dinghy in Palmyra's shark-filled lagoon and were missing, presumably drowned.

No evidence was found on Palmyra by U.S. investigators to indicate what had happened to the Grahams. While authorities suspected that Walker and Jenkins murdered the Grahams for their ketch and supplies, there was no evidence on which to base a trial for murder. So, Walker and Jenkins were tried in Hawaii for, and found guilty of, the theft of the *Sea Wind*.

Not until 1981 was forensic evidence found that placed the deaths of the Grahams at Palmyra Atoll. A South African woman, Sharon Jordan, who was visiting the island with her husband, found Muff Graham's skull and other bones washed up on the beach of the lagoon. Murder charges were filed against Walker and Jenkins, and Vincent Bugliosi was retained along with Leonard Weinglass to defend Jennifer Jenkins.

Vincent Bugliosi states, "I was characteristically reluctant to defend Jennifer Jenkins." (Bugliosi 1991a, 199). So before agreeing to defend Jennifer, he needed to be satisfied beyond reasonable doubt that she was indeed not a cold-blooded killer. The author further explains, "In a nutshell, although I've never been a law-and-order fanatic, I do believe that those who have committed serious crimes should be severely punished, and I do not want to be in a position of actively seeking to thwart this natural justice." (189).

Bugliosi knew that the case would involve a tremendously uphill legal battle for him, and he was hesitant to put his dedicated efforts along with his typical 100 hours per week of time into the cause of defending a guilty person. Even Vince's wife, Gail, suspected that Jennifer was guilty of murder. He, however, became convinced that although Jennifer Jenkins was guilty of bad judgment and guilty of loving the wrong man, "she was one of those rare criminal defendants who is not guilty as charged" (205), that is, not guilty of either premeditated or felony murder.

Bugliosi wrestled with what techniques he should use in defending Jenkins. He concluded in favor of doing what he is best at and aimed primarily at prosecuting Buck Walker in his defense of Jennifer Jenkins.

One of the major hurdles for Vince to overcome was that there were many inconsistencies in Jennifer's testimony. She had told detectives many things back when she and Buck were first arrested that differed greatly with what she was saying in her defense now—some of the earlier statements were outright lies. These statements compromised her as a witness, and Bugliosi felt that her testimony was critical for her defense in the murder trial. But Bugliosi was able during her trial to show that in that earlier time, Jennifer was unaware that a murder had been committed—that she was simply attempting to protect Walker, whom she loved, from charges stemming from his parole violations and drug infractions.

Jennifer proved also to be a difficult client: She acted as if she were doing Vince a favor by agreeing to meet with him. She did nothing toward her defense—was not a partner with Bugliosi and Weinglass in her defense—until the reality of her predicament hit her very late during her murder trial. Beyond that, Vince states that he had more problems in preparing Jennifer as a witness than he had experienced before with any other witness.

Because the Palmyra Murder was the most sensational crime story in Hawaii since the Massie Murder in 1931, most Hawaiians quickly became aware of the crime and the suspected murderers through the media. The unusual circumstances of the crime pointed toward the pair's guilt. Thus, Judge King agreed for a change of venue for the trials from Honolulu to San Francisco.

Vince Bugliosi was happy with his being teamed with Leonard Weinglass, a lawyer with much trial experience and expertise in defense of difficult cases. The author states that he held Weinglass in the highest regard for his professionalism. During the trial, Vince and Len interacted in ways that resulted in what could only be termed *a serendipitous defense*, but the defense team certainly could not rest on their laurels in this case. They faced the formidable federal prosecution team of Elliot Enoki and Walter Schroeder.

Because Buck Walker's murder trial was scheduled before Jennifer's, Bugliosi was in attendance during that trial to gain as much insight as he could for the purpose of defending Jennifer. The jury reached a verdict in the Walker trial in less than two hours, leading Bugliosi to conclude, "The unique circumstances of the case were a substitute for evidence." (Bugliosi 1991a, 299).

Judge King made a practice of showing disrespect to the defense lawyers during the Buck Walker trial. At the beginning of the Jennifer Jenkins trial in the judge's chambers, Bugliosi put the judge on notice that he would not be shown disrespect in the courtroom. As they left the judge's chambers, Leonard Weinglass exclaimed, "In all my years of practicing law, Vince, I've never heard a lawyer talk to a judge like you just did!" (Bugliosi 1991a).

Bugliosi continued to feel a sense of the lack of equilibrium throughout Jennifer's trial. As opposed to his confidence during all his other murder cases, and after hundreds of hours of preparation, at times he simply did not feel that he had a handle on this case.

Vincent Bugliosi produced a short, pithy overview for *And the Sea Will Tell* in the following words for his final summation to the jury:

> What we're dealing with here, ladies and gentlemen of the jury, is a real murder *mystery*, one that Agatha Christie could have conjured up only on her most inspired of days, the type of murder that rocking-chair sleuths like to ponder into the wee hours beside a crackling fire.

The only problem is that, unlike an Agatha Christie mystery, this nightmarish story, so tragically for Mac and Muff Graham, happens to be true.

Life is an endless series of inconsistencies, a bewildering mixture of contradictions, where the only thing stranger than fiction is reality. (Bugliosi 1991a, 555, 562)

Thus once again, in *And the Sea Will Tell*, Vincent Bugliosi has brought to the reader a compelling and engrossing true-crime murder mystery. He has excelled in making the lives of real humans manifest, in bringing to life the struggles and drama of the courtroom, in meticulous explanations of the intricacies of building a strong legal case for the defense, in clearly communicating his professional standards and stances, and in sharing the mysteries of the case—those solved, as well as those still unsolved.

And the Sea Will Tell became a number one seller on the New York Times hardcover bestseller list. When one asks why, the answer may be that the mystery continues. "Even after reading, however, *And the Sea Will Tell* refuses to relinquish its grip on our imaginations." (Dear 1995, 52).

What happened to Mac Graham? What happened to the sloop *Iola*, Walker and Jenkin's boat? Vincent Bugliosi answers these questions in the book's concluding sentence, "Someday, perhaps the sea will tell."

Reclaiming History: The Assassination of President John F. Kennedy (2007)

Vincent Bugliosi began in March of 1986 with six months of intensive study of the Kennedy assassination in preparation for the murder trial of Lee Harvey Oswald. He had been asked by the London Weekend Television to serve as prosecutor for the planned docutrial. He prepared for the trial exactly as he did for all his other murder trials. Gerry Spence, who had never lost a case up to that time, served as Oswald's defender. Since Oswald had been killed shortly after the Kennedy assassination by Jack Ruby, he was tried in absentia. A federal district court judge presided over the trial, original lay witnesses testified, and a Dallas, Texas, jury heard the case and decided on Oswald's guilt.

Reclaiming History is the twenty-year continuation and conclusion of the study Bugliosi began in preparation for the Oswald trial. The Kennedy assassination was not a murder mystery in the middle 1960s: At that time most American citizens believed that Lee Harvey Oswald was the sole individual responsible for the President's assassination. The Warren Commission and the House Select Committee on Assassinations had, after intense and lengthy investigations, determined that Oswald had planned to kill and then shot President Kennedy on his own, with help from no one else.

But by the mid-1980s, the minds of the public had been swayed by a myriad of speculations propounded and published as *theories*. Conspiracy buffs had created a demand for books on the subject, and conspiracy *theorists* rushed to satisfy that demand. Hundreds of conspiracy theory books had been published by 1985; and Americans began to doubt the Warren Commission report and the report of the House Select Committee on Assassinations. Today, most Americans believe that there was one or another assassination conspiracy that culminated in the death of President Kennedy.

In its 1,612 pages, *Reclaiming History* contains first Bugliosi's study of the facts of the Kennedy assassination and the definite conclusion that no one other than Lee Harvey Oswald was involved in the President's murder. Second, the book contains the author's explanation of conspiracy, history of the conspiracy movement, and the debunking of the major conspiracy theories. This latter task is amazing, for it is incredibly difficult to prove that something did not happen. Third, the book contains a book end section and a compact disk pocketed in its back cover that includes endnotes and source notes.

Thus, we have a presidential assassination that began as a solved murder. This became a murder mystery over time with much convincing of the American public by conspiracy buffs. Vincent Bugliosi gives conclusive proof that the murder is solved, and while he is at it, he disproves all of the major conspiracy theories. With *Reclaiming History*, Bugliosi has both solved the murder mystery and brought an end to uninformed speculations about the Kennedy assassination. History stands, indeed, reclaimed.

LEGAL AND POLITICAL CRITIC

"No Justice, No Peace" (1993)

Vince Bugliosi attempted to publish this article on police brutality and the effects on and reaction from the minority community in other venues, but all demanded that he shorten the article. Vince felt that, to completely cover the subject and explain his logic, the article had to remain as he had written it. *Playboy* magazine welcomed the police brutality article Vince had written—even telling him that it could be as long as he wished.

The basic theme of "No Justice, No Peace" is that a small percentage of police officers regularly brutalize minority persons and there is no punishment given to the officers who do so. The behaviors of these few violent officers put all officers under suspicion in the eyes of the minority community. Even when officers are reprimanded, the worst punishment they receive is a few days off with pay—administrative leave. Vince concludes that only when district attorneys begin to prosecute brutal officers for their crimes consistently, can we hope for police brutality against minority persons to cease.

Outrage: The Five Reasons Why O.J. Simpson Got Away With Murder (1996)

Initially, Vincent Bugliosi had little interest in the Simpson trial and certainly did not wish to write a critique of the same. Most of his books testify to his intense and almost exclusive interest in the true murder mystery. Having little interest in murders in and of themselves, "mystery" supplies the fuel for his creative energies. After contemplating the trial and reviewing the evidence available to the prosecution, Bugliosi concluded, "But there was no mystery in the Simpson case." (Bugliosi 1996b).

Dozens of books had been published before the writing of *Outrage* began. But since Bugliosi is a writer of true-crime books, many people urged him to write a book on the Simpson case. His answer to them was always, "No." Shortly after the Simpson trial verdict, his editor, Starling Lawrence, suggested that he consider writing a book about how Bugliosi would have prosecuted the case. Mr. Lawrence was persistent and finally persuaded him to write the book, although it was not to be the intense, true-crime mystery in which the author had excelled.

In *Outrage*, Vincent Bugliosi spares none of the key actors of the Simpson drama, but democratically applies his gifts of insight, evaluation, and critique to each and to all. The body of the book is staged between two short essays (an introduction and a conclusion) on the general, rampant, and staggering incompetence observable in our society today. The logic of *Outrage* is based on the assumption that actors in a courtroom are likely to be incompetent; and after careful analysis, the author finds them substantially so. Thus, the reader is not surprised when finding the charge of incompetence leveled at the defense, at Judge Ito, at the media and its "talking heads," and especially at the prosecution, in the expansion of the theme and the resultant conclusions.

A secondary theme, that of demythologizing or debunking many of society's common assumptions, is interwoven throughout the book. The author, sensitive to the illogic of many conventions, first exposes them as scientifically unsupported credos. Then he explains how the convention leads to faulty conclusions and ultimately, to injustice. One of the best examples of this may be found in the author's reaction to the Simpson supporters suggesting that God was on their side in the outcome of the trial, while Orenthal James Simpson smiled and held a Bible aloft in his hand. Infuriated by these words and action, Bugliosi responded in an Epilogue insertion titled, "God, where are you?" There he discusses theodicy, the questions of God's part in good and evil in relation to the commonly stated beliefs concerning human experience. Always totally honest, here almost brutally so, he openly states his own confusion in understanding theology and defines his perspective as that of an agnostic.

Outrage begins with a short and pithy editor's note, then follows the introduction in which Bugliosi explains why he decided to write the book and how his conclusions relate to the state of American society today. The five chapter headings express the five reasons given for why the Simpson trial ended with a not guilty verdict, when in fact, Orenthal James Simpson was guilty of a horrendous double murder. A lengthy epilogue follows in which the author wraps up the narrative and shares further insight.

The major murder evidence is given in the three appendices. This includes the police interrogation of O. J. Simpson, the suicide-note-like farewell letter of Simpson, and an explanation of the blood evidence and its presentation to the jury. *Outrage* concludes with copious and insightful endnotes, the hallmark of Vincent Bugliosi's writing, and probably the most important part of the book for dedicated students of the practice of criminal law.

Major issues that form the foundation on which the book is built are explained in the introduction: First, the author states that there existed abundant and clear evidence that O. J. Simpson, and O. J. Simpson alone, was guilty of the murders of his wife Nicole Brown Simpson and Ronald Goldman. Second, the murder evidence pointed to no one else. There were no other suspects; nor was any evidence available that pointed to another suspect. Third, none of the evidence supported the innocence of Simpson. Fourth, the author states that human incompetence and mediocrity are ubiquitous in American society today and that this is indeed the case in every walk of life, in every service, and in every profession. The reader is led to consider personal experiences of the incompetence of others and then is guided to the conclusion that general incompetence and mediocre professional performance ensured the not guilty verdict in the murder trial of O. J. Simpson.

The impact of media coverage of the case on the trial is explained in chapter one. While the author tends to view media coverage of the Simpson case as a mindless circus, he logically argues that the media coverage set the stage to trivialize the murders, to paint O. J. Simpson as a hero, to devalue the ability of the prosecution lawyers, and to question the strength of the prosecution's evidence. Further, the media was responsible for elevating the estimation of the rather ordinary lawyers of the defense who had little trial experience to the level of the *Dream Team* or *the best that money can buy*, to report the defense argument—consisting largely of innuendo and supposition, totally unsupported by evidence—as insightful and brilliant. Bugliosi states that the media "attributed to the defense lawyers star-celebrity qualities, while treating the prosecutors dismissively."

The media effect was from the beginning to convince the American public and the jury that although there existed conclusive evidence that Simpson was guilty of committing two brutal murders, he might get off with a not-guilty verdict. Bugliosi argues that this message became a self-fulfilling prophecy in the absence of a strong prosecution.

In chapter two, "The Change of Venue: Garcetti Transfers the Case Downtown," Bugliosi illuminates the first major error of the prosecution in terse and pithy style. With this change of venue, from an environment favorable (or at least neutral) to the prosecution's case to an unfavorable environment, the prosecution in essence shot itself in the foot before the courtroom battle began. No satisfactory argument has been offered for this colossal lapse of prosecutorial reason. The author concludes, "It was a monumental blunder, one that all by itself was a reason for the miscarriage of justice in the Simpson case."

The third reason for why Simpson got away with murder, a major judicial error, is presented in chapter three. Many of the judicial improprieties evidenced during this trial appear to have occurred due to Judge Ito's hiding his incompetence behind a facade of aloofness, sternness, and disrespect of others in the courtroom, but the most damaging judicial error was Ito's allowing the defense to play *the race card*. The defense played the race card for all it was worth, and the prosecution proved itself inept at dealing with the judge's ruling or with the issue once it was allowed, although race had no logical bearing on the issue of Simpson's guilt.

The pivotal issue, "the incredible incompetence of the prosecution," is the subject of chapter five. Vincent Bugliosi boldly brings to the reader's attention to incident after incident, example after example of an almost unbelievable level of prosecutorial incompetence displayed in serial episodes— before, during, and after the Simpson trial. He states, "The prosecution of O. J. Simpson was the most incompetent criminal prosecution I have ever seen. By far."

Already mentioned was the faulty decision to change venue. Other prosecutorial errors may be illustrated by the following examples: The use of faulty criteria for jury selection, failure of the lead prosecutor to excuse herself when learning of jury bias against her, failure to introduce a mass of very incriminating and easily presentable evidence, assuming that Simpson would testify, objecting to the defense bringing in evidence that was in effect favorable to the prosecution, bungling of the presentation of the bloody glove evidence, and at times during the trial and especially evident during the summation, totally inadequate preparation.

The fifth chapter, titled, "The Weak Voice of the People," considers the final summation. It concerns the district attorney's incompetence, as did chapter four. The prosecution's final argument is described by the author as grossly lacking in thought and preparation. The prosecution failed to counter many of the defense arguments, did little to shore up its own weaknesses, displayed several memory lapses in mid-argument, and made statements off the top of the head that favored the defense. Vincent Bugliosi illustrates his own prosecutorial skills in writing components of the final summation as he would have done it. His final summation in itself is well worth the cost of the book.

Outrage probably should be mandatory reading for lawyers, specifically for those representing the people through the district attorney's office. The book also will prove helpful to women law students desiring to become trial or criminal lawyers, for the author details an especially good example of an egregious example. Bugliosi concludes that for Prosecutor Marcia Clark, the O. J. Simpson trial represented the poorest performance of her legal career for a variety of reasons—some of which related to her gender and gender-based demeanor in the courtroom. Finally, all students of law, and all citizens who hold justice in high regard, will benefit greatly by the reading of *Outrage*; for in *Outrage*, Bugliosi has produced another legal masterpiece.

The Phoenix Solution: Getting Serious about Winning America's Drug War (1996)

In *The Phoenix Solution* (*Phoenix*), Vince Bugliosi offers proposals, which if adopted by the U.S. Government, would allow America to win the drug war quickly. Why has the man who is the best known felony trial prosecutor and the most accomplished true-crime mystery author, chosen to write a book—a blueprint, as it were—setting forth a plan that can solve the drug problem? It is because Bugliosi considers the drug problem to be the greatest crisis America has faced since the American Civil War and that the U.S. government, through its actions and by its proven track record of failing to even slow the ever-increasing influx of illicit drugs into America, is obviously not seriously engaged in an attempt to win the drug war.

The fans of popular lawyer Geoffrey Fieger have proffered a book review in a nutshell by stating, "He tackled one of the most serious threats to the American way of life, our illegal drug problem, in *The Phoenix Solution*. This is a no-holds-barred answer to how we can really win the drug war. He forgets the rhetoric and goes directly to supported solutions." (Bugliosi 2006b).

Bugliosi writes this book, an update of his earlier (1991) volume, *Drugs in America: The Case for Victory: A Citizen's Call to Action*, hoping that the federal government will carry out these solutions. The book is not intended for the general reader, but rather is offered as "a legal road map for the authorities to follow" should they choose to do so. It appears clear that our country is unaware that it has "the legal authority to employ the recommended proposals."

When asked on *The Today Show* if he believes that the U.S. government will follow the suggestions of *Phoenix*, Bugliosi replied that he believed that it was "extremely unlikely" that the government will implement the proposals offered in the book. The question followed, "Then why did you even bother to write the book?" Vince responded that the problem is severe enough to warrant the effort. He goes on to say that the only reason the United States has such a serious drug problem is that America is "not serious about solving it and never has been."

Probably the greatest credo supporting America's failure to stem the drug traffic is that the drug war is "perceived to be incapable of solution." Bugliosi exclaims, "Nothing is more cloying and smacks more of posturing and mere symbolism than our continued use of the 'war' metaphor to characterize our fight against the drug menace. The fight, of course, bears no resemblance to a real war."

The drug war is more of a never-ending game between the parties, with the drug traffickers remaining on top—ever winning. Their object is to get drugs into the United States, and they are accomplishing that goal exponentially. The U.S. government makes large seizures and records each as a winning point, when in reality, the seizures are evidence of the government's defeat. For each load of cocaine seized, ten more loads go undetected and make it to the streets of American cities for sale.

The illogic of the U.S. government war plan is startling: Since that which we have been doing is not working, we propose to do more of the same? This line of illogic appears to be endemic in governmental policy. Another obvious example can be found in the criminal justice system: Since it can be shown scientifically that prisons have, at best, a minute effect on crime rates and no has an effect on drug use, let us have a prison-building binge to incarcerate ever larger numbers of drug users. Thus when the U.S. government reports that it has had *the best year yet*, it ought to be reporting that it has had *the worst year yet!*

In summarizing America's willingness to fight to win the drug war, Bugliosi states:

> I believe the federal government will not adopt the measures recommended because for some unfathomable reason, in the area of fighting drugs, otherwise perfectly intelligent human beings have become virtual automatons who have unconsciously surrendered and forfeited their right to think in mindless obeisance to existing policies, as pathetically inept as they are. After a seventy-year fight, if the war on drugs were suspended at this very moment, the consensus of most knowledgeable observers would be that we have lost the war, badly. In fact, we've virtually conceded defeat by no longer even trying to win. (Bugliosi 1996b, 7)

The author explains that illicit drug use is of epidemic and extremely destructive proportions, that the National Household Survey on Drug Abuse found as many as 21.8 million used illicit drugs in 1994, and that as many as one third of American adults have used an illegal drug at least once in their lifetimes. Two realities are posited: First, that illicit drugs are the greatest scourge America faces domestically today. Second, that all efforts to curb illicit drug trafficking and use have failed. Bugliosi argues that not only are the $50 billion in drugs sold per year destroying the moral fabric of America, but in terms of deaths, murders, human suffering, illness, and lost productivity, drugs are destroying the physical fabric of America as well.

In part one, the author offers a short history of the creation of drug laws and their enforcement in the United States. And while enforcement has had little effect on drug use, virtually the only recommended solution offered has been legalization. Thus Bugliosi states the predicate of the book: The drug problem is extreme, therefore it will take "revolutionary measures" to solve.

Part one of the book is a review of the two means employed by the federal government to enforce federal drug laws, interdiction and eradication (and/or crop replacement). Ideally, interdiction is defined as stopping drugs from entering the country. The author gives evidence of how neither federal drug enforcement nor the American military has been able to, or can, stop the flow of drugs into this country through interdiction. Presently, with efforts of the Drug Enforcement Administration, the U.S. Border Patrol, the U.S. Customs, the U.S. Coast Guard, and related enforcement agencies, ten loads of illicit drugs pass into the United States undetected for every load that is *interdicted* by these agencies.

A policy of worldwide eradication of coca, poppy, and marijuana plants; of destroying methamphetamine labs; and of replacing drug-producing crops with food crops is shown by the author to be simply not feasible. The author points out that to make a major dent solely in South American cocaine production, all personnel of the American military would have to be stationed on that continent permanently. A policy of eradication is further handicapped by history and custom of coca-producing countries, local and international economics, government and law enforcement corruption, political sovereignty issues, and by the simple supply-and-demand business of the drug kingpins.

One factor, that of cocaine (and other illicit drug) production costs, is often misunderstood because of the simple fact that black market drug prices are so high on the streets of America. The cost of cocaine production is minimal. American drug laws themselves drive the high street prices through the underground economy that results from the response to the laws themselves. When large amounts of money are to be made, huge amounts of money, in which $100 bills are often counted by weight, entrepreneurs will arise who are willing to take advantage of the situation. Thus, if the drug lords lose a load to interdiction, they will find production sources that will produce the ten loads that arrive in America—as long as the great demand continues.

In ending part one, the author concludes that U.S. government efforts at interdiction and eradication have been a dismal failure. He further argues, by quoting Peter Reuter of the Rand Corporation, that both federal government programs are a "colossal waste of money." In effect, with interdiction and eradication programs, the federal government can neither defeat South American farmers, nor can it defeat the drug lords.

Part two includes Vincent Bugliosi's two proposals to win the war on drugs. Proposal one is to train and deploy a special forces unit on limited military search-and-find missions against the drug kingpins. Two corollary measures are proposed: (1) to continue the death penalty for drug lords, which is presently federal law; and (2) to create a "special federal court to expedite the trials and appeals of drug lords."

Bugliosi gives two major arguments for this proposal: First, he argues the "advisability and lawfulness of a military search-and-find mission." Second, he proposes that it is "the *explicit constitutional duty* of this nation's chief executive to pursue this course of action." In support of these arguments, the author shows that international law does not rule out this course of action.

Further, the U.S. Constitution supports the president in repelling attacks and in protecting the security and welfare of the country. The federal Posse Comitatus law does prohibit using the American military for policing on foreign soil. And the U.S. military is already involved in a similar endeavor: The U.S. Coast Guard currently seizes illicit drug shipments on the high seas.

There also exist historical precedents for similar presidential actions: President Wilson sent General Pershing into the country of Mexico to pursue Pancho Villa. Presidents took it on themselves to involve the American military in Grenada, Kuwait (the Gulf War) and in the war with Iraq. The American military invasion of Panama to arrest President Noriega on drug-trafficking charges was also under presidential order.

With a rather tongue-in-cheek manner, Vincent Bugliosi introduces his second proposal by stating that it is "for the more faint of heart." Proposal two is the interdiction of drug-profit monies. Another way to end the drug crisis in America, completely different and independent of the first proposal, is to make drug-trafficking unprofitable to the drug kingpins. At the present, the United States has no comprehensive strategy to stop money laundering.

The first action suggested to implement a serious national program of drug-money interdiction would be to create two separate U.S. currencies: Currency number one would be legal tender only outside the United States. Currency number two would be legal tender only inside the United States. Domestic currency—that which is used to distribute and purchase drugs in the street marketplace—then could not be smuggled out of the country; or at least, would not be due to its worthlessness on the international market.

The second action suggested is to develop an organized policy for the interdiction of drug-money wire transfers. To be laundered, drug money must find its way into the international banking system. Most drug moneys laundered are laundered through international wire transfers.

The third action proposed is to place resident federal agents into banks to interdict the drug money in the laundering process. Without money laundering, cocaine trafficking would cease to be a profitable enterprise.

The fourth and final component of this proposal is for the federal government to set up a computerized central command post. The author argues that if we are serious, let us stop drug trafficking. "If we are not, we should at least have the decency to stop the posturing." If we are unwilling to take the special steps proposed above, then we are not really serious about winning the drug war.

Finally, while Bugliosi does not formally endorse drug legalization, his exploration of the legalization theme in the last chapter of *Phoenix* leaves the reader questioning whether Vince intended legalization to be his third proposal—although to be given less weight than the first two.

He explains that there is only one logical and just reason to support drug laws—that drug laws protect people from themselves. On the other hand, Bugliosi lists eleven benefits that most likely would result from the legalization of drugs in America.

The author concludes with an explanation of why he believes his proposals in *Phoenix* probably will not be implemented by the federal government. The reader must take note of this section for it deals with the motivations of politicians and the actual (but unstated) goals and purposes of federal agencies.

The Phoenix Solution leaves the reader believing that the proposals suggested, if implemented, would allow the U.S. government to win the war on drugs once and for all. As a road map for policy makers, the book is at times tedious to read, but the proposals suggested are fresh, new, and innovative. The proposals are so logical in their applications, that if implemented, they simply should work!

No Island of Sanity: Paula Jones v. Bill Clinton: The Supreme Court on Trial (1998)

In *No Island of Sanity* Vince Bugliosi bravely offers a stunning critique of the U.S. Supreme Court for its decision in Paula Jones v. Bill Clinton to allow a private citizen to bring a private lawsuit against an acting president. In a sense there was no decision on this matter, because the Supreme Court chose to ignore the question. Vince compares and contrasts the action (or inertia) of the Court regarding this lawsuit with precedence and on constitutional law. In this book, Bugliosi himself puts the Supreme Court on trial. Bugliosi concludes that the U.S. Supreme Court acted improperly in valuing Jones's right to sue over and above the right of the American people to have a president's undivided attention directed toward the running of the country.

The Betrayal of America: How the Supreme Court Undermined the Constitution and Chose Our President (2001)

The title of this book explains its contents in a nutshell: Vincent Bugliosi tackles the U.S. Supreme Court once again in this volume. First, Bugliosi explains the Florida state constitution and Florida state election laws. Second, the author expounds the political intrigue that held up the recounting of presidential election ballots in Florida. Third, he shows precedence for state supreme courts determining issues relating to election vote recounts. And finally, Vince argues that the U.S. Supreme Court improperly wrested the decision from the Florida Supreme Court and went against the U.S. Constitution (which clearly states that undecided presidential contests are the domain of the U.S. Senate) and went on to choose the next president of the United States. Bugliosi feels that the action of the U.S. Supreme Court is criminal.

PRAISE: A PANEL OF HIS PEERS

Respected and successful trial lawyers hold Vincent T. Bugliosi in their highest regards: F. Lee Bailey concludes that Vince is "the quintessential prosecutor." (Bugliosi 2007b). Gerry Spence, after losing to Bugliosi at the docutrial of Lee Harvey Oswald for the Kennedy assassination, stated, "No other lawyer in America could have done what Vince did in this case." Alan Dershowitz stated, "Bugliosi is as good a prosecutor as there ever was." The veteran criminal defense attorney, Harry Weiss (who has faced Bugliosi in a criminal trial) explained, "I've seen all the great trial lawyers of the past thirty years and none of them are in Vince's class." And the top prosecutor for the Manhattan District Attorney's Office for years, Robert Tannenbaum, puts a finish to the Bugliosi tale when he states, "There is only one Vince Bugliosi. He's the best." (Bugliosi 1996a, 12).

FURTHER READING

Bugliosi, Vincent T., with Curt Gentry. 1974. *Helter Skelter: The True Story of the Manson Murders*. New York: W. W. Norton.

Bugliosi, Vincent T., with Ken Hurwitz. 1978. *Till Death Us Do Part: A True Murder Mystery*. New York: W. W. Norton.

Bugliosi, Vincent T. 1981a. Not guilty and innocent—The problem children of reasonable doubt. *Criminal Justice Journal* 4:349-74.

Bugliosi, Vincent T. and Ken Hurwitz. 1981b. *Shadow of Cain: A Novel*. New York: W. W. Norton.

Bugliosi, Vincent T., with William Stadiem. 1987. *Lullaby and Good Night: A Novel Inspired by the True Story of Vivian Gordon*. New York: NAL Books.

Bugliosi, Vincent T., with Bruce B. Henderson. 1991a. *And the Sea Will Tell*. New York: Ballantine.

Bugliosi, Vincent T. 1991b. *Drugs in America: The Case for Victory: A Citizen's Call to Action*. New York: Knightsbridge.

Bugliosi, Vincent T. 1993. No justice, no peace. *Playboy*, 40 (2): 66–68, 156–62.

Bugliosi, Vincent T. 1996a. *Outrage: The Five Reasons Why O.J. Simpson Got Away With Murder*. New York: W. W. Norton.

Bugliosi, Vincent T. 1996b. *The Phoenix Solution: Getting Serious about Winning America's Drug War*. Beverly Hills, CA: Dove Audio.

Bugliosi, Vincent T. 1998. *No Island of Sanity: Paula Jones v. Bill Clinton: The Supreme Court on Trial*. New York: Ballantine.

Bugliosi, Vincent T. 2001a, February 5. None Dare Call It Treason. *The Nation*. http://www.thenation.com/doc/20010205/bugliosi/ (accessed October 18, 2006).

Bugliosi, Vincent T. 2001b. *The Betrayal of America: How the Supreme Court Undermined the Constitution and Chose our President*. New York: Thunder's Mouth Press/Nation Books.

Bugliosi, Vincent T. 2007. *Reclaiming History: The Assassination of President John F. Kennedy*. New York: W. W. Norton.

Dear, Pamela S., ed. 1995. Bugliosi, Vincent (T.) 1934-. In *Contemporary Authors: New Revision Series,* Vol. 46, 50–52. Detroit, MI: Gale Research.

Manso, Peter. 1998. Kenneth Starr's war against America: An interview with Vincent Bugliosi. *Penthouse Magazine* (Reprinted), 1–12, December.

Schauer, Edward J. 2007a, May 31. Communication with Starling Lawrence.

Schauer, Edward J. 2007b, May 31. Interview with Gail T. Bugliosi.

Schauer, Edward J. 2007c, March 5; April 14; April 17; June 9. Interviews with Vincent T. Bugliosi.

Bugliosi, Vincent. 2006a, October 18. In *eBookMall.* http://www.ebookmall.com/alpha-authors/Vincent-Bugliosi.htm/ (accessed October 18, 2006).

Bugliosi, Vincent. 2006b, October 18. In *Fans of Fieger: Lawyer Hall of Fame.* http://www.fansoffieger.com/bugliosi.htm/ (accessed October 18, 2006).

Bugliosi, Vincent. 2007a, January 19. In *AEI Speakers Bureau.* http://www.aeispeakers.com/print.php?SpeakerID=164/ (accessed January 19, 2007).

Bugliosi, Vincent. 2007b, January 19. In *BookRags.* http://www.bookrags.com/printfriendly/?p=vincent-bugliosi-cri/ (accessed January 19, 2007).

Bugliosi, Vincent. 2007c, January 19. In *Wikipedia, The Free Encyclopedia.* http://en.wikipedia.org/w/index.php?title=Vincent_Bugliosi&oldid=101494954/ (accessed January 19, 2007).

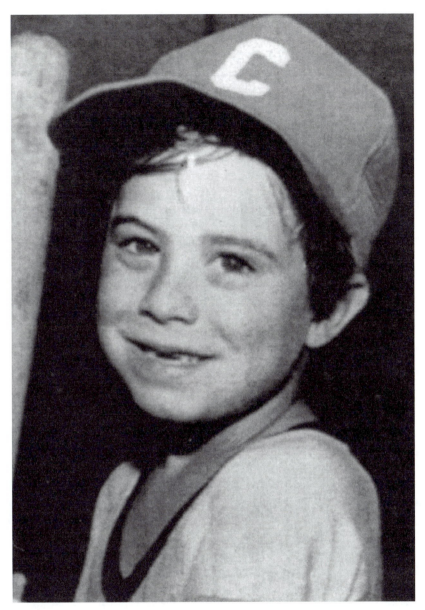

AP Images

For Adam: The John Walsh Story

Elizabeth Quinn DeValve

It is likely that most people are aware of the impact John Walsh has had on crime through his work on *America's Most Wanted*. It is also very likely that most people know of the kidnapping and brutal murder of his six-year-old son, Adam. What may not be as widely known is the impact he has had on crime victim legislation across the United States and his diligent advocacy for crime victims and children (victims and nonvictims). Since 1983 John Walsh has worked tirelessly, steadily, and mightily to prevent others from experiencing what he and his wife, Revé Walsh, experienced when their son was taken away from them. Education, legislation, and the establishment of centers for missing children (including the Adam Walsh Center and the National Center for Missing or Exploited Children) have all come to fruition under the watchful eye of John Walsh. One might suggest that this is not the road they would have chosen, that having Adam present in their lives is what they would have preferred. But for the millions of crime victims in the United States, and especially for the missing children and their parents or guardians, had it not been for John Walsh, their experiences may have been drastically different. This chapter introduces the reader to John Walsh and the impact he has had on crime through his various efforts.

JOHN WALSH—THE BEGINNING

John Walsh is the oldest of four children, born to Irish Catholic parents on December 26, 1945, in Auburn, New York. His father started out at Notre Dame but was drafted to fight in World War II as an Air Force pilot. His mother grew up in a wealthy household and lost both of her parents when she was quite young. The business that had supported her family so well seemed to crumble, and it took years for her brothers to reinvent it. John Walsh has two younger brothers, Jimmy and Joe, and one younger sister, Jane. By his own admission, John Walsh had a happy childhood. In his book, *Tears of Rage*, Walsh describes his life growing up in New York. He talks about how loving his parents were to each other, to their kids, and to anyone who needed it. He states that his father taught him about values and morality, and as he grew he began to feel a sense of responsibility "[T]hat it was my job to be in charge of the world." (Walsh and Schindehette 1997, 12). The role modeling of his father would certainly help him out later in life. Some people say that things happen for a reason, and they're usually referring to bad things, not good things. To use that saying but in a different way, one might suggest that John Walsh was blessed with such a wonderful childhood and young adult life because somewhere down the line he was going to suffer immeasurably. If he didn't have the strong foundation established in his youth, there might not be a John Walsh chapter in this volume.

John Walsh has been a fighter since his youth. Today he fights for legislation and programs that will aid children and crime victims; in the past he fought for honor, girls, Irish pride...anything. John Walsh attended Auburn Community College and moved on to the University of Buffalo to study English and, later, history. He was, in his terms, a big man on campus and hung out with fun-loving guys—mostly jocks who were also conscientious students. It was in Buffalo that he met Revé Drew. Revé was a bit younger than college age when she and John Walsh met at a bar called Brunner's, in Buffalo. She, like Walsh, had a love for life and was open to trying new experiences. Early in their relationship, Revé is described by Walsh as being interested in art and horses and as smart, serene, and "game." (Walsh and Schindehette 1997). The two would have what would now be called "an open relationship" where they dated each other and others, but even when John moved down to Florida after college they maintained contact and continued to spend time together.

GETTING OUT OF THE NORTH

After graduating from the University of Buffalo, John Walsh moved to Florida and worked as a cabana boy and head cabana boy at the Diplomat Hotel in Hollywood, Florida. There he would set up the beach for sunbathing and take care of the guests. He made great money and was able to play in the ocean and enjoy the nightlife. It was at the Diplomat that John met and established a life-long personal and professional relationship with John Monahan, Sr., a top executive at the Diplomat. Walsh saved the life of Monahan's son, Johnny, one day and that may well have cemented their relationship.

At some point while in Florida, Walsh decided he wanted to marry Revé and returned to New York to "surprise" propose. They were married in a large ceremony in Florida on July 10, 1971, which followed with a two-month, fly-by-the-seat-of-their-pants honeymoon in Europe. They settled in Miami Shores, Florida, soon after and Walsh began working as a cabana manager at a large beach hotel. He then decided to "get a real job" and began working in hotel marketing for Gulf American Corporation with John Monahan. Walsh worked with Monahan to promote island resorts to prospective clients across the globe. When Monahan quit Gulf American Corporation, Walsh left too. He landed a job with Bahamian Out Island Promotion Board and worked aggressively to promote some of the Bahamian Islands that weren't as popular as Nassau and Freeport. He worked to promote the islands, to entertain the clients, and to bring in more clients. It was a demanding job, but a lot of fun, according to Walsh.

After a few years of married life Revé became pregnant. Adam John Walsh was born on November 14, 1974, in Miami Shores, Florida. Their lives would change forever.

ADAM

No chapter about John Walsh could be complete without discussing his son, Adam. In *Tears of Rage*, John Walsh describes Adam as an "old soul"; he was someone who was laid back, grateful, sophisticated (for a little boy), curious, smart, fun, and engrossing. According to John Walsh, some of Adam's favorite things were drawing creepy crawlies, spending time in the ocean, and playing baseball. Adam was someone everyone wanted to be around.

On July 27, 1981, Adam Walsh was abducted while he and his mother were at Sears in the Hollywood Mall in Hollywood, Florida. From the information provided in *Tears of Rage*, a possible scenario of events is that Adam was watching some kids play video games in a display area in the toys section. One witness's account suggests that Ottis Toole approached Adam while he was watching the boys play a video game and spoke to him a bit. It was reported by a security guard that some of the boys playing the video game got rowdy, and she asked if their parents were around. Two of the boys said no and she told them to leave through the North entrance (the entrance Adam and Revé came through earlier), and one boy said his parents were in the store. It appears that the security guard may have thought Adam was with this last boy and sent them both out the West entrance. Perhaps as Adam was outside the store, maybe looking for his way back in, Ottis Toole either coaxed him into his car or pulled him by his arm into the car and drove off. Many people remember seeing the car that Ottis Toole was driving, and some people remember seeing Adam being pulled by the arm into the car. According to Revé, all these events happened in a very short period of time, maybe five to ten minutes. Revé ran around the store looking for Adam and asking people if they had seen him, to no avail. The Hollywood police were called after awhile and responded, but seemed to think that Adam had wandered off and would return shortly. What seems to be consistent is that there was no protocol for dealing with children who had gone missing, unless they were runaways. There was no protocol within the Sears store, within the mall, or within the police department. John Walsh appeared after being called by either Revé or his mother. (It is important to remember that the time period in which this all happened was the early 1980s and despite the Women's Movement in the 1970s, it was still a man's world and men listened to other men. Man = serious.) After finding out who was the officer in charge and what they had done and would continue to do, all parties moved across the street to the Hollywood Police Department.

Over the next two weeks a command center was set up by John Walsh in the Hollywood Police Department. The tireless efforts of friends, family, and volunteers resulted in searches, posting of fliers with Adam's picture and information, and answering phones. Walsh would learn this much later, but tips that came in to the Hollywood Police were not always recorded with the most diligence and were not always followed up on. People who should have been interviewed weren't. On August 11, 1981, after Revé and John Walsh appeared on *Good Morning America* so they would be able to post Adam's picture in a national forum, John Walsh received a phone call stating that they had found remains that belonged to Adam.

Because of the lack of assistance and protocol they received when Adam was abducted, the Walshes have fought for crime victims' and children's rights to improve the ability of law enforcement to respond to abducted children calls. In addition, they have helped to establish a national center for missing children, state-specific centers for missing children, national and state legislation improving treatment and other services to crime victims and children, databases for the collection of information on violent offenders, and statewide informational clearinghouses. In accordance with these monumental achievements, John Walsh has received numerous awards ranging from *People* magazine to honors from four presidents of the United States. John Walsh's crime-fighting efforts have taken place in the courtroom and the television screen with the production and/or hosting of ten television programs. The remainder of this chapter will focus on the achievements of John Walsh and discuss the impact of these achievements on the progression of the crime victims and children's movements.

WRITTEN AND MEDIA PROJECTS

John Walsh has been involved with the development, production, starring and/or hosting of ten television and film projects devoted to educating the public about crime and victimization in many different respects. The list of projects includes: *Adam* (1983), *Adam: His Song Continues* (1986), *A Parent's Greatest Fear* (1984), *America's Most Wanted* (1988–present), *Manhunter, America's Most Wanted: Final Justice, If Looks Could Kill* (1995), *Street Smart Kids* (nominated for an Emmy 1987), and *The John Walsh Show* (2002–2004). Most recently John Walsh has teamed up with the creator of *Baby Einstein*, Julie Clark, to create two DVDs educating children about stranger and Internet safety. The DVDs are called *Stranger Safety* and *Internet Safety*, and they teach children how to be safe in situations with strangers and while browsing the Internet. The DVDs have won a number of awards including the following:

Stranger Safety	Internet Safety
Emmy Award (2005)	
Parenting Mom-Tested DVD Video of the Year Award (2005)	
Dove Family Approved Seal (2005)	Dove Family Approved Seal (2006)
Kids First! Endorsement (2005)	Kids First! Endorsement (2006)
iParenting Media Award (2005)	iParenting Media Award (2007)
Mom's Choice Award (2005)	
Film Advisory Board Award of Excellence (2005)	Film Advisory Board Award of Excellence (2006)
Awarded Best Product by Orca Communications Unlimited, LLC (2005)	

John Walsh has cowritten three books, *Tears of Rage* (1997), *No Mercy* (1998), and *Public Enemies* (2001). *Tears of Rage* is both a mini-biography of John Walsh and the story of the Adam Walsh case. *No Mercy* and *Public Enemies* include chapters describing some of the most notorious criminals profiled on *America's Most Wanted*.

America's Most Wanted

America's Most Wanted is a weekly hour-long television program that profiles real crimes in an effort to capture fugitives, locate missing persons, and generally to solve crimes. The Fox Network, a new fledgling television network in the 1980s, created the show in its infancy as a TV network. The criminals profiled may have committed recent crimes or the crimes profiled may be "cold." John Walsh introduces the audience to the crime, a recreation is provided, and the viewing audience is instructed on how they can provide information if they have knowledge of the incident or the fugitive. *America's Most Wanted* aired its first show on February 7, 1988, and has been on the air since; it ties *Good Morning America* as the longest running show in television history. There was a brief period of time in which the program was cancelled and was off the air for about six weeks in 1996. September 21, 1996, was the last official show when it was originally cancelled, but it returned to the air on November 9, 1996. The Fox network picked up the show again on September 24, 1996, because of the outcry of viewers and law enforcement agencies.

The first criminal profiled, David James Roberts, was caught within days. Since its first airing, *America's Most Wanted* has been responsible for aiding in the capture of 944 fugitives and the recovery of fifty-three missing persons and children. Because the show received such an incredible response on its first airing, the network executives decided to air it on all 125 Fox-affiliated stations and seven owned-and-operated stations. Domestic and international excitement surrounded *America's Most Wanted* as well; the show is currently aired in multiple countries outside the United States and is responsible for the "capture of fugitives in 31 countries." (http://www.amw.com/about_amw/faw.cfm/)

John Walsh only agreed to host the show if he was able to secure that local, state, and federal law enforcement agencies would not be in competition with each other for resolving cases profiled, if a toll-free hotline could be established to take calls, and if victims were treated with care.

LEGISLATION AND ORGANIZATIONS

John Walsh has lobbied heavily for a great deal of legislation to be enacted at the state and federal levels. On the statewide level he has testified and helped to enact legislation establishing informational clearinghouses, requiring background checks for people working in day care centers, enacting repeat-offender bills, arguing for videotaping for children's testimony, and testifying for the improvement of victims' rights in all fifty states. This is an immense task, given the amount of time needed to devote to getting to know the special issues faced by each state. Recently, he helped to garner support for the Anti-Murder Act in Florida, which was enacted in 2007. He and Revé Walsh founded the first center for missing children in Florida to help people in situations similar to theirs. The center they opened was named the Adam Walsh Outreach Center for Missing Children.

Adam Walsh Outreach Center for Missing Children

The Adam Walsh Outreach Center for Missing Children, established in 1981, was the first statewide center that provided assistance to parents who had missing children. The three goals of the center were to offer a $100,000 reward for the apprehension of Adam's killer, to assist law enforcement agencies with finding missing children, and to work with Paula Hawkins on getting the Missing Children Act passed. The original Adam Walsh Outreach Center was based in Florida but three more Adam Walsh Outreach Centers were established in South Carolina, New York, and California. The Adam Walsh Centers have now merged with the National Center for Missing and Exploited (NCMEC) children and are branch centers of the national organization. The NCMEC Southeast location in Florida is still the center for all "child-protection education and prevention." (http://www.missingkids.com).

On the federal level, John Walsh is a symbol of both strength and the crime victims movement and he was integral in enacting and/or supporting the establishment of the Missing Children Act of 1982, the Missing

Children's Assistance Act (MCAA) of 1984, the NCMEC (through the MCAA of 1984), VI-CAP, Code Adam, Team Adam, the Amber Alert Network, the Adam Walsh Children Protection and Safety Act of 2006 and continues to fight for a Crime Victims' Rights Constitutional Amendment. Also, he testified in Congress against the North American Man/Boy Love Association, better known as NAMBLA. To better understand the impact on crime fighting of the bills and programs listed previously, a brief description of each of the federal pieces of legislation and established programs follow.

Missing Children Act of 1982

The *Missing Children Act of 1982*, 28 USC § 534(a), requires law enforcement to investigate thoroughly all missing children cases and input all information about the case in the National Crime Information Center (NCIC) Missing Person File. It also calls for the Federal Bureau of Investigation to assist local and state law enforcement if appropriate and confirm that the information has been placed in NCIC for the child's parents.

Missing Children's Assistance Act (1984)

The Missing Children's Assistance Act 42 USC § 5771 *et seq.*, enacted by Congress in 1984, directed the Office of Juvenile Justice and Delinquency Prevention to establish a national clearinghouse that would provide general information on missing and exploited children; maintain and operate a 24-hour hotline to collect information on missing and exploited children; provide technical assistance in the recovery of missing children to law enforcement, state nonprofit missing children's organizations, and parents; create and operate training programs for how law enforcement should conduct a missing child investigation; and to conduct an awareness campaign educating the public about issues related to missing and exploited children. John Walsh was hired as the vice chairman for the National Center for Missing and Exploited Children and was charged with getting the center off the ground and is listed to this day, along with Revé Walsh, as the Founders of the National Center.

National Center for Missing and Exploited Children

The NCMEC has grown tremendously in the last twenty-three years. The mission of the NCMEC is "to help prevent child abduction and sexual exploitation; help find missing children; and assist victims of child abduction and sexual exploitation, their families, and the professionals who serve them." (http://www.ncmec.org). The Center operates a clearinghouse for information on missing and exploited children, a twenty-four-hour hotline for reporting tips on current missing children, a CyberTipline that may be used to report tips on Internet-related sexual exploitation of children, offers training programs for law enforcement and social service personnel on how to deal with missing and exploited children cases, provides technical assistance to law enforcement and other agencies with missing child cases, distributes photographs and descriptive information about missing children worldwide, provides information on legislation related to protection of children, and works with nonprofit and private sector enterprises to manage child-protection efforts.

National Center for Missing and Exploited Children Fact Sheet

How many children are reported missing each year?

The U.S. Department of Justice reports the following:

- 797,500 children (younger than eighteen) were reported missing in a one-year period of time studied, resulting in an average of 2,185 children being reported missing each day.
- 203,900 children were the victims of family abductions.
- 58,200 children were the victims of nonfamily abductions.
- 115 children were the victims of "stereotypical" kidnapping. (These crimes involve someone the child does not know or someone of slight acquaintance, who holds the child overnight, transports the child 50 miles or more, kills the child, demands ransom, or intends to keep the child permanently.)

How many cases of missing children has NCMEC helped resolve?

Since 1984, NCMEC has assisted law enforcement with more than 138,400 missing-child cases, resulting in the recovery of more than 121,500 children.

How many calls does NCMEC's hotline (1-800-THE-LOST®) handle?

In the last quarter of 2007, the hotline handled an average of 258 service-related calls per day. Since its 1984 inception, the toll-free hotline has handled more than 2.2 million calls.

How many children have been recovered through AMBER ALERTS?

Since 1997, the AMBER Alert program has been credited with the safe recovery of 377 children. To date there is a network of 119 AMBER Plans across the country.

How many children are victims of online sexual exploitation?

According to the latest online victimization research,

- Approximately one in seven youth online (ten to seventeen years old) received a sexual solicitation or approach over the Internet.

(continued)

- Four percent (4%) received an aggressive sexual solicitation: a solicitor who asked to meet them somewhere; called them on the telephone; or sent them offline mail, money, or gifts.
- Thirty-four percent (34%) had an unwanted exposure to sexual material: pictures of naked people or people having sex.
- Twenty-seven percent (27%) of the youth who encountered unwanted sexual material told a parent or guardian. If the encounter was defined as distressing—episodes that made them feel very or extremely upset or afraid—42 percent (42%) told a parent or guardian.

How pervasive is the problem of child sexual exploitation?

Research indicates that 1 in 5 girls and 1 in 10 boys will be sexually victimized before adulthood.

How many reports of child exploitation have been made to CyberTipline?

CyberTipline has received more than 546,600 reports since it was established in March 1998.

Reports to CyberTipline involve the possession, manufacture and distribution of child pornography, the online enticement of children for sex acts, child prostitution, child sex-tourism, child molestation (not in the family), unsolicited obscene material sent to a child, and misleading domain names.

How many victims of child exploitation have been identified through the Child Victim Identification (CVIP) Program?

As of December 16, 2007, CVIP has information on more than 1,233 child victims from around the world seen in sexually abusive images.

Through the end of November 2007, CVIP Analysts reviewed seized child pornography collections from more than 11,650 investigations across the country, through the Child Recognition and Identification System (CRIS).

Source: http://www.ncmec.org/missingkids/.

The NCMEC has helped to introduce to the law enforcement community many technologies to aid in the recovery of missing children. In 1989 the NCMEC launched a new type of technology that age-progressed photos. Age-progression was a necessary tool because children develop at such a fast rate, and for those children who remained missing for years and years it could be very difficult to identify someone from a dated picture. Other innovative developments include the following:

1997—Establishment of the Jimmy Ryce Law Enforcement Training Center, which provides training to law enforcement agencies for dealing with missing child cases.

1998—Creation of the CyberTipline: an online tool that accepts reports of sexual exploitation related to "child pornography, online enticement of children for sex acts, molestation of children outside the family, sex tourism of children, child victims of prostitution, and unsolicited obscene material sent to a child." (CyberTipline link)

2002—Establishment of the Child Victim Identification Program: a program that identifies children who are victims of child pornography (which to date has resulted in the identification of more than 1,000 child pornography victims).

2004—Implementation of the Katrina Missing Persons Hotline. This hotline was created to aid in the recovery and reunification of persons gone missing as a result of Hurricanes Katrina and Rita. NCMEC was successful in finding all 5,192 children who were reported missing to them.

Lost Child Alert Technology Resource (LOCATER)—a free Web-based program for law enforcement agencies that helps them to create and disseminate images and information about missing children and adults rapidly to the general public. The posters can also be used to publicize "wanted" information, crime alerts, and rewards for information.

2007—NetSmartz411: a resource for parents and guardians to learn about Internet safety.

The NCMEC has improved its recovery rate from 62 percent in 1990 to 96 percent in 2006. It is responsible for aiding law enforcement in the recovery of more than 112,900 missing children and assistance on 130,300 cases. Additionally, the Center has received more than 475,000 leads on child sexual exploitation on its CyberTipline.

Violent Offender Criminal Apprehension Program

The Violent Offender Criminal Apprehension Program (ViCAP) is maintained by the Federal Bureau of Investigation and is a nationwide database that houses and analyzes information about violent offenses to identify patterns of serial offenders. This database is available to all law enforcement agencies: local, state, and federal.

Code Adam

The Code Adam program was created by Wal-Mart in 1994 with the purpose of finding a missing child in a business establishment. The response of the establishment's employees includes (1) receipt of a detailed description of the child, including the clothes he is wearing, (2) an announcement describing the child and his clothing and the coordinated effort of other employees to monitor entrances and begin the search for the child, (3) calling law enforcement after ten minutes if the child is not located, (4) reuniting a found child with the family member if he appears unscathed, (5) an attempt to delay the departure of an individual who is found to be with the child unauthorized, and (6) the cancellation of the Code Adam upon discovery of the child or the arrival of law enforcement.

Team Adam: Missing Child Rapid Response System

The Team Adam program is composed of retired law enforcement professionals from local, state, and federal agencies who assist law enforcement agencies with missing children cases. Starting in 2003 with a $3 million grant from the Michael and Susan Dell Foundation, Team Adam consultants travel to agencies that may need extra assistance in a missing child or child sexual exploitation case and/or may not have the expertise necessary to handle a missing child case effectively. They assist law enforcement with searches, computer forensics, investigation and analysis, resources and equipment, and technical assistance. Additionally, the team is there to support the family and work with the media as needed.

AMBER Alert Network

The AMBER Alert program, supported by the Wireless Association, is an emergency alert system whereby descriptions of abducted children and suspected abductors are aired over media sources to assist in the search and recovery of serious child abduction cases. This program consists of a partnership between broadcasters, law enforcement, and transportation agencies. The program is named after Amber Hagerman, a nine-year-old girl who was abducted while riding her bike. A neighbor heard her scream as she was being pulled off of her bike and forced into a pickup. The neighbor called the police who, along with the FBI, searched for the girl and interviewed neighbors. The media covered the story in their regular newscasts. Amber was found four miles from her neighborhood in a drainage ditch. Her case remains unsolved.

There are 121 AMBER Alert Plans nationwide (53 statewide, 28 regional, and 40 local). There are a number of guidelines specified for a case to be considered for an AMBER Alert Plan:

- There is reasonable belief by law enforcement an abduction has occurred
- The abduction is of a child age seventeen years or younger
- The law enforcement agency believes the child is in imminent danger of serious bodily injury or death

- There is enough descriptive information about the victim and abduction for law enforcement to issue an AMBER Alert to assist in the recovery of the child
- The child's name and other critical data elements, including the Child Abduction flag, have been entered into the National Crime Information Center (NCIC) computer.

Between 1996 and June 2007 there have been 333 successful recoveries resulting from AMBER Alerts.

Adam Walsh Children Protection and Safety Act of 2006

The Adam Walsh Children Protection and Safety Act of 2006 is a act that protects children from sexual predators, violent criminals, and child abuse via child pornography. The bill was introduced on December 8, 2005, and signed by President George W. Bush on July 27, 2006. The law expands the effectiveness of sex offender registries by integrating information stored in statewide sex offender registries into the National Sex Offender Registry so that a sex offender cannot evade law enforcement simply by moving from state to state. Additionally, this law increases mandatory minimum penalties for the most serious sex offenses against children, increases penalties for child sex trafficking and child pornography, and assists states in creating bills that will allow for states to institutionalize those sex offenders who are not reformed and are about to leave prison. Furthermore, the law authorizes the creation of Internet Crimes against Children taskforces that will help to train and assist law enforcement in combating child exploitation through use of the Internet. Finally, the law calls for the creation of a National Child Abuse Registry and requires that background checks be conducted on individuals interested in becoming foster or adoptive parents.

Crime Victims' Rights Constitutional Amendment

Discussion has existed for quite some time on amending the Constitution to add consideration for crime victims. John Walsh was a major proponent and advocate for the Crime Victims' Rights Constitutional Amendment and includes the text of a proposed amendment in his book, *Tears of Rage*. The Amendment was proposed to include services for victims including the following:

Protection provided for victims of violent crime without compromising the rights of defendants;

Notification of public proceedings about the crime that occurred to them in a reasonable and timely manner, the right to be included in those proceedings and the right to decisions that involve the victim's safety, delay of proceedings, and restitution by the offender;

All rights listed in the Amendment are applicable only to the victim or victim's representative, and thus no new trial or claim for damages will be allowed as a result of this Amendment;

This Amendment will not hamper the President's ability to grant pardons or reprieves.

The Amendment is only valid if it has been ratified by three-fourths of the states within seven years of the date of submission to Congress. It will take effect on the 180th day after ratification.

It appears that the push for a Constitutional Amendment has been set aside because of the lack of support from Congress. In its place, proponents advocated for an amendment to the Federal Rules of Criminal Procedure titled the Crime Victims' Rights Act, which would include the provisions listed above. The Crime Victims' Rights Act was enacted in 2004–2005 by the 108th Congress.

If one were to add the numbers presented in this section of the chapter, it appears that more than 700,000 individuals have been directly impacted by the efforts of John Walsh. The operative words in the previous sentence are "directly impacted." This says nothing about those who were aided because of legislation or a program he pioneered or for which he advocated. The actual number of individuals affected by Walsh's work is likely immeasurable.

AWARDS RECEIVED

John Walsh has been the recipient of numerous awards, honors, plaques, and so forth. According to both *Tears of Rage* and Avery Mann, Director of Media and Publications at *America's Most Wanted* and publicist to John Walsh, there are fifteen boxes of such honors and awards housed at the headquarters of *America's Most Wanted* (personal communication, May-June 2007).

Among those fifteen boxes the following are included:

Honored five times by four Presidents (Ronald Reagan [twice], George H.W. Bush, Bill Clinton, and George W. Bush);

National Father of the Year of 1984, Everyman category (received in 1985); in *Tears of Rage*, John Walsh remarks that this is the most special award he has ever received;

U.S. Marshals Man of the Year (1988);

Federal Bureau of Investigation Man of the Year (1990);

CBS Portraits: 1 of the "100 Americans Who Changed History";

People 1 of the "50 Most Beautiful People" (1996);

Citizen Action Award from the National Association Citizens on Patrol;

Director's Recognition Award from the U.S. Secret Service (2002);

Honorary U.S. Marshal (2003): This honor has been bestowed upon only seven other people throughout the history of the organization; among the other recipients are George Washington and Ronald Reagan.

Special Recognition Award from the U.S. Attorney General (2004);

David Angell Humanitarian Award by the American Screenwriters' Association (2005); and

Honorary Life Member of the International Police Association (2006).

CONCLUSION

John Walsh is first and foremost an advocate for the rights of children and crime victims. From the depths of grief, he and Revé Walsh have helped to focus society's attention on the needs and worth of the crime victim. Mr. Walsh has accomplished many things through congressional testimony at both the state and federal levels and through his many multimedia projects: clearinghouses, educational material, and opportunities for people to get involved. Mr. Walsh is the spokesperson for the word "action"; it's what he is all about. Mr. Walsh is a true icon in the fight against crime. He isn't a police officer, a district attorney, or a legislator—he is an advocate and his weapons are his words.

FURTHER READING

Criminal Justice Newsletter Hackensack: May 3, 2004, 1.

Federal Sentencing Reporter 19(1) October 2006.

Federal Sentencing Reporter 19(2) December 2006.

U.S. Congress. Crime Victims' Rights Act. 108th Congress. 18 U.S.C. Section 3771.

Walsh, John, with Philip Lerman. 1998. *No Mercy: The Host of America's Most Wanted Hunts the Worst Criminals in Our Time—in Shattering True Crime Cases.* New York: Pocket Books.

Walsh, John, with Philip Lerman. 2001. *Public Enemies: The Host of America's Most Wanted Targets the Nation's Most Notorious Criminals.* New York: Pocket Books.

Walsh, John, and Susan Schindehette. 1997. *Tears of Rage: From Grieving Father to Crusader for Justice: The Untold Story of Adam Walsh.* New York: Pocket Books.

Washington Post. "The TV Show America Still Wants; Despite Protests by Governors, Police, Last Episode Airs Tonight." September 21, 1996, A01.

Washington Post. "Stay of Execution for 'Most Wanted.'" September 25, 1996, B01.

Websites

http://www.amw.com/about_amw/faq.cfm (accessed June 6, 2007).

http://www.amw.com/safety (accessed June 6, 2007).

http://www.childsearch.us/site3/codeadam.html.

http://criminaljustice.state.ny.us/missing/graphics/federallawsummary.pdf (accessed June 7, 2007).

http://www.fbi.gov/hq/isd/cirg/ncavc.htm.

http://www.flgov.com/release/8709 (accessed July 25, 2007).

http://www.kepplerspeakers.com/speakers/speakers.asp?1+EV+457AboutJohnWalsh (accessed May 27, 2008).

http://www.missingkids.com/missingkids/servlet/PageServlet?LanguageCountry=en_US& PageId=381 (accessed June 12, 2007).

http://www.ncmec.org (accessed June 12, 2007).

http://www.ojp.usdoj.gov/aag/speeches/nmcday.htm (accessed May 31, 2007).

http:///www.thesafeside.com (accessed June 6, 2007).

http://www.whitehouse.gov/news/releases/2006/07/20060727-7.html.

Larry Stone Photography

FBI Profilers

Richard N. Kocsis

WHAT IS CRIMINAL PROFILING?

Unfortunately, defining what is *criminal profiling* is not as easy a task as one may initially expect, principally because the word "profiling" has become synonymous with a variety of contextually different tasks in contemporary society and law enforcement circles. Perhaps one of the best examples is the biological technique of DNA profiling whereby DNA matter from a crime scene is examined and compared for matches with DNA matter of potential suspects. Although distinctions here may seem readily easy to discern, the term profiling nonetheless emerges in a variety of differing behaviorally based contexts. For instance, there also exists the technique of racial profiling where sets of characteristics deemed to be indicative of an individual likely to perpetrate a certain form of crime are used as a screening tool to identify potential perpetrators. An example of this type of profiling occurs with customs officers attempting to discern individuals who may be smuggling narcotics through an international airport terminal. Many law enforcement agencies also make use of what are often termed offender or intelligence profiles wherein information about an individual (often a previously apprehended criminal) is compiled to provide an informative summation of the individual's particulars, known activities, and so on.

Within the context of this chapter and the work of FBI profilers, the term criminal profiling describes what is arguably the oldest form of profiling, that is, a behaviorally based forensic technique whereby exhibited behaviors in a crime or series of crimes are examined for the purpose of developing a composite description of the characteristics of the person or persons who committed the particular crime(s) under examination. The purpose of this criminal profile is to assist police officers with their investigations via a number of possible avenues. One avenue by which a criminal profile can be used is through a process of prioritization, whereby any previously developed list of suspects can be ordered in terms of how closely the features of the identified suspects match those predicted with the profile. Thus, suspects who closely match the profile can be afforded a high degree of priority, in terms of further investigation, whereas those who do not closely resemble the profile can be relegated to a lower degree of priority. Although perhaps not commonly known, criminal investigations by law enforcement need to be undertaken in an optimal manner whereby ideal outcomes can be obtained from the minimal expenditure of resources in terms of police personnel, time, and effort. Accordingly, a criminal profile in this context can act as a valuable tool in allowing chief officers to better focus where and who their detectives spend their time and resources investigating.

Beyond prioritizing any list of existing suspects, a criminal profile can also generate potential suspects for investigation. For example, a criminal profile may indicate that the probable offender responsible for the crime under investigation is likely to have a preexisting criminal record consisting of certain behaviors, for example, voyeurism. Equipped with this information, police personnel may check their records and investigate individuals in the vicinity of the crime who have exhibited a history of similar voyeuristic tendencies.

As previously mentioned, criminal profiling as discussed in this chapter is arguably the oldest form of profiling. Although criminal profiling is sometimes incorrectly hailed as a new and revolutionary crime fighting tool, it is in fact, indicative of a long-held fascination that the human race has always held in seeking to classify and predict criminality within its societies. Although fictional examples of criminal profiling can be found in classic literature such as Sir Arthur Conan Doyle's character Sherlock Holmes, various nonfictional accounts of profiling can also be traced throughout the annals of history. Indeed, it is somewhat ironic that one of the earliest examples of criminal profiling dates back to 1888 with the police investigation into what would ultimately prove to be one of the most notorious serial killers in history: Jack the Ripper.

Profiling Jack the Ripper

In 1888, the commander of the London Criminal Investigation Division (CID) consulted Dr. Thomas Bond for any insights he could offer into a series of brutal murders of young women that had occurred in the suburb of Whitechapel and had gripped the entire city with fear (Rumbelow 1988). These murders would ultimately become infamous as those committed by "Jack the Ripper." As a police surgeon, Dr. Bond's primary involvement with the matter was to undertake an autopsy of the fifth victim and provide his opinion on the murderer's likely knowledge of medicine or more precisely, surgical procedures, given the evident mutilation that had been perpetrated on the body.

However, given the intractable nature of the crimes, on this occasion Dr. Bond was also asked to hypothesize about the characteristics of the individual who could have committed such a series of abhorrent crimes. Following his examination Dr. Bond compiled a report summarizing his conclusions, which included the following information:

> ...all five murders were no doubt committed by the same hand. In the first four the throats appear to have been cut from left to right, in the last case owing to the extensive mutilation it is impossible to say in what direction the fatal cut was made. All the circumstances surrounding the murders lead me to form the opinion that the women must have been lying down when murdered. (Whittington-Egan 1975, 114)

(continued)

With respect to the likely characteristics of the offender Dr. Bond made the following comments:

> ...In each case the mutilation was implicated by a person who had no scientific nor anatomical knowledge. In my opinion he does not even possess the technical knowledge of a butcher or horse slaughterer or any person accustomed to cutting up dead animals. (115)
>   ...A man subject to periodical attacks of Homicidal and Erotic mania. The murderer in external appearance is quite likely to be a quiet inoffensive looking man, probably middle-aged and neatly and respectably dressed. He would be solitary and eccentric in his habits, also he is most likely to be a man without regular occupation, but with a small income or pension. (115)

Although the perpetrator of these murders has never been conclusively identified and thus we are prevented from making any definitive assessment of Dr. Bond's predictions, what is perhaps most remarkable is consideration of the "types" of predictions or information that is contained in Dr. Bond's report. That is, Dr. Bond offered various conclusions relating to whether the murders were committed by the same or different individuals, the likely modus operandi in committing the murders, and a series of demographic features including the murderer's likely age, gender, manner of dress, vocational history, demeanor, and even possible mental disorders. Despite these predictions having been made approximately 120 years ago, the criminal profiles that are compiled in this modern day and age essentially endeavor to offer police investigators the same insights and information about the likely offender.

Another historical example of profiling, not strictly within the field of police criminal investigation, however, occurred in the latter years of World War II. The U.S. Office of Strategic Services (the precursor to the Central Intelligence Agency) sought the services of Dr. Walter Langer to undertake a psychological evaluation of the German leader Adolf Hitler. Pivotal to this assessment was to profile, that is, make key predictions, concerning Hitler's likely choice of actions should the tide of the war turn against him and Germany. Some of the possibilities Dr. Langer predicted included Hitler personally leading his remaining armies into a final futile battle or ordering the total self-destruction of Germany's resources. However, Dr. Langer's foremost prediction was that Hitler would commit suicide to avoid the perceived humiliation of his capture by the allied forces. History would ultimately prove Dr. Langer's prediction to be correct. From these historical examples, it should be apparent that although a degree of technological sophistication and terminology has certainly evolved in recent years surrounding criminal profiling, its fundamental concept is, in fact, remarkably old.

MOTIVELESS CRIMES IN AMERICA AND THE FBI BEHAVIORAL SCIENCE UNIT

With the passing of prohibition and the era of McCarthyism, the frequency of a particular style of crime insidiously began to rise in America. Although violent crimes such as murder or rape were not unfamiliar to American law enforcement, the criminological patterns and interpersonal dynamics of how these crimes typically occurred had remained generally the same over the decades. For example, in a large proportion of circumstances a causal and often motivational nexus could be found to exist between murderers and their victims. However, what began to appear in growing prevalence were violent crimes, such as murder, which seemed increasingly to be perpetrated in a motiveless fashion and thus deviated from the conventional criminological patterns. This is not to suggest that such crimes had never been encountered previously, but the overall occurrence of such crimes was comparatively rare. The rise in these crimes was readily noticed by law enforcement, as the investigation and apprehension of perpetrators of these crimes was quite difficult in comparison.

This rise in these apparently motiveless crimes had not gone unnoticed by J. Edgar Hoover's premier law enforcement agency, the Federal Bureau of Investigation (FBI) and in particular its fledgling Behavioral Science Unit (BSU) based in the FBI Academy at Quantico, Virginia. Intended to be one of the premier law enforcement training facilities in America (as well as the training institution for FBI agents), the FBI Academy encompassed numerous innovative dimensions to law enforcement education and training well beyond traditional methods such as the instruction of law, operational practices, and firearms training. The most relevant to this chapter was the FBI's recognition of the contribution behavioral sciences could make to law enforcement and thus the creation of a department within the Academy faculty featuring agents who would provide instruction on various topics in this area.

Criminal profiling within the FBI principally began with two agents, Howard Tetan and Patrick Mullany, who were foundational members of the BSU. Both Tetan and Mullany were keenly interested in how the disciplines of criminology and psychology could be adapted and directly applied in a practical manner to assist ongoing criminal investigations. Indeed, Tetan's interest in this possibility led him to visit and draw some inspiration from the renowned psychiatrist, Dr. James Brussel, who had been consulted to apply his talents to a number of famous cases, with some remarkable results.

Method in their Madness: Dr. Brussel and the Mad Bomber of New York

November 1940 would mark the first incident in what would become a protracted and violent series of bombings in New York city spanning a period of two decades. An unexploded pipe bomb was discovered on the premises of the electric company Consolidated Edison, the main supplier of electricity to New York at that time. Alongside the bomb was a neatly transcribed note: "Con Edison crooks, this is for you!". With the luxury of hindsight it seems unfair to criticize the fact that little was made from this initial discovery. Indeed, following the attack on Pearl Harbor and the total commitment of America to the war effort, another letter was received (this time by police) from the author of the original note. This letter contained the message "I will make no more bomb units for the duration of the war—my patriotic feelings have made me decide this—I will bring Con Edison to justice later—they will pay for their dastardly deeds. F.P." (Brussel 1968).

For the duration of World War II and a number of years thereafter no further bombs were found (although some letters were sent to various sources such as newspapers). Unfortunately, this apparent reprieve in activities was not destined to last. On March 25, 1950 another unexploded pipe bomb was discovered, and that year marked the commencement of a destructive bombing campaign that would terrorize New Yorkers, with the destructive blast of each successive bomb growing larger.

By 1956 and with no clear suspects as to who might be the bomber, New York police decided to try a new tactic in their investigation by consulting Dr. James Brussel, a respected psychiatrist based in Greenwich Village. Interestingly, Dr. Brussel did not have much experience in the investigation of crime but had spent most of his career in the clinical treatment and care of the mentally ill. Nonetheless, investigators valued Dr. Brussel's opinions and were interested to see what different insights a man of his education and experience might make of the crimes. Presented with this request, Dr. Brussel dutifully examined all available case material concerning the bombings and compiled a description (what we would now call a criminal profile) of the type of individual he believed to be planting the bombs. Among the many features Dr. Brussel predicted was that the bomber would be a middle-aged man of foreign-born Slavic descent and most probably Catholic. Perhaps the most peculiar and seemingly esoteric prediction was Dr. Brussel's belief that when apprehended, the bomber would be a well-dressed individual, most likely wearing a blue double-breasted suit with the jacket buttons fastened.

After further investigation of the crimes, the bomber, George Metesky, was ultimately apprehended. Upon his arrest police noticed the remarkable similarity Metesky bore to Dr. Brussel's profile. Metesky was a middle-aged foreign man of Polish Roman Catholic descent. When police arrested Metesky at his home, he asked if he could change into some clothes (as he was in his pajamas at the time) before going to the police station and into custody. Astonishingly, when Metesky emerged from his bedroom he was impeccably dressed, wearing a blue double-breasted suit with all buttons on his jacket done up precisely as Dr. Brussel had predicted. Because of his uncanny insight into George Metesky, police would later consult Dr. Brussel on the murders of the Boston Strangler, and his work would later serve as inspiration for members of the FBI Behavioral Science Unit and their efforts in criminal profiling.

Drawing on their own studies and theories, Tetan and Mullany informally began to discuss unsolved cases that visiting police students brought to their attention in class. These informal discussions ultimately involved the development of various predictions concerning the probable offender, which the officers followed up on their return to their active duties. The input that Tetan and Mullany provided to investigators was appreciated, and knowledge of their profiles and the assistance they potentially offered to investigators gradually spread within the American law enforcement community.

Whereas Tetan and Mullany originally had considered the occasional case during the course of their classes, they soon found themselves receiving more and more requests from police inquiring whether they could offer some insight into unsolved cases. A significant proportion of these cases involved circumstances where no apparent motive was discernable. Consequently, something of a serendipitous union transpired whereby an investigative facility was emerging that seemed ready to assist police with the investigation of these motiveless violent crimes that were difficult to solve via conventional avenues. The benefit of these profiling techniques was that they did not rely entirely on typical criminalistic features of a crime such as physical evidence or witnesses. Instead, criminal profiles were derived simply through interpretations of the behavioral patterns evident in the crime.

With time, the number of agents within the BSU grew. Many of these agents taught classes in behavioral sciences and explored their application to criminal investigation much in the same fashion as Tetan and Mullany had done originally. However, toward the late 1970s these profiling activities had grown to such an extent that it was decided that they should be formalized into a core function of the BSU and not merely something that agents undertook in an informal capacity in addition to their teaching commitments. The decision to formalize these activities effectively marked the birth of a legacy that continues to this present day in terms of the FBI's role in providing criminal profiles to law enforcement agencies throughout the United States and the iconic status of FBI profilers. In an organizational restructure of the BSU, divisions were created not only for the traditional activities of law enforcement training but also for the dedicated provision of criminal profiles to assist police agencies as well as studying violent offenders to develop the FBI's criminal profiling capabilities. Although changes have transpired over the decades in terms of organizational structures, these fundamental functions of providing operationally orientated support to police (e.g., criminal profiles), researching violent crimes, and the training of law enforcement personnel continues today.

From quite humble and modest beginnings the provision of criminal profiles by FBI profilers now operates via a well-structured consultation process starting with trained FBI agents stationed in most U.S. states. These agents serve as an initial screening point whereby local police can submit their case and gain some feedback about whether the case is suited to profiling. Assuming the case is suitable for profiling and further analysis is desired, it is then forwarded to the operational profiling division for analysis and the development of a criminal profile that may assist the police investigators.

THE CONTRIBUTION OF FBI PROFILERS TO THE LAW ENFORCEMENT AND SCIENTIFIC COMMUNITY

FBI profilers have made a number of important contributions to the practice of criminal profiling. They can be credited with popularizing the practice of criminal profiling in the public's consciousness and within the law enforcement and scientific communities throughout the world. The importance of this popularization should not be underestimated as it has had several significant effects on the development and practice of criminal profiling in assisting law enforcement agencies and in potentially reducing violent crime.

First, it should be recognized that through the promotion of their activities and publication of books and articles describing their endeavors, FBI profilers have created an awareness of potential investigative capabilities for profiling the characteristics of offenders of violent crimes in ways that never used to be reported in days gone by. This public awareness arguably has promoted greater understanding of the complexities involved in identifying the perpetrator(s) of violent crimes and may have an effect on deterring some crime for fear of apprehension via the advanced investigative techniques shown on television.

Second, owing to the popularization of criminal profiling, FBI profilers can be credited for building on investigative practices available to law enforcement personnel. By the promotion of their activities and the documentation of their research, FBI profilers have generated a broader knowledge of criminal profiling as an investigative resource that detectives can avail themselves of and thus potentially have expanded the repertoire of tools for police personnel anywhere in the world.

Third, and perhaps the most significant accomplishment to arise from the popularization of profiling by FBI profilers, has been the generation of greater scholarly interest in the technique by the international scientific community. That is, FBI profilers through their activities have provided impetus for others around the globe to engage in coherent research studying violent crimes to advance profiling techniques. This is an important dimension to the scientific evolution of any technique or discipline to which FBI profilers are deserving of praise as it is debatable at what rate the technique of criminal profiling would have developed without them. It should be understood that although examples of criminal profiling can be found sprinkled throughout history (e.g., Dr. Bond with Jack the Ripper or Dr. Brussel with the Mad Bomber), they represent instances where individuals have applied their own specialized training to profile crimes on an ad hoc basis. Lacking in such instances, however, is any cohesion or conceptual approach to how these individuals attempted to construct criminal profiles. In contrast, the endeavors of FBI profilers arguably represent the first cohesive attempt to describe how crimes may be profiled. It is from the development of their own approach to profiling via the conduct of systematic research that has led others to consider possibilities in how criminal profiles may be constructed.

THE RESEARCH OF FBI PROFILERS: TO UNDERSTAND THE ARTIST YOU MUST STUDY THEIR WORK

Underpinning much of the research developed by FBI profilers is one fundamental principle. Rather than studying mental disorders and their relevance to violent crimes, it was decided that for the needs of law enforcement the way to better understand and profile violent criminals would be through the study of their crimes. Thus, in metaphorical terms it was concluded that the best method to understand the artist would be the careful study of his work. From this simple principle an extensive program of research has emerged on numerous forms of violent crime that were considered amenable to the technique of criminal profiling. The common feature of many of these studies first involved the collection of case materials concerning solved cases. These materials were then studied at length by FBI profilers who subsequently visited the incarcerated offenders. These visits involved conducting carefully developed interviews that were designed to elicit as much information as possible about the offender and the mindset and reasoning in perpetrating the crime. The information from all of these cases was then collated and formed the data for the study. The data was then subjected to various forms of statistical analysis in an attempt to identify coherent patterns in how offenders perpetrated their crimes and what these patterns might typically suggest about the offender in terms of common characteristics that could in turn form the basis of a criminal profile.

One of the most prominent studies of this type undertaken by FBI profilers was that involving a sample of thirty-six sexual murderers. The data collected from this study produced what is, arguably, one of the most renowned pieces of research relevant to criminal profiling and one of the cornerstone pieces of research relied on by FBI profilers when constructing criminal profiles. This study found that the offenders of these sexual murders could be distinguished and thus differentiated into one of two broad categories. One category was titled the *Organized* offender and was typically characterized by individuals who were organized in all aspects of their life in the sense that their activities are generally planned and they take great care with their personnel appearance/grooming and belongings. In direct contrast to this was the other category, the *Disorganized* offender, which was indicative of individuals who typically demonstrated a haphazard approach to life. Thus, the activities of disorganized offenders were often poorly planned and executed and sometimes even impetuous. The personal appearance of these *Disorganized* offenders also was found to often be of a disheveled, untidy nature. Incumbent to each of these two offender categories was a set of crime scene behavior patterns that were found to be indicative of the respective patterns. Accordingly, crime scenes committed by an Organized offender were indicative of planning and premeditation and could be distinguished by various attributes such as whether there were any indications that the offenders brought along weapons or tools to perpetrate the crime. Conversely, the crime scenes committed by a Disorganized offender were found to be reflective of a haphazard, unplanned, or even spontaneous crime that may have been committed simply through some impromptu initiative or opportunity. Thus, attributes within a crime scene that are said to be suggestive of a Disorganized offender would be evidence that objects located at the crime scene were used as a weapon (i.e., the offender did not have the foresight to bring a weapon with them).

With the development of these behavioral categories, FBI profilers could use them to evaluate and profile the characteristics of a probable offender to a case presented to them by a police agency requesting their assistance. Thus, the principle inherent to profiling is one somewhat analogous to retro-classification. The features of an unsolved case could be examined to determine whether the evident modus operandi of the crime matched the

The Organized/Disorganized Dichotomy to Sexual Murderers

Organized offender characteristics include the following:

- Good intelligence
- Socially competent
- Skilled work preferred
- Sexually competent
- A high birth-order status
- Father's work is stable
- Presence of inconsistent childhood discipline
- Controlled mood during crime
- Use of alcohol with crime
- Precipitating situational stress
- Living with a partner
- Mobility and with a car in good condition
- Follows the crime in the news media
- May change jobs or leave town

Disorganized offender characteristics include the following:

- Average intelligence
- Socially immature
- Poor work history
- Sexually incompetent
- A low birth-order status
- Father's work unstable
- Harsh discipline in childhood
- Anxious mood during the crime
- Minimal use of alcohol
- Minimal situational stress
- Living alone
- Living or working near the crime scene
- Minimal interest in news media
- Minimal changes in lifestyle

Corresponding to the offender profiles of Organized and Disorganized sexual murderers were their crime scenes, which could also be distinguished.

(continued)

Organized crime scene features include the following:

- A planned offense
- Victim a targeted stranger
- Victim personalized
- Controlled conversations
- Demands submissive victim
- Restraints used
- Aggressive acts prior to death
- Body hidden
- Weapon or other evidence absent
- Transports victim or body

Disorganized crime scenes features include the following:

- A spontaneous offense
- Victim or location known
- Victim depersonalized
- Minimal conversation
- Crime scene random and sloppy
- Sudden violence to victim
- Minimal use of restraints
- Sexual acts after death
- Body left in view
- Evidence of weapon often present
- Body left at death scene

behavioral features of either an organized or disorganized offense style. Once such a determination had been made, the profiler could draw on the characteristic features that were indicative of either an Organized or Disorganized offender in the construction of a criminal profile.

CONSTRUCTING A CRIMINAL PROFILE

The exact process whereby FBI profilers evaluate a crime for the purpose of constructing a criminal profile is very much dependent upon the particular circumstances of the crime under examination in combination with the

Crime Classification Manual: The "DSM" of Crime

Perhaps one of the crowning achievements of the research undertaken into criminal profiling by the personnel of the FBI Behavioral Science Unit (BSU) is the development of the *Crime Classification Manual* or the "*CCM*" (Douglas et al. 2006). Now into its second edition, the CCM represents a veritable cornucopia for cataloging how various forms of crime have been previously committed. The concept of the *CCM* was derived from the *Diagnostic and Statistic Manual of Mental Disorder,* more commonly referred to as the *DSM* (American Psychiatric Association 1994). Within the mental health professions of psychiatry and psychology throughout the world the *DSM* has become recognized as one of the standard indexes by which mental disorders are classified in terms of detailed criteria for diagnosis. The creation of this index has had enormous benefits for the mental health profession in collating information on the various forms of mental disease.

In an analogous context the development of the *CCM* was undertaken to create a standardized index whereby offenses could be evaluated and through such assessment a better understanding of the crime gained that would ultimately assist police investigators with their inquiries. Given the FBI Behavioral Science Unit's involvement predominantly with violent crimes, the *CCM* is not an all-encompassing compendium of every imaginable form of crime but is instead focused on three broad categories: murder, rape, and arson. Within each of these three main areas a wide variety of motivational taxonomies are presented, detailing characteristic circumstances of specific methods employed in crimes committed before (similar to diagnostic criteria for assessing mental disorders in the *DSM*). Beyond simply outlining characteristic features inherent to various forms of crime, however, the *CCM* indexes these criteria with useful information for police personnel, such as investigative considerations of how to examine the crime scene as well as suggestions for search warrants and common forensic findings. Thus, in a sense the *CCM* is not only a tool for diagnosis but also represents a tentative guide for prognosis and possible cure, with the provision of factors that may assist in the investigation and apprehension of the perpetrator of the crime.

specific issues of the police investigation. Nonetheless, there is a general procedure that FBI profilers follow in constructing a criminal profile that combines much of the aforementioned research conducted by FBI Behavioral Science Unit. This procedure principally involves five steps that operate in a loop until a criminal profile has been developed and the unknown offender apprehended. The five steps in criminal profile construction are Profiling Inputs, Decision Process Models, Crime Assessment, Criminal Profile, and Investigation and are explained below.

Step 1. Profiling Inputs

As one might expect, the very first step in the FBI process of constructing a criminal profile involves the systematic collection and evaluation of all available evidence pertinent to the crime in question. Thus, this initial step can in one sense be viewed as a data collation step wherein as much information as possible is collected and examined for the purpose of subsequent steps in the process. The types of information that are evaluated in this phase can be quite extensive. First, information pertaining to the crime scene needs to be carefully considered and includes such things as the presence of any physical evidence, the specific position of the body (in the circumstance of a homicide), and the type and/or presence of any weapon involved in the crime. Next are issues related to victimology, which involves a careful consideration of the victim of the crime. Issues typically considered include the victim's background, habits, family structure, age, and occupation.

Unsurprisingly, another crucial input is the forensic information relevant to the crime. This naturally includes issues such as the circumstance of the murder, the cause of death, the wounds evident on the victim, the findings of an autopsy report, and any other relevant laboratory reports. Another important set of inputs are the various reports that the police officers investigating the crime have made. These may include reports on general background information, the time of the crime, who reported it, and the general neighborhood (such as its socioeconomic status and the prevailing crime rates). The final type of profiling input consists of any visual information that may assist in the evaluation of the crime. These inputs include such things as photos of the crime scene and the victim and even aerial shots that may give some broader impression of the overall setting in which the crime occurred.

Step 2. Decision Process Models

Having collected all the profile inputs relevant to the crime, the next step involves the initial interpretation of this information in terms of any meaningful patterns. Thus, the evident *type* and *style* of crime that has transpired is considered. There can potentially be any number of possible contingencies dependent on the evident number of victims (using murder as an example once again) or the setting of the crime (a home as opposed to a public area). Also taken into consideration at this point is the apparent primary intent of the crime, the level of risk the victim associated with (i.e. activities indulged in by the victim that may expose them to danger), and the degree of risk the offender may be considered to have assumed in perpetrating the crime. These risk variables are considered concomitantly with a host of other factors such as the time and location of the crime.

Step 3. Crime Assessment

The third step in the FBI profile construction process involves reconstructing the behavior of the offender, the victim, and the overall sequence of events that led to the perpetration of the crime. Thus, information from the previous stages are evaluated and judged in different terms. These include a potentially appropriate classification of the crime such as whether the crime is of an organized or disorganized type, the possible selection and method of controlling the victim, and the degree to which staging may be present in the crime. Also considered in this reconstruction step are any motivations inherent to the crime and more generally, any other factors that are pertinent to the dynamics of the crime scene.

Step 4. Criminal Profile

With the crime assessment complete, the next step in the process involves the actual compilation of a profile wherein pertinent characteristics of the probable offender as well as other behavioral aspects that may prove useful to the criminal investigation are compiled. Thus, the profile ideally will contain such information as anticipated demographic features of the offender, physical characteristics, and habits. Beyond the prescriptive listing of attributes believed to describe the offender there will also be indications of the offender's likely behavior subsequent to the commission of the crime as well as some suggestions, where appropriate, on how consulting police officers optimally may investigate the crime.

It is in this phase of the construction process where the loop of reevaluation commences. Attributes of the criminal profile that are considered in the context of steps two and three are reconsidered to ascertain whether the predictions of the criminal profile logically agree with the deduced elements of the crime. For example, with all available evidence taken into account, the criminal profile is considered in terms of whether such an individual could have perpetrated the crime in the way it occurred.

Step 5. Investigation

With the criminal profile developed, the process shifts to the police officers directly involved with the investigation of the crime to determine who among their established suspects demonstrates some resemblance to the profile and thus the prioritization of their inquiries accordingly. Assuming no suspects have been established, the profile may be considered in terms of how the predictions concerning the type of person who may have perpetrated the crime can be identified through various investigative avenues.

FBI Profiling in Action

On the 23rd of January 1978, Sacramento police officers entered the modest home of David Wallin to commence the investigation of a horrific crime. Inside the home was the mutilated body of his 22-year-old pregnant wife, Theresa, who had been shot through the head and her partially clad body left mutilated. Adding to the horror was the discovery of an empty blood-spattered yogurt carton at the crime scene that had evidently been used to drink blood from Theresa's eviscerated body cavity.

The investigating officers were quite unaccustomed to crimes of such heinous savagery, particularly because there was no evident motive to Theresa's murder. However, circumstances quickly deteriorated for the Sacramento police, because no sooner had they embarked on their investigation into Theresa's murder, when another group of brutal murders was discovered three days later in a home less than one mile away. On the 26th of January an elderly woman knocked on her neighbor's partially ajar front door. As no response was heard from inside, she entered the home, only to make a horrific discovery similar to that of the murder of Theresa Wallin. Inside the home were the bodies of a woman in her late twenties and her middle-aged father, both of whom had been shot through the head. Akin to Theresa Wallin, the woman's body was mutilated, with indications that cannibalistic acts had occurred. Given the abhorrent nature of these brutal murders, FBI profilers were consulted to see what insights they could derive from the murders. After carefully considering the circumstances of the crimes, a profile was developed that read in part:

> Killer is white, male, twenty-seven years old, living within a mile of the area. Has probably been treated in a mental institution and recently released. He is single and unemployed or working at a menial job. He has no friends. Unusual behavior includes being withdrawn and reclusive. Has a high school education or less. He is psychotic, probably schizophrenic. He and his residence are slovenly and unkempt. Evidence of his crimes will be present. He is thin and undernourished. He probably tortures animals. (DeNivi and Campbell 2004, 25)

Equipped with this profile, Sacramento police continued their investigation and canvassed the local suburbs questioning residents about whether they knew of anyone who matched the profile description. Remarkably, within hours of commencing these inquiries, one resident identified an individual by the name of Richard Trenton Chase who resembled their description. Chase's residence was placed under surveillance, and when he was observed leaving his apartment with a box under his arm, he was immediately arrested and his premises searched. With his arrest the remarkable similarities between Chase and the FBI criminal profile seemed evident. Chase's apartment was located within a mile of the murders and was a complete mess. Inside the kitchen police found three dirty kitchen blenders that contained traces of human blood and tissue as well as several plates on which human body parts were being kept in the refrigerator. As for Chase himself, he was twenty-eight years old, emaciated, and slovenly as described in the profile. He had a history of treatment for schizophrenia from a psychiatric hospital and had been released into the care of his parents who provided the apartment for him (which he occupied alone) because he was unable to maintain steady employment. Chase had a history of torturing and disembowelling small animals and drinking their blood in the delusional belief that this would prevent radiation from drying his own blood and shrinking his heart (Ressler and Schactmann 1992).

CRIMES WITHOUT BORDERS

Although not a form of criminal profiling, the work of the FBI BSU is also renowned for developing a crime-fighting tool known as the Violent Criminal Apprehension Program (ViCAP), a computer database capable of analyzing and linking crimes by the behavior patterns exhibited at the crime scene. Ironically, the initial impetus for the development of ViCAP did not originate from within the FBI BSU but rather with a retired chief of police and former homicide commander, Pierce Brooks. In the 1950s Brooks was concerned with two phenomena. First, he was concerned about the difficulty in effectively communicating the large volume of information typically generated during the investigation of violent crimes such as a murder. Second, he was concerned about the mobility of criminals to travel undetected into different police jurisdictions and commit further offenses. That is, given the difficulty in communication among different police agencies, Brooks was acutely aware that criminals potentially could elude apprehension for crimes by simply traveling to different police jurisdiction where investigators may have been oblivious to the individual's previous offenses.

This circumstance is not an issue of fault on the part of any police investigator. Rather, it is an unfortunate artifact arising from the existence of numerous independent police agencies throughout the United States and the logistical difficulties involved in adequately communicating details of all cases under investigation to all other jurisdictions. These difficulties in communication are compounded by the sheer volume of crimes that can occur and indeed accumulate in any given year. For example, in the 1950s and 60s there were on average approximately 10,000 homicides committed in America. However, by 1980 this figure had more than doubled to over 23,000. Consequently, the number of these crimes was likely to make the communication of their circumstances, particularly unsolved cases still under investigation, difficult between police jurisdictions. This unfortunate phenomenon of investigators being oblivious to the existence of multiple crimes committed by the same perpetrator has been termed *linkage blindness*.

It was from this circumstance that the idea of a tracking system was developed, wherein details pertaining to unsolved crimes across many jurisdictions could be collated. Once assembled together, all cases could be systematically assessed for similarities that would indicate that any number of crimes previously thought to be separate could in fact have been perpetrated by the same offender, the idea being to alert the relevant police investigators in their respective jurisdictions to this circumstance. In the 1950s the idea of such a tracking mechanism was something more within the realm of science fiction. However, by the 1980s and the advent of relatively cheap and yet powerful computers that could analyze large amounts of data, this idea was soon to become a reality, with Brooks collaborating with the members of the FBI BSI for the development of the ViCAP tracking system.

It is important to appreciate the distinction between ViCAP and the various previous criminal record indexes that continue to exist. Criminal record systems allow police officers to identify the criminal history of individuals. Consequently, these systems are essentially retrospective databases in determining any history of prior convictions recorded for a particular individual. These systems, however, do not offer investigators much in terms of assessing the circumstances (such as the modus operandi) of crimes that are

Tracking a Mad Man: The Murders of Henry Lee Lucas?

In June 1983 police arrested a man named Henry Lee Lucas for illegal gun possession. While in his jail cell Lucas wrote a note pleading for help, because he believed that he suffered from some form of illness, which had compelled him to commit multiple murders over the past years. Subsequent to this note, Lucas took police officers to the locations where he had deposited the bodies of Kate Rich, an eighty-year-old woman whom Lucas had worked for as a handyman, and Frieda Powell, one of Lucas's own nieces. With the discovery of these bodies began an extensive videotaped confession by Lucas wherein he claimed to have been killing people over the past decade and could recollect some 200 murders committed in virtually every state in America (Norris 1988).

News of this homicidal odyssey quickly spread throughout the U.S. law enforcement community and detectives from differing jurisdictions wanted an opportunity to interview Lucas to establish whether any number of unsolved cases in their jurisdiction was one of the many murders Lucas was readily confessing to have committed. Unfortunately, this interest in Lucas quickly and quite inadvertently bestowed on him a pseudo-celebrity status and many privileges not typically accorded with incarcerated murderers (such as opportunities to leave his jail cell and be transported to distant locations across the country while being accommodated in hotels and served good meals). Naturally, this special treatment for Lucas came at great expense to the American tax-paying public.

Normally, such expenditure could be justified because it was made for the valid pursuit of justice—the potential resolution of a previously unsolved murder. However, the real dilemma began when the reliability of Lucas' forthright confessions started to come into question. On one notable occasion Lucas was questioned as to whether he was responsible for the murders committed in Guyana. Lucas readily confessed to this, although he claimed to be unsure whether Guyana was in Louisiana or Texas. In offering the confession Lucas was clearly unaware that Guyana is located in South America and the murders were those perpetrated by the cult leader Jim Jones, who persuaded his followers to drink poison (Innes 2003).

The case of Henry Lee Lucas highlights that had ViCAP been in existence at the time of Lucas' supposed killing rampage across America, law enforcement officials would have been able to verify his claims more readily and reliably. Despite claiming to have killed hundreds of persons, it now appears that Lucas may have murdered a much smaller number.

currently unsolved and under investigation. It is this task of acting not only as a database but as a proactive means of analyzing and linking multiple crimes previously thought to be separate that has made ViCAP a valuable tool for crime fighters in the United States.

HITS AND MISSES

Although the efforts of FBI profilers in assisting American law enforcement agencies are well known and commendable, they have, unfortunately, not gone without incident and at times criticism. Despite the best of intentions in the provision of a forensic technique to help combat aberrant violent crimes in America, there exists, at times, strong debate about the overall value and benefit of FBI profilers. However, when appraising these criticisms, it is important to distinguish between criticisms that are specifically indicative of FBI profilers per se and those more broadly conceived as problems related to the validity of criminal profiling in general.

Given the renown surrounding criminal profiling, its frequent portrayals of success in television, movies, and novels, as well as the numerous semi-autobiographical accounts of how profiles have been beneficial to criminal investigations, it is perhaps difficult to appreciate that impartial, scientifically vetted studies that may endorse the accuracy of criminal profiles are remarkably scarce. Indeed, it is of some concern that within the limited scientific literature currently available, there are indications that the accuracy and validity of criminal profiling may be nowhere near as favorable as anticipated.

Deciphering the precise reasons as to how a forensic technique has come into use without its capabilities first having been demonstrated scientifically is difficult. Two factors, however, that may account for this circumstance are the operational needs of law enforcement combined with the general perception of the value or worth of criminal profiles. As indicated at the start of this chapter, there existed an imperative for additional mechanisms to assist American law enforcement investigations into aberrant violence crimes. Consequently, from a pragmatic viewpoint, it has been suggested that it was of greater importance to expend resources in addressing operational needs in providing criminal profiles to assist police investigators than to expend these same resources in academic exercises of testing the validity of profiling.

This imperative to provide criminal profiles seems to have been concomitantly buttressed with a utilitarian argument that the validity of criminal profiles can be demonstrated vicariously by their continued use. The logic behind this argument is essentially an adaptation of the old English proverb: the proof is in the pudding. That is, if the provided criminal profiles were not deemed to be accurate and thus of some use, then police investigators would not continue to request and use them to assist with their investigations. Although there is certainly very strong intuitive appeal to the logic of such an argument, a handful of recent studies have found some troubling results that highlight the unreliability of this notion. Specifically, these studies have indicated that perceptions concerning the accuracy of criminal profiles can be distorted easily, based on a variety of simple factors. If the perceptions concerning the merit of a criminal profile can be distorted easily, then these perceptions are an unreliable measure of their accuracy and all arguments supporting the validity of criminal profiles based on their continued use via such perceptions are similarly unreliable and invalid.

Given the debate that surrounds the validity of criminal profiling, it is therefore unsurprising that there are instances where the input and methods for constructing criminal profiles by FBI profilers have been criticized as hindering criminal investigations.

It must however again be emphasized that instances where the merit and accuracy of criminal profiles have been brought into question are not indicative of the work of FBI profilers only. Indeed, the FBI is one of the few organizations to have undertaken some focused assessment of their procedures. Although some scientific research has, over recent years, emerged

The U.S.S. *Iowa*: Disaster or Murder-Suicide?

On the April 19, 1989, the battleship U.S.S. *Iowa* was conducting routine training exercises off the coast of Puerto Rico. Part of these exercises involved the test firing of the main sixteen-inch cannons aboard the ship, each of which weighed approximately 120 tons. These cannons were housed in three large turrets aboard the ship. Two turrets were positioned at the front of the ship, with the third located at the ship's rear. The firing procedures for these cannons involved a sophisticated set of steps involving not only the gunnery crews who operated the cannons within the turrets but also numerous sailors many decks below within the ship who handled the loading of the powder charges used to fire the cannons. As a seasoned ship in the U.S. Navy, the *Iowa* had used its cannons in numerous military campaigns dating as far back as the 1950s and the conflict in North Korea. Within all this time the procedures for firing the cannons had remained effectively the same and had operated without significant incident. However, on April 19, 1989, this impeccable safety record dramatically changed.

After the cannons of the first turret had fired, it was the turn of the second turret to commence firing its cannons. The orders were given to load the cannons in preparation and then abruptly just before firing was meant to commence, one of the gun crew members was heard through the on-board communication system as saying, "Hold up just a minute. We've got a problem here" (DeNivi and Campbell 2004, 289). A seemingly motionless pause transpired for approximately thirty seconds. Then, abruptly, a tumultuous blast occurred as the second turret exploded, killing all forty-seven crew members within the turret and crippling the ship.

In light of the Iowa's unblemished safety record, the cause of such a catastrophe was of great concern. The Pentagon commenced an investigation into the incident to scrutinize how the guns could have possibly malfunctioned in such a dramatic manner. As the investigation progressed, suggestions began to emerge that the explosion may not have been due to a mechanical failure. At approximately the same time as this notion was beginning to emerge, a relative of one of the deceased crew members was noted as making inquiries concerning eligibility for payment on a life insurance policy. These circumstances began to arouse suspicions, and investigation shifted to exploring the possibility that the explosion was no accident but perhaps was deliberately caused by one of the crew members on board the ship. As one component of this investigation Navy investigators consulted FBI profilers to evaluate one of the crew members whom they suspected may have caused the explosion. After some consideration the profilers came to the conclusion that it was possible that the deceased crew member may have caused the explosion aboard the *Iowa* deliberately, and thus the incident was no accident but instead a form of murder-suicide. Unsurprisingly,

(*continued*)

this conclusion was an issue of immense contention by the relatives of the deceased crew man. Ultimately, the matter of the explosion aboard the *Iowa* was brought before a committee of the U.S. House of Representatives, where the circumstances of the incident and the subsequent investigation were independently and closely scrutinized. One component of the committee's review involved an examination of the procedures used by the FBI profilers. From this review a number of highly critical observations of the FBI profilers were made, including that their procedures were considered inadequate and unprofessional. It was further noted that, in the view of the review committee, the profilers had not sufficiently indicated the speculative basis to their analysis (U.S. House of Representatives 1999).

The 1996 Atlanta Olympic Games: An Accidental Villain

Just after noon on July 27, 1996, during the summer Olympic Games hosted in Atlanta, a security guard noticed an unattended backpack in one of the venues. Suspecting that the backpack might contain a bomb, he alerted law enforcement officials of this possibility and then participated in efforts to clear the area. Unfortunately, the guard's suspicions were not unfounded, and before the area could be properly evacuated, a pipe bomb concealed inside the backpack exploded, killing two and injuring more than 100 people in the vicinity of the blast.

Initially, the security guard who had noticed the backpack received praise from the media as a hero who had attempted to avert disaster. Unfortunately, this praise was to be short-lived. Concerns began to emerge that perhaps the guard may have been involved in the bombing itself. That is, some analogy was drawn between the perceived actions of the guard and circumstances where firefighters had been found to initiate fires they themselves had lit. Investigators consulted FBI profilers about the circumstance of the bombing, and after some consideration the profilers agreed that the security guard matched the profile of the type of individual who may orchestrate a situation whereby he could engage in a heroic act. Thus, they concluded that the guard had some involvement in planting the bomb so he could participate in the evacuation and be perceived as a hero for his actions.

Thereafter a deleterious cycle ensued. The public media in observing the actions of investigators questioning and searching the guard's home increasingly focused their attention on the hapless guard as no longer a hero, but rather, the perpetrator of the crime. After enduring intense media scrutiny and vilification, it was found that the guard was not the bomber, no matter how well he matched the profile. Subsequently, and with tragic irony to the distress these events had on the guard and his family, the actual bomber was apprehended.

critically evaluating the technique of criminal profiling (in general), the work of the FBI remains one of the few organizations to have embarked on some assessment of their own specific techniques for criminal profiling. Although the outcomes of these studies are a far cry from the popular reputation of criminal profiling, they are nonetheless demonstrative of a willingness for self-evaluation and improvement.

CONCLUSION

There can be no doubt that the FBI and its personnel have contributed greatly over the years to the development of profiling techniques aimed at identifying the perpetrators of society's most heinous crimes. Although the FBI cannot be credited with inventing profiling per se, the institution can be credited with enhancing and popularizing the technique. This has been achieved largely by a commitment on the part of its members to explore and understand criminal behavior through studying key criminal populations and their motivations for perpetrating heinous crimes such as murder and rape. By interviewing offenders, cataloguing their responses, and examining their deeds, the FBI has developed templates that are still used today by criminal investigators in law enforcement agencies throughout the world.

Although some attempts to assess the efficacy of their approach to criminal investigation using their techniques have been undertaken, there is still much work to be done in terms of developing the practice of profiling generally and its useful application. In order for criminal profiling as a technique to develop, greater scientific investigation on a global scale is warranted. As has been discussed already, a dearth of sound scientific analysis has characterized the field of criminal profiling to date. Indeed, scholarly research on the efficacy of profiling as a technique has been disappointingly limited. However, just as the FBI as an institution has been a maverick in pioneering approaches to criminal profiling and popularizing its practice the FBI may in the future be at the forefront of moving the practice of criminal profiling towards a more scientific endeavor capable of better assisting in the investigation of crime and the apprehension of its perpetrators. Only through continued, focused scientific research can the use and limitations of criminal profiling be understood.

FURTHER READING

Bullock, J. A., G. D. Haddow, D. P. Coppola, E. Ergin, L. Westerman, and S. Yele-taysi. 2005. *Introduction to Homeland Security.* London, UK: Elsevier.

DeNevi, D., and J. E. Campbell. 2004. *Into the Minds of Madmen.* Amherst, NY: Prometheous Books.

Douglas, J. E., and A. E. Burgess. 1986. Criminal profiling: A viable investigative tool against violent crime. *FBI Law Enforcement Bulletin* 9:32–36.

Douglas, J. E., A. W. Burgess, A. G. Burgess, and R. K. Ressler. 2006. *Crime Classification Manual.* San Francisco, CA: Jossey-Bass.

Douglas, J. E., A. W. Burgess, and R. K. Ressler. 1983. Rape and rape murder: One offender and twelve victims. *American Journal of Psychiatry* 140:36–40.

Douglas, J. E., and R. Hazelwood. 1980. The lust murderer. *FBI Law Enforcement Bulletin* 49:8–12.

Douglas, J. E., and C. Munn. 1992. Violent crime scene analysis: Modus operandi, signature and staging. *FBI Law Enforcement Bulletin* 61:1–10.

Douglas, J. E., and M. Olshaker. 1995. *Mindhunter.* New York: Scribner.

Douglas, J. E., R. K. Ressler, A. W. Burgess, and C. R. Hartman. 1986. Criminal profiling from crime scene analysis. *Behavioral Sciences & The Law* 4: 401–421.

Doyle, A. C. 1891. *The Original Illustrated Sherlock Holmes.* Secaucus, NJ: Castle.

Egger, S. A. 1998. *The Killers among Us: An Examination of Serial Murder and Its Investigation.* Upper Saddle River, NJ: Prentice Hall.

Fisher, A. J. 1993. *Techniques of Crime Scene Investigation.* 5th ed. New York: Elsevier.

Harris, T. 1985. *The Red Dragon.* New York: Heinemann.

Harris, T. 1986. *The Silence of the Lambs.* New York: Heinemann.

Harris, T. 1999. *Hannibal.* New York: Heinemann.

Hazelwood, R. R., S. Michael, and J. Warren. 1989. The serial rapist: His characteristics and victims (Part I). *FBI Law Enforcement Bulletin* 57:11–17.

Hazelwood, R. R., and S. Michaud. 1999. *The Evil That Men Do.* New York: St. Martin's Press.

Howlett, J. B., K. A. Hanfland, and R. K. Ressler. 1986. The violent criminal apprehension program—ViCAP: A progress report. *FBI Law Enforcement Bulletin* 14:9–11.

Icove, D. J., and J. H. Estepp. 1987. Motive based offender profiles of arson and fire-related crimes. *FBI Law Enforcement Bulletin* 17:28–31.

Innes, B. 2003. *Profile of a Criminal Mind: How Psychological Profiling Helps Solve True Crimes.* Leicester, UK: Silverdale Books.

Jeffers, H. P. 1992. *Profiles in Evil.* London: Warner Bros.

Kocsis, R. N. 2006. *Criminal Profiling: Principles and Practice.* Tottowa, NJ: Humana Press.

Langer, W. 1972. *The Mind of Adolf Hitler.* New York: New American Library.

Lazer, D., ed. 2004. *DNA and the Criminal Justice System: The Technology of Justice.* Boston: MIT Press.

McCary, G., and K. Ramsland. 2003. *The Unknown Darkness.* New York: Morrow.

Norris, J. 1988. *Serial Killers.* London: Arrow Publications.

Palermo, G. B., and R. N. Kocsis. 2005. *Offender Profiling: An Introduction to the Sociopsychological Analysis of Violent Crime.* Springfield, IL: Charles C. Thomas.

Pinizzotto, A. J. 1984. Forensic psychology: Criminal personality profiling. *Journal of Police Science and Administration* 12 (1), 32–40.

Pinizzotto, A. J., and N. J. Finkel. 1990. Criminal personality profiling: An outcome and process study. *Law and Human Behavior* 14:215–233.

R v. Guilfoyle. 2001. 2 Cr. App. Rep. 57.

Ressler, R. K., and A. W. Burgess. 1985a. Violent crime: The men who murdered. *FBI Law Enforcement Bulletin* 2:32–39.

Ressler, R. K., and A. W. Burgess. 1985b. Crime scene and profile characteristics of organized and disorganized murderers. *FBI Law Enforcement Bulletin* 18: 7–15.

Ressler, R. K., and T. Shachtman. 1992. *Whoever Fights Monsters.* London: Simon & Schuster.

Risinger, D. M., and J. L. Loop. 2002. Three card Monte, Monty Hall, modus operandi and "offender profiling": Some lessons of modern cognitive science for the law of evidence. *Cardozo Law Review* 24:193–185.

Rumbelow, D. 1988. *The Complete Jack the Ripper.* London: Penguin.

Turco, R. N. 1990. Psychological profiling. *International Journal of Offender Therapy & Comparative Criminology* 34:147–154.

Tyler, T. R., and C. J. Wakslak. 2004. Profiling and police legitimacy: Procedural justice attributions of motive and acceptance of police authority. *Criminology* 42 (2), 253–281.

U.S. House of Representatives. 1990. *U.S.S. Iowa Tragedy: An Investigative Failure.* Report of the investigations subcommittee and the Defense Policy Panel of the Committee on Armed Services, House of Representatives, 101st Congress, 2nd Session.

Vorpagel, R. E., and J. Harrington. 1998. *Profiles in Murder.* New York: Plenum.

Whittington-Egan, R. 1975. *A Casebook on Jack the Ripper.* London: Wiley.

Wolfgang, M. E., and N. A. Weiner, eds. 1982. *Criminal Violence.* Thousand Oaks, CA: Sage.

Sheriff Joe Arpaio

Kelli Stevens

The desire to punish criminals is not a new concept. As long as there have been criminals, societies from ancient times to modern day have wanted them punished. In the United States the pendulum swings back and forth with regard to the best way to handle lawbreakers. In the 1950s and 1960s the American criminal justice system was based on a medical model that espoused the concept of rehabilitation. However, in the 1970s the pendulum began to swing toward harsher punishments for criminals, mainly because it was believed that rehabilitation did not work and that something needed to be done.[1] So in the last twenty-five to thirty years, the criminal justice system has seen an increase in harsher sentencing laws to include longer prison terms, increases in executions, and punitive treatment of offenders. This shift in ideology has boded well for many Americans, including politicians.

Historically, politicians capitalize on the popular sentiments held by society as they run for office, and the get-tough sentiment is no exception. For example, consider the Willie Horton incident during Vice President George H. W. Bush's quest for the White House. Bush used to his advantage the murder of a law-abiding citizen by Horton, a convict on furlough from prison. Bush used the politicized nature of the Horton furlough effectively in his bid for the presidency, basically making his opponent Michael Dukakis appear "soft on crime" because he allowed this furlough to take place. Local politicians in the 1990s often used the get-tough platform in their campaigns as well.

A former regional director for the Drug Enforcement Administration (DEA) and soldier in the "War on Drugs," Joe Arpaio ran for sheriff of Maricopa County, Arizona in 1992, at the right time—the height of the get-tough era in criminal justice. Arpaio's campaign platform consisted of the familiar get-tough stance typical of this period, but some, especially the citizens of Maricopa County, do not consider what he said simply rhetoric, but rather promises that have been transformed into reality. His innovative, albeit controversial, reforms in the county's jails and law enforcement practices are part of American popular culture, and he has attained the status of a crime-fighting icon and "America's Toughest Sheriff." But who is this tough lawman? Where did he come from? How did he become so popular in the desert of Arizona, as well as around the world? These questions will be answered, followed by an examination of Arpaio's popular but controversial policies, not so widely known policies, and criticisms and problems. This chapter also seeks to give the reader a broader perspective of the changes that occurred in penal philosophy in the United States beginning in the 1980s to the present day, along with a brief discussion of popular culture and crime and how Arpaio is a significant figure in these areas.

ONE TOUGH LAWMAN

Arpaio the Man

Joe Arpaio was born in Springfield, Massachusetts in 1932. His parents were Italian immigrants from Naples, Italy. Sadly, his mother died while giving birth to him. So, from birth to three years, Arpaio and his father lived with one Italian family and then from three to twelve with another family. His father was busy trying to run a business and worked many long hours, so he needed help raising Arpaio.[2] When Arpaio was twelve his father remarried. Arpaio attended two different high schools in Massachusetts, Classico and Commerce. While at Classico, Arpaio played sports, but was not on the "first team." He switched to Commerce High his senior year. He recalls being a "C" student who had to study because he worked in his father's grocery store and he was more interested in playing sports—football, basketball, and baseball—than academics. He joked about faring better in sports at Commerce because there were only about one hundred boys attending the school. There were many more girls attending the school, which for some teenaged boys would be a distraction, but Arpaio didn't go out with girls much in high school. He said girls would call him, wanting to go out, and they would tell him they liked his legs! But he remained focused on sports and studied to make a C average, as he was not a good test taker. According to Arpaio, the most important class he took in high school was typing.[3] That skill would serve him well in both the army and in his career as a law enforcement officer.

In 1950, the year Arpaio graduated from high school, the Korean War began; he joined the U.S. Army. He felt it was time to move on and leave behind his not-so-happy childhood, even though his father had the money for him to attend college and wanted him to attend college. While in basic training he met a young lady named Angela from New Jersey and got engaged. His engagement didn't work out for several reasons—Angela was an only child of a very close-knit Sicilian family. They did not want their daughter marrying someone who wanted to become a cop and move her away.

After enlisting in the army, Arpaio was sent to France and spent two years there; he eventually attained the rank of sergeant. He served in an administrative capacity for a two-officer, eight-man medical detachment. Arpaio recalls having charge of quarters duty at night; servicemen would come in for shots for venereal diseases and he would give them the shots. Although he wasn't a medic, he would tell them to bend over and then jab them in the buttocks with a needle. He found this task quite amusing. Later, Arpaio received an honorable discharge at the age of twenty-one and decided it was time to pursue his dream of becoming a federal agent. He had always wanted to be an agent for the Federal Bureau of Investigation, but he cannot specifically recall why other than that he had a toy gun and badge as a child.

After leaving the Army, he moved to Washington, D.C. in 1954 and took the entrance tests for both the Border Patrol and the Washington, D.C. Police Department (DCPD). He did not pass the test for the Border Patrol, but did pass the test for DCPD, so his law enforcement career began. During the 1950s police officers were true "beat cops," and they walked the streets, getting to know the citizens in the beat they were assigned to protect and serve. Arpaio asked his captain for a beat with some action, so he got what he asked for. He worked a tough beat in a predominantly African-American community, armed with a nightstick and a .38 caliber handgun. He "locked everybody up." A young Arpaio enjoyed his job immensely even though he obtained the unofficial status of "most assaulted cop in D.C." in 1957. He said one of the reasons he obtained this title was because he wouldn't walk around the hoodlums congregating on the sidewalks, but instead would walk right through them, and "if you didn't move you were under arrest." He gave everybody tickets: "You spit on the sidewalk, you get locked up. You urinate in public; you get locked up."[4] With all of these arrests came reports to write; Arpaio typed his own reports. This is where his high school typing class became very useful. He was able to type his reports quickly and head back out to the streets to make more arrests, but he also made a little time for socialization.

Arpaio met his wife Ava while in D.C.; she lived in the same building as he and his roommate, George. George, a fellow officer, actually had Ava's number and said he didn't have any luck getting through. Arpaio said, "Give me the number; I'll take care of it." So, he gave Ava a call, and they began dating. In the meantime, Arpaio's career was about to take a different turn.

While employed with DCPD, Arpaio met the sheriff of Clark County, Nevada, while working at a parade for President Eisenhower. The sheriff was impressed with Arpaio and encouraged him to move to Nevada. At first Arpaio was not keen on the idea, but he wanted to advance in his career and there seemed to be more opportunities for advancement in Nevada. Thus, he accepted the offer not long after and moved to Las Vegas where he was hired by the Las Vegas Police Department. Las Vegas certainly was not a boring place and Arpaio recalls meeting Elvis Presley while on patrol. Arpaio stopped Presley and a female companion who were riding on a motorcycle—they were driving at a high rate of speed. By the time the encounter was over Elvis was at the police station signing autographs and having a police department mechanic check out his motorcycle.[5] During his stint with Las Vegas Police Department Arpaio's attitude changed. He realized the law was not so black and white and that citing everyone for every single violation of the law, no matter how minute, was "chicken."[6] His new-found philosophy would serve him well in the future. Arpaio worked for the Las Vegas Police Department for only six months before fulfilling his dream of becoming a federal agent.

In 1957, after serving as a police officer at the local level, Arpaio took a job with the Bureau of Narcotics, now known as the Drug Enforcement Administration (DEA). His old friend, George, had gotten hired by the Bureau of Narcotics, so Arpaio had a contact on the inside. He and Ava relocated to Chicago, Illinois, where they eventually married and he began work as an undercover agent. The Bureau of Narcotics needed Italian agents to infiltrate the drug scene in Chicago and Arpaio was a perfect fit. He had never worked undercover and this was an exciting opportunity that was the beginning of a three-decade-long career as a federal agent fighting the war against crime and drugs. Arpaio was quite adept at undercover work and there was no group he could not penetrate, no criminal he could not earn the trust of, and he maintained his integrity all the while. He earned the nickname "Nickelbag Joe" because no deal was too small.[7] His philosophy was to start out small and work his way up to the top members of the operation. He even arrested a corrupt police officer in the officer's own police car because the officer sold him heroin. He worked long and hard and in 1961 was reassigned to undercover work in Turkey to stop the heroin and opium trade to the United States.

Arpaio recounts being dropped off in Istanbul, Turkey, with no police authority, no backup, no connections, no language training, no information, and only a few hundred dollars and his Smith & Wesson firearm. Ava and his son remained in the United States and he was alone in a foreign country. This did not stop Arpaio; he quickly adapted and began making connections in the underworld of narcotics. He would make deals that took place in the mountains with armed opium farmers delivering the product by horse, mule, or whatever mode of transportation was most suited for the terrain. And, on more than one occasion, these deals did not go exactly as planned; gun battles would often erupt. Arpaio escaped death more times than he'd like to count.[8] After about six months, he was working with the Turkish National Police to take down a dominant drug ring that exported phenomenal amounts of heroin to the United States. The operation was a success and went down as the largest seizure ever made in Turkish history, more than 2,000 pounds of opium.

Arpaio's exemplary undercover work in Turkey yielded a number of honors and awards, including the Exceptional Service Award from the general director of the Turkish National Police, a Special Service Award from the U.S. Treasury Department, and the Superior Performance Award from the U.S. Treasury Department.[9] His career continued to flourish as he was promoted to Special Agent in Charge of the DEA San Antonio, Texas, field office to tackle the drug trade increasing along the United States-Mexico border.

While in San Antonio, Arpaio achieved such successes as leading the raid against members of a drug operation in which more than $1 million worth of pure heroin was seized and a drug dealer was arrested right in front of the federal building. He then moved on to be the special agent in charge in Washington, D.C., where he was instrumental in the investigation and arrest of a bureau deputy director in Baltimore, Maryland, who had gone bad, which led to the uncovering of other agents inside the Bureau of Narcotics who were selling heroin. Arpaio finally landed in Phoenix, Arizona, in 1978 as the regional director of the DEA. In 1982 he retired from the DEA, after a long rewarding career in law enforcement, to help his wife run a travel agency.

Their son Rocko came home from college to help run the business as well, and it was no small business. In fact, the family business took in more than $6 million one year. Arpaio says that people kept asking him during this time, "Why don't you run for sheriff?" He gave little thought to it until he lost the travel account with the sheriff's department. At this point, it would no longer be a conflict of interest, so he tossed his hat in the ring for the sheriff's race in 1992 and won.

Popular Policies

After Arpaio was elected sheriff in Maricopa County, Arizona in 1992, he was faced with the daunting task of operating the county jail facilities and carrying out law enforcement duties after the budget suffered a $10 million cut; although the Sheriff's Department had an $82 million budget, it was

Arpaio Timeline

1932	Born in Springfield, Massachusetts
1950	Graduates from high school; joins the U.S. Army
1953	Honorable discharge from U.S. Army
1954	Joins Washington, D.C., police force
1957	Most assaulted D.C. cop; joins Las Vegas Police Department; special appointment to the Bureau of Narcotics
1961	Bureau of Narcotics special assignment in Istanbul, Turkey
1964	Special Agent in Charge, San Antonio, Texas
1968	Deputy Regional Director for the Bureau of Narcotics and Dangerous Drugs, Baltimore, Maryland; Regional Director, Mexico City, Mexico
1973	Section Chief, Office of Intelligence for the DEA, Washington, D.C.
1978	Regional Director for DEA, Phoenix, Arizona
1982	Retired from DEA
1992	Elected sheriff of Maricopa County, Arizona

not an easy task.[10] Maricopa County had roughly 2.5 million residents at the time and covered 9,200 square miles; the county is as large as the state of New Jersey. It is the fourth most populous county in the United States. Because of tougher sentences for drug offenders and sweeping legal reforms in the criminal justice system, federal, state and local correctional institutions across the country were strapped to house inmates with little or no extra available bed spaces. Arpaio had to be creative and he succeeded.

One of the first major reforms he made in office that gained worldwide attention was to create 1,000 new bed spaces to house inmates. What is so spectacular about that? one might ask. Well, the fact that the new bed spaces were located in the Arizona desert in old army tents, mainly Korean War era tents, surrounded by razor barbed wire, might have had something to do with it. Arpaio secured the old tents, which were worn and full of holes, from the government free of charge. After spending only about $80,000 to prepare the land space to secure the inmates and provide basic needs (electricity, plumbing, etc.), the Tent City Jail was ready to take on inmates in August of 1993. He had saved the taxpayers millions and succeeded in building a new facility to house inmates that would not detract from property values in a residential area. Interestingly, the Tent City Jail is located just outside of Phoenix between the city dump and the animal pound.

After the Tent City Jail was constructed, the media swarmed to the desert to get a firsthand look at the innovative camp. Of course there were critics, but they were told by Arpaio, when asked about the cruelty of such a place, that if American troops can go to the Middle East and live in the desert in tents, then our inmates should not have it any better than our soldiers. This comment struck a cord with the public, as the Persian Gulf War had ended just a couple of years before. This was only just the beginning of media coverage concerning Arpaio's policies.

Another bold decision made early in office by Arpaio was to take away amenities such as coffee, tobacco products, pornographic materials—magazines and movies—and to severely limit cable television programming in all penal facilities in the county. Notably, Arpaio only allowed television channels such as the Disney Channel, the Weather Channel, ESPN, C-SPAN, and the Phoenix municipal government channel to broadcast. He also discontinued the use of salt and pepper, which saved the taxpayers around $20,000 a year.[11] The Maricopa County Sheriff's Office's (MCSO) vision statement includes terminology regarding being a leader in the field of law enforcement, and some of Arpaio's decisions certainly led the way to getting tough on inmates.

Arpaio decided to cut spending even further by reducing meals to two a day and serving only one hot meal, thereby reducing the cost to taxpayers. Inmates receive a sack lunch consisting of two sandwiches, one bologna and one peanut butter sandwich, fruit, vegetables, and Kool-Aid.[12] The bologna

Maricopa County Sheriff's Office Vision Statement

The Maricopa County Sheriff's Office is a fully integrated law enforcement agency committed to being the leader in establishing the standards for providing professional quality law enforcement, detention, and support services to the citizens of Maricopa County and to other criminal justice agencies.

Source: Maricopa County Sheriff's Department, used with permission.

sandwich has received worldwide media attention because the outside press discovered that a batch of it was green. A fluke in the processing of the meat turned it green, and the Sheriff was touted as being so tough that he feeds the inmates green bologna. But Arpaio is not heartless; the evening meal is hot and there are a wide variety of foods served with adequate portions. Again, media sources from all over the world scrambled to report on how the removal of amenities was faring with inmates and to question the humaneness of Arpaio's policies. Of course, the inmates complained about not being given what they wanted, but the Sheriff contended, and still does, that "they should not live better in jail than on the outside," and "jails shouldn't be hotels." Arpaio continued to make innovative changes with much success.

In November of 1993, the mall patrol posse was formed because of several highly publicized carjackings around the malls during the height of the Christmas shopping season. Arpaio decided to take action and called on his posse members to assist. It should be noted that he did not create the use of the posse in Maricopa County, as it had been in existence fifty years or so before he took office, but while in office he has greatly expanded the use of volunteers. So, more than 700 posse members rose to the occasion to make the citizens feel safe and deter crime in the malls and parking lots. They assisted deputies in making arrests, responded to calls from other law enforcement agencies, and helped shoppers and motorists.[13] The money this operation saved taxpayers was phenomenal, considering the posse members do not get paid. The success of this operation led to the formation of many other special posses.

Several other posse projects popular with the citizens of Maricopa County include Operation Zero Tolerance, Operation Take Away Graffiti, and the Deadbeat Parent Posse. Operation Zero Tolerance, designed to thwart prostitution in the Van Buren Street District of Phoenix, was launched in April 1994. With the help of armed posse members, the MCSO and the Phoenix Police Department inundated Van Buren Street for sixty days. Posse members patrolled on foot, on horseback, and in vehicles day and night. During this time, calls to the police department regarding prostitution decreased significantly.[14] Although it was not a permanent solution, the operation met with much success and support from local businesses and residents.

The next successful venture was Operation Take Away Graffiti. Arpaio does not view graffiti as a legitimate form of art, but rather a blight on the city's buildings and other structures, as well as a telltale sign of gang activity.[15] Once again to save taxpayers money, he approved the formation of a posse to tackle this problem and planned Operation Take Away Graffiti. On March 24, 1995, more than 500 posse members hit the city streets armed with night-vision scopes. For three months, the posse patrolled the areas most known for graffiti and gang activity, and, as expected, calls to police regarding this problem almost ceased. Posse members donated thousands of hours to clean up buildings, bridges, and billboards. Why stop here? Arpaio, with the help of staff, has created about sixty special posses since being elected in 1992.

The use of volunteers from the community empowered with law enforcement authority seemed to be unsettling for members of the press and civil rights organizations who accused Arpaio of creating a police state. However, not just anyone wanting to become a member of the sheriff's posse is allowed. MCSO has strict guidelines for posse applicants. They must undergo a stringent background investigation, submit to urine testing for detection of illegal substances, and participate in classroom instruction on subjects such as law and first aid, and some members must undergo a psychological evaluation and weapons and firearms training. Today, there are more than 3,000 men and women serving on the posses, and they pay for all of their own equipment and uniforms.

One of Arpaio's most notable policies, aside from the Tent City Jail, was to reestablish chain gangs in 1995. He began by creating an all-male chain gang comprised of inmates who volunteered to participate. Arpaio received criticism, as one might imagine, as chain gangs historically have been associated with cruelty and prejudice. However, one of the main purposes of the chain gang, Arpaio touts, is rehabilitation. Inmates who have had disciplinary problems while incarcerated can volunteer to participate on the chain gang in order to regain entrance into the general population from lockdown or to get their jobs back that they lost because of their disciplinary problems; they are not forced to work on the chain gang. Arpaio says this is the Last Chance Program, and "the program is meant to help the inmates contribute to the community and do something productive."[16] Inmates are chained together in groups of five and are overseen by detention officers and armed posse members while they work out in the desert heat. The chain gangs perform a multitude of meaningful tasks such as clearing brush, burying the indigent of the county, cleaning the streets in Phoenix and surrounding areas, and painting over graffiti, helping reduce costs for taxpayers. If the inmates complete the program they are awarded a graduation certificate and are allowed to participate in normal activities

Maricopa County Sheriff's Office Posses

Special Operations	Areas of the County
Air	Anthem
Cold Case	Desert Foothills
Communications	Desert Search
Community Services	Fountain Hills
Crime Prevention	Fountain Hills Mounted
Cyber	Gilbert
Dares	Litchfield Park
Divers	Mesa Mounted
Enforcement Support	Mesa Southside
Executive	Metro Assistance
Helicopter	Mountain Rescue
Instructor	New River Search and Rescue
Jeep	Queen Creek Crime Prevention
Maricopa K-9	Queen Creek Mounted
Medical Rescue	Rio Salado Mounted
Motors	Scottsdale Mounted
Operations	Sun City
Pioneer Search and Rescue	Sun City West
Ranger	Sun Lakes
Search and Rescue KHOR	Surprise
Special Assignment Unit	West Valley
Special Forces	Westbrook Village
Special Operations Air	Westside Mounted
Special Projects	Whitetank Mounted
Street Crime Prevention	Wickenburg Search and Rescue
Tactical Support	
Tactical Vehicle	

Source: Maricopa County Sheriff's Office Web site, http://www.mcso.org/, used with permission.

within the jail such as education classes, recreation time, and religious ceremonies.[17]

Since Arpaio is an equal opportunity sheriff, in 1996 he created the world's first chain gang for females. The female chain gang performs many of the same tasks as the male chain gang, and the purpose of the chain gang is also the same. Female inmates who have had disciplinary problems can apply to be on the chain gang and earn back privileges of having a job and being housed in the general population. The women clean the streets of

Phoenix and clear brush, the same as the men. And why stop there? Arpaio is the only sheriff in history to institute a chain gang for juvenile offenders. This bold step again drew criticism from organizations such as the American Civil Liberties Union. This did not stop the sheriff from establishing other controversial policies.

Arpaio felt that inmates should be easily recognizable and discernable while working out in the community on the chain gangs so he replaced the scrub-like uniforms with the old black and white striped uniforms. Arpaio's critics again sounded their trumpets, citing Arpaio as a man who enjoyed humiliating the inmates, but he stood by his decision, stating it's a matter of security.

Another change in prison garb would also prove to be a security measure, although it wasn't originally thought of in that manner. Pink underwear. Yes, pink underwear was another popular change instituted by Arpaio in 1995 after he discovered inmates were stealing the white boxer shorts and selling them for cash. So, Arpaio had the boxers died pink because it was less likely the male inmates would insult their manhood by selling pink underwear; little did he know the pink boxers would also serve as a security measure. In February of 2000 an inmate escaped from custody while being transported from one jail facility to another.[18] The inmate, Sergio Verdugo-Lopez, took off the black and white striped uniform, but was still wearing the pink underwear. His pink underwear was spotted by a sheriff's deputy only thirty minutes or so after the escape, at which time he was apprehended. The pink underwear was not only popular among the jail staff, but also the public.

The word spread in the community about the pink underwear, and MCSO began receiving calls from citizens wanting to purchase the pink boxer shorts. This turned into a great opportunity for the MCSO, and almost half a million dollars worth of the boxers were sold in no time. This money was poured back into the agency to purchase fuel and pay other expenses within the department. The pink boxer shorts can still be purchased today.

Aside from changes in prison clothing, technology would spur other major changes within the department. With the advances in technology in our society, Arpaio and his staff decided to capitalize on this by installing a "jail cam" (to be broadcast via the Internet) in the booking area to capture live video of lawbreakers being processed into the jail, partly because of accusations of misconduct on behalf of jail staff. Arpaio stated he had nothing to hide and people were welcome to see what goes on in the jails. Much controversy arose from this and has now transformed into mug shots being posted for offenders arrested. Mug shots for a three-day time period are posted on the department's Web site and then new ones are uploaded. This has become so popular that almost one million hits a day are recorded to the Web site. But there are many more programs that have received less publicity, which will be discussed in the following section.

Not So Widely Known Policies

Because of the extensive publicity on Arpaio's controversial programs, the less debatable programs have not received much attention, but deserve their own spotlight. Arpaio's long career in federal law enforcement brought him face to face with the plight of the human condition, and made an impact on him, as evidenced in the establishment of numerous rehabilitation-oriented classes and curriculum designed to address the treatment needs of inmates.

The ALPHA program (Aware, Learn, Plan, Help, and Accept) is a substance abuse treatment program for sentenced inmates. Implemented in 1996 and led by licensed therapists and counselors, ALPHA is one of the most successful programs Arpaio has instituted. This program is offered to both male and female adult inmates, as well as juveniles, and lasts for six months. Inmates wanting to participate in the program must also agree to enroll in other adjunct programs such as anger management, job preparedness, and GED/Computer Learning Lab while keeping a perfect disciplinary record. Those inmates who fail to adhere to the program guidelines are discharged. Since its inception, the ALPHA program has had more than 4,000 successful graduates and a recidivism rate of only 14 percent.[19] Many other programs aimed at successfully reintegrating the offender into the community were sanctioned by Arpaio while in office.

Cognitive Restructuring is a program attended by those who graduate from the ALPHA program and is designed to change the pattern of criminal thinking and cognitive distortions that lead to law-breaking behavior. ALPHA graduates attend this class twice a week. Anger management classes are offered to inmates, especially those arrested for assaultive offenses, and incorporate a life skills component to increase inmates' ability to be independent and responsible citizens.

Another interesting program in Arpaio's Estrella Jail is the Girl Scouts Beyond Bars program in which mothers who are incarcerated can participate in their daughters' Girl Scout troop activities; this is the only jail in America that has such a program.[20] The local Girl Scout troop sponsors the program, and those girls whose mothers are incarcerated go to see their mothers in jail and engage in various activities such as arts and crafts. The hope is to "break the cycle of crime between generations." Arpaio has other programs within the walls of his jails to encourage youth, strengthen families, and hold parents accountable.

Hard Knocks High is the only accredited high school inside a jail in the United States and it's in three of the county's jails: Madison, Towers, and Lower Buckeye. In addition to education and learning, Arpaio aims to hold parents accountable. He instituted a "Deadbeat Parent" posse to round up parents who fail to pay child support and take responsibility for their family. The posse obtains information through the warrants division regarding outstanding warrants for failure to pay child support, and then posse members scour the community looking for deadbeat parents to arrest. This program has netted thousands of dollars in child support for children in the community.

Arpaio not only has a soft spot in his heart for children, but also for animals. Arpaio had one of the jail facilities converted into an animal shelter, known as the MASH Unit (MCSO Animal Safe Hospice) to house animals that have been recovered through the department's Animal Cruelty Investigative Unit. Ironically, the animals live in a facility with central heat and air, while thousands of inmates live in tents with neither. Inmates care for these abused and neglected animals. The hope is to instill a sense of responsibility and accomplishment, thereby rehabilitating inmates. The inmates who work in the MASH Unit feed, water, bathe, and train the animals, which can be adopted for a small donation by members of the community. The donations help to fund the operation and provide basic care for the animals. Other evidence of his soft spot for animals has come in the form of a recent increase in arrests for those suspected of animal cruelty. Several professionals have been arrested for animal cruelty, including a veterinarian and a charter school teacher. Arpaio doesn't care who you are; if you break the law, you will be arrested.

Other inventive programs instituted in Maricopa County jails since Arpaio took office include Dignity, a special program for prostitutes, designed to teach self-worth, self-esteem, and independence for women who have found themselves in the profession. Additionally, education programs such as English as a Second Language, English Learning Instruction, health education and HIV awareness, literacy tutoring, and a learning lab with computers to assist those who struggle with traditional classroom instruction have been instituted. Parenting classes, twelve-step programs, and special curricula for women—Winning Opportunities for Working and Women Healing Ever New—are also an important part of the programming. In addition to creating classes to help rehabilitate inmates, Arpaio established several other policies that are not so widely known to improve safety inside and outside of the jails.

In May 2007 Arpaio no longer allowed sealed mail into his jails. Inmates are only allowed to receive postcards. Any letters or packages received are returned to the senders. Back in 2002 inmates were required to use only postcards for their outgoing personal correspondence. This move was designed to save taxpayers money by using reduced postage mail. The recent switch from postcards for incoming personal mail will also save taxpayers money, according to Arpaio. He cited security as the main reason for the switch though, because contraband is placed inside the sealed envelopes and packages. In a news release in March 2007 Arpaio stated that employees searching the mail have found illegal drugs such as methamphetamines inside envelopes, as well as handcuff keys and pornography. Because of the high volume of mail through the jails, more than two million pieces per year, it takes eight full-time employees to search the mail. Switching to allowing only postcards to be sent to inmates will again save the taxpayers money and reduce the amount of contraband being smuggled into the jails. Arpaio has accomplished many great things as the sheriff of Maricopa County, Arizona, but he has also garnered much criticism.

Criticisms and Problems

Not everyone is a fan of Arpaio. Because of his bold and unapologetic stance toward crime and criminals and his constant media exposure, he has had his fair share of condemnation. There are Web sites on the Internet, political action committees, and other private organizations dedicated to opposing him and ousting him from office. There are hundreds of articles criticizing Arpaio for allowing inmates in Maricopa County jails to be treated as "subhuman," although he does not condone this, and there have been lawsuits filed against him on numerous occasions, including wrongful death suits.

There are hundreds of Web sites on the Internet about Arpaio, but one in particular dedicated to driving him out of office in the 2004 election, www.arpaio.com, features his political opponent Dan Saban, claiming he could "improve the operation of the Sheriff's office." The Web site offers reasons to recall Joe Arpaio from office:

1. With Arpaio, real law enforcement takes a back seat to publicity stunts.
2. He lives in a fantasy world of self-importance.
3. Millions of tax dollars have been wasted on lawsuits.
4. He is responsible for a critical and dangerous shortage of personnel in both the jails and on patrol.
5. Hundreds of current sheriff's office employees, represented by a number of employee organizations, have expressed a vote of no confidence for Sheriff Arpaio.
6. The self-proclaimed "Toughest Sheriff in America" is too fearful to debate other candidates....[21]

Additional criticism from the Web site relays a story about an eighteen-year-old boy accused of plotting to kill the sheriff who was entrapped by MCSO employees. The boy's mother formed a group called Mothers Against Arpaio in hopes of getting him out of office. Mothers Against Arpaio contends that many inmates have been "injured, beaten, and even killed while in jail," and that Arpaio "lacks respect for human life and dignity."[22] Despite these criticisms, it should be noted that Arpaio has been reelected three times since taking office.

Even more critics have voiced their opinions and concerns about Arpaio. Some of the most damning criticism of Arpaio has been in the form of lawsuits regarding the treatment of inmates and pretrial detainees in his jails. Arpaio has been sued thousands—some sources say between 1,500 and 6,700—of times for a variety of allegations.[23] The most serious suits include wrongful death suits. Brian Crenshaw, a legally blind inmate arrested for shoplifting, died after allegedly falling from his bunk. Crenshaw purportedly assaulted a detention officer and was placed in lockdown for six days. On the sixth day, he fell from his bunk, suffering a perforated intestine and a broken neck; officers found him unconscious in his cell. The family of Charles Agster, a mentally disturbed man, filed a lawsuit against the county for his death after he was restrained improperly. Phillip Wilson died after being assaulted by other inmates; Pearl Wilson, his mother, claims the staff allowed this to happen.

In 1996, an inmate, Scott Norberg, allegedly was handcuffed, dragged from his cell, and placed in a restraint chair with a towel over his face. He later died from "positional asphyxia," according to medical reports. Norberg had been arrested for chasing and trying to kill two young girls; he was high on methamphetamines. MCSO employees contended Norberg was combative and uncooperative, and officers were trying to restrain him after he attacked them. The Norberg family filed a civil lawsuit against MCSO and Arpaio, which led to an investigation into jail conditions by several outside agencies.

The U.S. Department of Justice (DOJ) issued a report in March 1996 conveying that conditions at the county's jails were unconstitutional with regard to the use of excessive force against inmates and inmates' medical needs. A year later Amnesty International launched an investigation into jail operations by sending representatives to tour the facilities. They concluded, "Detention officers appeared to resort to levels of force out of all proportion to the threat posed by the inmate. Where cases were investigated, however, the use of force was usually found to be justified by the jail authorities, despite questionable circumstances."[24]

The report also detailed concerns about the lack of security measures in the Tent City Jail, the use of chain gangs as a form of inhumane punishment, the misuse of restraint devices, the prevalent use of stun guns as a means of controlling inmates, the lack of privacy for female inmates, and treatment of juveniles. Amnesty International recommended changes such as delineating a clear policy regarding use of force, including a zero tolerance policy for excessive force, ensuring MCSO policies conformed to international standards on the use of force, ceasing to use the Tent City Jail, ceasing the issuance of stun guns to correctional staff, revising and strictly monitoring the use of restraint chairs, providing educational and rehabilitative opportunities to juveniles, and much more.

In October 1997, the DOJ released a statement saying it had reached an agreement with MCSO for steps to be taken to "ensure guards do not engage in excessive force or misuse mechanical restraints against their prisoners." Arpaio agreed to take steps such as obtaining additional funds from the county to increase its number of staff, increasing training aimed at dealing with difficult inmates, improving conditions of the Tent City Jail, revising procedures regarding the use of restraint chairs, and revising policy related to the use of nonlethal weapons by staff.[25] Eventually, the lawsuit filed by the Norberg family was settled for $8.25 million, but more complaints were forthcoming.

In 1999, the DOJ filed a complaint under the Civil Rights of Institutionalized Persons Act, 42 U.S.C. §§ 1997–1997, in *United States v. Maricopa County* (D. Ariz.) regarding the medical and mental health services of inmates housed in the county's penal facilities. "Simultaneously, the parties filed a settlement agreement that provided for hiring of additional medical and mental health staff; improved medical evaluation services both for intake and routine care; additional space for the provision of medical services; an improved distribution system for medications and monitoring of possible side effects; creation of an Infection Control Committee; and improved quality assurance mechanisms to assess the quality of medical and mental health services provided at the facilities."[26] Despite Arpaio's commitment to improving services of his agency as any elected official would do, subsequent lawsuits were filed.

Arpaio has been sued regarding MCSO's high-speed pursuit policy that was revised after two deaths, although it was in compliance with the International Association of Chiefs of Police model pursuit policy. Interestingly, many of the department's policies are reviewed and updated periodically to ensure high standards and compliance with changing laws. The high-speed pursuit policy was due for its review and subsequently was changed, coincidentally at the time of the aforementioned deaths. MCSO is not the only law enforcement agency sued regarding pursuit policy. A recent Supreme Court case, *Scott v. Harris*, addresses this issue. In Georgia, Deputy Timothy Scott attempted to end a high-speed pursuit in order to safeguard other motorists by bumping the fleeing suspect's vehicle and forcing it off the road. The vehicle crashed, rendering its driver paralyzed. The suspect sued the deputy, claiming his fourth amendment rights were violated, but the Court held Scott's actions reasonable.[27] Most recently, in 2007, Arpaio was sued for not taking a female inmate to an abortion clinic; the results of this lawsuit are still pending. Arpaio states he doesn't mind the lawsuits, because he has not done anything wrong, and anyone can sue another person for anything these days.

Inmate lawsuits are prevalent across the country in federal, state, and local institutions. The Prison Litigation Reform Act of 1995 passed by the U.S. Congress was an effort to stem the tide of lawsuits filed by inmates. Inmates file thousands of lawsuits, many of them frivolous, each year. One inmate sued the state of Oklahoma because he wanted to wear women's underwear, while others have sued claiming their religious beliefs called for a diet of steak and shrimp. A federal prisoner filed suit when a sweatsuit valued at twenty-five dollars was lost in the laundry; this suit was dismissed as frivolous. A court placed restrictions on one inmate from filing suits, considering that he had previously filed forty-seven suits, all of them unsuccessful.[28] The point is that inmates have nothing but time on their hands, and many spend time suing the state, sheriffs, or other law enforcement officials instead of using their time wisely to rehabilitate themselves.

Not only are inmate lawsuits common, but so too are deaths of inmates while in custody. The DOJ implemented the Death in Custody Reporting Program after the passage of the Death in Custody Reporting Act in 2000 (PL-106-297). This program has improved data collection methods from state prisons and local jails regarding inmate deaths to include specific causes of deaths such as cancer, heart diseases, hepatitis C, and AIDS, as well as specific inmate characteristics. Findings from the first report published since the implementation of the Death in Custody Reporting Program indicate that homicide rates in local jails have slightly declined from five per 100,000 in 1983 to three per 100,000 in 2002.[29] Suicide accounted for more deaths than did homicide, forty-seven per 100,000 in 2002. The report also explains that the nation's fifty largest jail jurisdictions reported a total of 1,037 deaths from all causes. Critics of Arpaio would like to paint the picture that inmates dying in his jails is an unusual phenomenon, when it is not. Los Angeles, New York, and Cook County, Illinois, the top three largest jail jurisdictions in the country, aggregately reported 252 deaths between 2000 and 2002. Maricopa County, being the fourth most populous jail system in the country, reported thirty-one deaths. The death count includes suicide, homicide, and other causes such as various illnesses. Considering the problems often associated with the criminal lifestyle, inmates are an unhealthy population, and this undoubtedly contributes to a higher mortality rate for this population when compared to general society. Deaths in Maricopa county jails are not all Arpaio is being criticized for; most recently it is regarding his stance toward illegal immigrants.

Arpaio has been criticized for his policies on illegal immigration, an issue viewed by many as a federal problem. He disagrees with the plan supported by the U.S. Congress to address illegal immigration, so he devised his own method of dealing with it. He created a special force called the Illegal Immigration Interdiction (Triple I) Strike Force dedicated to arresting smugglers and illegal immigrants, and deputies have been cross-trained by Bureau of Immigration and Customs Enforcement staff. As of May 2007, 546 arrests have been made, which were allowed under state law, for human smugglers.

The most recent move in which Arpaio anticipates criticism is the implementation of an inmate organ donation program, the only of its kind in the country. Arpaio wants inmates to "have a heart" and sign up via the "I.DO!" program to voluntarily donate their hearts (and other vital organs and body parts). The program goals are to increase awareness for organ

Policy Changes and Major Events During Office

1992   Elected Sheriff of Maricopa County, Arizona
1993   Restrictions on amenities, Tent City Jail, mall patrol posse
1994   Operation Zero Tolerance, Girl Scouts Beyond Bars
1995   Operation TAG, male chain gang, pink underwear
1996   Reelected sheriff, female chain gang, ALPHA program, Scott Norberg incident
1997   Hard Knocks High
1998   Pup tents for incarcerated teens
1999   U.S. Supreme Court ruling that Arpaio can ban pornography
2000   Reelected sheriff
2001   American flags painted in 2,000 cells after the 9–11 terrorist attacks
2002   Arrests made for plot to murder Arpaio
2003   Major animal cruelty investigation
2004   Reelected sheriff
2005   Sheriff's posse helps Gulf Coast victims of Hurricanes Rita and Katrina
2006   English Learning Instruction
2007   KJOE Radio, Inmate Idle, Triple I Strike Force

donation and to motivate inmates to do something good for others. Inmates watch educational videos via the jail's television programming, and staff are available to answer questions. Inmates are not pressured into donating their organs, and if they choose to do so, a postcard is sent to their family notifying them of the decision.

The following section of this chapter discusses changes in federal crime policies that trickled down to affect the nation on local and state levels. A brief overview of several major pieces of legislation is provided, lending insight into the development of the get-tough stance toward crime and Arpaio's place in the movement.

NATIONWIDE SHIFT IN PENOLOGY: HARSHER IS BETTER

The last several decades have seen conservative crime policies in which get-tough sentencing reforms were implemented throughout the country and masses of people were incarcerated. The "War on Drugs" was in full swing and many of the federal crime initiatives focused on increasing penalties for drug law violators. There have been many examples of get-tough legislation, one of which was the Comprehensive Crime Control Act of 1984. This act resulted in changes in increased punitiveness in various areas of crime policies to include sentencing, forfeiture of assets associated with illegal activity, penalties for drug laws, and prosecution of certain juveniles as adults. For instance, the 1984 statute repealed the Youth Corrections Act, abolishing all special forms of treatment and release, and replaced indeterminate sentencing with determinate sentencing. Because Maryland passed a life-without-parole statute in 1987 representing the just-deserts stance taken by society, other federal initiatives further increased the powers of both federal and local law enforcement agencies in the quest to win the war on drugs. The point here is that both state and federal governments exhibited a commitment to reduce crime rates with increased sanctions.

Shortly after the passage of the Comprehensive Crime Control Act of 1984, the Anti-Drug Abuse Act of 1986 became law. This legislation enabled federal agencies to increase focus on the reduction of supply and demand, and moreover, many drug-related activities such as growing, manufacturing, and trafficking in drugs were criminalized. Under the Act, new crimes were identified, making it illegal to utilize juveniles in selling drugs, to sell drugs to pregnant women, to sell drugs near educational institutions, and to launder drug money. Increasingly punitive legislation continued into the 1990s.

During the presidency of Bill Clinton, the Violent Crime Control and Law Enforcement Act of 1994 authorized mandatory life imprisonment for persons convicted of two or more felonies, serious violent felonies, and serious drug offenses. Subsequent to passage of this act, the nation saw a multitude of new laws enacted in numerous states embracing this get-tough position on repeat offenders. For instance, life-without-parole statutes were passed in some states, Minnesota sentencing guidelines incorporated a grid for determining punishment of offenders based in part on prior criminal records, and California's governor Pete Wilson approved Assembly Bill 971 that contained three-strikes legislation. These three-strikes laws placed considerable limitations on discretion of judges and prosecutors, who before were less limited by indeterminate sentencing laws.

Subsequently, some scholars postulated that penal thinking and the ensuing policies had gone through an important model change to a "new penology" focusing on the management of aggregates instead of emphasis on the individual offender.[30] Criminologist David Shichor's study draws a correlation between three-strikes laws and the cultural model of fast-food restaurant management philosophy, "McDonaldization."[31] He states this philosophy is utilized in other sectors of society, such as the criminal justice system, whereby values of efficiency, consistency, and control by technology are significant factors in the operation of the criminal justice system. The system places less emphasis on individuals and more on the masses. Consequently, the three-strikes laws are not only indicative of a new penology, but also an increasing trend toward "penal harm."

The penal harm movement refers to harsh treatment of criminals evidenced in legislation and both institutional and community correctional policies. The three-strikes legislation, life-without-parole statutes, policy changes within the correctional institutions, and increases in probation and parole revocations are all presented as examples of contributing factors of the movement. Researchers in a variety of disciplines such as criminal justice, politics, and psychology, cited many policies such as elimination of television privileges, exercise equipment, hot meals, and access to grants for college, as well as reinstitution of chain gangs as evidence of the momentum of the penal harm movement. Arpaio early on had implemented programs and policies that seemingly fell into this category of penal harm, but the intentions behind these changes were not as evil as thought at first glance. Arpaio admitted openly his penal philosophy: hard work, discipline, and no frills. But at the same time, he pointed out the positive benefits of these changes for inmates: increased sense of responsibility, instillation of a work ethic, and improvements in physical and mental health of inmates.

Public opinion polls conducted in 1994 and 1995 indicated support for the penal harm movement, citing crime as the main problem in the United States, and touting overwhelming support for get-tough crime legislation. As a result many states, such as California, Georgia, Florida, and Washington followed, adopting three-strikes legislation supporting the punitive trend. Public support for Arpaio was and still is based on his get-tough stance and his commitment to treating inmates as inmates. Arpaio has consistently stated that jails should not be hotels.

With respect to this new legislation, California was the first state to implement a mandatory three-strikes law. In March 1994, Assembly Bill 971 was passed, and its most notable provision was a requirement that judges impose "an indeterminate sentence of a minimum of twenty-five years to life, or triple the normal sentence, whichever is greater, on offenders convicted of certain serious or violent felonies if they have two previous convictions for any felony."[32] Also, Assembly Bill 971 requires consecutive prison sentences for multiple-count convictions and limits good-time credits to 20 percent after the first strike. Slogans such as "do the crime, do the time" became popular, and under some of these new mandatory sentences, offenders were serving 85 percent of their sentences. The trend continued with other states enacting similar statutes.

The Sentence Reform Act of 1994 was passed "authorizing life imprisonment without possibility of parole, pardon, early release, leave, or any other measure designed to reduce the sentence for any person convicted of a second serious violent felony."[33] Thus, Georgia's law is the most restrictive, by containing the "two-strikes" provision, as opposed to the normal three strikes. Unlike other states, though, Georgia's law specifically pertains to violent felonies. Similarly, the state of Washington has strict and severe laws regarding "persistent offenders." Washington's law, for instance, stipulates that the governor is discouraged from pardoning offenders until they have reached a certain age and no longer pose a serious risk. Moreover, the governor of Washington must submit a report twice a year regarding "the persistent offenders he or she released during his or her term of office and that the reports continue to be made for as long as the offender lives or at least ten years after his or her release from prison."[34] Additional expressions of harsher punishments for offenders continued to materialize in sentencing.

Another manifestation of this just-deserts or determinate sentencing model can be seen via life-without-parole statutes. This model was prevalent in most states, especially the southern states. In these instances two models are prevalent: statutes designed to incapacitate career criminals and others pertaining to society's need for revenge on serious offenders. Cheatwood maintains that the American public has become increasingly dissatisfied with crime rates and, further, perceived judicial/correctional leniency has contributed to enactment of tougher sentences for criminal offenders.[35] The state of Florida passed several mandatory sentencing statutes in 1988 and 1989, making it difficult, if not impossible, for offenders to earn good time credit. Also in Florida, several highly publicized crimes that occurred in 1993 and the murder of a female police officer and the murders of several tourists in 1994 and early 1995 sparked the passing of the 1995 Crime Control Act, which increased punishments for all types of offenses including nonviolent ones. Evelyn Gort, a Miami police officer, was off duty when she was killed by Wilber Mitchell, a parolee who had served only two months and seventeen days of his one-year sentence. The "Officer Evelyn Gort and All Fallen Officers Career Criminal Act" was enacted during a special session of the legislature in May 1995. The adult population of offenders was not the only group to feel the effects of tougher sentences; juveniles as well were affected.

The juvenile justice system began a shift from rehabilitation toward punishment as juvenile crime rates increased. More and more juveniles were committing adult crimes, such as murder, rape, aggravated assault, and robbery. Critics of the juvenile system felt that the rehabilitative stance toward juveniles was hampering law enforcement goals of retribution and deterrence and called for a shift away from rehabilitation.[36] Many states, including Texas, modified their judicial waiver statutes by expanding the offenses eligible for judicial waiver. Also, the age at which a juvenile may be waived to adult court was lowered to permit the allocation of more severe sanctions. Florida enhanced punishments for juveniles after the murder of British tourist Gary Colley during a failed robbery attempt at a rest stop in rural north Florida in September 1993 in which four juveniles, including a thirteen-year-old, were arrested for the murder. Arpaio's jails hold about two hundred juveniles charged as adults; these juveniles are either awaiting trial or have been sentenced for serious felony or misdemeanor offenses. Arpaio believes their criminal behavior should not stand in the way of obtaining an education. If juvenile inmates are disruptive or have disciplinary problems while attending Hard Knocks High, they will not be kicked out; their education will just be delivered to them in a different way. They are not allowed to quit.

The harsher penalties for juveniles combined with get-tough legislation led to an increase in incarceration rates across the nation. According to the Bureau of Justice Statistics, in 1985 the incarceration rate for jails and prisons combined was 313 inmates per 100,000 residents. By 1996, this rate had almost doubled to 615 inmates per 100,000 residents. Mid-year in 2000, the nation's jails and prisons housed 1,931,859 inmates, a rate of 702 inmates per 100,000 residents. The incarceration rate continued to increase, and by mid-year 2005, 2,186,230 inmates were held in jails and prisons in the United States, with an imprisonment rate of 738 inmates per 100,000 residents. Maricopa County's jail population mirrored the increasing national trends, as did many local jail populations. In 1993, when Arpaio took office, the county jail system held 3,000 inmates and by 1996 held approximately 5,600. By the year 2000, the jail population had increased to around 7,000, and by year-end 2004 to approximately 9,148.[37] Arpaio wanted his officers to be able to arrest lawbreakers without fearing that not enough space was available in the county's jail system, so he made sure there was room to hold everyone arrested. New facilities were constructed, including Tent City Jail, to house the increasing number of law violators.

Taken together, various legislation enacted over the past thirty years has become increasingly punitive, as society and politicians have demanded harsher sentences for offenders, in turn increasing the number of individuals incarcerated. It is clear that treatment, prevention, and education regarding drug abuse was not a top priority during the 1980s and 1990s, yet the rehabilitative ideal was not completely dormant. In fact, some research during those decades revealed that citizens wanted offenders not only to be punished, but also rehabilitated.[38] Several reasons, ranging from the need to reduce prison crowding to cost-effectiveness, have been cited in the literature for increase in support of rehabilitative measures for offenders.

Although the Violent Crime Control and Law Enforcement Act of 1994 promised to put 100,000 more police officers on the streets, it also was the first bill in years to provide a substantial sum for treatment of inmates in both state and local correctional facilities. Some states such as Texas had already begun to fund community-based substance abuse treatment for probationers in need of rehabilitation. This carte blanche funding for community supervision and corrections departments across the state again revealed increasing support for rehabilitation of offenders. In addition to funding for community-based treatment, Texas legislators expanded correctional capacity by increasing its bed space by 90,000 between 1989 and 1995. Interestingly, of the 90,000 beds, 6,000 of those were assigned as treatment bed space for the large number of incarcerated substance abusers. It had become clear that drug abuse was a significant problem which needed to be addressed.

Since the war on drugs, research shows that a large percentage of offenders incarcerated have drug or alcohol problems. In 1997, a survey of inmates in state and federal correctional facilities indicated that 83 percent had a history of drug use, and about one in six reported committing their current offense to obtain money for drugs. A 2002 Bureau of Justice Statistics report indicates that in the year prior to incarceration, 68 percent of jail inmates reported symptoms that met substance abuse or dependence criteria.[39] Arpaio knew all too well the effects drugs could have on people and with the support of staff implemented a variety of substance abuse programs inside Maricopa County jails to address the staggering numbers of inmates with these issues.

Researchers began studying both the in-prison and community-based therapeutic community model treatment programs in hopes of positive outcomes. These studies have consistently shown that defendants who successfully complete the phases of a therapeutic community program have lower recidivism rates than those who have not undergone treatment.[40] In one such study, Hartmann found that of clients who received treatment, only 14 percent had been arrested or convicted during the follow-up period, while those in the control group had been arrested twice as many times as the experimental group. Another study found decreased rates of recidivism, including relapse for offenders who continued treatment after work release.[41] Arpaio's programs have similar success rates, as the ALPHA program boasts only a 14 percent recidivism rate of its graduates.

ARPAIO AND POPULAR CULTURE

Arpaio has attained the status of a crime-fighting icon, and rightly so. His achievement of this status can be explained by examining the influence of popular culture on the criminal justice arena and particular factors that have given rise to his status. Surette defines popular culture as "a common shared set of world knowledge that is pervasively distributed via the mass media."[42] Mass media outlets such as movies, television, radio, the Internet, and print are chock full of crime stories. Hollywood has produced countless crime dramas: *12 Angry Men, Along Came a Spider, Beverly Hills Cop, Dead Man Walking, The Godfather, Goodfellas, Pulp Fiction, Scarface, Silence of the Lambs, The Untouchables,* and *U.S. Marshals* to name a few. There are hundreds of crime-related television programs such as *America's Most Wanted, American Justice, Boston Legal, The Closer, Cops, CSI: Miami, Dog the Bounty Hunter, FBI Files, The First 48, Law and Order,* and *NYPD Blue,* and the list goes on. There is even a specific television station devoted solely to crime, *truTV* (formerly, *Court TV*). Every national and local news station airs at least one crime-related story almost every single day. The World Wide Web is host to millions of sites about crime and criminal justice. Information and news are able to travel at phenomenal speeds, so a large number of people read or hear about events almost instantaneously around the world. Because of the inundation of crime stories via the mass media, fascination with crime has become part of popular culture and has made Arpaio an icon of crime fighting.

There are many definitions of icon, but the most appropriate that comes to mind here is a definition from the art world: things or persons that are considered the most admirable or recognizable examples of something.[43] Perhaps because Arpaio has fought corruption in his forty-plus years as a law enforcement officer and stood up for what is right and ethical (including arresting "dirty cops") or perhaps because he dared to institute changes in the jails of Maricopa County that would no doubt spark criticism, has he achieved the status of an icon of crime fighting. He seems to be the most recognizable and admirable example of a law enforcement officer fighting crime in today's society.

Arpaio has actually achieved the status of crime-fighting icon based on numerous factors including controversial policies, innovative programs, and widespread media attention. In the early 1990s news of Arpaio's controversial changes in Maricopa County spread around the globe. He first garnered worldwide attention after the construction of the Tent City Jail in 1993. News reporters from as far away as the Netherlands came to Arizona to catch a glimpse of the tent compound. The implementation of chain gangs for men, women, and juveniles helped boost his popularity, as did the scrapping of amenities for inmates (no pornography, no tobacco, etc.) Then when he ran for reelection in 1996, Arpaio was the first Republican sheriff reelected in Maricopa County since 1919. His approval rating by citizens of the county consistently hovers around 65 percent despite negative press coverage, criticisms by civil rights organizations such as Amnesty International and the American Civil Liberties Union, and lawsuits. And he would not be a part of popular culture unless someone had tried to kill him, right? Well, Arpaio has had his life threatened numerous times; several people have even plotted to kill him, but were arrested. Despite the death threats he continues to carry out his job in the public eye.

Sheriff Arpaio has been featured in more than 2,000 national and international print sources and radio and television programs. He has been written about in such respected publications as *The New York Times*, *Time* magazine, *The Washington Post*, and the *Los Angeles Times*. In fact, he has been written about in almost every developed country in the world. He has guest-starred on television programs including *The Donahue Show*, *Politically Incorrect*, *Good Morning America*, and *The Today Show* and has been featured on other programs such as *20/20* and *60 Minutes*. In 2004 Arpaio was a guest on *Penn & Teller's Bullshit* show on cable television, which featured an episode about the war on the drugs and other guests such as a Harvard Medical School professor, the president of the National Organization for the Reform of Marijuana Laws, the editor of *High Times* magazine, and a former drug smuggler. In May 2007, Arpaio made national news when he offered Los Angeles County Sheriff's officials to transfer Hollywood party girl Paris Hilton to his jail to serve her DUI sentence. She would not get special treatment in Arizona; Arpaio said he would put her in Tent City Jail, and she could even volunteer to work on the chain gang. His request, however, was declined by Los Angeles County officials.

In addition to television appearances, Arpaio has dabbled in radio as well. In February 2007, he launched his own radio station called KJOE radio inside the county jails. Partnering with Tim and Willy of KNIX radio, KJOE radio is broadcast from the Fourth Avenue Jail four hours a day, five days a week. Arpaio said the radio station features educational programming, wholesome music, and live chat forums with local community leaders, business people, and health specialists.

Arpaio has met important political figures such as President George W. Bush, Senator Bob Dole, Utah governor and 2008 presidential candidate Mitt Romney, Senator Phil Gramm of Texas, and Senator John McCain. He has also met celebrities such as John Walsh, host of *America's Most Wanted*. Walsh's son, Adam, was abducted from a mall in Florida in 1981 and subsequently murdered. Walsh became a high-profile victim's advocate, went on to host *America's Most Wanted*, and was instrumental in the formation of the National Center for Missing and Exploited Children. Walsh and *America's Most Wanted* worked on several local stories, and Arpaio's tough stance toward crime naturally drew their attention. Arpaio and Walsh became friends early in Arpaio's career, and they have supported each other throughout the years. Walsh conducted the swearing-in ceremony after the last election, and recently Arpaio launched the use of facial recognition technology in a local elementary school in June 2007 in support of the efforts of many, including Walsh, with missing children. The technology is designed to identify sexual predators who attempt to enter schools and to compare children's faces to those in the database of the National Center for Missing and Exploited Children.

Early in 2007, Arpaio met Paula Abdul, singer, choreographer, and celebrity judge on *American Idol*. Arpaio launched his own version of the popular television program, calling his *Inmate Idle* in March 2007. Inmates cast their votes for their favorites and the six final contestants showcased their singing talents in front a panel of celebrity judges, including Arpaio, rock and roll singer Alice Cooper, and an Elvis impersonator. Arpaio said this program helped to make use of inmates' idle time, hence the name of the program. He also stated that the contest helped to build inmates' self-esteem and promote positive interactions among inmates and did not cost the taxpayers anything.

Ty Pennington, host of ABC's *Extreme Makeover: Home Edition* and former carpenter on TLC's popular reality show *Trading Spaces,* paid a visit to Arizona and met the sheriff while in town. The television show needed manpower to help with the home for a young cancer survivor, and Arpaio called on his posse to help with the task. Additionally, Arpaio has met John W. Teets, former owner of the Dial Corporation; Steve Elman, former owner of the Phoenix Coyotes minor league hockey team; and local celebrity chef Eddie Matney.

Despite the negative publicity and criticisms, Arpaio is still the sheriff of Maricopa County. He has been in office since 1993 and has instituted many changes and faced many challenges. He is seventy-five years old and does not have plans to retire anytime soon. He credits much of his success to the steadfast support of his wife Ava, to whom he has been married for fifty years. Despite the long work hours, the dangers of the job, and the constant moving around the country, she has stood by his side. Because he does not have any hobbies, he works twelve to fourteen hours a day. Surprisingly though, he admits to being a fan of romantic movies, so he goes to the theater with his wife. They go to the mall together and she attends many work-related functions with him; they go everywhere together. The position as sheriff of Maricopa County is Arpaio's favorite position of all the positions he's held throughout his career. He truly loves being a "beat cop," and Maricopa County is his beat. He takes pride in his position and would not be doing it if he could not do it his way. In fact, his cell phone ring tone is Elvis' rendition of "My Way."

He is tough; he is passionate about his job, and even though he may be viewed as a politician, he does not like politicians. He said he is not going to let any politician tell him what to do because he serves the people. Consider these voter statistics: In 1992, during the primary election for the sheriff's race, Arpaio won 52 percent (77,000 votes) of the vote while his opponent had 47 percent. In the general election that same year Arpaio received 428,575 votes while his opponent received 318,774 votes. In 1996 Arpaio ran for sheriff unopposed and received 651,073 votes; he received more votes statewide than any other candidate except President Clinton who garnered 653,288 votes. In 2000, Arpaio received 74 percent of the votes in the primary and 66 percent of the votes in the general election, defeating his opponent by a landslide. He won both the primary and general elections in 2004 with 56 percent. As long as people continue to vote for him, he will continue to implement programs to improve Maricopa County.

NOTES

1. Robert Martinson, "What Works: Questions and Answers About Prison Reform," *The Public Interest* 22 (1974).

2. Joe Arpaio (Sheriff of Maricopa County, Arizona), interview by Kelli D. Stevens, February 23, 2007, Phoenix, AZ (hereafter cited as Arpaio Interview).

3. Ibid.

4. Ibid.

5. Sheriff Joe Arpaio and Len Sherman, *America's Toughest Sheriff: How to Win the War Against Crime* (Arlington, TX: Summit Publishing Group, 1996), 168 (hereafter cited as *America's Toughest Sheriff*).

6. Arpaio Interview.

7. *America's Toughest Sheriff*, 171.

8. Arpaio Interview.

9. *America's Toughest Sheriff*, 186.

10. Ibid, 30.

11. Maricopa County Sheriff's Office, *Sheriff Joe Arpaio*, Official Biography, (Phoenix, 2006).

12. *America's Toughest Sheriff*, 47.

13. *America's Toughest Sheriff*, 107.

14. Maricopa County Sheriff's Office, *The Posse Battles an Age-Old Problem: Prostitution* (Phoenix, [1996?]).

15. Maricopa County Sheriff's Office, *A Return to Chain Gangs* (Phoenix, Arizona [1996?]).

16. Ibid.

17. Ibid.

18. Stacey Opland, *Pink Underwear Reveal Prison Escapee* (Coeur d'Alene, ID: The Backup Training Corporation, 2000), http://www.thebackup.com/archives_newsdetail.asp?id=753/.

19. Maricopa County Sheriff's Office, *Inmate Programs: Alpha Programs* (Phoenix, 2005), http://www.mcso.org/index.php?a=GetModule&mn=Inmate_Programs&page=Alpha/.

20. Maricopa County Sheriff's Office, *Adult Inmate Programs* (Phoenix, 2005), http://www.mcso.org/index.php?a=GetModule&mn=Inmate_Programs&page=Adult/.

21. Arpaio.com: Recall Arpaio in 2005!, "Top Ten Reasons to RECALL Joe Arpaio," (2004), http://www.arpaio.com/index.htm/.

22. Mothers Against Arpaio official Web site, http://www.mothersagainstarpaio.com/.

23. Linda Bentley, "Sheriff Joe Featured in 'Torture: America's Brutal Prisons'," *Sonoran News*, March 2, 2005, http://www.november.org/stayinfo/breaking3/SheriffJoeBBC.html/.

24. Amnesty International Online Library, *Ill Treatment of Inmates in Maricopa County Jail, Arizona*, (1997), AMR 51/051/1997, http://web.amnesty.org/library/index/engAMR510511997?open&of=eng-2am/.

25. U.S. Department of Justice, "Jails in Maricopa County, Arizona to take steps to reduce excessive force and use of improper restraints under justice department agreement," news release, October 31, 1997, http://news.bbc.co.uk/1/hi/default.stm/.

26. U.S. Department of Justice, "CRIPA Activities in FY 2000," http://www.usdoj.gov/crt/split/documents/cripa00.htm/.

27. *Scott v. Harris*, 550 U.S. (2007).

28. *Nagy v. FMC Butner*, No. 03-6736, 2004 U.S. App. Lexis 15042 (4th Cir.). 2004 JB Sep, *Sims v. Scopelitis*, No. 50A03-0211-CV-399, 797 N.E.2d 348 (Ind. App. 2003).

29. Christopher J. Mumola, "Suicide and Homicide in State Prisons and Local Jails," (August, 2005 NCJ 210036), U.S. Department of Justice, Office of Justice Programs, 1.

30. David Shichor, "Three Strikes as Public Policy: The Convergence of the New Penology and the McDonaldization of Punishment," *Crime & Delinquency* 43(4)

(1997): 470–92; Craig Haney and Philip Zimbardo, "The Past and Future of U.S. Prison Policy: Twenty-five Years after the Stanford Prison Experiment," *American Psychologist* 53(7) (1998): 709–27.

31. David Shichor, *Crime & Delinquency* 470–92.

32. Peter J. Benekos and Alida V. Merlo, "Three Strikes and You're Out!: The Political Sentencing Game," *Federal Probation* 59(1) (1995): 5.

33. Ibid.

34. Ibid.

35. Derral Cheatwood, "The Life-without-Parole Sanction: Its Current Status and a Research Agenda," *Crime & Delinquency* 34(1) (1998): 43.

36. Eric J. Fritsch, Tory J. Caeti, and C. Hemmens, "Spare the Needle But Not the Punishment: The Incarceration of Waived Youth in Texas Prisons," *Crime & Delinquency* 42(4) (1996), 593–609.

37. Darrell K. Gilliard and Allen J. Beck, "Prison and Jail Inmates at Midyear 1996," U.S. Department of Justice Bureau of Justice Statistics bulletin, January, 1997, NCJ 162843, 1; Allen J. Beck and Jennifer C. Karberg, "Prison and Jail Inmates at Midyear 2000," U.S. Department of Justice Bureau of Justice Statistics bulletin, March, 2001, NCJ 185989, 1; Paige M. Harrison and Allen J. Beck, "Prison and Jail Inmates at Midyear 2005," U.S. Department of Justice Bureau of Justice Statistics bulletin, May, 2006, NCJ 213133, 1; Paige M. Harrison and Allen J. Beck, "Prison and Jail Inmates at Yearend 2004," U.S. Department of Justice Bureau of Justice Statistics bulletin, April, 2005, NCJ 208801, 10.

38. Jody L. Sundt, Francis T. Cullen, Brandon K. Applegate, and Michael G. Turner, "The Tenacity of the Rehabilitative Ideal Revisted: Have Attitudes Toward Offender Treatment Changed?" *Criminal Justice & Behavior* 25(4) (1998): 426–42.

39. James D. Griffith, Matthew L. Hiller, Kevin Knight, and Donald D. Simpson, "A Cost-Effective Analysis of In-Prison Therapeutic Community Treatment and Risk Classification," *Prison Journal* 79(3) (1999): 352; Christopher J. Mumola, "Substance Abuse and Treatment, State and Federal Prisoners, (1997) U.S. Department of Justice Bureau of Justice Statistics bulletin, January, 1999, NCJ 172871, 1; Jennifer C. Karberg and Doris J. James, "Substance Dependence, Abuse, and Treatment of Jail Inmates, 2002," U.S. Department of Justice Bureau of Justice Statistics bulletin, July, 2005, NCJ 209588, 1.

40. William D. Bales, Shann Van Slyke, and Thomas G. Bloomberg, "Substance abuse treatment in prison and community reentry: Breaking the Cycle of Drugs, Crime, Incarceration, and Recidivism?" *Georgetown Journal on Poverty Law and Policy* 13(2) (2006): 1; Matthew L. Hiller, Kevin Knight, and D. Dwayne Simpson, "Recidivism following Mandated Residential Substance Abuse Treatment for Felony Probationers," *Prison Journal* 86(2) (2006): 230; David J. Hartmann, James L. Wolk, Scott Johnston, and Corey J. Colyer, "Recidivism and Substance Abuse Outcomes in a Prison-based Therapeutic Community," *Federal Probation* 61(4) (1997): 18–25.

41. Hartmann, Recidivism and Substance Abuse Outcomes, 25; Steven S. Martin, Clifford A. Butzin, Christine A. Saum, and James A. Inciardi, "Three-year Outcomes of Therapeutic Community Treatment for Drug-involved Offenders in Delaware: From Prison to Work Release to Aftercare," *Prison Journal* 79(3) (1999): 294.

42. R. Surette, *Media, Crime and Criminal Justice: Images and realities* (Pacific Grove, CA: Brooks/Cole Publishing Company, 1992).

43. Art & Framing Designs, http://www.artandframingdesigns.com/resources_art.html/.

FURTHER READING

Arpaio.com: Recall Arpaio in 2005!, Top Ten Reasons to RECALL Joe Arpaio. 2004. http://www.arpaio.com/index.htm/.

Arpaio, Joe, and Len Sherman. 1996. *America's Toughest Sheriff: How to Win the War Against Crime*. Arlington, TX: Summit Publishing Group.

Art & Framing Designs. http://www.artandframingdesigns.com/resources_art.html/.

Bales, William D., Shann Van Slyke, and Thomas G. Bloomberg. 2006. Substance abuse treatment in prison and community reentry: Breaking the cycle of drugs, crime, incarceration, and recidivism? *Georgetown Journal on Poverty Law and Policy* 13(2): 1.

Beck, Allen J., and Jennifer C. Karberg. 2001. Prison and Jail Inmates at Midyear 2000. U.S. Department of Justice Bureau of Justice Statistics Bulletin March, NCJ 185989, 1.

Benekos, Peter J., and Alida V. Merlo. 1995. Three strikes and you're out!: The political sentencing game. *Federal Probation* 59(1): 5.

Cheatwood, Derral. 1998. The life-without-parole sanction: Its current status and a research agenda. *Crime & Delinquency* 34(1): 43.

Fritsch, Eric J., Tory J. Caeti, and C. Hemmens. 1996. Spare the needle but not the punishment: The incarceration of waived youth in Texas prisons. *Crime & Delinquency* 42(4), 593–609.

Gilliard, Darrell K., and Allen J. Beck, 1997. Prison and Jail Inmates at Midyear 1996. U.S. Department of Justice Bureau of Justice Statistics Bulletin, January, NCJ 162843, 1.

Griffith, James D., Matthew L. Hiller, Kevin Knight, and Donald D. Simpson. 1999. A cost-effective analysis of in-prison therapeutic community treatment and risk classification. *Prison Journal* 79(3): 352.

Haney, Craig, and Philip Zimbardo. 1998. The past and future of U.S. prison policy: Twenty-five years after the Stanford Prison Experiment. *American Psychologist* 53(7): 709–727.

Harrison, Paige M., and Allen J. Beck. 2005. Prison and Jail Inmates at Yearend 2004. U.S. Department of Justice Bureau of Justice Statistics Bulletin, April, NCJ 208801, 10.

Harrison, Paige M., and Allen J. Beck. 2006. Prison and Jail Inmates at Midyear 2005. U.S. Department of Justice Bureau of Justice Statistics Bulletin, May, NCJ 213133, 1.

Hartmann, David J., James L. Wolk, Scott Johnston, and Corey J. Colyer. 1997. Recidivism and substance abuse outcomes in a prison-based therapeutic community. *Federal Probation* 61(4): 18–25.

Hiller, Matthew L., Kevin Knight, and D. Dwayne Simpson. 2006. Recidivism following mandated residential substance abuse treatment for felony probationers. *Prison Journal* 86(2): 230.

Karberg, Jennifer C., and Doris J. James. 2005. Substance dependence, abuse, and treatment of jail inmates, 2002. U.S. Department of Justice Bureau of Justice Statistics Bulletin, July, NCJ 209588, 1.

Maricopa County Sheriff's Office. 1996. *The Posse Battles an Age-Old Problem: Prostitution.* Phoenix, Arizona.

Maricopa County Sheriff's Office. 1996. *A Return to Chain Gangs.* Phoenix, Arizona.

Maricopa County Sheriff's Office. 2005. *Adult Inmate Programs.* Phoenix, Arizona. http://www.mcso.org/index.php?a=GetModule&mn=Inmate_Programs&page=Adult/.

Maricopa County Sheriff's Office. *Inmate Programs: Alpha Programs.* Phoenix, Arizona. http://www.mcso.org/index.php?a=GetModule&mn=Inmate_Programs&page=Alpha/.

Martin, Steven S., Clifford A. Butzin, Christine A. Saum, and James A. Inciardi. 1999. Three-year outcomes of therapeutic community treatment for drug-involved offenders in Delaware: From prison to work release to aftercare. *Prison Journal* 79(3): 294.

Martinson, Robert. 1974. What Works: Questions and Answers About Prison Reform. *The Public Interest* 22.

Mumola, Christopher J. 2005. Suicide and Homicide in State Prisons and Local Jails. (August, 2005 NCJ 210036), U.S. Department of Justice, Office of Justice Programs, 1.

Mumola, Christopher J. Substance Abuse and Treatment, State and Federal Prisoners. 1997. U.S. Department of Justice Bureau of Justice Statistics Bulletin, January, 1999, NCJ 172871, 1.

Opland, Stacey. 2000. *Pink Underwear Reveal Prison Escapee.* Coeur d'Alene, IH: The Backup Training Corporation. http://www.thebackup.com/archives_news detail.asp?id=753/.

Shichor, David. 1997. Three strikes as public policy: The convergence of the new penology and the McDonaldization of punishment. *Crime & Delinquency* 43(4): 470–492.

Sundt, Jody L., Francis T. Cullen, Brandon K. Applegate, and Michael G. Turner. 1998. The tenacity of the rehabilitative ideal revisited: Have attitudes toward offender treatment changed? *Criminal Justice & Behavior* 25(4): 426–442.

Surette, R. 1992. *Media, Crime and Criminal Justice: Images and Realities.* Pacific Grove, CA: Brooks/Cole Publishing Company.

Mark Fuhrman

Scott H. Belshaw

In the field of criminal justice there have been a lot of people who have made many contributions, both good and bad. For former Los Angeles Police detective Mark Fuhrman, his contributions to the field have been legendary. In 1995 Mark Fuhrman served as a state's witness in the trial of former pro football player, O. J. Simpson. Mark Fuhrman was a detective assigned to the homicide division investigating a murder that took place in the upscale neighborhood of Brentwood located just inside Los Angeles, California. This detective was called to the stand to testify about the crime scene and the evidence that he found. However, this trial began to take a turn for the worse. This police detective began to be the target of the defense. Mark Furhman's past began to catch up with him. When he made racist comments into an audio recorder, he never thought that they would come back to haunt him in a court of law. This highly decorated police officer then became the butt of every joke about racists in the United States. When detective Fuhrman was placed on the stand to testify regarding the Simpson and Goldman murders, he thought that it was going to be about his crime scene investigation techniques or how well he preserved any evidence that was obtained while investigating the murders. One of the most famous criminal defense attorneys in the country, F. Lee Bailey, began to ask detective Fuhrman questions regarding his role as the lead homicide detective. Bailey then began to ask him questions regarding his views toward African Americans and how he felt about them. Detective Fuhrman just assumed the defense attorney was fishing for something—anything that would discredit him. Fuhrman was asked if he had ever used any racist slang or words such as the "n-word" in describing African Americans. Mark Fuhrman adamantly stated "no."

Most professors of law will state that a first-year law student is taught while cross examining a witness not to ask a question to which you do not know the answer or cannot prove the answer. Detective Fuhrman was dealing with a defense attorney with impeccable credentials and experience. Mark Fuhrman underestimated F. Lee Bailey. After Detective Fuhrman adamantly denied using racial slurs toward minorities, the defense team produced tapes of Fuhrman using numerous racial slurs and demeaning remarks toward people of different races and backgrounds, particularly African Americans. The defense team was also successful at convincing the jury that Fuhrman planted the infamous bloody glove in the case. This put into serious question his credibility and motives. The defense exploited this doubt and was able to convince a jury to find O. J. Simpson not guilty of the murder of his ex-wife and Ronald Goldman. Fuhrman was subsequently charged with perjury and pled guilty, becoming a probationer. He was now on the other side of the fence within the criminal justice system. He was ordered to retire from the police department and moved to Idaho to start a new life for himself. Throughout Mark Fuhrman's life he will be known as the "racist cop from the O. J. Simpson trial."

Mark Fuhrman Plea Agreement for Perjury Committed during O. J. Simpson Trial: Dated October 2, 1996

Superior Court of the State of California, County of Los Angeles, Central District

The People of the State of California, Plaintiff, v. Mark Fuhrman, Defendant

Original Charge: Count I: Violation of Penal Code section 118 (a felony)
Convicted Of: One Count, Count I of Information, of Penal Code sec. 118
Date of Offense: On or about March 15, 1995.
Guilty by: Plea of nolo contendre.
Date: 10/2/96
Judge: Ouderkirk
Actual Time In Custody: 0 days 4019 P.C. Time: 0 days
No. BA 109275

Personal History in Lieu of Probation Report
Hearing: 10/2/96 Time: 9:00 Dept.: 109
Bail: O.R.
Negotiated Plea: People v. West plea: Defendant plead no contest with an understanding:

1. no jail time;
2. three years probation;
3. probation supervision in defendant's current state of residence;
4. the minimum restitution fine;
5. the single term of probation that defendant violate no laws; and
6. entry of a plea of nolo contendre.

Defendant has entered a waiver pursuant to People v. Harvey.
Co-Defendants: None
Attorney: Darryl Mounger

Personal History
Legal Name: Mark Fuhrman A.K.A.: None
Address: [REDACTED]
Telephone:
Age: 44 Date of Birth: February 5, 1952
Birthplace: Tacoma, Washington
Race/Ethnicity: White
Citizenship: United States of America

(continued)

Date Arrived in L.A. County: 1975
Date Arrived in State: 1970
Sex: M Height: 6′ 2″ Weight: 205 Hair: Brown Eyes: Brown
Driver's License No.: [REDACTED]
State of Issuance: [REDACTED]
Social Security No.: [REDACTED]
Education: High school and approximately 2 years college
Military Service: U. S. Marine Corps: 1970–1975
Type of Discharge: Honorable
Health/Handicaps: None known
Alcohol/Drug Use: No drugs, non-abusive occasional alcohol consumption
Father's Name: [REDACTED]
Address: [REDACTED]
Mother's Name: [REDACTED]
No. of Brothers: [REDACTED]; No. of Sisters: [REDACTED]
Ages: [REDACTED]
Present Spouse: [REDACTED]
Address: Same
Former spouse(s): [REDACTED]
Addresses: Unknown
Defendant's Children
Name . . . . Age . . . . Custody . . . . Supported by [REDACTED]

Employment Record
From . . . To: 1975 . . . 1995
Employer: Los Angeles Police Department
Type of Work: Law Enforcement
Salary [REDACTED] 1995

Criminal History
Present Requesting Agency: California Department of Justice
Date: 10/2/96 Surrendered
BI No.: . . .; CII No.: . . .; FBI No: . . .
No Criminal Record

Circumstance of the Offense
Defendant was one of the two detectives originally assigned to investigate the murder of Nicole Brown Simpson and Ronald Goldman. He arrived at the crime scene located on Bundy Drive in Brentwood in the early morning hours of June 12, 1994. Upon arrival, Defendant began his investigation.

Within an hour of his arrival, defendant was notified two more senior detectives had been assigned responsibility for the case.

When the two senior detectives arrived, they requested defendant accompany them to the house of the deceased woman's husband. At this second location, Rockingham Drive, defendant made several evidentiary discoveries which eventually led to the arrest of O. J. Simpson, the former husband of the deceased woman.

In July 1994, defendant appeared as a witness for the prosecution in the preliminary hearing of the homicide case against Simpson.

Defendant was called as a prosecution witness in the homicide trial of *People v. Simpson* (Los Angeles Superior Court No. BA 097211) in March 1995. Defendant was cross-examined on March 14 and 15, 1995. On March 15, 1995, defendant was asked the following questions by the cross-examiner and gave the following answers:

Q. "I will rephrase it. I want you to assume that perhaps at sometime since 1985 or 6, you addressed a member of the African American race as a nigger. Is it possible that you have forgotten that act on your part?"

A. "No, it is not possible."

Q. "Are you therefore saying that you have not used that word in the past ten years, Detective Fuhrman?"

A. "Yes, that is what I'm saying."

Q. "And you say under oath that you have not addressed any black person as a nigger or spoken about black people as niggers in the past ten years, Detective Fuhrman."

A. "That's what I'm saying, sir."

Q. "So that anyone who comes to this court and quotes you as using that word in dealing with African Americans would be a liar, would they not, Detective Fuhrman?"

A. "Yes, they would."

Q. "All of them, correct."

A. "All of them."

Source: People v. Simpson, Vol. 107, p. 18899.

On September 5, 1995, Laura Hart McKinney testified. In her testimony she laid the foundation for two tape-recorded excerpts which, in Defendant's own statements as recorded, impeached Defendant's denial of any use of the racial epithet during the ten-year period. She also testified that Defendant had used the epithet in nonrecorded conversations during the ten-year time period.

Three other witnesses, Kathleen Bell, Natalie Singer, and Roderick Hodge, each testified to instances of Defendant's use of the racial epithet within the ten-year period.

On September 6, 1995, Defendant was recalled to the witness stand as a defense witness. Out of the presence of the trial jury, Defendant asserted his constitutional right not to incriminate himself.

Defendant's Statement

Through his attorney, Defendant has stated he is entering a *People v. West* plea because he believes it is in his best interest to do so. Defendant deeply regrets the effect his testimony has had on the general public, the Los Angeles Police Department and its employees, and his family.

Sentencing Considerations

Violation of Penal Code section 118 is a felony punishable by a term of two, three, or four years in prison. A person convicted of the offense is eligible for probation and may be supervised out of state pursuant to the interstate compact.

Criteria Affecting Probation [Rule of Court 414]

(a) Crime-related facts:

(1) Seriousness as compared to other instances of the same crime.

While perjury is always a serious offense, it is rare that a witness who has given testimony is prosecuted for that perjury. When there is prosecution, the usual case involves a situation in which the witness has given false testimony about an event related to the crime or provided a false alibi.

Here there is no evidence that defendant gave any false testimony about his investigative efforts. The false testimony related to personal use of a racial epithet during a time period that pre-dated the criminal investigation. An argument can be made that this type of perjury is less serious than giving false testimony about the investigation.

(a)(2) No weapon was involved.

(a)(3) No individual victim was involved.

(a)(4) No injury was inflicted on any person.

(a)(5) There was no individual who suffered monetary loss.

(a)(6) Defendant was an active participant in the crime.

(a)(7) There are unique circumstances in the commission of the offense.

(a)(8) No criminal sophistication was demonstrated.

(a)(9) The Defendant did take advantage of a position of trust and confidence in the commission of the offense.

(b) Defendant-related facts

(b)(1) No prior criminal record.

(b)(2) Not applicable because defendant has never before been placed on parole or probation.

(b)(3) Defendant is willing to comply with the terms and conditions of probation.

(b)(4) Defendant is able to comply with the terms of probation.

(b)(5) Imprisonment would create financial hardship on the Defendant's dependents. Because of his background as a police officer Defendant would be at risk in prison. There is no evidence that Defendant needs to be incarcerated to deter him from future similar criminal conduct.

(b)(6) Defendant's primary adult employment was as a peace officer. One result of this conviction is Defendant is precluded from ever again being a peace officer in California. (Government Code, Section 1029.) The high profile that resulted from the events surrounding the crime as well as the news focus that the conviction will create will make it difficult for Defendant to find employment at any professional level.

(b)(7) The remarks of defendant as reported by his counsel indicate remorse.

(b)(8) Defendant presents no danger to others.

It would appear that defendant is an appropriate candidate for probation.

Circumstances in Aggravation [Rule of Court 421]
The factors which appear to be circumstances in aggravation are:
Rule 421(a)(6): Defendant's perjury illegally interfered with the judicial process.
Rule 421 (a)(11): Defendant took advantage of a position of trust.

Circumstances in Mitigation [Rule of Court 423]
The factors which appear to be circumstances in mitigation are:
Rule 423(a)(6): There was no physical harm to any persons or property.
Rule 423 (b)(1): The Defendant has no prior criminal record.
Rule 423(b)(3): The Defendant has voluntarily acknowledged wrongdoing at an early stage of the criminal process.

Submitted by: John A. Gordnier
Sr. Assistant Attorney General, Counsel For The People
/s/ John A. Gordnier
John A. Gordnier

Darryl Mounger
Counsel for Defendant
/s/Darryl Mounger
Darryl Mounger

(continued)

The within and foregoing history in lieu of probation report has been read and considered by me this 2nd day of October, 1996.
/s/John W. Ouderkirk
John W. Ouderkirk
Judge of the Superior Court

Source: http://www.lectlaw.com/files/case63.htm/

After this infamous trial everyone thought that Mark Fuhrman would disappear from the public light. After a few years had passed, however, Mark Fuhrman wanted to put his investigative skills to good use. He still had the training and knowledge of a homicide cop. He decided to put down all he had experienced in the O. J. Simpson case into a book titled *Murder in Brentwood*. In the wake of the nation's interest in the JonBenet Ramsey case, Fuhrman was later approached by distinguished crime author Dominick Dunne to look into a murder of a young teen some thirty years before. Not too sure if he wanted to get back into the public eye, he reluctantly accepted the assignment to write a book about the murder of Martha Moxley, a teenager who lived in the upscale neighborhood of Greenwich, Connecticut. Hopefully this book would be redemption for the wrongs that he had done in the past. The book garnered national attention and led to the eventual arrest and charge of Fuhrman's named prime suspect for the murder. After the success of *Murder in Greenwich: Who Killed Martha Moxley?* Mark Fuhrman found himself examining other unsolved cases, utilizing his detective skills and his newfound writing ones. Since the O. J. Simpson trial, Mark Fuhrman has authored four books on various cases with a unique analysis. In his latest book, *Death and Justice*, Fuhrman examines the Oklahoma death penalty system and comes to a remarkable transformation. He begins to change his view of the death penalty in the United States. In this book he notices the flaws of discretion within the Oklahoma Court and Corrections systems. He uncovers corruption within the District Attorney's office and policing agencies. He states that, as a police officer, he always believed in the death penalty and believes that we do not use it enough. However in *Death and Justice* he makes a 180-degree turn on this stance. He states that the death penalty is racist and corrupted and needs serious reform. He even goes to suggest a moratorium on all death penalty cases and has become a supporter of abolishing the death penalty.

From the trials and tribulations of the O. J. Simpson case to his reexamination of unsolved cases that eventually produced convictions and to his transformation from death penalty supporter to abolitionism advocate, Mark Fuhrman has become a person in search of redemption from his past problems. Is the public still willing, however, to give this man a second chance?

This chapter gives a historical background of this infamous icon of criminal justice. It will also describe Mark Fuhrman's role in the O. J. Simpson case, which catalyzed his professional demise, and his reinvestigation of the Martha Moxley murder, which placed Fuhrman tentatively on the path toward professional redemption. It will also address his involvement with the capital punishment system in Oklahoma, which completely reversed his view about the death penalty.

HISTORICAL BACKGROUND

Mark Fuhrman was born February 5, 1952, in Eatonville, Washington. His parents were Ralph, a truck driver, and Billie. Mark and his younger brother were descended from a German immigrant family. In 1970, at the age of eighteen, Fuhrman enlisted in the U.S. Marine Corps. After rising through the ranks to that of sergeant, Fuhrman was honorably discharged in 1975. Later that year he joined the Los Angeles Police Department (LAPD) as a police officer. Fuhrman worked his way up from a "beat cop" to the role of detective and served on the force for twenty years. By 1980, Fuhrman had been married and divorced twice, before marrying Caroline Lody, the wife who saw him through most of the LAPD years and the O. J. Simpson trial. They had two children, a daughter and a son. Fuhrman earned more than fifty-five commendations in the line of duty before retiring, an act that is itself shrouded in controversy, much like the rest of Fuhrman's career, both past and present. Fuhrman, now divorced, lives in Idaho, where he moved, and is an avid outdoorsman. Rumors abound that the area of Idaho where Fuhrman moved his family is populated by white supremacist separatists, further casting suspicion on his status as a racist in the eyes of some.

Mark Fuhrman spent many months in the spotlight of the public fury surrounding the murder trial of O. J. Simpson. The detective became one of the trial's most easily recognized players when the criminal trial's prosecution used evidence that he collected as a key factor in their case. The evidence included blood drops on Simpson's car and outside his guest house as well as the "bloody glove" that he discovered at Simpson's estate. The contribution that this evidence made to their case eventually was outweighed by the focus of the defense on the character of Detective Fuhrman. Specifically, they implied that he may have been the lynchpin in the police frame-up of Mr. Simpson by having planted evidence like the bloody glove. The defense team made claims that Fuhrman had racially motivated intentions by bringing to light statements that he had made previously in which he used racial slurs. Mr. Fuhrman had denied using such terms on the stand in front of the jury, but was proven incorrect when audio evidence was presented in court. In this evidence, Fuhrman was heard to use racial slurs such as the infamous "n-word."

THE SIMPSON-GOLDMAN MURDERS: THE DRAMA BEGINS

Late on a Sunday night, a dog barked relentlessly. Neighbors first noticed the dog, a white Akita, at approximately 10:15 P.M. By 11:00 P.M., a neighbor walking his own dog encountered the obviously distressed pooch pacing back and forth on the sidewalk. The Akita followed him home, and when the neighbor attended to the poor animal, he noticed that the dog's underbelly and paws were covered with a sticky red substance that could only be blood. Other neighbors intended to care for the dog overnight, but the Akita was so restless, they tried to walk the dog in an attempt to calm it down. The dog steered the pair directly to 875 Bundy, where it stopped and gazed into the blackness at the side of the condominium. The neighbors carefully peered in the direction where the dog was looking and thought they could make out a body lying at the foot of the steps. The couple immediately contacted police, and a story that would hold a nation spellbound as it unraveled and divide a country with its twists and turns was set in motion.

THE CASE OF A LIFETIME

In the wee hours of June 13, 1994, LAPD Detective Mark Fuhrman received the assignment that would forever change the course of his life and people's views of race and crime in the United States. He, along with his partner Brad Roberts, was called to investigate a double murder at a condominium located at 875 Bundy. Little did he know that the investigation of two Brentwood killings would lead him to the home of a former professional football superstar and American icon before sunrise.

Fuhrman and his supervisor, Ron Phillips, arrived at the residence at 2:10 A.M. The two conducted a visual inspection of the crime scene, "eyeballing" it, without getting too close to the two bodies or their immediate surroundings. Roberts arrived during this time, making him the eighteenth police officer to sign in at the scene of the crime. Fuhrman dug out his notepad and began making notes of the things he saw—a bloody fingerprint on the rear gate; what he thought was a ski mask near the male victim; a blood trail that led from the back of the property down an adjacent alley, stopping abruptly; a bloodstained left-hand leather glove lying inches from Nicole Brown Simpson's body, underneath a plant. Fuhrman's keen attention to detail would later come to haunt him during the trial.

Not long after Roberts' arrival, approximately ten to fifteen minutes, Phillips was informed that the investigation of the case would be conducted by Homicide Special Section of the Robbery/Homicide Division of the

LAPD, which was considered to be the foremost murder investigation team in the Los Angeles area. Fuhrman and Roberts would remain at the scene but were no longer to lead the investigation. Fuhrman wrote more details in his notebook in anticipation of being asked about them later. According to Fuhrman, when he was interviewed about his involvement with the investigation, he was never asked about many of the details he documented.

Vannatter and Phillips walked the crime scene without disturbing the decedents, which could only be done by the investigators from the county coroner's office. The officers would not be able to determine the cause of death of the victims until they arrived. Nicole Brown Simpson and her as-yet-unidentified male companion lay in pools of blood outside Nicole's home, where her two children were sleeping upstairs, oblivious to the commotion. As detectives Fuhrman, Lange, Phillips, and Vannatter discussed their next moves, they received word that the operations chief for the LAPD West Bureau, Commander Keith Bushey, wanted the four to contact O. J. Simpson personally to make arrangements for the care of his children. Fuhrman knew the location of Simpson's home, having responded to a call at the address in 1985 while he was a patrolman. At that time, Nicole called police because Simpson reportedly had attacked her car with a baseball bat, causing body damage in a fit of anger against his then-wife.

At 5:00 A.M., Fuhrman and the other investigators went to the home of Nicole's former husband, former National Football League superstar Orenthal James "O.J." Simpson. They drove in two cars, for less than five minutes, to the gated estate on Rockingham Drive. Simpson's vehicle, a white Ford Bronco, was parked outside the gates on the narrow street. Trying the buzzer next to the gates, the detectives were unable to wake anyone inside the home. Fuhrman wandered near the edge of the property, running his flashlight's beam over the Bronco. Packages inside the Bronco were clearly marked "Orenthal Products," but the detectives ran a check on the license plate through the radio to be sure the vehicle was indeed Simpson's. After determining that the Bronco was licensed to the Hertz Corporation, who used Simpson as a spokesperson, Fuhrman called Lange back to the Bronco. The two looked at a spot near the driver's door handle, which appeared to be blood. The other detectives had found the phone number to the Simpson home and were calling it with their cell phones, but they were not receiving an answer.

Fuhrman and the other detectives found themselves in a difficult situation. Barely two miles away, a woman and her companion lay murdered in pools of blood, and the police found themselves outside the home of the woman's former husband, a famous sports personality, whose car had bloodstains on it. There were cars parked inside and outside the fence surrounding his home, but nobody answered the door buzzer or the telephones when the police rang. The police were allowed to enter premises without a search warrant if urgency permitted, and whether the urgency was real or perceived, this situation was certainly urgent. A private security officer arrived and confirmed for the detectives that Simpson and his live-in maid should have been on the premises. As nobody answered the phone or the gates at the residence, the decision was made for Fuhrman to climb the fence and unlock the gate from the inside. Entering the premises without a search warrant would cause difficult entanglements in the prosecution's argument and it, along with the racially inflammatory statements from his past, would help contribute to Fuhrman's professional downfall.

Just before 6:00 A.M., the detectives knocked on the door and rang the doorbell of O. J. Simpson's home. Still receiving no answer, the four walked to the side of the house, where they saw three guest cottages. The first guest house held a male guest, who identified himself as Kato Kaelin. A young woman, who identified herself as Arnelle Simpson, O.J.'s adult daughter, was in the second cottage. Fuhrman remained with Kaelin while Arnelle took the other three policemen in the home to check on any occupants. The home appeared empty, with Simpson nowhere to be found, and all four policemen took the opportunity to interview first Kaelin, then Arnelle Simpson. Arnelle contacted her father's personal assistant and provided the detectives with Simpson's contact information at his Chicago hotel. Arnelle then called Al Cowlings, her father's lifelong friend, to notify him that her stepmother had been murdered. Phillips contacted Simpson, who was concerned and upset at the news, but did not ask for any details concerning his ex-wife's death. He reported that he would take the next available flight back to Los Angeles. It was up to Tom Lange to contact the Brown family and notify them of the murder before the media obtained the news. Lange arrived at the Browns' home in Orange County at approximately 6:21 A.M. and broke the devastating news to her parents and sister.

Ten to fifteen minutes later, Fuhrman found Vannatter in the house and brought him to the garden behind Kaelin's bungalow to tell him about a discovery on the property. Resting on the walkway among the leaves was a bloodstained right-handed leather glove that appeared to be the match to the left-handed one found at Nicole Brown Simpson's condominium. Phillips and Fuhrman returned to the South Bundy address, leaving Lange and Vannatter at the Rockingham home to determine whether it was the second of two related crime scenes. After Lange left for the Bundy condominium, Vannatter discovered a trail of blood droplets connecting the two vehicles parked in Simpson's driveway, the front door and walkway to the house, and the Ford Bronco outside the gates. Fuhrman and Brad Roberts, his partner, returned around 7:00 A.M. with a police photographer who had been taking photos at the condominium. The photographer took photos of the glove found at the Rockingham home and the numerous blood droplets found between the vehicles on the Rockingham property. It seemed apparent to all the detectives that the glove at Rockingham was a match for the glove at Bundy. Since the glove and the blood drops at Rockingham were in plain view of the public, they were classified as evidence that could be taken without a search warrant.

The Rockingham mansion was labeled as a crime scene due to the evidence that was found. An LAPD criminalist and his assistant arrived at Rockingham at 7:10 A.M. to collect and document evidence, including the blood spots, the glove, and the Bronco, which was to be towed to the police garage for further investigation. Vannatter left the Rockingham estate to retrieve his partner, Lange, and obtain a search warrant for the Rockingham property belonging to Simpson. Fuhrman remained at the Rockingham home to maintain the security of the crime scene there.

The media had heard word of the murders and began assembling across the street from the Bundy condominium around 8:00 in the morning. Officers recorded the license plate numbers of the neighborhood vehicles and searched the area, hoping to find a hidden murder weapon. At 9:10 A.M., the coroner's investigator and her assistant arrived to examine the two bodies. An hour later, the criminalist and assistant who had been at the Simpson house arrived at the Bundy condominium. The team completed their examinations of the bodies of Nicole Brown Simpson and Ronald Goldman as well as the cataloguing and photographing of their surroundings.

Vannatter arrived at Simpson's Rockingham home just before 12:00 noon with a signed search warrant. He was met there by Howard Weitzman, a criminal attorney who had been contacted by Simpson, and Bert Luper, from the LAPD Homicide Special Section. As the three discussed the methods by which the house would be searched, Simpson arrived at the home. Initially, he was handcuffed and detained by Roberts, Fuhrman's partner. After being reminded that Simpson was not under arrest, Simpson was released and taken downtown to be questioned by detectives about the murders of his ex-wife and her young friend.

THE DOWNWARD SPIRAL BEGINS

After a whirlwind of events including the funeral of Nicole Brown Simpson, at which her ex-husband made an appearance, and a low-speed police chase of a reportedly suicidal Simpson and his friend, Al Cowlings, in Simpson's Bronco, Orenthal James Simpson was arrested on June 17, 1994, for the murders of Nicole Brown Simpson and Ronald Goldman.

Simpson armed himself with a team of high-profile, high-dollar attorneys, some of whom, however, had never tried murder cases, to proffer his defense. The prosecution went with three seasoned assistant district attorneys who were reputedly tough and thorough and who had lost few trials. The state's case, the prosecution argued, was simple: a "mountain of evidence" showed that Simpson and his deceased ex-wife had a stormy relationship; Simpson had dropped his bloody gloves, which he had been wearing when he'd committed the murders, at his home and at Nicole's; and his blood, sometimes mixed with the victims', was at both locations. The argument for the defense was even simpler: Simpson was just another black man at the mercy of lying, corrupt police officers and law enforcement professionals and was a victim of the white-run judicial system. The judicial system began, according to Simpson's defense team, with Detective Mark Fuhrman.

An article published in *The New Yorker* magazine on July 25, 1994, levied some serious allegations at Fuhrman. Reporter Jeffrey Toobin had written an article titled "Annals of an incendiary defense—a surprising and dangerous defense strategy under consideration by O. J. Simpson's legal team, led by Robert Shapiro, centers on Detective Mark Fuhrman, the police officer who jumped over Simpson's wall—and found the bloody glove." In the article, Toobin claimed to have spoken to the Simpson defense team, allegedly attorney Robert Shapiro, about strategy, which included insisting that it was Fuhrman who planted the bloody right-hand glove at the Rockingham home of Simpson. The article alleged there was "evidence of a police conspiracy," and one of the defense attorneys stated to Toobin of Fuhrman: "This is a bad cop."

The article also referred to disturbing behavior and racist views demonstrated by Fuhrman. Simpson's defense team insisted, repeatedly, that Fuhrman had planted the second "bloody glove" at Simpson's Rockingham estate. Fuhrman, the defense argued, had collected the bloody glove at the Brentwood condominium and deposited it at the Rockingham home when he hopped the fence, without a search warrant, to gain access to the Simpson house. The other detectives involved in the investigation could not believe that Fuhrman would have been able to plant the glove. He had been the seventeenth police officer to log in at the Bundy crime scene, and none of the other officers who had examined the area had reported seeing a second glove near the bodies.

In August, the defense filed a motion requesting the release of Fuhrman's personnel records from LAPD. On September 26, the defense requested hair samples from Vannatter, Lange, and Fuhrman, as well as an examination of the clothing they had worn and the vehicles they had driven on the day of the murders. They asked to have photographs of the detectives' shoe soles to see if one of them had left the bloody footprints at Nicole Simpson's condominium. All this was done in an effort to prepare for the dissection of Fuhrman's investigation as well as his personal character.

A jury of twelve, with twelve alternates, was finally selected to hear the case. The jurors consisted of eight African Americans, two of mixed heritage, one Hispanic, and one white. The alternates were seven African Americans, one Hispanic, and four whites. Only six of the original jurors would still be serving in the trial. On Monday, January 23, 1995, exactly ten years to the day that O. J. Simpson had become the first Heisman Trophy winner to be elected to the Pro Football Hall of Fame, Simpson's trial for the murders of his ex-wife and her companion began.

Mark Fuhrman's involvement with the investigation and trial spiraled out of control when the defense strategy became apparent. Simpson's lawyers—Johnnie Cochran, Robert Shapiro, F. Lee Bailey, Barry Scheck, Peter Neufeld, and Alan Dershowitz—focused on Fuhrman's supposed racism. No facet of Fuhrman's involvement in the case was safe from examination. Fuhrman was asked about his personal beliefs and how they affected his professionalism. Fuhrman insisted that he was an ethical officer and investigator and did not verbalize racial epithets for the ten years prior to the trial.

Fuhrman took the witness stand again on March 9, 1996, to explain himself to the court outside the presence of the jury. He testified to never having met Kathleen Bell or making racist statements in her presence. He also testified regarding the 1985 incident to which he had responded as a patrol officer, when Simpson allegedly had damaged his wife's car with a baseball bat. The following day, Fuhrman testified to the evidence found at the Rockingham home, including some items found in Simpson's Bronco. Fuhrman also testified to his actions at Nicole Simpson's condominium through the night, leading up to the decision to climb the fence at O. J. Simpson's mansion.

On March 13, the defense began cross-examining Fuhrman. F. Lee Bailey asked detailed questions about Fuhrman's encounters with persons who would state that he had made racist remarks and comments about African Americans in their presence. Fuhrman denied meeting these individuals, but conceded that it was possible that he could have met them; however, he stated, it was not possible for him to have uttered racial epithets. In an attempt to demonstrate that he had ample opportunity to plant evidence, framing Simpson for the murders, Fuhrman was then asked, in great detail, about the actions he took on June 13 at both the South Bundy and Rockingham addresses. Bailey implied that Fuhrman had planted evidence because he'd lost an important case to detectives from another division. Fuhrman conceded that he was disappointed in losing what looked like an "interesting and very complex" case. Bailey, in return, attempted to show that Fuhrman planted evidence to further his career. Bailey and Clark battled over whether evidence could be presented in front of the jury to show that Fuhrman once called a black Marine sergeant "nigger." Judge Ito did not immediately allow the defense to enter into this line of questioning with Fuhrman, but after weeks of argument, the arguments became moot, inasmuch as the jury was allowed to hear firsthand the evidence of Fuhrman's racism. Fuhrman left the witness stand after five days of testimony. Philip Vannatter testified shortly thereafter that Fuhrman was asked to leap over the fence at Simpson's mansion because he was the fittest and lowest-ranked of the four detectives at the scene. Vannatter also testified that it was his idea, and not Fuhrman's, for Fuhrman to enter the property.

A private investigator hired to assist the defense team made the discovery that contributed directly to Fuhrman's uselessness as a prosecution witness. Laura Hart McKinney, a professor at the North Carolina School of Arts, had once been an aspiring screenwriter living in the Los Angeles area. She had interviewed—and audiotaped—Fuhrman in 1985 while working on a screenplay about female police officers. The tapes were found and, after court battles in North Carolina and Los Angeles, turned over to the Simpson defense team, who utilized the damning statements within to shred Fuhrman's credibility. On the tapes, Fuhrman bragged about his membership in a secret LAPD organization called Men Against Women or MAW. That, however, proved to be one of the least damaging admissions on the tape. Numerous times, Fuhrman's voice could be heard using the word, "nigger." In one quote Fuhrman stated, "Yeah, we work with niggers and gangs. You can take one of these niggers, drag 'em into the alley, and beat the shit out of them and kick them. You can see them twitch. It really relieves your tension." Even though only two limited portions of the tapes were admitted into the Simpson trial in front of the jury, the remainder of the tape excerpts, all sixty-one of them, were played in open court outside the presence of the jury. By playing the tapes, Judge Ito commented that he could not be accused of withholding information of "vital public interest," but playing the Fuhrman tapes served only to incense the African American community. Although the statements in the tapes were horrific and inflammatory, it was difficult for many to conceive that Fuhrman's use of the word "nigger" meant that he tried to frame Simpson for the murders.

Why, claimed the defense, would Fuhrman be so adamant about framing Simpson for the murders? Along with Fuhrman's reported prejudice against mixed-race couples, particularly in which the male was African American, Fuhrman had been assigned to the case of a lifetime—and then promptly unassigned, in favor of more "elite" police investigators, within a matter of minutes.

The tapes cast immediate doubts on Detective Fuhrman's motives. He appeared to be, as the defense argued, a racist, rogue police officer who often took the law into his own hands as he saw fit. He had investigated a murder of a white woman in which the prime suspect was her ex-husband, an African American man. People who had interacted with Fuhrman came forward with tales of Fuhrman's repeated vocalization of his hatred of mixed-race couples in which the man was African American and the woman was white.

A real estate agent named Kathleen Bell wrote a letter to Simpson's defense lawyers describing what Fuhrman had told her in one interaction with him: "When he sees a nigger (as he called it) driving with a white woman, he would pull them over. I asked, would he if he didn't have a reason, and he said that he would find one."

Fuhrman returned once again to the witness stand on September 6, 1995. When asked if he had planted or manufactured evidence or lied in his reports concerning the Simpson murder investigation, Fuhrman repeatedly pled, "I wish to assert my Fifth Amendment privilege." The following day, the defense attempted to have Fuhrman testify again before the jury. Judge Ito ruled against this, but he did rule that the jury would be notified of Fuhrman's unavailability to testify further. Ito advised the jury that Fuhrman was unavailable to testify further in the trial and that the jurors could consider his unavailability when deliberating. The prosecution was unhappy with the rulings, but Ito also stated that it would be inappropriate to place a witness on the stand when it was apparent that the witness would invoke the Fifth Amendment in response to each question.

Judge Lance Ito denied the defense the opportunity to bring up other reported instances of alleged conduct by Fuhrman, stating, "the underlying assumption that Fuhrman planted the Rockingham glove for the purpose of incriminating Simpson in the brutal and savage murders required a leap in both logic and law too broad to be made based on the evidence before the jury." The damage, however, had been done. A deadly blow had been dealt to the prosecution's case. With Fuhrman exposed as an apparent racist and liar, much of the prosecution's argument flew out the window. The state turned against him. Lead prosecutor Marcia Clark dubbed him "the worst LAPD has to offer" and later pleaded with the jury not to find Simpson "not guilty" based on Fuhrman's views and practices. Defense attorney Johnnie Cochran had become renowned for successfully suing municipalities in suits involving excessive force or sexual abuse by police officers, and with the negative evidence toward Fuhrman, Cochran made a passionate argument. In closing arguments, Cochran insisted the jury take a stand against a "lying, genocidal racist cop" and "America's worst nightmare." Cochran compared Fuhrman to Adolf Hitler, stating that his beliefs condoned the brutal beating and burning of African Americans, particularly those involved in mixed-race marriages.

Simpson further alleged that all of the most incriminating pieces of evidence against him were planted by corrupt officers or were mishandled by the LAPD. This evidence included the trail of Simpson's blood at the Bundy address; Simpson's blood on the back gate of the Bundy property; the blood of Simpson and the two victims in Simpson's Ford Bronco; Simpson's blood inside and outside of his home on Rockingham; and Simpson's and Nicole's blood on Simpson's socks in his bedroom at his Rockingham home. Despite the fact that the blood at the crime scene had been collected earlier in the day than Simpson supplied a blood sample for comparison, the blood at the Bundy address matched Simpson's blood. Although Simpson admitted that the blood matched, he took matters a step further and alleged that his own blood had been planted in place of the blood of the "real" killer. Further, Simpson's defense attorneys argued that all forensic tests done on the blood and other evidence yielded questionable results because of the alleged mishandling of the evidence. The defense spent the entire month of May 1996 arguing that the DNA evidence linking Simpson to the murders was suspect.

In response, Fuhrman reported that he never had time to plant the glove. There were too many police officers and other personnel around. He had been the seventeenth officer to sign in at the murder scene and would have had to snatch the second glove, from a secured location, in plain sight of numerous other police officers.

Despite Christopher Darden's attempt to remind the jury that the only "n-word" they should consider when determining their verdict was Nicole Brown Simpson, the damage had been done.

The Simpson trial, and Fuhrman's involvement in it, divided the nation. To many in the minority communities, the trial's purpose of finding a man guilty or innocent of two murders was secondary to the question of whether an African American man could receive fairness and justice in a legal system largely created and administered by whites. In other areas, the populace wondered whether a jury comprised of mostly minorities would convict a male African American celebrity of a crime in spite of the multitude of evidence against him. To still more people, the murder victims were shoved aside in favor of their accused killer, whose famous legal team commanded such presence in the courtroom—and the media—to demonstrate that racism and bigotry were the real issues at stake, rather than resolving the deaths of Nicole Brown Simpson and Ronald Goldman.

The twelve-member jury, comprised of ten women and two men, of whom nine were African American, two were white, and one was Hispanic, acquitted O. J. Simpson of the murders of his ex-wife and her companion.

THE SPIRAL CONTINUES: AFTERMATH OF THE SIMPSON TRIAL

After Fuhrman retired, the LAPD intended to find out whether his claims on those infamous McKinney tapes were true. The internal affairs division of the LAPD spent half a year interviewing people who had been arrested by Fuhrman during his tenure on the police force. They also spoke with current and former prosecutors who handled those cases. Many of the interviewees were minority individuals who had nothing negative to say about the way Fuhrman had conducted himself when dealing with them. In the end, internal affairs could find nothing to substantiate the taped statements made by Fuhrman. Some speculated that he had been exaggerating to impress McKinney or, as Fuhrman had explained previously, that he was assuming a character to fit in with McKinney's screenplay in progress.

Fuhrman sued Toobin and *The New Yorker* magazine, citing seven total counts of libel, invasion of privacy, and infliction of emotional distress.

In 1996, Fuhrman was charged with one felony count of perjury for his denial during the Simpson trial of ever having used the word "nigger." Fuhrman pled no contest to the charge and was placed on probation and fined $200. As part of his plea agreement, Fuhrman also was never again allowed to be a police officer in California.

Fuhrman wrote a memoir about his involvement in the Simpson investigation and trial titled *Murder in Brentwood*. In it, he first apologizes, saying he is ashamed and sorry for his past remarks and behavior. Then, in an unemotional chronology, Fuhrman brought the case back to its sordid beginning and described the crime scene, from his first impressions through the beginnings of his investigation. He describes the enormous amount of blood that flowed down the cobblestone walk at Nicole Simpson's home. Bloody shoe prints, sometimes displaying the entire soles of the shoes, led toward the heavy gate at the rear, which was smudged with more blood. A trail of blood led into the alley next to the home and then suddenly vanished. Either the attacker had stopped bleeding, said Fuhrman, or had gotten into a vehicle. The blood trail resumed at O. J. Simpson's home, where more bloodstains were found on his Ford Bronco in numerous places. Inside Simpson's house, there were freshly cleaned black sweat clothes in a washing machine, and the light switch near the washing machine displayed more smears of blood. Also within Fuhrman's notes prepared inside Nicole's home, he had documented the appearance of a bloody fingerprint on the deadbolt lock of the heavy gate at the rear of her yard.

Fuhrman continued, insisting that he never had the opportunity to plant the bloody glove at Simpson's home. Lead detectives Vannatter and Lange overlooked crucial evidence, Fuhrman alleged, and did not read Fuhrman's notes until much later. This is how the bloody fingerprint outside Nicole Simpson's home was lost. Vannatter and Lange, according to Fuhrman, even gave Simpson enough information to fabricate a mild alibi during his half-hour interrogation on the day after the murders. Most of Furhman's ire was directed at the state's attorneys, who abandoned him and left him with little choice but to plead the Fifth Amendment when he was recalled to the stand after the release of the McKinney tapes. Fuhrman speculated that although he might have been called racist by the defense, Clark would have done better to revive him as a witness rather than to further discredit him. However, in order to do that, Clark would have had to open up questioning about all of the evidence missing from the case, including that missing fingerprint on the gate, which would have damaged the credibility of her lead detective and new star witness after Fuhrman's disparagement, Vannatter. Clark apparently was unwilling to trade Vannatter's credibility for Fuhrman's evidence.

The Simpson criminal trial had ended, but civil lawsuits were filed by Ron Goldman's father and Nicole Brown's family, citing that Simpson should be held liable for the deaths of Ron and Nicole. Although Fuhrman testified in the civil lawsuit, the presiding judge issued rulings that the civil jury would not be allowed to hear any of his testimony in the criminal trial, nor would they hear about his no-contest plea to perjury resulting from his testimony in the criminal trial. In the end, the jury unanimously determined that O. J. Simpson was to be held liable for the deaths of Nicole Brown

Simpson and Ronald Goldman, and he was ordered to pay a total settlement of $33.5 million to the families of the victims.

A MOVE TOWARD REDEMPTION: A REINVESTIGATION OF THE MARTHA MOXLEY MURDER

After the success of *Murder in Brentwood,* Fuhrman was contacted by true-crime author Dominick Dunne, father of murdered actress Dominique Dunne of *Poltergeist* movie fame. Dunne had written a book, *A Season in Purgatory,* based on the murder of a Greenwich, Connecticut, teenager. The murder had remained unsolved since 1975. Dunne had been impressed with Fuhrman's work in *Murder in Brentwood,* and he wanted Fuhrman to investigate the unsolved Greenwich killing.

On October 31, 1975, fifteen-year-old Martha Moxley was found underneath a Japanese elm tree at the rear of her Greenwich, Connecticut home. She had apparently been beaten to death the night before, on "mischief night." The discovery shook the private Belle Haven community to its core, for it was perhaps only the second murder that had been committed in recent memory. The Moxleys had relocated from California the previous year and had been assimilated readily into the community. On the night of October 30, Martha and several friends were playing pranks—spraying shaving cream in neighbors' yards and ringing doorbells—when they headed to the home of the Skakel family to continue the party. Martha reportedly left the Skakel house to return to her own home sometime between 9:30 and 11:00 P.M., but she never made it. Her body was discovered at midday, with blood everywhere and genital and buttock area exposed, her life having been cut short by a bludgeoning by her enraged attacker.

Several suspects were identified by local authorities. Robert Mathers, a neighbor who lived in his mother's home nearby, was one of the first suspects considered. One reason for suspecting him initially was that a package of condoms found in his room had one missing. Mathers was subjected to a polygraph examination and failed it, saying that the medicine he was taking affected the results. Tommy Skakel, relative of Robert F. Kennedy, was listed as the next suspect, because other youths reported that Martha was last seen alive with him. His father, Rushton Skakel, was out of town on business, but he returned home quickly and readily gave police access to his home and children. Tommy Skakel and Robert later both took polygraph examinations and passed. Rushton Skakel later forbade any further access to his children after authorities wanted access to Tommy's school and medical records. Ken Littleton, a new tutor hired by Rushton Skakel, was also interviewed as a possible suspect. On the night of Martha's murder, Littleton was spending his first night in Skakel home. He had taken all the Skakel children to dinner at the country club, where he allowed them to drink alcohol. The family went back to the Skakel home at approximately 9:00 P.M. Littleton was made the main suspect eleven months later because of a failed polygraph exam. According to Littleton, he failed because he was nervous about having been arrested for burglary and not being entirely truthful about it. Michael Skakel, Tommy's younger brother, was ruled out as a suspect. Michael had an alibi, as he was reportedly at a friend's house at the time of the murder.

In 1991, interest in the Moxley murder briefly sparked when a cousin of the Kennedys, William Kennedy Smith, was tried for rape in Florida. The media immediately made a connection between Smith and his rabble-rousing Skakel cousins in Connecticut, and it was rumored that Smith had actually been in the Skakel home on the night of the Moxley girl's murder. The revelation of the common bloodline between the families renewed interest in the Moxley case and spurred another look at the murder. Many of the original players in the case were reinterviewed. Alas, the new investigation did not reveal any new information, and the allegation of Smith's presence at the Skakel home on October 30, 1975, proved to be false. The case, although still open, once again retreated to a back burner.

In 1992, weary of the speculation and repeated questioning of his family, Rushton Skakel hired Sutton Associates, a private investigations firm, to investigate the murder and determine once and for all that Tommy and Michael had had nothing to do with Moxley's death. During the Sutton investigation, Michael and Tommy changed their alibis that substantiated their whereabouts during the time that the girl died. Again, no arrest was made by authorities. Mark Fuhrman finally entered the picture several years later.

Fuhrman met with Dorothy Moxley, Martha's mother, and became intrigued with the case. Fuhrman believed he could solve the case and get the Greenwich authorities to take another look at the murder. Fuhrman's reinvestigation of the Moxley murder initially met opposition from the local and state law enforcement agencies. Greenwich police refused to let an "outsider" like Fuhrman, especially one with his tarnished reputation, have access to their records, their documents, their conclusions. The community of Belle Haven proved to be more tightly knit than most small communities. A subcommunity of the already well-to-do Greenwich, Belle Haven was comprised of approximately forty homes belonging to the richest of the rich families in the area. Belle Haven lay on a peninsula that poked into Long Island Sound. The neighborhood was protected from the outside world by two gates connected by one major street, along which the houses were built. A private security force regularly patrolled the properties each night.

Dorothy Moxley wanted an independent forensic pathologist to review Martha's autopsy records. Despite negativity from the community and the law enforcement community (Fuhrman was, after all, that "racist cop" from the Simpson trial), Dorothy wanted his help with solving her daughter's murder. After much opposition, Fuhrman was able to get the state attorney's office to release the autopsy report, and it was reviewed by a forensic pathologist, the same one Fuhrman had encountered in the past during the O. J. Simpson trial. With the new review of the autopsy report, Martha's potential time of death changed significantly. Police had reported time of death as occurring between 9:30 and 10:00 P.M., when Dorothy Moxley heard a dog barking frantically outside. The forensic pathologist believed Martha's time of death, based on her blood loss and stomach contents, could have been as late as 1:30 A.M. on Halloween. This revelation once again refocused attention on the Skakel brothers and their reported alibis for the night.

On October 11, 1997, Fuhrman interviewed Millard Jones, who had been one of the first two policemen on the Moxley murder scene in 1975. Now a minister, Jones dropped a surprise on Fuhrman: when he had arrived on the scene, Jones stated, the handle of the murder weapon was still stuck in the girl's neck. This long-believed "missing piece" of the murder weapon had been cited as the reason local police could not solve the murder conclusively, for they could not get the killer's fingerprints off the handle if the handle were missing. Fuhrman couldn't believe it. The missing piece of the murder weapon had been in Martha's body when she was discovered, and yet the case had remained unsolved largely because the handle of the golf club, which was determined to have belonged to the Skakel brothers' deceased mother, could not be found. Fuhrman had Dan Hickman, the second policeman to arrive at the murder scene, interviewed as well. His story corroborated Jones' account; he, too, had seen the handle of the broken golf club stuck in the girl's neck. Both Jones and Hickman stated that they had never been interviewed formally by the detectives investigating the murder, so they had never had a chance to confirm that crucial detail. Fuhrman contacted Dr. Richard Danehower, the Moxleys' personal doctor, who had arrived on the scene some hours later to confirm that Martha was indeed dead. Dr. Danehower told Fuhrman that he had seen a shiny metal object on the ground next to Martha's body when he arrived and that the object looked like the handle of a golf club.

In 1998, two books were published that instantly renewed interest in the Moxley case: Fuhrman's work and *Greentown*, penned by Greenwich native Timothy Dumas. Fuhrman's book grabbed national attention not only for his reputation as the "racist cop" from the O. J. Simpson trial, but also because of the identity of the murderer. Fuhrman named Michael Skakel, a neighbor of the Moxleys in Belle Haven and a relative of Robert F. Kennedy, as Martha Moxley's murderer. In Fuhrman's opinion, Michael Skakel was the most likely candidate for the murder due in part to his anger at his brother Tommy, because Tommy had kissed Martha and Michael had harbored teenage romantic feelings for Martha. In addition, Michael had reportedly confessed to the killing while attending a therapeutic boarding school in Maine a few years after the murder.

The accusation seemed to light a fire under the Greenwich authorities. In June 1998, the state of Connecticut appointed a one-man grand jury to investigate the Moxley matter. With an eighteen-month deadline, Superior Court Judge George Thim was charged with the task of providing a report as to whether the Moxley murder could be prosecuted. During the investigation, several past teachers, classmates, and friends of Michael Skakel were interviewed. In January 2000, Judge Thim released his report, which concluded that there was, indeed, enough reasonable cause to believe that Michael Skakel was the murderer of Martha Moxley.

In 2002, Michael Skakel was charged with the murder of Martha Moxley, a crime that had occurred twenty-seven years earlier. He flew from his home in Florida to surrender to the Connecticut authorities. Because Michael was fifteen years old when the murder occurred, the case originally was filed as a juvenile action. A judge ruled that Skakel was to be tried as an adult. On May 7, 2002, the trial began, lasting four weeks. On June 7, 2002, nearly three decades after Martha Moxley's death, Michael Skakel was found guilty of her murder. He was sentenced to twenty years to life in prison. Fuhrman, present at the trial, was interviewed by the press and appeared on camera and in the newspapers numerous times, being cited as a driving force behind the criminal conviction, the culmination of the previously unsolved case. In some opinions, Fuhrman placed himself on the path to redemption by solving the 30-year-old murder of an all-American teenage girl.

OTHER BOOKS AND ENDEAVORS BY MARK FURHMAN

Fuhrman has revitalized his career by becoming a best-selling true-crime author who still invites water-cooler discussion by writing books about controversial subjects. For his next project after the conclusion of the Moxley matter, Fuhrman tackled the unsolved deaths of sixteen women, mostly prostitutes, all located barely ninety miles from his home, in *Murder in Spokane*. Fuhrman blamed sloppy and delayed police work and the failure by the police to share pertinent details about the victims with the public for the continued deaths of other women. When Fuhrman attempted to help the police with their investigation, he was met, as he had been in the past, by opposition from law enforcement because of the fact that he was a convicted perjurer. In the end, Robert Yates, Jr., was tracked through his white Corvette, in which one of the victims had been spotted, and arrested for the murder of one of the victims. Through DNA evidence, Yates was linked to nine more of the deceased women. Fuhrman exposed the fact that Yates had been interviewed by police three times during the investigation, but was not considered a suspect until several years had passed.

EVEN COPS CHANGE THEIR MINDS

In 2003, Fuhrman's book *Death and Justice*, an examination of the capital punishment system in the state of Oklahoma, was published. Examining one jurisdiction in particular, Oklahoma County, which includes Oklahoma City, Fuhrman discussed the death penalty process and its machine-like operation. The president of an Oklahoma defense attorneys' organization who appeared on Fuhrman's KXLY radio show invited Fuhrman to come to Oklahoma and check things out after calling the state "a regular death factory." As a former police officer, Fuhrman believed in capital punishment and its process until he researched and wrote *Death and Justice*. Initially, Fuhrman stated that he believed that any problems with the capital punishment system were rare and were unintentional mistakes. He also assumed that there was a very low rate of wrongful convictions due to the higher standards to which capital murder cases are held. During his research, Fuhrman encountered numerous people whose everyday actions caused him to question his beliefs. In his dealings with the father of one executed prisoner, Fuhrman wrote: "When I was a cop, I only had compassion for the victims of crime. I could not allow myself to feel anything but contempt for those who were responsible. Jim Fowler helped me realize that it was possible to feel compassion even for criminals, which is right and necessary, yet only makes the rendering of justice more difficult."

Fuhrman took notice of the Oklahoma capital punishment system when Jack Pointer, a guest on his radio show, when a scandal involving a forensic chemist and manager of the Oklahoma City Police Department crime lab, Joyce Gilchrist, hit the presses. DNA testing performed by the Oklahoma Indigent Defense Service and the Innocent Project—run, ironically, by Barry Scheck, whom Fuhrman knew from the O.J. Simpson trial—proved that Gilchrist and other chemists had caused errors in some murder and rape cases in which the defendants were convicted wrongfully. Among the wrongfully convicted were three death row inmates. Fuhrman followed the family of one of the inmates, Mark Fowler, who was put to death during his work on the book.

Also highlighted by Fuhrman in his book was Bob Macy, former district attorney for Oklahoma County, who bragged about the number of people sent to death row from his jurisdiction. Macy, according to Fuhrman, believed that the accidental execution of a truly innocent person was a fitting price to pay to keep the capital punishment system moving. Fuhrman disagreed with Macy and wrote that he no longer believed in the death penalty because death penalty cases are not "investigated or prosecuted at a level that can guarantee justice, or even that the accused is actually guilty."

Following his death penalty study, Fuhrman forayed into the civil and family law arena by producing *Silent Witness: The Untold Story of Terri Schiavo's Death*. Fuhrman, with assistance and cooperation from Terri's parents, siblings, and medical and legal experts, analyzed medical records, legal documents, and case files to discuss the extraordinary case. The book drew criticism from many by being released before the final autopsy results on Schiavo were available. Fuhrman, however, took his book beyond the public division of opinion her case caused and presented an argument against Michael Schiavo, who chose to let his long-disabled wife die an unconventional death after years of life-sustaining treatment.

Fuhrman's latest book, *A Simple Act of Murder*, concerns the John F. Kennedy assassination. In it he advances a theory debunking the "Single Bullet Theory" while still maintaining that Lee Harvey Oswald acted alone. He claims that the Warren Commission was forced to adopt the Single Bullet Theory for political reasons. However, he says that a dent in the chrome above the windshield in the presidential limousine used that day vindicates the story told by John Connally, that a first shot at President John Kennedy did not hit him. Fuhrman opines that the death of President Kennedy itself was not a conspiracy, but that the aftermath of the killing—the hiding or destroying of evidence by those with personal or political motivations—was.

Fuhrman is a frequent guest of conservative commentator Sean Hannity and a sometime contributor for FOX News. He is also the host of the Spokane, Washington, radio show "The Mark Fuhrman Show." The show covers local and national topics and includes many guest callers and listeners. Fuhrman makes it clear that he doesn't think much of the Spokane County Sheriff's Department, regularly offering diatribes that describe them as lazy, undertrained, and inept at investigations. "You know," Fuhrman says, "I love cops. Most of these guys aren't cops. They're not doing the job. You know a good rule of thumb is, watch 'NYPD Blue.' Would Andy Sipowicz tolerate this (stuff)? He'd go ballistic."

In response to the proposed book *If I Did It* written by O. J. Simpson and to be published by ReganBooks, an imprint of HarperCollins, Fuhrman reportedly stated that he would drop HarperCollins as publisher of his own books in the future. However, Simpson's book has since been cancelled. Most recently, the family of Ronald Goldman has been awarded the transcript of the book as part of an effort to collect their portion of the wrongful death suit settlement.

Mark Fuhrman's reputation can be pinned, in the eyes of many, directly on his professional destruction during the O. J. Simpson trial. With a few ill-spoken words from his past, Fuhrman unintentionally rocketed himself in public opinion from a detective on a celebrity murder case to a law-skirting, racist government official. His investigative skills and talents were forgotten in the resulting media madness. Disgraced, retired, and on probation, Fuhrman sought to rebuild his life quietly in another state, but he could not pass up the opportunity to explain himself and his actions, and thus his book *Murder in Brentwood* was born. The book caught national attention once again and directly led to his involvement with the reinvestigation of the

Martha Moxley killing in Connecticut. The subsequent release of the result-ing book, *Murder in Greenwich*, redeemed Fuhrman in some ways after he identified the most likely suspect to have committed the murder. Fuhrman's involvement in the Moxley matter caused a resurgence of interest in the case and led to the eventual arrest and prosecution of Michael Skakel, the man named in Fuhrman's book as Martha's killer. Fuhrman's career has been reborn as a popular and successful true-crime author. He has since penned several more books, including *Murder in Spokane* (2002); *Death & Justice* (2003); *Silent Witness: The Untold Story of Terri Schiavo's Death* (2005); and *A Simple Act of Murder: November 22, 1963* (2006). After years of liv-ing with controversy, Fuhrman tries to keep his private life out of the scru-tiny of the mass media and the public, still living quietly in Idaho. Despite his attempts to exist outside of the spotlight, Fuhrman's love for investigat-ing the unknown and unsolved continues to draw him into the public eye. For his persistence and desire while solving previously unsolved crimes, Mark Fuhrman is an icon of crime fighting.

ACKNOWLEDGMENTS

I want to thank my wife, Amanda, for her help with this project. I appreci-ate all that she has done for me with this project and in my life. I am truly lucky to have her in my life. Also I want to thank John Rodriguez for his support of this project. Lastly, I cannot forget my Dad and Mom. I want to make you proud.

FURTHER READING

August, Bob. The Real OJ. http://www.bobaugust.com/index.htm/.

Buckley, William F., Jr. 1995. "Where does Fuhrman take us?" (Editorial) *National Review*. September 25.

CBS News. 2001. *48 Hours Mystery*: Mark Fuhrman Biography. http://www.cbsnews.com/stories/2001/07/13/48hours/main301303.shtml/.

CBS News. 2002. Murder, They Wrote: Murder in Spokane, A Serial Killer on the Loose. February 15. http://www.cbsnews.com/stories/2002/02/15/48hours/murder/main329534.shtml/.

Chua-Eoan, Howard, and Elizabeth Gleick. 1995. Making the Case. *Time*. October 16. http://www.time.com/time/magazine/article/0,9171,983569,00.html/.

CNN. Simpson Civil Trial Special Section. "Jury: OJ Is Liable." http://www.cnn.com/US/OJ/simpson.civil.trial/index.html.

Fuhrman, Mark. 1997. *Murder in Brentwood*. New York: Regnery.

Fuhrman, Mark. 1998. *Murder in Greenwich: Who Killed Martha Moxley?* New York: HarperCollins.

Fuhrman, Mark. 2001. *Murder in Spokane: Catching a Serial Killer*. New York: Avon.

Fuhrman, Mark. 2003. *Death and Justice: An Expose of Oklahoma's Death Row Machine*. New York: HarperCollins.

Fuhrman, Mark. 2005. *Silent Witness: The Untold Story of Terri Schiavo's Death*. New York: HarperCollins.

Fuhrman, Mark. 2006. *A Simple Act of Murder: November 22, 1963*. New York: HarperCollins.

Geringer, Joseph. The Martha Moxley Murder. http://www.crimelibrary.com/notorious_murders/famous/moxley/index_1.html/.

Gleick, Elizabeth. 1995. Headliners. *Time*. December 25. http://www.time.com/time/magazine/article/0,9171,983884,00.html/.

Gleick, Elizabeth. 1996. A Simpson remake. *Time*. September 23. http://www.time.com/time/magazine/article/0,9171,985192,00.html/.

Goska, Danusha. Mark Fuhrman. http://www.codypublishing.com/goska/furman.html/.

Jones, Thomas L. Notorious Murders. Most Famous. OJ Simpson. http://www.crimelibrary.com/notorious_murders/famous/simpson/index_1.html/.

Lafferty, Elaine. 1996. Glove story II. *Time*. October 21. http://www.time.com/time/magazine/article/0,9171,985336,00.html/.

'Lectric Law Library. Mark Fuhrman's 10/2/96 Plea Agreement to Felony Perjury at OJ Simpson's Criminal Trial. http://www.lectlaw.com/files/case63.htm/. http://www.law.umkc.edu/faculty/projects/ftrials/Simpson/Fuhrman.htm/.

Montaldo, Charles. Profile of Michael Skakel. http://crime.about.com/od/murder/p/michael_skakel.htm/.

NewsHounds. 2006. FOX News Taps Mark Fuhrman to Analyze Duke Rape Case. How Racially Insensitive Can You Get? http://www.newshounds.us/2006/04/18/fox_news_taps_mark_fuhrman_to_analyze_duke_rape_case_how_racially_insensitive_can_you_get.php/.

NewsMax.Com. 2005. Mark Fuhrman Probing Schiavo Case. http://www.newsmax.com/archives/ic/2005/5/6/230418.shtml/.

One People's Project. Mark Fuhrman. December 2, 2006. http://www.onepeoplesproject.com/index.php?option=content&task=view&id=83&Itemid=29/.

Reaves, Jessica. 2000. The murder case that just wouldn't go away. *Time*. January 19. http://www.time.com/time/nation/article/0,8599,37804,00.html/.

Revolutionary Worker Online. Fuhrman: Play the Tapes Again! *Revolutionary Worker #896*. March 2, 1997.

Van Biema, David. 2000. A crime in the clan. *Time*. January 31. http://www.time.com/time/magazine/article/0,9171,995999,00.html/.

Walsh, James. 1995. The lessons of the trial. *Time*. October 16. http://www.time.com/time/magazine/article/0,9171,983570,00.html/.

Wolff, Craig. 1997. Look who's talking: Defending himself, Mark Fuhrman returns to the scene of the crime. *The New York Times*. March 23. http://www.nytimes.com/books/97/03/23/reviews/970323.23wolfft.html/.

Rudolph "Rudy" Giuliani

Camille Gibson

THE EARLY YEARS

Wayne Barrett in his biography *Rudy! An Investigative Biography of Rudolph Giuliani* (2000) and Eleanor Fremont (2002) in her book *America's Mayor: Rudolph W. Giuliani* have offered a thorough history of Rudolph "Rudy" Giuliani's background. Indeed, it was Barrett who uncovered Giuliani's father's criminal past and Mafia ties. According to Fremont, these revelations were news to Giuliani himself, who reported thereafter that he had been aware of a grave family secret—but had not been told the specifics. The following details in this section on Giuliani's background come from Barrett and Fremont's investigative works.

Rudolph "Rudy" Giuliani was named after his grandfather Rodolfo Giuliani, "an opera lover" with a "stubborn and stormy disposition" (Fremont 2002, 3). Rodolfo was from Montecatini, a northern Italian village. He emigrated to New York in 1880 at age seventeen. Thereafter, he married a young woman, Evangelina Giuliani, with the same surname. He and Evangelina settled on 123rd Street, which was at the time an Italian section of Harlem. Rodolfo was a tailor and his wife Evangelina a dressmaker. Evangelina worked at a garment factory, while Rodolfo worked at home. Rodolfo expected his eldest child, Harold to make deliveries for the family business. However, Harold was often distracted and consequently received regular harsh beatings from his father. Rodolfo died February 1946, shortly before his grandson Rudy would turn two years old.

Giuliani's parents Harold Giuliani and Helen D'Avanzo met at a party around 1929 in New York City. They lived a thrifty existence like many of those about them given the harshness of the Great Depression and the Prohibition era. Harold Giuliani was a large fellow, about five feet, eleven inches, rough in appearance and somewhat hot-tempered. He had four siblings, Charles, Marie, Olga, and Rudolph. He dropped out of school at age fifteen. As a juvenile he was arrested for burglary and sanctioned with juvenile probation. At a young age he tried boxing but his poor vision hindered his success. He was also a plumber's assistant at one point. Helen was shy and ladylike and an excellent student. She had five older and rather protective brothers: one a firefighter, three police officers, and brother Leo, a bar owner. Helen's parents, Luigi and Adelina D'Avanzo, were southern Italian immigrants from Avellino and Naples, respectively. Luigi died in 1925, leaving forty-three-year-old Adelina to raise their seven children (Vincent, Fanny, William, Helen, Leo, Edward, and Roberto) with very limited means.

Harold and Helen courted for seven years. That they had a relationship appears significant because historically many Northern Italians have considered their darker-complexioned countrymen, the southern Italians, to be inferior to them. Plausibly, the fact that a northern Italian, Harold, married a southern Italian, Helen, is suggestive of the type of home in which Rudy

Giuliani grew up, a home that may have communicated messages about surpassing racial bias. This may explain Rudy Giuliani's early leanings to an apparently more inclusive Democratic party and his deep and apparently sustained hurt over what he seemed to perceive as rejection by New York City's black community when he lost his first run for mayor in 1989 against the African-American candidate, David Dinkins.

Giuliani's father Harold was far from perfect. If he thought another fellow was being disrespectful to his wife, he would often respond with violence; hence, one of Helen's monikers for him: "savage." Indeed, Helen married Harold a year after he was released from Sing Sing Prison. Unemployed at age twenty-six, Harold Giuliani had succumbed to the lure of crime on April 2, 1934. While with a companion, he robbed a Borden Farm milkman by sticking a gun in his stomach as the milkman made rounds in a residential building. They pulled down their victim's pants, but while they were attempting to bind the man, a police officer entered the building. Harold Giuliani was arrested, but his companion escaped. When arrested, Harold lied about his age, address, and name, stating that he was Joseph Starrett. On April 12, 1934, he was charged with assault, robbery, larceny, and receiving stolen property.

Although Harold had no apparent funds, he had connections who, in a matter of days, had him out on $5,000 bail. The milkman, Harold Hall, was apparently threatened into changing his story by later claiming that it was Harold Giuliani's accomplice who had put the gun to his stomach. Harold Giuliani then pled guilty to a single reduced charge of third-degree robbery. He refused to give up his accomplice and so on May 29, 1934, he was sentenced to two to five years at Sing Sing Prison. He began his sentence on May 31 of that year. His prison psychiatric report described him as an "aggressive, egocentric type." It suggested that he had a sense of inferiority from childhood that had grown worse with "his prolonged idleness and dependence on parents." (Barrett 2000, 17). Harold was released on about four years parole on September 24, 1935, having served a year and four months at Sing Sing. Thereafter, Harold worked for some time with Helen's brother Leo, who owned a bar in Brooklyn called Vincent's and who was associated with the mob. Harold provided protection from unruly patrons, and he did collection for Leo's side business—loan-sharking.

Rudolph William Louis Giuliani, the first and only child of his parents, was born on Sunday May 28, 1944, during wartime. The Giulianis were mature parents by the time their son was born. Helen was thirty-five years old and had been trying to conceive for six years. It was a time of lack, politics, history, and missing young males, off at war—a world where children were taught their place, which was helping the adults around them. In his earliest years, Rudy's family lived with his grandmother Adelina, who often cared for him at 419 Hawthorne Street, Brooklyn. Typical of the time, many people had extended family nearby.

When Rudy Giuliani turned seven, his father moved the family to Long Island. The impetus for the move was Harold's observation of Rudy's cousin and frequent playmate Lewis (Leo's son). Lewis was being influenced by the mob life about him. Harold did not want this for his son. It turns out Harold's instincts were right. Lewis later became a gangster and was dead by age thirty-six.

Giuliani's mother Helen died September 8, 2002, at age ninety-two with her son and his two children (Andrew, then sixteen, and Caroline, then thirteen) by her side. His father Harold had passed away in 1981 from cancer.

TOWARD WHO HE IS: GIULIANI'S CHARACTER

Except for law school, all of Giuliani's education occurred at Catholic schools. He attended the all-male Bishop Loughlin Memorial High School in Brooklyn on scholarship. There he was taught by the very strict De La Salle Christian Brothers. He graduated in 1961. Then he attended Manhattan College, majoring in political science and graduating in 1965. New York University Law School followed, where he made the law review. He graduated in 1968.

Giuliani biographer, Andrew Kirtzman, describes Giuliani's sometimes rigid allegiance to the Catholic faith as part of his attraction to law, given its required rigidity. In both Catholicism and law there are clear rules and penalties. Not surprisingly then, as a young college student Giuliani considered entering the priesthood and expressed much disgust at the lies, hypocrisy, selfishness, and incompetence of local politicians. About his choice of a legal career, Giuliani has said:

> I wanted to be a doctor. I wanted to be a journalist...I thought about being an Air Force pilot and I had a lot of different dreams and ambitions, and finally, toward the end of college, decided to go to law school, ended up at NYU Law School. And after a week or two of being in law school, I said to myself, "I found the profession that I like and enjoy and really feel fulfilled with." And I was very lucky; I mean, I found something that...sort of fit me. (Giuliani 2002, 101)

His mentors included Brother Jack O'Leary, a high school teacher who helped to develop his interest in music and reading despite the fact that many considered those interests less than manly then. Later there was Lloyd Mac-Mahon, chief judge of the Southern District of New York for whom he clerked after law school. MacMahon pointed out mistakes that were not to be made on a case. This same MacMahon wrote a letter to have Giuliani spared military service during the Vietnam War. Also a mentor to Giuliani while he was a young prosecutor was Carl Bogen, the New York Police Department (NYPD) detective on whom the television character Kojak was based.

His role models included John F. Kennedy, whom he admired for being a white politician who managed to have rare success at navigating both minority and white circles. From Deputy Attorney General Harold Tyler, Giuliani learned to remain calm under pressure; from Martin Luther King, Jr., he learned to expect progress, and from Joe DiMaggio that "the struggle is constant." (70–71). From Ronald Reagan, for whom he worked two and a half years, he learned resoluteness in handling an office. Giuliani also admired New York archbishop John Cardinal O'Connor whom he considered brilliant both in public and in private and, New York's 103rd mayor (from 1965 to 1973) John V. Lindsey, whom Giuliani considered an independent, outspoken reformer who managed the city well at a turbulent time.

Other influences on who he has become include books like John Kennedy's *Profiles in Courage* and being raised around his father's youngest brother Rudolph, a police officer and his mother' three police officer brothers and her fire captain brother. Apparently, Giuliani grew up hearing his uncles' heroic stories. Courage, his father told him, was "being afraid but then doing what you have to do anyway." (70).

Giuliani asserted in 2002 that "I have a pretty good sense that I'm very, very human, that I make a lot of mistakes, and that I got to keep working on it. And if I don't, my mother reminds me of it all the time." (56). Nevertheless, while mayor of New York, Giuliani was not known for admitting to mistakes or for making apologies. In more recent times, under a national microscope he has. For example, when President George W. Bush solicited Giuliani's input on a candidate to be the head of the Department of Homeland Security in 2004, Giuliani recommended his loyal friend and former New York Police Commissioner, Bernard Kerik. As it turns out, Kerik was a poor choice, given a less than stellar legal history. Later in 2007, he was indicated on federal corruption charges. Giuliani then admitted he had indeed made a mistake—but requested balance in judging him given his many other successful decisions. He has referred to himself as an independent, a reformer, a maverick, an optimist, reasonable, honest, honorable, courageous, compassionate, passionate, a good judge of people, an excitable Italian, and a hard worker who likes to be surrounded by hard workers. His work ethic came from his father, who taught him to "do the job in front of you. If you do a good job of it, you have a future, if you don't, then you don't have a future doing much of anything." (66).

Giuliani enjoys comedy, opera, music in general, baseball, golf, and life. His sense of humor is evident in his many photographs in drag and his television appearances on comedic television programs like *Seinfeld, David Letterman,* and *Saturday Night Live.* He is also infectiously passionate about New York City and about New Yorkers. After the September 11, 2001, (9/11) World Trade Center terrorist attacks, he repeatedly called them "the most wonderful people in the world."

Of course, many people have offered their descriptions of Rudy Giuliani. Some of them have been positive, but many of them have been much less so. Common adjectives for Giuliani include captivating (there are at least ten books about him); charismatic, diligent, persistent, courageous, circumspect, emotional, bully, opportunist, ruthless, defiant, opinionated, intolerant, suspicious, fascist, blind, scrappy, brash, duplicitous, immoral, heartless, mean, and wrong. Edward "Ed" Koch, one of New York City's longest serving mayors (1978–1989) called Giuliani "mean-spirited," "traitor," "vindictive," and a "nasty man" and "villain" but also "mayor of America" and a "visionary." Giuliani had played an active part in uncovering various scandals associated with the Koch administration.

Many who know Giuliani personally have said that he would often argue with those who opposed him and demonize and demean his critics. To noted biographer Wayne Barrett, Giuliani "was a mesh of half-truths, double agendas and secrets, wins that had to be transformed into records, losses that had to be imagined as wins, flaws that were depicted as misunderstood strengths, opponents who could only be explained as evil" (Barrett 2000, 11).

Significantly, although Giuliani has changed his mind on significant issues (for example, opposing school vouchers to endorsing them; opposing abortion to supporting abortion choice and his endorsement of equal rights for homosexuals), he is definitely not wishy-washy. He is capable of making and sticking with difficult decisions that he thinks are best, despite protests to the contrary. For example, as mayor he had to make sharp budget cuts, actions that drew several protests, but he remain unperturbed. Also, after 9/11 during the recovery efforts as safety concerns emerged, despite protests to the contrary, he reduced the number of workers at Ground Zero (the site of the incident). In hindsight, this turned out to have been the best thing, given health problems that have since manifested. Out of his desire to be respected and to leave a mark in history Giuliani describes himself as being "willing to make decisions...one of the ways in which I've helped turn the city around is I do make decisions and I'm not afraid of controversy if I believe this is the right direction for the city." (Giuliani 2002, 80). So, where did he get this stubborn disposition?

One insight is offered by Eleanor Fremont, who wrote that when Giuliani was a boy growing up in Brooklyn, ten minutes from the Brooklyn Dodgers' Ebbets Field, his father, an ardent Yankee fan, dressed his son in Yankee attire and sent him down the street. The neighborhood youth, incensed by this action, set upon young Rudy. He perceived himself as a martyr Yankee fan, who in the face of opposition would remain steadfast despite the cost. This love of the Yankees that he shared with his father began at age four when he saw Joe DiMaggio play. He remains a very ardent fan, and as mayor of New York had the joy of hosting parades in honor of Yankee World Series' victories. He took his passion for the Yankees even further as mayor by attempting to extend the city's income tax surtax to finance a relocation of Yankee Stadium.

Giuliani is clearly a man of courage, as evidenced by his early days as a federal prosecutor in both Washington, D.C. and New York. He was brave enough to take on the mob (organized crime) and the powerful but corrupt. In the aftermath of 9/11 as President George Bush and Vice President Dick Cheney were rushed into hiding, Giuliani was the leader that the media was able to locate and to show to the world at a time when Americans in particular seemed desperately to need to see a leader in action.

Nonetheless, Giuliani's crudeness or incivility is classic. It apparently has two dimensions: a crude public persona and a more private manipulative kind of crudeness to handle opposition among his insiders. Examples of the crude public persona include the September 1992 episode of Giuliani's joining a rowdy crowd of police officers to protest then Mayor Dinkins Civilian Complaint Review (an independent group of people who would investigate civilian complaints against the police). The officers were discontented because the board had all civilians, no officers in the membership. At the protest, Giuliani shouted epithets through a bull horn, further instigating the crowd. Another example of Giuliani's public crudeness occurred in October 1995 when, to the shock of many, Mayor Giuliani ordered Palestinian leader Yasir Arafat to leave a United Nations function of world leaders held at Lincoln Center. Many thought Giuliani did this for his own personal gain to appeal to the many Jews in the city, given the longstanding conflicts between Jews and Palestinians in the Middle East. Another incident that cost him several approval points with the public was his May 2000 announcement to the press that he was leaving his wife and the mother of his two children for his mistress, Judith Nathan, before he told wife Donna Hanover about these plans.

His crude private behaviors have involved incidents where his staff assisted him in efforts to intimidate those who opposed him into compliance. Examples of these crude private tactics have been reported by two of his education commissioners. The first, Ramon "Ray" Cortines felt forced to resign; the other, Rudy Crew, was terminated. First, Ray Cortines, a sixty-two-year-old from California, began his post as education commissioner the summer of 1993. Giuliani apparently considered Cortines too independent a reformer and perhaps, given Cortines' quiet demeanor, difficult to read and subsequently to trust. The relationship between Cortines and Giuliani became particularly poor when Cortines refused to terminate 2,500 Board of Education employees, including his press aide John Beckman, who had been an ardent supporter of the Dinkins administration, and Leonard Hellenbrand, who had opposed the mayor publicly. Cortines and the mayor also disagreed about the mayor's push to have the NYPD in charge of school security.

Consequently, one evening in April 1994, Giuliani had Cortines summoned to Gracie Mansion late in the day. Cortines was made to wait more than an hour and then was hassled by Giuliani and staff to make the required terminations and to accept Herman Badillo as a monitor of the school system and in essence, as Cortines' supervisor. The next day Giuliani's best friend and deputy mayor, Peter Powers, made repeated calls to Cortines' office to see if Beckman and Hellenbrand had been fired. When they were not, Giuliani announced to the media that Badillo would indeed be the school system's monitor. Cortines then drafted a resignation, but on the appeal of Board of Education president Carol Gresser and Governor Mario Cuomo, he stayed. However, Giuliani called Cortines "precious," "playing the little victim," and "whining," apparent inferences to Cortines' sexual orientation. Cortines resigned in September 1995. His replacement was Rudy Crew.

Rudy Crew, a forty-five-year-old African American from Tacoma, Washington, fast became friendly with Giuliani. He did as the mayor wanted. This included efforts to end the lifelong tenure of public school administrators and the social promotion of students (grade promotions based on age as opposed to student achievement). As some interpret things, Crew even attempted to make Giuliani appear to be a successful education reformer by excluding the low scores of the city's non-English-speaking students from the Regents examination (New York's test of student achievement) success statistics. However, three years into his post, Crew found himself at odds with the mayor's new position of endorsing vouchers or efforts to divert public school education dollars to private schools. Previously, Giuliani had made a number of speeches against vouchers and according to Crew (in an interview with Wayne Barrett), he had told Crew that his novel position was "just politics." Apparently, with his eyes on a statewide Senate run, Giuliani wanted to appeal to the statewide Catholic electorate and the Republican National Party. Yet, Giuliani went further than a mere verbal endorsement. He set aside millions for the voucher plan and apparently leaked confidences about Crew's marital troubles and other matters to the press. By December 23, 1999, Giuliani had garnered the necessary Board of Education votes to terminate Crew. Thereafter, Crew spoke to Wayne Barrett about Giuliani:

> He had no pedagogical commitment, no education philosophy, no grounding in a belief system...When Rudy sees a need to take someone out, he has a machine, a room full of henchmen, nicking away at you, leaking crazy stories. He is not bound by truth. I have studied animal life, and their predator/prey relations are more graceful than his...There is a very powerful pathology operating inside this man...I believe he feels an anger about some piece of his life that just takes over.(Newfield 2002, 57)

Ed Koch described Giuliani this way: "Rudy Giuliani has two moral compasses. On the one hand he is an honest man, fiscally incorruptible and fearless in the face of organized crime. On the other, he'll say almost anything to get his way." (Koch 1999, 111). Also, several persons who knew Giuliani while he was mayor said that he saw people who criticized him as his enemies. Also, when things went bad he would scapegoat others.

There has also been Giuliani's classic jealousy. For anything positive on his watch, he apparently wanted the credit. This was clearly the case with his first police commissioner, William "Bill" Bratton, who often has been called "a cop's cop" by fellow officers, referring to his understanding and care for fellow officers. Bratton's career in New York began with him as head of New York's transit police. Later as New York's Police Commissioner he merged the transit police with the NYPD, putting them in the same uniform for a omnipresent police effect. Indeed, officers could often be seen day and night on the streets, in the subways and other public places. Bratton also called his approach "community policing," although the officers were not known for much community interaction besides simply being present. Bratton was instrumental in putting George Kelling's "broken windows theory" approach into effect, and crime was indubitably in substantial decline. For this and more, Bratton received a lot of adulation in the press and from various groups. But he had transgressed in overshadowing his boss, the mayor, on crime fighting. Apparently jealous of Bratton, Giuliani required that Bratton fire his press secretary, John Miller. He also berated Bratton in the press for his time at the popular restaurant, Elaine's. When Ed Koch mentioned to Giuliani that Bratton would leave his position if demeaned, Giuliani responded "I don't care if he leaves. I run the police department." (Koch 1999, 61). Bratton resigned March 1996. His replacement was Giuliani's loyal fire commissioner, Howard Safir.

Giuliani's jealousy was coupled with a very controlling leadership style. As mayor, he micromanaged extensively. This was most evident in his efforts to terminate government employees whom he perceived to be disloyal, often because they had endorsed a Giuliani campaign rival or had disagreed with the Mayor on an issue. He had at least 300 city employees who reported to his commissioners fired for being "off agenda" (that is, not supportive of the Mayor's agenda for the city). Thus, the commissioners and their people operated out of fear and resentment. Giuliani also took care to have loyalty in the ranks by insisting on approving all high-level staff hires who would be working for his deputy mayors.

Noted private practice civil liberties attorney Richard Emery, who argued successfully against some of Giuliani's attempts to curtail free speech, considered Giuliani's micromanagement to be arrogance. Emery described Giuliani to writer Jack Newfield as thinking himself so smart that he avoided delegating, believed he was never wrong, and had a position of moral rectitude. Giuliani argued "respect for the rule of law" but then often attempted to change the laws for himself, for example, attempts to extend his time as mayor after 9/11 and his efforts to change city laws so that public advocate

Mark Green, a Democrat, would not succeed him if he failed to finish his term as mayor in the event of success in a U.S. Senate race. Nevertheless, after Giuliani's diagnosis with prostate cancer, which he revealed publicly in spring 2000, he claimed that he had changed for the better.

THE WOMEN

For the most part, Giuliani has maintained that his personal life is personal. Nevertheless, since it is often said that behind every successful man there is a woman, the women in Rudy Giuliani's life are discussed here. These women include his mother, three wives, and various rumored mistresses.

His mother, Helen Giuliani, was raised by her widowed mother of seven. Helen was a bright and doting woman. She maintained well into the 1990s that her son Rudy was a liberal at heart. She was the person whom Rudy Giuliani claimed reminded him on occasion that he was not perfect.

Regina, Giuliani's first wife, was the daughter of his father's cousin Salvatore Peruggi. They had been frequent playmates after Rudy's family moved to Long Island when he was seven. His mother thought the union was ill-fated from the beginning because Giuliani and Regina had such different personalities: he, an extrovert who liked to socialize, and she, a quiet home body. But Giuliani refused to listen to his mother and got married in October 1968. In 1982, after fourteen years of marriage he was successful in getting their marriage annulled, divorce being forbidden in the Catholic Church. For the annulment Giuliani claimed that he thought Regina was his third cousin, but then found out she was his second cousin. However, many witnesses to the union claimed that Giuliani had been dishonest in his claim of ignorance.

Next was second wife Donna Hanover. Giuliani met Donna in 1981 when, as a prosecutor for the Reagan administration, he made frequent trips to Miami to address the Haitian refuge crisis. Hanover was a television anchor in Miami. Unlike with Regina, Donna and Rudy's personalities matched. They married in 1983 and became the parents of a son, Andrew, born in 1986 and a daughter, Caroline, born in 1989. Donna Hanover was an ardent supporter of her husband's career. By 1995, that had changed after Cristyne Lategano came into Mayor Giuliani's world.

Cristyne Lategano was a young Italian in her twenties when she began working for Mayor Giuliani. She exercised considerable influence at City Hall. For this, and for her reputation as a malicious gossip, fellow staffers disliked her. She was part of the mayor's executive committee, his communications director, responsible for constructing his image in the media. Giuliani apparently admired her diligence and her ability to discern people. In 1995 after a news story appeared with the caption "The woman behind the Mayor," featuring a picture of Giuliani and Lategano, Donna Hanover accused them of having an affair. Both Lategano and Giuliani denied having one, and there are no reports of a sexual consummation. Nevertheless, the spirit of an affair, emotional intimacy, clearly existed between them as the two spent almost all their days and late nights together, working. Thereafter, Donna and the children remained at Gracie Mansion (the Mayor's residence), but Donna stopped making public appearances with her husband.

Lategano had managed to come between Giuliani and his closest aides, and by 1999 most of Giuliani's closest staffers had left his administration, including long-time best friend and deputy mayor Peter Powers. Then, in February 2000 Lategano herself left the administration, moving to South Carolina to be close to her mother and to marry Nicholas Stratis, a sportswriter. Promptly taking her place as a frequent companion of the mayor was Judith Nathan, a forty-five-year-old health company executive. By this time, Donna Hanover was truly off of her husband's calendar, but evidently she did not realize just how far off. So, on April 27, 2000, Giuliani announced that he had prostate cancer; on May 6, 2000, his wife Donna announced to the media, "I will be supportive of Rudy in his fight against his illness, as this marriage and this man have been very precious to me" (Kirtzman 2001, 315). Four days later, to Donna's surprise, Giuliani told the press that he was leaving his wife, clearly to be with his mistress. By this time, he had been seeing Nathan for about ten months. Biographer Wayne Barrett suspects that the timing of the announcement of the affair was an effort to preempt the release of Barrett's investigative biography, *Rudy*. Giuliani and Donna were divorced in 2002. Thereafter, Giuliani married Judith Nathan on May 24, 2003.

Giuliani has asserted that he values family: "The reason I am such a fortunate man is I have people that love me and I love them, and they care for me and I care for them. And that's the greatest support that you can have in life" (Giuliani 2002, 55). Nevertheless, his relationship with his two children has been a strained one in recent years, so much so that son Andrew, an aspiring golfer, supported his father's presidential campaign from a distance and daughter Caroline, a self-proclaimed liberal, supports Barack Obama for President of the United States.

POLITICS AND CAREER

Giuliani has gone back and forth between working in the public and the private sector. After law school in 1968, he clerked for Judge MacMahon, U.S. District Judge for the Southern District of New York. Then, in 1970 he worked as one of the federal U.S. attorneys in New York. He was soon promoted to executive assistant U.S. attorney and chief of the office's narcotics unit. Then, in 1975 he left New York to work in Washington, D.C., as an associate deputy attorney general and chief of staff to the deputy attorney general under Gerald Ford's presidency. He returned to New York in 1977 to work at the private practice law firm Patterson, Belknap, Webb, and Tyler. In 1981, under the Ronald Reagan presidency, he returned to Washington, D.C. as an associate attorney general in the Department of Justice. In that capacity he supervised the U.S. Marshals, the Drug Enforcement Agency, and the Bureau of Corrections. His most high-profile task at this point was handling the Haitian refugee crisis, the return of thousands of refugees to Haiti.

Nevertheless, much of Giuliani's most significant crime fighting occurred in 1983 when he returned to New York after being appointed U.S. Attorney for the Southern District of New York. In that capacity he had 540 dismissals and more than 4,152 convictions, with only twenty-five of them overturned. These cases involved organized crime figures, drug dealers, white collar criminals, and politically corrupt persons. In 1989, amidst praise, but also considerable criticism over a few high-profile acquittals, Giuliani resigned as a federal prosecutor to prepare for a mayoral run and consequently work for the same law firm (White and Case) that defended Panamanian dictator Manual Noriega. He left White and Case in 1990 for another private law firm, Anderson, Kill, Olick, and Oshinsky, where he stayed until becoming the 107th mayor of New York in 1994, serving two terms, and leaving office at the end of 2001.

He had remained unscathed by the decadence of the 1980s—the drugs, money, and nightlife—which put him at odds with many on Wall Street and in City Hall. On becoming mayor, he had inherited the remains of both the Koch and Dinkins mayoral administrations. Democrat Edward Irving Koch had been mayor for three terms (from 1977 to 1989). He left office marred by scandal involving persons in his administration, deteriorating quality of life in the city, and conflicts with minority leaders. Democrat David Norman Dinkins followed as mayor from 1989 to 1993. Dinkins was the city's first African-American mayor. He had a narrow win over Giuliani, with less than 50,000 votes in a city of more than seven million. Giuliani had been ignorant of the workings of the New York political machine. Winning an election in New York City has often necessitated having the right endorsements in words and in funds. Andrew Kirtzman, a Giuliani biographer, characterized the loss as Giuliani's failing to take advantage of relationships like his friendship with the very powerful Republican Senator Al D'Amato and the influence of liberal party leader Ray Harding. Instead, he was doing things his own way, with an awkward public persona, an intimidating presence, and his harsh public criticism of other public figures. This gained him an early lead in the polls. Nevertheless, the Giuliani machine was unwieldy. He had a huge campaign headquarter, numerous staff in mid-town Manhattan, and hardly any financial backers.

To many observers, it was the racial unrest in the city that won Dinkins the 1989 mayoral election. The flames of racial contention became particularly hot when in August 1989, Gina Feliciano, from the predominantly white Bensonhurst area of Brooklyn, had bragged about her black boy-friend, sixteen-year-old African American Yusef Hawkins, who was from the predominantly black Bedford Stuyvesant, Brooklyn. Her ex-boyfriend, Keith Mondello, was most unhappy about this, and on the night of Gina's eighteenth birthday Mondello stood with friends outside her party in case Hawkins showed up. Before the night was through, Hawkins was dead. In the aftermath, many criticized then-mayor Ed Koch for his mishandling of the racial unrest that followed this and previous such incidents. It was time for change.

While campaigning for mayor, both David Dinkins and Rudy Giuliani attempted to meet with the grieving Hawkins family. The family, perturbed by what appeared to be efforts to politicize and exploit their loss, refused to meet with the candidates. Later, with the urging of black community leaders, they reluctantly agreed to meet with David Dinkins. The meeting with Dinkins did not go well. Nevertheless, there was a boost in the polls for the Dinkins campaign.

To make matters worse for Giuliani, Andrew Kirtzman reported that without consulting his campaign advisors, Giuliani named comedian Jackie Mason as his honorary campaign chair. In that capacity Mason made a number of public racially inflammatory remarks regarding Jews supporting black candidates regardless of the candidates' competence. Mason was forced to resign from the Giuliani campaign, but the damage was done. Mason had apparently been a vain attempt by Giuliani to gain Jewish support.

Dinkins eventually was victorious as mayor. Some believe that Giuliani has maintained a grudge against the black community for the Hawkins slight and his loss of the 1989 mayoral campaign. Giuliani himself told Jack Newfield, "They stole that election from me. They stole votes in the black parts of Brooklyn, and in Washington Heights. Illegal Dominican immigrants were allowed to vote in Washington Heights" (Newfield 2002, 65). Newfield concluded from this conversation and his observations of Giuliani that "...this twist of fate—having to run against Dinkins instead of Koch—was the turning point in Giuliani's emotional life about race...Giuliani thought of himself as a 'man of destiny,' who was going to be president someday. Losing his first bid for public office to an African American he felt superior to, fractured his psyche. His ego had a hard time accepting the judgment of the people" (64).

Two years into the Dinkins administration, racial tensions remained a major issue. Violence erupted again in the Brooklyn community of Crown Heights on August 19, 1991, and continued for three days as blacks rioted. The incident began when a car that was a part of a Jewish motorcade ran a red light, killing a seven-year-old black child, Gavin Kato. Shouts followed to "kill the Jew," and twenty-nine-year-old Jewish student Yankel Rosenbaum was killed.

Indubitably, by his second run for City Hall in 1993, Giuliani had learned a lot. During the Dinkins administration, while working for the law firm

Anderson, Kill, Olick, and Oshinsky, he studied politics and policy. His advisors included a history professor and senior editor of the *City Journal,* Fred Siegel; Yale University president emeritus Benno Schmidt; Harvard lecturer George Kelling; long-time political maverick Ray Harding (Liberal Party Leader); and Andrew Cuomo, an expert on homelessness. He apparently also was influenced by the work of New York University professor Larry Mead, who had published about putting welfare recipients to work cleaning parks and picking up garbage. He also managed to surround himself with *bricoleurs* capable of smearing the competition.

He was able to criticize Dinkins for his inept handling of racial conflict involving Jews, and in so doing painted Dinkins as more of the old Koch administration; he also exposed persons in the Dinkins camp who held racially intolerant views, from which it appears he harvested substantial Jewish support. Thus, although Dinkins spent much of his administration making necessary but unpopular decisions to improve the city's economic status, curb violence, and abate racial unrest, he was not particularly media savvy about it, leaving the Giuliani administration to reap the benefits. The public blamed Dinkins for their discomforts and ignored the substantial decline in violence during the second half of the Dinkins administration. This was an error that Giuliani would be sure not to repeat as mayor, with the assistance of his close associate and communications director Cristyne Lategano.

November 2, 1993, in his second election against David Dinkins, Giuliani became New York City's 107th mayor. He won by a 2 percent margin, about as much as he had lost to Dinkins four years earlier. To some, including Giuliani, liberal dominant New Yorkers were sending a message; they wanted something new: law and order. As Kirtzman put it, it was a move "against the indignities of daily life...that the ways of vagrants and petty thieves who filled the streets would cause citizens for the first time to think of themselves as victims and the less fortunate as the victimizers" (Kirtzman 2001, 23). To others, Giuliani won because more Staten Island residents than usual showed up to vote on a referendum about Staten Island seceding from New York City. Whatever the story, Giuliani finally was at the helm of a very diverse city of more than 7.5 million people, with 250,000 employees and a $31 billion budget.

He promised New Yorkers, "no deals for jobs, no deals for contributors, no patronage" (Giuliani 2002, 89). Yet his administration included several patronage appointments of close friends and their family members. These were people who Giuliani thought he could trust, those loyal to his agenda regardless of capability. His initial inner circle of advisors or his "yes" people included Peter Powers, Giuliani's best friend since high school; wife Donna Hanover, a WPIX television reporter; his Justice Department friends Arnie Burns and Randy Levine (both also of Proskauer, Rose, Goetz, and Mendelsohn law firm); Ken Caruso (of Sherman and Sterling); and his U.S.

attorney office subordinate Dennison "Denny" Young (also of White and Case law firm). According to Giuliani biographer Fred Siegel, Giuliani surrounds himself with persons who are intelligent, loyal, and energetic. The harmony among the initial Giuliani work group was severely diminished by the presence of his young communications director Cristyne Lategano, whom the mayor seems to have placed on a special pedestal of confidence, so much so, that before the end of Giuliani's time as mayor, most of the initial inner circle had left his administration.

In his first term, Giuliani centralized administrative decisions out of his office. With this move, documents previously available to the public became functionally off limits, making it difficult to investigate the mayor's claims of success. The positive side of this was that it put Giuliani in frequent contact with his deputy mayors, which facilitated a quicker process for getting tasks completed. Reportedly, in his 8:00 A.M. staff meetings, he could be persuaded to change his mind with the right evidence. He was also willing to cross party lines, for example, in giving his endorsement to Democratic gubernatorial candidate Mario Cuomo in 1994, a miscalculation since George Pataki won the election and the new governor was not quick to forgive. Relations between the two remained clearly contentious. Yet, true to himself, if not to his political party agenda, mayor Giuliani continued to disagree with the national party on gay rights, abortion choice, and gun control. He is, after all, a New Yorker.

Undeniably, the Giuliani years were times of prosperity for many. The city looked inviting and crime was significantly on the decline. There were, however, significant weaknesses in the Giuliani administration. These included his efforts to reform education, to address a housing shortage, and to reduce poverty. Nonetheless, in 1997 Giuliani won reelection to a second term as mayor (but with 172,000 fewer votes than his previous win). His primary opponent was Democrat and former Manhattan borough president Ruth Messinger. This was an unusual victory in New York, which rarely grants a Republican mayor two terms.

Except for law school, all of Giuliani's education had occurred at Catholic schools. The same was true for his closest friends. Thus, it was apparently devoid of true multicultural appreciation. The result was his later embrace of a "color-blindness" stance. As he described it: "I don't care about people as minorities, or as majorities or as subgroups. I care about people as people. I think the thing wrong with this city is people cared about people as members of subgroups: Italian Americans, Irish Americans, African Americans, this American, that kind of American, some other kind of American" (Giuliani 2002, 78). Such colorblindness refuses to acknowledge that people's circumstances and experiences in life can be affected by their color; this is a social effect, not a biological one.

Giuliani's narrow academic exposure proved significant later when he attempted to improve a rather unique, but dismal public school system. This was something that he had not experienced and evidently knew little about. His efforts included using Herman Badillo, a City University of New York graduate himself, to attempt to reform his alma mater. In the midst of student protests to the mayor's reform efforts, Giuliani's comments demonstrated how out of touch he was with this largely minority-serving institution. He insisted that tuition was rather low and that protestors were simply cutting class. In so doing, the mayor appeared unappreciative of the value and impact of the public university's significant role in educating low-income city residents and new immigrants.

The situation for the city's 1.1 million children in its 1,100 public schools was much worse. Many of them were in overcrowded classrooms, with no air conditioning on hot days (so classes were often conducted in the dark), few computers, irregular maintenance, and several very unhappy teachers. There were nonetheless, lavish facilities in pockets of the city that served predominantly white students. The statement that seemed to characterize the mayor's stance on public education in New York was that the "whole school system should be blown up" (Koch, 1997).

The problem, according to some, was the mayor's management style. He was not a collaborator, and collaboration with parents, teachers, unions, administrators, and the community is necessary to accomplish most things in education. Thus, at the end of the two-term Giuliani administration, less than 30 percent of the city's eighth graders passed the New York Standardized Test (called the "Regents") in reading and mathematics. There were also significant declines in the graduation rate.

Then there were the mayor's efforts at welfare reform. After President William "Bill" Clinton's welfare reform bill passed in 1996, Giuliani stepped up his implementation of workfare based on the ideas of New York University professor Larry Mead. It involved moving able-bodied persons off of welfare and onto workfare, where they were required to work for the city in exchange for benefits. The work largely involved cleaning parks and city streets. The result was mixed. Workfare reduced the welfare rolls and encouraged more people to find their own employment (to avoid being relegated to cleaning the parks). However, absent real skills and education and forced to make poor choices for childcare in order to do workfare, it appears that some women turned to less desirable, illicit means of making income. Prostitution increased. Many churches and charities saw the numbers that they served surge. Yet, this was a city in the midst of a Wall Street "bull market" with many overnight millionaires. Corporations threatening to leave the city also got substantial tax breaks as incentives to remain. Indeed, the Giuliani years were good times for commercial real estate developers, like Donald Trump, but the city's housing shortage remained.

When on occasion the disparate life circumstances of the rich were compared to the poor, the mayor's response was that the poor benefited perhaps the most from the reductions in crime under his administration. Yet it appears that although crime was down overall in the city, in some pockets of the city where the poor were, crime numbers had remained high. The mayor also did not appear particularly compassionate to the poor when in 1998 he refused to meet with striking taxi drivers and ordered crackdowns on the homeless, panhandlers, and street vendors. To many, Giuliani began to look like a mayor of the rich masquerading under a cloak of "law and order."

His frequent efforts to curtail free speech in a rather liberal city further alienated him from many because they seemed a calculated effort to garner support beyond the city, given his broader political ambitions. The most noted free speech battle had him at odds with the publicly funded Brooklyn Museum in a move that some considered contrived to garner Catholic votes from the state's 40 percent Catholic electorate. Giuliani threatened to evict and de-fund the Brooklyn Museum if it did not cancel an upcoming exhibit. The October 1999 exhibit was called "Sensation: Young British Artists from the Saatchi Collection." It included a piece by African artist Chris Ofili depicting a Black Madonna with elephant dung, vaginas, and anuses suspended about her. Many high-profile persons supported the museum's right to free speech. The mayor had called himself a "keeper of morals," which was quite hypocritical to some given his rather public affair with his mistress at the time, Judith Nathan. Jack Newfield characterized the mayor's response to the exhibit as an example of the mayor's many failings at separating his private perspective from the requirements of his office and the law.

Giuliani's other unsuccessful free speech battles included the following:

Housing Works v. Police Commissioner Howard Safir on efforts to limit the size of demonstrations.

Marten v. Giuliani on holding persons overnight for minor violations during a peaceful protest.

Walton v. Safir on the firing of black female officer Yvette Walton in the aftermath of the Amadou Diallo shooting by police officers. Walton had spoken out against the racial profiling practices of NYPD's Street Crime Unit.

Harmen v. City of New York on requiring child welfare workers to get city consent before speaking to the press.

Latino Officers Association v. Safir on a requirement that police officers get the police commissioner's permission before making public statements about department policies and practices.

Latino Officers Association v. City of New York on not allowing a Latino officers group to march in uniform in parades as other ethnic and national groups had been able to do.

Metropolitan Council on Housing v. Safir on a refusal to let protestors sleep on a sidewalk outside of Gracie Mansion (the mayor's public residence).

Tunick v. Safir over refusal to let a photographer shoot nude models on a public street.

New York Magazine v. City of New York over attempts to keep *New York Magazine's* satirized advertisements about the mayor off of New York City Transit buses.

Kalke v. City of New York over the Parks Department ban of a church's distribution of free condoms as part of a HIV prevention program.

People v. Lyons, Sanchez and Schenk after members of the Socialist Workers Party received a summons for gathering signatures on a petition to be on a ballot.

Million Youth March v. Safir after Nation of Islam activist Khallid Mohammed was denied a permit for a Labor Day weekend rally.

Fifth Avenue Presbyterian Church v. City of New York after homeless persons who had the permission of a church to sleep outside the church building and on church grounds were threatened with arrest (Newfield 2002, 21–25).

Giuliani characterized his time as mayor as a period in which accountability and leadership were emphasized. As he put it:

Accountability replaces unmanageability. Accountability basically says a city is no more difficult to run than any organization. Every organization is difficult to run. Every organization has difficulties in getting to the precise goal that is intended for it, but that doesn't make them unmanageable. It means you have to be accountable, you have to be honest, you have to lay out what you can achieve, and then try to proceed in order to accomplish that. And in doing that you rebuild people's confidence in government (Giuliani 2002, 92).

Of leadership, he said: " …leadership means taking unpopular positions…rejecting harmful political fads…sometimes leadership requires challenging myths" (92).

In 2000, there was the first serious public talk of Rudy Giuliani as a possible presidential candidate. As it turns out, Giuliani had long set his sights on the presidency and had even considered whether being New York's mayor might help or hurt his ambitions for higher office. Regarding the matter he said in a 1998 NBC interview: "No, I haven't always wanted to be president…I think it's a very daunting—it's almost something that I don't like to talk about…[T]here's like a sacredness to it that you shouldn't really talk about it unless at some point in your life you decide to do it, then you should do it…I don't give it a great deal of thought. It seems like a very remote kind of thing" (93). Many perceive the U.S. Senate as a step that facilitates a run for the office of President of the United States. However, in May 2000, Giuliani withdrew from a Senate race where his prime contender was Hillary Clinton. His stated reason was to battle his recently diagnosed prostate cancer, a disease to which his father had succumbed in 1981. This was his second time walking away from a Senate run. The earlier occasion was in 1988, when he was a U.S. attorney. At that time he had a number of significant cases that he felt obligated to handle himself.

Regardless, Giuliani served as mayor of "the capital of the world," New York City, from 1994 to 2001. He left the mayor's office as a 9/11 hero, so much so that he became the frontrunner for the Republican nomination for president in 2007. However, Giuliani's campaign faltered, and he withdrew from the race after finishing third in the January 29, 2008, Florida primary. He has made a fortune from public-speaking engagements and his Giuliani Partners leadership, security and investment consulting jobs, which have included the country of Mexico as a client. In 2005 he became a part of the prominent international law firm Bracewell and Patterson, which was renamed Bracewell and Giuliani in his honor. His book *Leadership* became a national best seller. These events have all overshadowed the racial and class discontent during his administration in New York City. Giuliani had inherited a city with a surplus, but left it with a deficit, which he blamed on 9/11 even though the deficit existed before 9/11.

CRIME FIGHTING

Rudy Giuliani, crime fighter? Undeniably so, although some have challenged just how much credit is due to him, and him alone, for bringing law and order to a once very chaotic city. As a prosecutor, his aim was "to make the justice system a reality for the criminal" (Giuliani 2002, 101). He continued this posture as New York's 107th mayor. Wayne Barrett, author of three books on Rudy Giuliani, described him in 2000 as the "best known law enforcement figure in America since J. Edgar Hoover" (2002, 1). His life as a prosecutor even inspired two classic movies, *Serpico* and *Prince of the City*.

Giuliani became prominent as a crime fighter in 1974 when in *Perry Mason* fashion, as a young prosecutor, he conducted a grueling cross-examination of a three-term Democratic congressman Bertram Podell, who dissolved into tears on the stand, pleading guilty to conflict of interest and conspiracy to defraud the government. Thereafter, his prominence grew with further successful prosecutions of high-level organized-crime figures under the Racketeer Influenced and Corrupt Organizations (RICO) Act of 1970.

As an Italian himself, he battled the stereotype that all Italians are involved with the Mafia. In all, he prosecuted several Mafiosi. However, his legal colleagues have been known to disagree when Giuliani seemingly takes all of the credit for investigations and prosecutions that were already under-way by the time he got involved. One such case was the Bonanno crime family prosecution, which was underway for a year before Giuliani got involved; another was the Colombo crime family prosecution.

His cases also included the prosecution of the rich and famous such as Drexel Burnham and Michael Milken, financiers (on junk bonds, racketeering, and securities fraud); Imelda Marcos, wife of Philippines' president Ferdinand Marcos (on federal corruption charges); Leona Helmsley, hotel mogul (on tax evasion); E. Robert Wallach, corporate consultant (for conspiracy and fraud); Dennis Levine, investment banker (on insider trading); and Ivan Boesky, banker (on insider trading).

Another of Giuliani's famous cases involved Marc Rich, billionaire finan-
cier and twenty-year fugitive from justice, who had fled to Switzerland to
avoid prosecution. The allegations in this 1983 case included fraud, illegal oil
dealings with Iran, and owing $48 million in U.S. taxes. To Giuliani's aston-
ishment, years later Bill Clinton granted Rich a presidential pardon in January 2001, to which Giuliani responded: "When I first heard about it, my
reaction quite honestly was, no, no, it's a mistake. They must be confused
with somebody else. No president would pardon a fugitive. No president
would pardon someone on the FBI top number one list of fugitives for a long,
long time. No president would ever pardon someone where the charges are
still open that he traded with Iran during the hostage crisis." He emphasized
however, that he did not object to pardons in general, having recommended
several for people he thought had straightened themselves out (97).

Giuliani did not shy away from investigating his own. His assistant attorney Daniel Perlmutter pleaded guilty in 1986 to stealing more than $41,000
and about five pounds of drug evidence, at which time Giuliani said, "We
have to investigate ourselves. We have to aggressively investigate agents,
police officers, assistant U.S. attorneys. We're in a dangerous business, and
that's one of the prices you pay" (90). Maverick prosecutor Giuliani also
targeted political corruption. While Ed Koch was mayor and Giuliani was
U.S. Attorney of the Southern District of New York, many of those around
Koch went down for corruption, e.g., Congressman Mario Biaggio (1969–
1988, for accepting bribes and obstructing justice); Bess Myerson, a former
Miss America who was Mayor Ed Koch's Cultural Affairs Commissioner
(for conspiracy, mail fraud, and obstruction of justice); and Bronx Democrat
Stanley Friedman and others (for racketeering, conspiracy, and mail fraud).

As a prosecutor Giuliani thought it important to communicate with the
public and is extremely proud of having a part in convicting more high-level
offenders than his predecessors. Part of this joy was that he thought prosecuting such offenders had more of a deterrent effect than prosecuting street
offenders for violence. A large part of the deterrence effort was prosecuting
in the public eye. To this end, his tactics were harsh, including having suspects handcuffed and seized at work, such as in his efforts against some
Wall Street traders, namely Robert Freeman, a Goldman Sachs investor;
Timothy Tabor, a Merrill Lynch executive; and Richard Wigton, a Peabody
investment executive. Of such persons Giuliani remarked, "I can understand
how a young investment banker has been led astray, but do not ask me to
sympathize with him" (106). Clearly, he delighted in prosecuting greed. He
says of himself:

> I had this youthful conviction that all human beings were basically good. If
> you just turned on the right switch, goodness and rationality would flow
> forth. I came to realize that rationality does not necessarily rule and that some
> people were simply evil. There was very little you could do to change them,

and if you entertained the romantic notion that they could be changed, you would wind up endangering innocent people (56)

As a federal prosecutor in New York's Southern District, he started Federal Day—one day a month where drug arrests in Manhattan and the Bronx went to federal as opposed to state court, which meant that a conviction was more likely followed by harsher penalties. Ed Koch believed that this had a deterrent effect even though the drug cases that went this route were few compared to those handled in state court.

Later, as mayor and no longer prosecuting criminals himself, Giuliani remained as a leader to federal prosecutors. In this capacity he used his office to facilitate the prosecutions of organized-crime figures involved in criminal activities at the Fulton Fish Market, Hunts Point Market, and the city's annual San Gennaro Italian Festival (which claimed to raise funds for charity). The latter was in fact a front for Genovese crime family operations. He also prosecuted "Fat Tony" Salerno and the heads of five crime families (Barrett 2000,1): the Bonanno, Colombo, Genovese, Gambino, and Lucchese crime families. His prosecutions included Sicilian Mafia leader Gaetano Badalamenti for using New York pizzerias as heroin distribution fronts. The fish market prosecutions involved price fixing on fish entering the city. Giuliani would orchestrate sweeps of arrests of fishermen and threatened on occasion to close the area totally. He also got organized crime out of the city's garbage collection business (where the Lucchese and Gambino crime families had a stronghold on commercial garbage collection, inflating the cost as much as 40 percent). Giuliani insisted on open competition for garbage collection, and businesses benefited. He was undeterred by at least two hits put out on his life for $200,000 and for $400,000. In jest, he claimed to be insulted that the hit money was so little!

Indubitably, Giuliani's reputation as a crime fighter was substantial in getting him into City Hall. He was an antidote for disorder, riots, drug crime, violence, local government scandals, and Wall Street troubles, and possibly, for poorly performing schools, declining public service, and increasing homelessness. As a prosecutor he could empathize with the city's police officers. He had the opportunity to see Dinkins alienate himself from members of the NYPD by instituting an all-civilian Civilian Complaint Review Board (CCRB) and by too quickly taking the side of civilians in conflicts with the police. Giuliani was sure to do the reverse. Under his administration the CCRB did very little, and Giuliani quickly gave officers the benefit of the doubt in all conflicts with civilians.

Earlier, in 1992, during the Dinkins administration, Giuliani had even joined a rowdy group of protesting officers outside of City Hall, yelling epithets about the Dinkins approach to law and order. Yet, as mayor, Giuliani was not a favorite of many New York police officers. He was often at odds with many Latino and black police officers, who perceived him to be biased against them. Giuliani had also refused recommendations for police salary increases and other contractual changes. Many officers were also unhappy with the low morale that seemed to come from the Compstat process. Compstat (short for Computer Statistics) refers to the NYPD initiative of having weekly meetings with NYPD precinct commanders to assess crime-mapping data in areas where various crimes seemed to be increasing. Precinct commanders then were held accountable for reducing the crime statistics. The pressure on precinct commanders was passed all the way down to the patrol officers and seemingly, this impacted officer morale negatively.

Facts about Compstat

Bill Bratton, the architect of Compstat and an advocate of a "Broken Windows" approach to policing, is the current police chief of Los Angeles, California. He has served as the police chief in Boston, Massachusetts, and New York City under Mayor Rudolph Giuliani. During his tenure as the police chief of New York City under Giuliani, violent crime rates dropped precipitously. Bratton has transferred his vision of policing to the Los Angeles Police Department. Below is a summary of the principles of Compstat, which was one of Bratton's most notable elements of police management in New York City under Giuliani.

The elements of Compstat consist of the following four distinct principles.

Accurate and Timely Intelligence. Accurate and timely intelligence, or information, is absolutely essential in effectively responding to any problem or crisis. Since today's policing techniques nearly always consist of vast amounts of information, it is necessary to provide a vehicle wherein essential information can easily and effectively be shared with all levels of the organization. Often times, detectives have information on suspects or crime trends and patterns, but the actual field patrol officers who may be in contact with potential suspects have no idea of what information detective personnel possess or need to clear a case. Just as important, this principle also provides for an early warning system to identify emerging crime trends and patterns. In today's environment of ever-shrinking resources, being able to apply the necessary resources to an identified problem area is crucial in successfully reducing crime. Historically, marked police vehicles have randomly been deployed in hopes of deterring potential criminals who see the black and white police vehicles on patrol. This principle suggests that the intelligence/information be used as a radar screen to direct police resources to the exact problem area.

Effective Tactics. Traditional policing tactics have always dictated that most problems may be solved at a superficial level. In other words, take care of the suspect and don't worry about the social or environmental situation that may be adding to or creating the problem. Compstat tactics encourage "thinking outside the box" and mandates that every resource, both internal and external, is considered in responding to a problem. Compstat tactics also provide for a sense of urgency in responding to problems. The old attitudes of public entities responding at slow speed are no longer acceptable. Every case or call for service is handled as the traditional "Big Case" and is thoroughly and rapidly investigated in a systematic manner.

Rapid Deployment. For decades, police departments have been driven by calls for service and respond their limited resources in a reactive manner. With Compstat, the police department is now armed with vital intelligence regarding emerging crime trends or patterns that allows for a strategic police response. The strategic response can be in many forms, both traditional uniformed or plainclothes officer response as well as nontraditional decoys and sting operations.

Relentless Follow-up and Assessment. An essential element in any crucial operation is the need to critically assess past tactics and review what was successfully employed and what just didn't work. One of the main differences between private enterprise and the public sector is the bottom line of positive returns. The public sector and police departments have rarely been evaluated on their results. On the other hand, if a business implements an unsuccessful strategy or provides an unacceptable level of customer service, it isn't long before bankruptcy is filed. The bottom line with Compstat is results. Everything that the police department does, whether administrative, operational or investigative in nature, is evaluated by the results achieved. Static operations that do not provide for successful results are immediately assessed for their value and necessity to the overall operation of the department.

Source: Los Angeles Police Department Compstat Unit. http://www.lapdonline. org/crime_maps_and_compstat/content_basic_view/6363/.

Regardless, crime declined substantially, most notably, murder. In 1993, there were 1,927 homicides, but in 2000, there were 671. The decline had begun under the Dinkins administration with police commissioner Lee P. Brown and his assistant commissioner Jeremy Travis. Also, the declining crime numbers were occurring nationwide, so how much of the New York declines is attributable to Giuliani is hard to say. Experts have attributed New York's reduced crime numbers to "a demographic age reduction, reduced use of crack cocaine, and mandatory, longer prison sentences…[and] better and more sophisticated use of police resources" (Koch 1999, 10). Jimmy Breslin, Pulitzer winning journalist, saw things this way:

Giuliani named Bill Bratton the police commissioner. Bratton asked for a report on crime in the city. It was done by two working cops, Bill Gorta, a captain and John Yohe, a sergeant, whose interest was computers. Their report started a system that was called Compstat. It identified the places where the crimes were and had the precinct commanders held accountable.

The crime was—what a shock!—almost all in poor neighborhoods. For the first time in the city's modern years, the non-white neighborhoods had law enforcement. This brought the crime down so far and so fast that people called this normal policing a miracle" (Polner 2005, xvi)

Sounds simple enough, but it was a new and apparently effective approach in policing. Giuliani clearly cared about the criminal victimization of the poor. Under his administration, residents in some low-income communities, such as Washington Heights, had the opportunity to experience a taste of suburban security when drug-invested city blocks were closed by police officers such that no one could get onto the block without an identification and a clear legitimate reason to be there. Unfortunately, the cost of such efforts could not be sustained long term.

But what was this new approach to crime fighting? It was the "broken windows theory" in action. Before becoming mayor, Giuliani had kept up on the criminology literature. In 1982 university professors James Q. Wilson and George Kelling published an article in the *Atlantic Monthly*, "Broken Windows: The Police and Neighborhood Safety." The idea of broken windows is that if a window is broken in a building and not promptly fixed, then persons going by will see the broken window and assume that those in the building and the area do not care about their space. This assumption will encourage others to treat the property with similar disregard and soon, that building will have more broken windows. The law and order implication therefore is that fixing signs of disorder promptly prevents criminals from moving into an area to commit crime. What was unique about the approach was that it required warrant checks on petty offenders since statistics indicated that petty offenders were also serious offenders. Indeed, arresting petty offenders and then running warrant checks on them paid off. Between 1990 and 1994 New York's subway felonies fell 75 percent, and robbery fell 64 percent under transit police chief Bill Bratton, who was using the broken windows idea. Thereafter, Bratton left New York to return to Boston as Chief of Police, but months later, at the beginning of 1994, he returned to New York City to accept Giuliani's invitation to be New York City's police commissioner.

Bill Bratton had been a transit officer in Boston, working closely with George Kelling at the Harvard School of Government on the broken windows idea. Bratton had utilized the approach to reduce crime on Boston's trolleys. He was considered "a cop's cop," largely for walking the beat with officers and thus demonstrating an understanding of the issues that officers at all levels of the force had to address. He had tremendous success; crime decreased on the trolleys by 27 percent. Thereafter, Bratton became New York's new transit police chief in April 1990. The subways had been "overrun with hustlers, hoodlums, and the homeless" (Siegel 2005, 94). By 1991, George Kelling was heralding Bratton's success in another noteworthy article in the *City Journal* titled "Reclaiming the Subway."

Further, in the spirit of broken windows Giuliani took aim at "panhandlers, sex shop purveyors, cabbies, jaywalkers, street vendors, cop-bashers, un-reconstructed liberals, black radicals, black moderates, anti-Catholic art exhibitors, drunk drivers, methadone users, graffiti artists, public school bureaucrats, and, of course, welfare freeloaders" (Barrett 2000, 1–2). He barricaded certain streets to block jaywalkers, who could also find themselves with a summons. He also utilized shaming tactics to deter less than circumspect, if not illegal, activity. For example he had patrons of sex shops photographed, even though frequenting such establishments was not illegal.

But did Giuliani go too far? Some think so. He encouraged his police commissioners (William "Bill" Bratton, 1994–1996; Howard Safir, 1996–2000; and Bernard Kerik, 2000–2001) to tackle crime aggressively. For example, the morning of January 23, 2000, at 4:00 A.M., plainclothes officers entered Fort Washington Armory homeless shelter to arrest people who had failed to appear in court for offenses such as begging in public, public urination, and sleeping in the subway. Of the eighteen arrested, seven were schizophrenics.

In the wider city, broken windows efforts at cleaning up signs of disrepair were possible from the economic vibrancy of the city that Giuliani had inherited. He saw to the replacement of many sex shops with more widely appealing retail establishments such as the placement of Disney stores in Times Square, Manhattan. However, some insiders report that many of the negotiations for the Times Square revitalization occurred prior to Giuliani, under the Dinkins administration.

To further illustrate care, Giuliani tackled *in rem* housing (that is, real estate abandoned by the owners and thus the responsibility of government). He appointed former Dinkins administration staffer, African American Deborah Wright, to Housing Preservation and Development. She agreed with Giuliani that such properties should be unloaded from the city promptly into the hands of private enterprise, which would see to a community's upkeep.

To his credit, Giuliani appears to have been one of the few public officials to have taken threats of terrorism on United States soil seriously. He actively supported Andrew McCarthy, who led the prosecution of the blind sheikh Omar Abdel Rahman for the 1993 World Trade Center bombings, where six died and more than a thousand were injured. The sheikh was convicted but his coconspirator, Osama bin Laden, remained at large. Bin Laden threatened another attack to demolish the World Trade Center. Given this threat, in hindsight, Giuliani miscalculated in locating the city's $13 million emergency command center on the twenty-third floor of one of the World Trade Center Towers. His reason was that the Secret Service and the Central Intelligence

Agency were already located there. In 1998 he had City Hall reinforced with barbed wire and concrete barricades, and on occasion he had snipers on the roof of City Hall to protect it against terrorist attacks, all despite being severely criticized in the press for limiting access to a public building.

On the morning of 9/11, Giuliani received word of the possible attacks while at breakfast at the Peninsula Hotel in mid-town Manhattan. He proceeded quickly to the site. That day 2,974 people were killed; of those, twenty-three were police officers and 343 were firefighters. However, an estimated 25,000 lives were spared. Giuliani's stated that his inspiration in leading the city out of the horrific tragedy was Winston Churchill:

> I was trying to think, "Where can I go for some comparison to this, some lesson about how to handle it?" So I started thinking about Churchill, started thinking that we're going to have to rebuild the spirit of the city, and what better example than Churchill and the people of London during the Blitz in 1940… (Giuliani 2002, 13)

In the immediate aftermath, when the people of the world needed to see a hero, the cameras had found Rudolph Giuliani. Thereafter, he worked diligently to get the tourist economy back into the city and he was successful in doing so. In December 2001, *Time* magazine called him "Man of the Year" and "Mayor of the World." Queen Elizabeth selected Giuliani for knighthood, which he graciously accepted on behalf of the people of the city, and he also received Italy's highest civilian honor, the Cavaliere di Gran Croce.

But was he a hero? Apparently, many think so, but in New York City, among those who had the opportunity to observe events unfold more closely, some blame him for the deaths of hundreds of firefighters and others who died—in large part because the radios for emergency communications did not work and so commands to evacuate the towers before their collapse went unheard inside the towers. Two years earlier there had been City Council hearings about the poor condition of the radios. Nothing had been done.

Giuliani's crime-fighting efforts also included reforming New York City's judiciary. His posture suggests that he wanted judges to operate from a more crime-control (as opposed to due process or concern for legal technicalities) posture. Ed Koch had created a merit-based judicial selection and reappointment system, which required that the mayor accept the recommendations of a new mayor's Judiciary Committee and the New York Bar Association. But Giuliani reclaimed the mayor's right to select and appoint judges regardless of the committee or bar association's opinions. For example, he refused to reappoint Criminal Court Judges Eugene Schwartzwald and Jerome Kay despite their favorable recommendations. Giuliani was also insistent in the mid-1990s that Criminal Court Judge Loren Duckman retire and be investigated after his decision to release a suspect on bail resulted in the suspect committing murder in a domestic dispute. Hence, Giuliani may have made some judges very concerned about pleasing the mayor.

Although the numbers have not been thoroughly examined and the NYPD has admitted that their statistics are not infallible, crime declined drastically while Rudy Giuliani was mayor. However, the decline began before Giuliani. Dinkins had hired more officers and Giuliani hired even more; the drug wars were also on the decline, given more stringent enforcement efforts and longer sentences for offenders. Law and order had replaced chaos and drabness, for many, but not all who frequented New York City.

POLICE BRUTALITY

Although Rudy Giuliani has never encouraged police misconduct, his brash no-nonsense posture may have been misinterpreted by police officers already inclined to roguery. There were a number of high-profile cases of clear police brutality on his watch to which, regrettably, he was slow to respond apologetically. In fact, he refused to meet with minority leaders (who represented the victims) during the media frenzy around most of the incidents. This created a deep rift with local African Americans, Latinos, and civil rights advocates that continued through his entire mayoral administration. Giuliani's administration began with a rocky racial bent. On January 9, 1994, there was a hoax 911 call of a robbery at a mosque in Harlem. Responding police went charging into the mosque. Angry at the invasion into their place of worship and ignorant about the call, members of the Nation of Islam forcefully removed the officers. The scuffle was resolved peacefully, but Giuliani was most perturbed that arrests had not been made. Bratton, who was new on the job as police commissioner, was instantly at odds with the mayor who wanted a more aggressive law and order posture. The responding officers had chosen to resolve the matter with negotiations as opposed to arrests. Giuliani also tripled the size of the NYPD's Street Crimes Unit (to almost 400) in 1997. This unit, which had existed since 1971, held the motto "We own the night." Their primary focus was to get guns off of the streets and to pursue specific dangerous criminals. As a smaller group, the officers in the unit were trained and mentored carefully, which diminished when the group's size was inflated suddenly. The result was that certain persons apparently were profiled and mistreated. Blacks, Latinos, and gay men were strip-searched and held overnight while they were checked for warrants. Bratton had characterized the problem of police brutality as a "knucklehead" problem. He meant that police brutality was a matter of the actions of a few who were not the city's finest and whose presence on the force was a result of a lowered standard in police recruitment practices.

The following are a few of the many racial and ethnic minority members who were victims of police indignities during the Giuliani administration:

Alton Fitzgerald White, a 35-year-old black male and Broadway leading actor, in July 1999 was taken into custody, strip-searched, and not allowed any telephone calls for two hours after opening the door to let officers into his building. He thought that the officers were there to assist someone. The officers, who later apologized, claimed that they were looking for drug dealers.

Anthony Baez, a 29-year-old Latino Bronx resident, was playing football with others in the street on December 22, 1994. After his ball hit a squad car, an officer ordered the players to go home. Instead the players moved to another area of the street to continue their sport. A scuffle between the players and the officers followed and Baez, who suffered from asthma, was choked to death.

Abner Louima, a 33-year-old Haitian immigrant, on August 9, 1997, attempted to break up a fight outside a Brooklyn nightclub popular with Haitian immigrants. In the scuffle, one of the police officers arriving on the scene was punched. The officer mistakenly assumed that Louima was involved. Louima was taken to the precinct house, which had supervisors (sergeants) in the building. Therein, four officers participated in a severe beating and sodomy of Louima with a toilet plunger stick such that Louima's intestines were punctured, his bladder was injured, and several of his teeth were knocked out. Reportedly, one of the officers involved said, "This is Giuliani time. This is not David Dinkins time anymore." The officers involved then suggested that Louima's injuries were the result of gay sex. Four officers, Justin Volpe, Charles Schwarz, Thomas Weise, and Thomas Bruder, were convicted for the attack.

After the Abner Louima attack, which clearly shocked the city's conscience, Giuliani appointed a committee to examine police-community relations. The committee worked seven months to issue more than 100 recommendations that included better psychological screening of officers, more diversity in the police force, better pay, greater emphasis on courtesy, and requiring that new hires live in the city. Yet, instead of expressing gratitude, the mayor was largely dismissive of the work.

Then there was the Amadou Diallo shooting. On February 4, 1999, Diallo, a 22-year-old African immigrant, was killed while unarmed and reaching for his keys and identification. He was fired on by police 41 times, with nineteen bullets striking him after a Street Crimes Unit plainclothes officer had yelled "gun." In the aftermath, thousands protested the police actions and hundreds submitted to an arrest in protest. Yet Giuliani refused, as was his pattern then and now, to meet with black leaders. One exception was Giuliani's friend and ardent supporter, an African-American former congressman and a pastor of a substantial African-American congregation in Queens, New York, the Reverend Floyd Flake. The meeting ostensibly ended their friendship. Flake told Giuliani about being pulled over and called "nigger" by a police officer.

Giuliani seemed unmoved. Thus, the meeting ended with Flake telling Giuliani, "You've got a mean streak in you" (Kirtzman 2001, 247–248).

The incidents continued. On March 15, 2000, Patrick Dorismond, a 26-year-old black male security guard and father of two, was killed by police. As plainclothes officers attempted to engage Dorismond in a drug transaction, Dorismond, who had recently taken steps to become a police officer himself, refused their advances and out of his annoyance, a scuffle followed during which Dorismond was fatally shot. Thereafter, Giuliani attempted to demonize Dorismond by releasing his sealed juvenile record, which showed that at age thirteen Dorismond had been a delinquent. Giuliani went further, saying that this latest victim of alleged brutality was "no altar boy." As it turns out, Dorismond had been an altar boy, but the mayor refused to apologize for the remark, claiming it was a matter of unimportant semantics.

In all the above examples, the victims were racial minorities and the officers were white. Even Giuliani's African-American Deputy Mayor Raymond Washington had negative police encounters. Giuliani's response was to have him issued a special identification to ward off the police. The mayor appeared to have failed to understand minority concerns for their safety at the hands of police. He was, of course, capable of sympathy, but this seemed largely reserved for the police. For insight on the mayor's thinking in minority versus police disputes, newswriter Andrew Kirtzman offered this recount of comments that Giuliani made at the dedication of a street in honor of slain Police Officer Vincent Guidice in 1996:

> We have a right to demand more respect from the citizens of the city for police officers of the City of New York. It's about time to stop carrying signs pretending that they're racist, it's about time to stop carrying signs equating them to the KKK...They have to make decisions that I don't know that I'd be capable of making, and they're second guessed by some of the worst in society...the aggressive, appropriate police strategies of this department have saved thousands and thousands of lives (Kirtzman 2001, xii).

Yet, how could it be that Giuliani might appear so racially insensitive? Although his high school graduating class of 378 had only four blacks, he told writer Jack Newfield that he had a picture of Martin Luther King, Jr., in his high school room. Reportedly, while a law student in the 1960s, Giuliani sympathized with black rioters in Newark and Detroit. His friend Peter King claims he was "blacker than the blacks."

Yet, in a diverse city none of Giuliani's initial aides were black. In his second term there was one, Rudy Washington, the Deputy Mayor for Community Development and Business Services (from 1996 to 2001). Giuliani even had clear racists in his inner circle while mayor. These included Deputy Mayor for Economic Development John Dyson and Parks Commissioner Henry Stern, who each made remarks that blacks were inferior.

Overall, Giuliani himself appears to have made a point of avoiding black people. The mayor, who could make it to just about any police officer or firefighter's funeral at a moment's notice, often had some excuse about why he could not meet with noted black elected officials (such as U.S. Congressmen Charlie Rangel and Gregory Meeks, Manhattan Borough President Virginia Fields, and State Comptroller Carl McCall). He claimed that ignoring black leaders and what he called their pandering allowed him to serve the black community more effectively. Recently, as a candidate for the Republican nomination for President of the United States, he refused to participate in an All American Presidential debate at Morgan State University, for a largely African-American audience, choosing instead to attend a fundraiser elsewhere.

CONCLUSION

From the start to the end of his career in public service to New York City, Rudy Giuliani has exercised significant control over his public persona, at times through attacks on free speech in terms of limiting the comments of city employees to the press and pitching story angles to movie and television producers about his image. While in office, a number of public documents on his performance as mayor became unofficially unavailable, and when he left office, much of the paperwork on his administration was moved to a secure location. This being the case, the full story of Giuliani's successes and failures is unknown.

Perhaps Rudy Giuliani was a genius mayor or just a very lucky man. Jack Newfield, who knows him well, believes the latter to be the case. He calls Giuliani a "C-plus mayor of New York who became an A-plus myth in the world." He is referring to the fact that as mayor, Giuliani succeeded in putting himself at odds with many in the city: "blacks, black leaders, victims of police brutality, free speech and civil liberty advocates, AIDS activists, school teachers, schools chancellors, taxi drivers, community gardeners, museum artists, [and] sidewalk artists," to mention a few. Pre-9/11, Giuliani's approval rating was less than 50 percent, damaged in part by his revelation to the media earlier that year that he was leaving Donna Hanover, his second wife and mother of his two children, for his mistress Judith Nathan—all before telling wife Donna of these plans. Newfield attributes what he calls the "great mayor myth" to the power of television, in that after the 9/11 attacks the public's psyche desperately needed a hero. The President, who might have been the usual choice of hero, seemed lost and was even scuttled away into hiding. So too was the Vice President Dick Cheney, but the television cameras found and embraced Rudy Giuliani. Thus, Ground Zero became like a shrine, and Giuliani like its saint. A hero? "No," says Newfield, "he did nothing heroic; he merely did his job" (2002, 37).

Could it be pure luck that someone so ridiculed by so many has come so far politically? Likely not. He has managed to accomplish some significant positive changes as a courageous prosecutor and a hard-nosed, controlling mayor. Clearly he was not successful at all things, being human after all. It is more likely that his style has simply been very different from all those before him. His style carries a caustic flavor, suggesting entrenched issues with trust, loyalty, and race. However, to accomplish some things that needed to be done, namely, to bring law and order to a chaotic city, he was definitely the man for that job. The success with crime numbers, however, came at a grave and costly price for many innocent young minority males and their families. Regrettably, the mayor's sympathy for these families fell short. This remains a stain on a great legacy, but the story of Rudy Giuliani continues.

FURTHER READING

Barrett, Wayne. 2000. *Rudy! An Investigative Biography of Rudolph Giuliani*. New York: Basic Books.

Breslin, Jimmy. Preface. 2005. In *America's Mayor: The Hidden History of Rudy Giuliani's New York*, xvi. ed. Robert Polner, New York: Soft Skull Press.

Capeci, Jerry, and Tom Robbins. 2005. Prosecution. In *America's Mayor: The Hidden History of Rudy Giuliani's New York*, 11–12. ed. Robert Polner, New York: Soft Skull Press.

Fremont, Eleanor. 2002. *America's Mayor: Rudy W. Giuliani*. New York: Aladdin Paperbacks.

Giuliani, Rudolph. 2002. *The Mayor of America in His Own Words: The Quotable Giuliani*. ed. Bill Adler and Bill Adler, Jr. New York: Pocket Books.

Kelling, George. 1991. Reclaiming the subway. *City Journal* Winter, 17–28.

Kirtzman, Andrew. 2001. *Rudy Giuliani: Emperor of the City*. New York: Perennial.

Koch, Edward. 1999. *Giuliani: Nasty Man*. New York: Barricade Books.

Newfield, Jack. 2002. *The Full Rudy: The Man, the Myth, the Mania*. New York: Thunder's Mouth Press/Nation Books.

NYC. Gov, A Biography of Mayor Rudolph W. Giuliani. http://www.nyc.gov/html/ records/rwg/ html/bio.html/.

Parrott, James, and David Dyssegaard Kallick. 2005. Economy. In *America's Mayor: The Hidden History of Rudy Giuliani's New York*, 75. ed. Robert Polner. New York: Soft Skull Press.

Pearson, Hugh. 2005. Enforcement. In *America's Mayor: The Hidden History of Rudy Giuliani's New York*, 118. ed. Robert Polner. New York: Soft Skull Press.

Polner, Robert. 2005. Introduction. In *America's Mayor: The Hidden History of Rudy Giuliani's New York*, xxxii. ed. Robert Polner. New York: Soft Skull Press.

Siegel, Fred. 2005. *The Prince of the City: Giuliani, New York and the Genius of American Life*. San Francisco: Encounter Books.

Wilson, James Q., and George Kelling. 1982. Broken windows: The police and neighborhood safety. *Atlantic Monthly*. March. http://www.theatlantic.com/ doc/198203/broken-windows (accessed May 12, 2008)

Curtis Sliwa: Vigilantism, Victims' Rights, and the Guardian Angels

Brion Sever, with Al Gorman and Greg Coram

Curtis Sliwa is a long-time crime fighter and the founder of the Guardian Angels, an organization that is devoted to the safety of citizens. He created this organization in New York City in the late 1970s in the midst of a movement toward greater victims' rights and vigilantism, and it has grown from a handful of friends to a thriving organization. The success of the Guardian Angels has brought considerable fame to Sliwa, and though he still remains controversial to many observers, he is undeniably an icon of crime fighting.

Today, the Guardian Angels have an international presence, with groups now established in Japan, the United Kingdom, Canada, South Africa, New Zealand, and so on. Sliwa's popularity has continued to grow in congruence with the increased presence of the Guardian Angels, and through the trial of John Gotti, Jr. in connection with an assassination attempt made on his life. Sliwa regularly makes guest speaking appearances and currently hosts a radio talk show with cohost Ron Kuby.

This chapter will review Curtis Sliwa's contribution to criminal justice within a historical context of the larger social and political movements present during his rise to fame. It will explore the origins of vigilantism as well as the victims' rights movement, particularly in the 1960s and 70s in the United States. Included in this discussion will be a focus on sensational media coverage of crimes, popular television programs and movies centering on vigilantism and justice, the Nixon administration's movement of the criminal justice system back toward the crime control model, and vigilantes such as Bernard Goetz who have gained media attention. All of these phenomena were present during the development of the guardian angels and their influence on the rise of the Guardian Angels will be examined.

DEFINING VIGILANTISM

To better understand Curtis Sliwa's Guardian Angels' group, it is necessary to have a wide historical view of the concept of vigilantism and its relation to victims' rights. A historical perspective is not possible, however, without first attempting to clarify the term "vigilante." According to Merriam-Webster's dictionary, vigilante can be traced back to the Spanish and its original meaning was watchman or guard. People of ancient Rome used the Latin word "vigilans" with regard to Rome's own night watchmen who were assigned to keep an eye out for criminals drifting through the streets at night. Vigilante more recently has been used to describe someone who is a member of a volunteer committee organized to suppress and punish crime summarily, a self-appointed doer of justice. This is consistent with traditional conceptions of vigilantes as being those who take justice into their own hands.

In historical terms, vigilante has often had a judgmental connotation. This concept is underscored in Shotland's definition, who defines vigilantes as victims or family or friends of victims who seek revenge and overreact in their pursuing such revenge. For example, victims may use greater force than would be allowed by conventional law enforcement. This would include historic examples of blood feuds developing over harsh reactions by victims that were problematic enough to necessitate governmental authority of criminal offenses.

Perhaps one of the more influential researchers on the subject has been Les Johnson, who describes vigilantism as social movements that use force, violence, corporal punishment, or the threat of such. Johnson's definition explicates that vigilante acts are performed by groups that are not supported by the state and whose activities are in contrast to the standard norms of institutions. Accordingly, these groups attempt to impact crime or social control by providing security to members of society.

As Johnson demonstrates, the complexity involved in vigilantism combined with its evolving nature make it a difficult phenomenon to describe in one single definition. It is not a phenomenon that easily allows groups to be dichotomized into vigilantes or victims' rights advocates. There will be some overlap between the two groups, and whether a group is considered vigilantes or victims' advocates can vary with the time period and who is classifying them.

Because there is significant discord in the manner in which vigilantism is used by sociologists, criminologists, psychologists, criminal justice professionals, and political scientists, it is also difficult to conceptualize its merit. Although some sociologists tend to focus on a broad functional definition of vigilantism, viewing society's need for vengeance as a functional aspect of a society that values justice, others have viewed it as a negative phenomenon that occurs because of the character flaws of the people undertaking the act or because of a lack of proper oversight or effectiveness of law enforcement.

Criminologists and victimologists frequently have considered vigilantism within a discussion of its potential to impact crime and the criminal justice system. Some have emphasized its potential to impact crime through greater reporting practices or decrease it via deterrence. Others view vigilantism as a secondary issue or as a theoretical issue within debates over gun laws, the death penalty, neighborhood watch groups, juvenile justice, and self-defense, but have not placed as much emphasis on clarifying its definition.

Another complication emerging from this discussion is in establishing the scope of vigilantism: This obviously can hinge on the definition that is used. For instance, if the Webster's dictionary definition of vigilantism is used, whereby it is defined as a person who is a member of a volunteer committee organized to suppress and punish crime summarily, then a number of groups conceivably could be included. Indeed, some who have been referred to as terrorists or hate crime groups could be classified under this definition. Many political scientists would include these groups under the definition because they are inclined to study vigilantism as a form of political violence, while they would include nonviolent vigilantism as part of an internal critique of state government and thus as a function of politics.

Other definitions of vigilantism tend to be more case-specific, providing different types of vigilantes. Vigilantes incorporated under such typologies include social control vigilantes and crime control vigilantes. Social control vigilantes are motivated by issues that they believe impact the quality of life, values, or sense of decency in society. Under this definition, a vigilante could include those who seek equality for minorities at any cost, members of the Ku Klux Klan, or those seeking to influence special interests by ridding society of abortion, decreasing pollution, and so on.

Crime control vigilantes include those people or groups who believe that justice is not being upheld and that there needs to be intervention to rectify the injustices taking place. These groups may seek to aid law enforcement in their patrols and searches for fugitives or may try to influence the punishment that a criminal has received. For instance, crime control vigilante groups may patrol the streets to protect citizens or they may attempt to influence the everyday life of a rapist who has been released from prison by tracking his whereabouts or informing neighbors of his background. The line on which these actions border on the illegal is often a very fine one, particularly in the views of many within the criminal justice system. Moreover, vigilante groups typically do not fall strictly under crime control or social control classifications, because the two are not mutually exclusive. Indeed, Curtis Sliwa's Guardian Angels have undertaken strategies that are encompassed by both crime control and social control vigilantism.

One of the factors separating the definitions across the various fields studying vigilantism is the motivation necessary for a person or group of people to be included as vigilantes. Those in criminal justice and criminology tend to hold a narrow definition that includes people whose motivations are focused on justice or social order. Although hate would not be included as a primary motivation of vigilantes, it may be true that vigilantes often hate criminals or people they perceive to be criminals. The fields of criminal justice and criminology would place hate groups and terrorists in categories separate from vigilantism, whereas sociologists and political scientists are not as concerned with the legal barriers separating groups.

Although the victims' rights movement is often identified with vigilantism, the two are separate phenomena. Under some definitions of vigilantism, it certainly could be included within the goals and functions of the victims' rights movement. There are certain actions of vigilantes, however, that are not in line with the mainstream victims' rights movement.

The authors of this article do not use the term vigilante with the negative connotation with which it has commonly been associated. History has shown that those who were once considered vigilantes may now be

Citizen Patrols

In recent years, police departments have recognized the value in tapping into the motivation and enthusiasm of citizens desiring to volunteer in the effort against crime in their neighborhoods. In contrast to the notion of vigilantism, police departments have formed citizen patrols to work under the supervision of the police for the purpose of adding "eyes and ears" in the fight against crime. Below is a description of a typical citizen patrol program—in this case, from the Minneapolis (Minnesota) Police Department.

A Brief Guide to Citizen Patrols

Community Crime Prevention/SAFE believes that citizen patrols can be an appropriate extension of a block club. Having pairs of residents walking around the block at various times makes their watch force more visible. This is a more effective deterrent to crime.

Sponsorship

We advise residents to run their patrol under the auspices of their neighborhood association or some other group that will monitor the patrol's activities and provide support.

Management of the Citizen Patrol

The block club(s) or other group that organizes the patrol is responsible for recruiting potential participants and screening them. CCP/SAFE encourages patrol sponsors/organizers to do criminal history checks on those interested. All patrollers should be thoroughly briefed before they begin patrolling. This should include mission, appropriate activities, limits of authority, proper reporting procedures, and personal safety information. CCP/SAFE offers a four-hour workshop that provides the basic information needed to organize and run a citizen patrol. Contact your SAFE team for more information. The organizing group is responsible for the ongoing management of the patrol. This includes setting up the patrol schedule, monitoring the conduct of the patrollers, and informing the precinct of the activities of the patrol.

The Minneapolis Police Department and the City of Minneapolis do not license and are not responsible for the activity of citizen patrols or any loss or injury suffered as a part of their activities. Any liability incurred as a result of the patrol's activities is the responsibility of the individual patroller.

Role of Patrollers

Patrollers create a positive, watchful presence. When they identify situations where crime is occurring or appears about to occur (suspicious activity), they

(continued)

call 911 and continue to monitor the situation until a squad arrives, updating the telecommunicator as necessary. Patrollers are not expected to physically intervene in dangerous situations, but must use their judgment to decide on appropriate action. CCP/SAFE's citizen patrol workshop will provide guidance in assessing situations.

Equipment

For the safety of the patrollers, we advise them to carry either portable radios or cellular phones. This enables those on patrol to contact 911 quickly if they see an incident or need assistance.

Weapons

Carrying knives, guns, etc. is illegal. The only weapon patrollers can legally carry is tear gas (Mace). Screech alarms can also be carried.

Source: Minneapolis Police Department. Crime Prevention Resources. http://www.ci.minneapolis.mn.us/police/crime-prevention/docs/CITIZEN-PATROLS.pdf/.

endorsed by government officials and referred to as victims' advocates. The actions of these groups that were once considered extreme may become accepted over time, or they may tone down their strategies to gain greater government acceptance. Regardless, many groups begin as radicals but then gain greater acceptance from mainstream society over time. Thus, when we use the term vigilantism to refer to groups such as the Guardian Angels, this is a historical rather than a political or ideological interpretation.

THE CAUSES OF VIGILANTISM AND VICTIMS' ADVOCATES: MICRO AND MACRO EXPLANATIONS

Before discussing the history of vigilantism and victims' rights, we will assess some of the reasons that these phenomena occur. This analysis will review potential causes of vigilantism as well as victims' advocacy, and compare and contrast some of the sources of these behaviors. This discussion will emphasize both the macro and micro potential causes of vigilantism and victims' advocacy and how the impact of the time period changes these explanations.

In this chapter, we will separate vigilantes from victims' advocates via the motivations of the two groups and the strategies that they undertake. As the discussion above demonstrated, there is a great deal of overlap between the motivations and actions of the two groups, so we will use generalities in categorizing them. In essence, we will classify victims' advocates as those who focus strictly on issues or policies that impact the rights and lifestyles of victims, while vigilantes may include justice and retribution in their objectives. Moreover, victims' advocates do not use violence or threat of violence to obtain their desired results, while vigilantes sometimes use whatever means is necessary.

Because victims' advocates are primarily a function of modern criminal justice systems, vigilantism has a much longer history. Indeed, the use of violence and force by private citizens arguably provides a function in society when there is a limited organized system of criminal justice in place. Private citizens formulated the original police patrols, and thus, it is odd to some observers that law enforcement and government originally viewed them as outsiders or instigators. When private citizens use their own discretion in applying the law with no overriding legal guidelines to follow, vigilantism is an almost inevitable result, and increased reports of injustice and brutality typically have coincided. Thus, vigilantism eventually became a negative term that was used to describe unjust and discretionary violence and intimidation used against criminals by those who resist conventional avenues. However, one cannot ignore the functional aspect that vigilantism sometimes provides in societies that lack a strong central government or system of criminal justice.

Arguably, vigilantism is functional and even beneficial when there are increases in aggregate level perceptions of fear, victimization risks, and injustice resulting from weak criminal justice systems. Accordingly, the weaker the criminal justice system is perceived to be in protecting citizens against all victimization, the more likely vigilante behavior will originate and the more accepting society is when it does originate. In contrast, societies with strong criminal justice systems view citizen involvement with a more critical eye. For example, in the Old West of the United States, where law enforcement coverage was sometimes sparse, citizens moved to fill the gaps.

The United States has, however, more macrolevel determinates of vigilantism than the mere perception of an understaffed criminal justice system, and many theorists focus on the country's unique history. Indeed, a number of theorists believe that America has its own distinctive culture of violence: a subculture of violence per se. For instance, Brown asserts that violence has been a part of American culture since its inception and that violence has been used in several instances to preserve this nation. Accordingly, because of this initial reliance on violence, it has been relied on more in the United States than in other industrialized countries, with threats to law and order being met with a strong use of force. Brown contends that the use of force was also critical in maintaining the cultural values of America's three-class system, particularly when rioting began after the establishment of unions.

As with time period surrounding vigilantism, the theory used to explain macro level vigilantism differs depending on the location of the vigilantism. For instance, while undeveloped and disorganized areas with unsubstantial police presence led to much vigilantism in the West, vigilantism found in the South may have different causes. A number of additional theories may be used to explain much of the vigilante justice that existed in the Old South and many states in the North. For instance, subculture theories are instrumental explanatory tools in that small groups were typically responsible for the majority of vigilante acts occurring in the South throughout the 1800s and 1900s. Within some groups, the use of violence to control black populations become common, as seen in white citizens' societies and the Ku Klux Klan. Such subcultures involve a cycle in which ideology and tactics are learned socially by younger generations who have differential opportunities for inclusion in such groups. At a higher level, attempts were made to alienate black members of society to maintain the distinctions that had existed before the Civil War. These actions fall closely in line with the focus of racial conflict theory, which asserts that the elite will direct attention, laws, resources, force, etc., to control minority populations.

Another facet of vigilantism in America stems from the sacred right of gun ownership after the Revolutionary War. This right has led to the formation of heavily armed militia groups that are readying themselves for an overabundance of governmental intrusion or governmental indifference or inaction in a time of chaos. These groups would be on the fringe of the vigilante cultures in our definition, because they do not focus simply on crime and justice, but on governmental actions and policies. There is little doubt that the Second Amendment and its related history have an impact on vigilante justice. One of the facets of vigilante justice is arguably the overuse of force in protecting oneself or others from crime. More than 75 million Americans own guns today; 70 million of which are handguns. This high gun ownership rate allows for a higher potential of violent vigilante acts in the United States.

Victim advocacy is an increasingly common phenomenon in developed societies, particularly those with a long tradition of fundamental rights provided to the accused. Victim advocates are a function of the greater focus on the victim over the past fifty years, and they typically enjoy a more legitimate role within society today, with many of these positions included within the criminal justice system. While the causes of vigilantism are more complex at the aggregate level, victims' advocacy is mostly the result of the victims' rights movement and the turn-back to a crime control model. The number of victims' advocates also may increase relative to the numbers of vigilantes, as evolving societal standards dictate which behaviors denote advocacy and vigilantism.

As with most phenomena, the factors impacting macro level incidence differ from the individual level explanations of those participating in the phenomena. This is no different for vigilantism and victim advocacy. There are a number of alternative theories that could be used to explain why an individual becomes a vigilante or a victims' advocate. For instance, the behavior could be socially learned, as is commonly seen in families of police officers or firefighters who have been influenced by the elder generations. Similarly, joining a group with a controversial objective often can lure those who are seeking an exciting self-concept or greater involvement in an objective they hold in high esteem. Indeed, the original Guardian Angels could have had much of the same appeal for its members as a gang would provide. It granted an extended family and a direction for many young and poor minority youth at the time.

While the Guardian Angels may have provided for much of its original members' need for security, friendship, purpose, and so on, members joining today may have different backgrounds and rationales. The Guardian Angels are viewed more today as victims' advocates than they originally were, and they have more legitimate pathways to follow in accomplishing their tasks, simply because times have changed and opinions toward them have changed. Indeed, many in law enforcement and government now see the advantage of civilian groups in aiding the fight against crime. For instance, civilian agencies are cheap and can be particularly cost effective when its very members include members of society who were at risk for unconventional behavior. In this regard, these groups provide another outlet for youth besides deviance and offer a cheap resource for police. The greater the evolution between police and citizens groups like the Angels, the less they overlap with one another and understand their boundaries. This eventually leads to greater efficiency. Moreover, with the greater legitimacy of civilian groups and the greater prestige of becoming involved in the groups, recruitment ultimately becomes a more simple process.

Another aspect of civilian groups is that they provide an avenue to those who are ambitious about community involvement, yet lack the background, credentials, or even stability to become a government officer. They also provide an opportunity for those who are either too young or too old for traditional law enforcement activity, tapping into a resource that has not always been utilized. With the increasing older populations expected in the United States over the next fifty years, volunteer groups have the opportunity for greater numbers of members who could serve as mentors for the youth in the group.

One cannot ignore the influence of the media in a discussion of the causes of vigilantism and victims' advocacy. As will be discussed later in this chapter, television crime shows and movies may have an impact on the attitudes of members of society surrounding the criminal justice system and even the decisions of some of the initial Guardian Angels to become involved in the group. In this regard, these shows could also impact one's desire to be involved in the system. Indeed, the unprecedented numbers of law enforcement shows on television today have corresponded with an increasing number of criminal justice departments at universities across the country and those desiring to be involved in criminal justice. Although not all teens with an interest in criminal justice have the opportunity to go to college or have a desire to take out loans, they do have the opportunity to become involved in the fight against crime. Citizens groups can provide this opportunity for teens who are seeking involvement.

ORIGINS OF VIGILANTISM AND VICTIMS' RIGHTS

The term vigilante can be traced back to ancient society, although there is little documentation of organized vigilante groups that can be classified under a crime control model. This is unsurprising because of the sparse criminal justice literature remaining from the period and because vigilantism was a way of life at this time and nothing out of the ordinary. Indeed, blood feuds resulting from vigilante acts by one family against another were so common in ancient society that they contributed to the criminal justice system's being organized into an objective third party that would handle disputes over injustice or crime. The impact of crime control vigilante acts on the current state of the criminal justice system, though largely undocumented, should not be underestimated.

Although acts that were considered crime control vigilantism were common to ancient society, vigilantism with a social focus has commonly been associated with larger paradigm shifts throughout history. Slave rebellions, religious movements, and upheavals against governments can all be classified as social vigilantism and can be dated back to ancient times before the Roman Empire.

Vigilantism in the United States emanates from the Deep South and Old West during the 1700s. Lacking a formal system of criminal justice, groups from small towns began forming, calling themselves vigilance committees. As these committees evolved, members began harassing, torturing, or killing people who were seen, justifiably or not, as threats to their communities. Later in the eighteenth century, vigilante justice gave rise to the notorious lynch mobs, which were known for hanging people with little or no evidence of wrongdoing and with no concern for due process.

Perhaps no place or time period has molded our perceptions of vigilante justice more than the American West of the 1800s. This custom occurred in part because of the transitory nature of the West, the willingness to allow some groups such as slaves and Native Americans fewer rights than others (which translated over to suspected criminals), the historic use of violence to settle economic disputes, and the nature of the open frontier and settlements and the accompanying disorganized and sometimes nearly nonexistent criminal justice system. Vigilance committees were common within the West from the mid-1800s to the twentieth century. Vigilantism seemed to fill a need in areas where justice was a day's ride away. Vigilance committees were typically made up of merchants, ranchers, farmers, bankers, and other citizens who had clout in the area. They were developed as a method to protect one's family, land, and business interests, in some ways analogous to the formulation of feudal societies in the Dark Ages. Although these groups did attempt to stay within the governing laws of the time, they shared some other common threads with justice in the Dark Ages: corruption and brutality.

Perhaps the first well-known vigilance committee in the western United States was formed in 1851 in San Francisco on its waterfront district, or Barbary Coast as it was known at the time. The Barbary Coast was famous for its high crime rate, swindlers, murder, and corruption in government, although crime and corruption was found to some extent in most western cities at the time. San Francisco's problem was amplified by the influx of 49ers seeking a quick profit, leading to further disorganization of values, morality, and trust in one's neighbor. Vigilante committees were formed to stabilize the area and to bring justice to the large number of criminals who could not be apprehended and/or processed by the conventional system. The parallels between this environment and those found in the Bronx during the 1970s when the Guardian Angels originated provide tantalizing clues to the formulation of vigilance groups.

Although much of the historical attention has focused on the corrupt and violent side of vigilance committees, San Francisco's committee had success in cracking down on corrupt government officials and carpetbaggers. Other vigilante committees were formed in Montana and nearby settlements in the West, as well as in Southern states such as Tennessee, New Orleans, and Georgia after the Civil War. One particular group was formed in Tennessee and the members originally were hailed as vigilantes. This group originally fought against Northern Carpetbaggers during the instability in the South after the war, eventually becoming known more for their racism and brutality toward blacks: The Ku Klux Klan.

Vigilantism was not limited simply to the deep South and the West in the developing United States. As Brown contends, vigilantism arose in areas that were absent of effective law enforcement, a problem common in developing areas. Accordingly, at least 326 cases of vigilante groups have been identified from the mid-1700s until 1900.

The San Francisco vigilance committee was critical in that it marked a turning point whereby vigilance committees were no longer merely a phenomena found only in rural developing areas, but now were being established in the urban areas that were forming during the Industrial Revolution. During this time, there was considerable expansion in industry and immigration of the Irish and other groups into the country to assume the new jobs. These groups often moved into the low rent areas and took low salary jobs, working long hours and often having customs more accepting toward alcohol use than many of the surrounding inhabitants. When crime and lawlessness increased in these areas, vigilance committees were established and a new problem arose that was perceived to be beyond the control of law enforcement by themselves: the urban slum.

Because of the technological and societal changes that took place in the early 1900s and because of America's preoccupation with World War I and events leading up to it, vigilantism reemerged under a different focus in a country now considered a post-war power. A form of social control vigilantism called neovigilantism surfaced, triggering increased bounty hunting for fugitives of justice, lynching of minorities, and the formulation of neighborhood groups. This era also saw an escalation of groups that sought to decrease violence caused by alcohol as well as other social ills, particularly during federal prohibition in the 1920s and 1930s.

The vigilante movement became stagnant in the late 1930s and into the 1940s, as most of the world became immersed in the Second World War. After the end of the war, however, several factors influenced the direction of vigilantism, including social and political movements, theoretical paradigm shifts, and technological advances. It was during this time that the concept of victimology began to splinter out of the field of criminology, and more attention began to be placed on victims, their roles in society, and the impact of crime on their lives. At the same time, the civil rights movement gained momentum, with focus being placed on the treatment of blacks in the South.

In a sense, the civil rights movement was a form of social control vigilantism, whereby private citizens did not rely on the law or criminal justice system to correct an ill of society. This movement allowed citizens to better understand their own roles in fighting for the rights of victims and in correcting injustice. This movement also coincided with a time period in which citizens had a decreased faith in the government and saw it as a dispenser of punishment rather than a protector of justice. This perception was further solidified during the Vietnam War with the government's reluctance to leave Vietnam despite public protest and with the corruption in the Watergate scandal.

The civil rights and antiwar movements were of vital importance in the creation of the ideology that eventually underlined the victims' rights movement. Indeed, they demonstrated some of the failures of relying on government to settle disputes or to seek justice. The dissatisfaction with the approach in which the government handled the war translated into a greater mistrust in all government-run institutions and an awareness of the absence of citizen participation in governmental decisions. Indeed, many began to view the government as a cold and faceless organization concerned more with bureaucratic rules than for the citizens it represented.

Just as the women's rights movement was able to impact temperance in the 1700s and prohibition in the 1800 and 1900s, their impact on the victims' rights movement was just as profound. Although the movement had been in place and made linear strides since the inception of the United States, it experienced a revival of sorts in the late 1960s and early 1970s. Highly publicized events such as Billie Jean King's victory over Bobbie Riggs in tennis in 1973 simply provided fuel to a movement that had already gained momentum through the progress made in the civil rights movement, women's greater inclusion in the workplace, their involvement in legal debates surrounding abortion, and the strength of their voice in the antiwar movement.

The goals of the women's rights movement had evolved throughout history, but its impact on the victims' rights movement was strikingly similar to its impact in past movements surrounding alcohol. One of the primary motivations in those prior movements had been the perceived impact of alcohol on violence by men against women and on the family union. Similarly, this new movement centered on violence of men against women and what they viewed as the government's indifference to such domestic matters. Thus, many of the goals of the women's rights movement were congruent with the emerging focus on the neglect of victims by the government-run criminal justice system and the increasing crime control and social control vigilante movement.

THE CLIMATE OF THE 1960S AND 1970S AND ITS IMPACT ON VIGILANTISM AND THE VICTIMS' RIGHTS MOVEMENT

The organized movements that had formed by the 1960s were not the result of the victims' rights movement, nor were they the sole cause. These reforms did have a significant impact on the speed and efficiency with which the victims' rights movement was able to impact policy, however, and there may have never been an organized "movement" if it were not for the work of these groups. For instance, the civil rights and women's rights movements were already established and organized when victims' rights came into focus, allowing their knowledge and structure to be utilized more effectively in the victims' right movement. Could Mothers against Drunk Driving (MADD) have made such a powerful impact against drinking and driving without members who knew how to impact special interests? Moreover, could protections against police brutality and civilian review boards have developed as quickly without the use of the existing resources and connections with the civil rights movement?

The climate that existed in the 1960s and 70s brought together the right ingredients to increase concerns about the treatment of victims to the point that groups with opposing political ideologies took up the cause. While the civil rights and women's movement were placing greater focus on victims, the due-process model that had been popular in the 1960s was beginning to create a backlash and bring more conservative groups into the victims' rights movement. Fourth Amendment procedures such as the exclusionary rule were resulting in defendants' having cases dismissed because of what many perceived as technicalities unrelated to their guilt or innocence. This outrage was further amplified by sensational murder cases of the late 1960s and early 70s, a perception that not enough was being done to counteract crime, particularly drug crime, and a change in political ideology in the country.

In the early 1970s, the United States turned back toward what is now referred to as a crime control model. Under this model, more resources were devoted to building prisons, longer sentences were employed against criminals, and a number of agencies were created in an effort to counteract the growing drug problem. Anger was also brewing because of the number of rights defendants were receiving in relation to those granted to victims. The media further fueled this outrage by covering stories of sensational crimes that were disproportionate to their actual incidence, and sensationalizing cases where defendants had charges dismissed because of procedural issues.

Media sensationalism, particularly that which is focused on crime, has by no means decreased over the years. Its impact during the 1970s, however, may have produced a greater impact on viewer perceptions and criminal justice policy because of the novelty of this type of media exposure. Americans were becoming acquainted with the new expanding media market and the over-saturation of contemporary issues. They were not privy to the knowledge of the blurry line that sometimes exists between fiction and the facts provided by the media, particularly from a media that had become revered through its coverage of the war and role in uncovering the Watergate scandal.

Although vigilantism can be seen throughout the history of storytelling in works such as Robin Hood, the topic may have reached its apex in the 1970s and 80s. The entertainment industry of the 1960s and 70s seemed to be fixated on crime and justice. Books such as Truman Capote's *In Cold Blood*, and Vincent Bugliosi's *Helter Skelter* rehashed mass murders in real life, and they were later developed into motion pictures. A number of motion pictures centered on vigilantism, including the *Dirty Harry* and *Death Wish* series.

Some theorists contend that the *Dirty Harry* and *Death Wish* movies were not an influence on society during the 1970s, but rather a symptom of the perceptions about law and order that were gaining momentum. Lenz asserts that these films demonstrate that the concepts of law and order do not always coincide and are at times at odds with one another. Accordingly, these two movies portray a system that has become too law oriented, which necessitates unconventional approaches to achieve order. Such movies have come under criticism as glorifying tactics of vigilante violence, the potential impact on viewer perceptions being difficult to measure. Some movies such as *Magnum Force* and *The Star Chamber* even countered the growing movement in Hollywood toward vigilantism and victims' rights ideology by dramatizing some of the potential dangers of these ideologies.

The movement toward victim frustration in Hollywood was not limited to movies, and it began to gain momentum in television in the late 1970s. Television shows such as *The Rockford Files* and *Hill Street Blues* emphasized frustrations with law enforcement and criminal justice and their tendency to overemphasize red tape while ignoring victims. Theorists have contended that crime dramas can impact viewer perception of justice and stimulate moral deliberation about the criminal justice system and its legitimacy.

With the growing civil rights movement, feminist movement, a heightened media attention on crime, a turn to the crime control model, and vigilantism taking the forefront in entertainment, the victims' rights movement began to organize and make progress. Along with the creation of the field of victimology, there were a number of enhancements to the fate of victims in the criminal justice system in the 1960s and 70s. For instance, victims' compensation programs began in the 1960s, marking an initial attempt to compensate all victims of crime, not simply those who could afford crime insurance. The establishment of restitution programs that had become popular in Europe, with its greater use of fines and monetary penalties, coincided with the use of compensation to bring the victim back into the punishment process.

The attention to crime victims spread to crime data in the early 1970s with the National Crime Victimization Survey (NCVS). Until this time, crime statistics such as the Uniform Crime Reports (UCR) had focused primarily on reported crime and arrests, without recording many details about the attributes of the crime victim. The NCVS changed this by surveying a national sample of households about their victimization rather than their crime. The survey's rationale was to provide a better understanding of crime victimization and to assess the dark side of crime, the amount of crime occurring that was not reported to police.

The women's rights movement has had much impact on victims' rights, particularly through increased attention to domestic violence and rape. Feminists, victims of rape, and others in the victims' rights movement were instrumental in the formation of the first rape and battered women's shelters, as well as educating the public about these supposed taboo crimes. Since these programs began in the 1970s, police departments have established special rape units to process rape victims and have seen a significant increase in the number of women who feel comfortable enough to come forward and report rape. Police reaction to domestic violence also has been scrutinized since the 1970s, with a number of studies focusing on the effectiveness of the different police responses of arrest and warnings. Moreover, the right of victims to fight back against their attackers became a popular issue, with the battered-women's syndrome coming to the forefront as a self-defense strategy for many battered wives who injured or killed their husbands.

The 1980s brought greater victim involvement in the criminal justice system. As previously mentioned, MADD was successful in changing perceptions about drinking and driving and achieving tougher penalties against offenders. Attention to hate-based crimes also came to the forefront in the 1980s, with particular emphasis on crimes that are motivated by hatred of race and gender.

Finally, the 1980s saw more attention devoted to victims' rights within the court process, with victim-witness programs developed that acted as a liaison between victims and the prosecution. These programs concentrated on bringing victim awareness and impact back into the system. Now victims were kept up to date routinely on the progress of their cases and were even asked for their input in some cases.

New York City was a worldwide leader in the vigilante movement, stemming from the media publicity of its crime, a high fear of crime, and a police force that had been hampered by cutbacks. Famous cases of vigilantism also occurred, such as Bernhard Goetz, who shot four black youths on a subway train in 1984. The Goetz case polarized views on the subject and brought vigilantism into the spotlight in America, as Goetz was hailed as a subway vigilante by some and a criminal by others. Goetz was eventually acquitted of any illegality surrounding the shootings of the youths, but did serve time in prison for carrying illegal weapons.

CURTIS SLIWA AND THE ORIGINS OF THE GUARDIAN ANGELS

The Bernhard Goetz case highlighted frustrations about crime that had been brewing for a number of years in New York in 1970s. Drug dealing was common in New York City in the 70s, and the crack cocaine panic was on the horizon. Cases like "Son of Sam" had kept New York in fear for months at a time, and more citizens began to have supportive views toward vigilante behavior. It was under these circumstances that Curtis Sliwa originated the Guardian Angels in the late 1970s.

Curtis "The Rock" Sliwa founded what would become known as the Guardian Angels in 1979, when he was a manager at a McDonalds in the Bronx (www.guardianangels.org). The Guardian Angels were not the first community watch group created in New York, nor were they a group that was created simply on a whim by a man who was fed up with crime as many commonly perceive. Rather, the Angels were part of a process toward citizen involvement in law enforcement that was fledging, and they were an extension of other community groups that Sliwa had begun several years earlier. Sliwa became known as "The Rock" in high school in the early 1970s, because of his fighting and tenacious personality and also his sense of community activism. He was known for a strong sense of justice and being opinionated about crime and civic duty, eventually forming a neighborhood clean-up group called the "Rock Brigade" in 1977.

Sliwa remained close to many in the Rock Brigade in the late 1970s, even working alongside some of them at McDonalds. Partly because of his outrage over crime and its role in the deterioration of his neighborhood, Sliwa turned to the members of his Rock Brigade to help achieve his vision of a new group that would focus its attention more closely on crime, originally named the "Magnificent 13" in 1979. On February 13, 1979, the thirteen members officially began patrolling subways in the Bronx. At this time, these members were mostly a collection of minority teens who were trained to make citizen's arrests and patrol the subways, alleys, and neighborhood streets. They soon created uniforms, donning berets, red jackets, and white t-shirts. When they began to grow in numbers, they changed their name to the Guardian Angels, after the name given to angels who watch over people and deliver them from danger.

Some of the original Guardian Angels had been gang members in the past, a factor that Sliwa did not view as an inhibitor to inclusion into his group. Many of the Angels admitted that they had been inspired by the 1979 movie *The Warriors,* which centered on gang members who had a plan to take over the streets of New York. However, these Angels differed in that they desired to take back the streets for the law-abiding citizens of New York.

To be included into the Guardian Angels, prospects had to maintain a job or be a registered student and have no desire for revenge against criminals. Sliwa wanted the members to serve as protectors of society, rather than appear to fight crime. Although some of the original group carried knives as protection, none of them carried walkie-talkie radios because they did not want to be perceived as extensions of the police force. The Angels received training in martial arts and self-defense, and Sliwa also readied them for the harassment that they would encounter from citizens, by harassing them during training to ensure that they would not lose their temper under duress.

Because of citizen anger over crime at the time of the Angels' creation, particularly in New York City, the reaction to the Angels was sometimes positive. Many saw them as a much overdue aid to local law enforcement and welcomed them into their communities. Some were not as receptive, however, with claims made that they were overly aggressive and with then-mayor Koch describing them as "vigilantes" in a negative connotation. He has since reversed his stance against the group. This initial negative reaction was not surprising, because it had occurred throughout the 1960s when the first crime watch patrols in Brooklyn were dubbed vigilante groups. Sliwa did not help heal the divide when he openly criticized the procedures of police in some cities. Despite their detractors, the group did enjoy some immediate success, being credited with helping create safer environments for subway users.

Part of the resistance encountered by the original Guardian Angels was due to a perception of those in government about crime and other governmental issues. Some in government and law enforcement believed that vigilante and other neighborhood advocate groups decrease the overall authority of law enforcement. The neighborhood and multicultural community restoration projects that that exist today were not as common, and citizen involvement in what were perceived as government issues was not as encouraged. Moreover, the monopoly that government agencies had on law enforcement was economically beneficial in that it reduces duplication of enforcement efforts, which could potentially be more efficient for society if correctly allocated. This was similar to the arguments made surrounding the efficiency of centralized agencies compared to more personal, decentralized agencies that compete against and often overlap one another's efforts.

The Guardian Angels were not viewed by most in government and law enforcement as beneficial groups, but rather as novices who were overstretching their boundaries as citizens and whose potential negatives outweighed their positives. Thus, a factor existing today that was missing during the origins of the Guardian Angels is the increased governmental acceptance of community groups and a functioning relationship with law enforcement. As Johnson contends (1996), one of the key factors establishing whether groups are viewed as victim advocates or vigilantes is the support they receive from state and federal agencies.

GROWTH AND LEGITIMACY OF THE GUARDIAN ANGELS

Sliwa's Angels gained popularity despite their criticism, and they grew from thirteen members to forty-eight in the first year. Sliwa did not only encounter resistance from law enforcement and government officials, but gang members as well. He had to clarify to local gangs that the Guardian Angels were not attempting to take over their territory, but just make it safe for citizens.

Although many, even some of its original members, believed that the Guardian Angels would be a short-lived phenomenon, the organization has expanded to more than 5,000 members and fifty national offices and even international bases. According to Sliwa, by 1996 the Angels had made more than 4,000 citizen's arrests, on cases ranging from theft to murder. Typically, the Angels hold a suspect until police arrive or escort the suspect to a police precinct.

The journey of the Guardian Angels has included some bumps in the road, with the organization encountering friction when they attempted to open chapters in cities outside of New York. The doubts that haunted their original formation still exist in some areas today, as witnessed in Boston where government officials and law enforcement have not endorsed the group. But such resistance has turned to welcome in most cities, and now the Angels enjoy a more legitimized status in the United States. Indeed, the police chief and mayor of Minneapolis have been enthused by their recent coordination with the Angels.

The international growth of the Guardian Angels now has expanded to a number of countries including Canada, the United Kingdom, Japan, South Africa, and some Scandinavian countries. These international bases have generally coincided with increases in the crime rate in these countries. Not surprisingly, the Angels encountered struggles in their expansion into other countries, just as they had across the United States. They have made greater strides in Japan than in England and Canada. The organization has failed a few times in Canada in the past and has only a handful of members in England.

The Guardian Angels typically come to the attention of the general public when they are involved in high profile criminal cases, such as their shaming of the preppie murderer Robert Chambers or their volunteer efforts to pump gas in Washington, D.C., during the sniper shootings. In fact, one of the simultaneous criticisms by some and acknowledgements by others of the Angels has been their tendency to force involvement in high-profile issues. This could include their recent patrol of Mardi Gras after Hurricane Katrina and patrol of the borders near Mexico in search of illegal immigrants, but the Guardian Angels have a number of objectives today that are not in the public eye and do not involve street crime. While the objectives of the Angels may differ depending on the city in which they exist, the general goals of the group include safety patrol, education, and cyber security. Because the Angels are well known for their safety patrol, their efforts in education and cyber security are less well known. They offer a number of professional development seminars to police as well as seminars to students and teachers. Some of the subjects of their programs include school violence prevention, classroom management techniques, bullying in schools, gang recognition, Internet safety, and diversity awareness.

The Guardian Angels was one of the leading victims' advocate groups that recognized the crime problem existing over the Internet. After Curtis Sliwa had discussed cyber crime with some Internet experts on his radio show in 1995, he became convinced that the Internet was nearly an anarchist society that received little oversight or law enforcement. Although he knew very little about computers or the Internet, Sliwa decided that the Angels should begin patrolling the net much as they had the city streets in 1979.

Sliwa established the CyberAngels in 1995, referring to it as the first cyber neighborhood watch. The CyberAngels have worked with local law enforcement as well as the FBI and now have established connections with law enforcement in more than thirty countries in their attempt to patrol the Internet. The main focus of the group today is on online fraud, hacking, identity theft, cyber stalking, and tracking pedophiles. Similar to the Angel's safety patrol wing, the CyberAngels also provide classes and workshops. In fact, the Angels received a $200,000 state grant in 2006 to teach children around the state about the dangers of surfing the Internet and the existence of online predators. The grant is also being used to help train teachers about the warning signs of online bullying.

CURTIS SLIWA AND THE FUTURE OF THE GUARDIAN ANGELS AND VICTIMS' RIGHTS

Curtis Sliwa has achieved fame through means other than the Guardian Angels over the past twenty years, hosting radio shows and himself being a victim in a publicized criminal case. Sliwa was cohost of a talk show with Lisa Evers (his wife at the time) on WABC-AM radio in the early 1990s. He had been critical of the Mafia on his talk show, particularly the Gotti and Gambino families, when he was attacked by two men in 1992 and shot multiple times. The shooting was just four days before John Gotti was sentenced to prison and occurred when Sliwa was picked up outside his home in the East Village by two men who had stolen a taxi. One man was crouching down in the front seat of the car and sat up and began firing just seconds after Sliwa had sat down in the cab. He was shot in the legs and back while attempting to escape through the window. The doors to the taxi had been wired shut to impede any escape. The two men involved in the attack were later linked back to John Gotti, Jr., and he was tried three times for attempted murder in the failed assassination attempt. The first two trials resulted in hung juries and Gotti, Jr. was acquitted in the third trial.

Sliwa's radio program was cancelled after his assassination attempt, but he continued his work with the Guardian Angels in the 1990s, helping their transition to a global organization. Sliwa currently cohosts the "Curtis and Kuby in the Morning" program on WABC-AM radio and occasionally serves as guest host on the Sean Hannity Show.

With the Guardian Angels now well entrenched as a victims' advocate group, it is likely that they will continue to confront crime over the next twenty years. During the Angels' existence, there have been great strides in victims' rights, with some of the more notable programs including the establishment of victim witness programs, various forms of neighborhood watch programs, victim impact statements, extended victim compensation and restitution programs, protection from sex offenders, and a number of other initiatives. As technological changes generate new forms of crime, victims' advocates will continue to be called on to counter these criminals and protect their victims. In this regard, the victims' rights movement may not be a simple movement at all, but rather a natural and functional part of the criminal justice system that aids victims and protects potential victims. What exact role the Guardian Angels will have in this response to crime and victims is yet to be determined.

FURTHER READING

Abrahams, Ray. 1998. *Vigilant Citizens: Vigilantism and the State*. Oxford: Polity Press.
Anonymous. 2006. Guardian Angels Partnering With New York State to Keep Kids Safe on the Internet. *Associated Press*. http://222.wcbs880.com/pages/101038.php?contentType=4&contentID=219665.

Austern, D. 1987. *The Crime Victim's Handbook*. New York: Penguin Publishing.

Barker, Joshua. 2006. Vigilantes and the state. *Social Analysis* 50:203–207.

Brown, Richard. 1975. *Strain of Violence*. NY: Oxford University Press.

Brown, Richard. 2002. *Strain of Violence: Historical Studies of American Violence and Vigilantism*. Oxford, UK: Oxford University Press.

Buckler, K., and L. Travis. 2005. Assessing the news-worthiness of homicide events. *Journal of Criminal Justice and Popular Culture* 12:1–25.

Capeci, Jerry. 2003. Junior Don Behind Curtis Sliwa Shooting. *Gang Land News* June 26. http://www.ganglandnews.com/column336.htm.

Carrigan, William. 2004. *The Making of a Lynching Culture: Violence and Vigilantism in Central Texas, 1836–1916*. Urbana: University of Illinois Press.

Cloward, Richard. 1994. Illegitimate means, anomie, and deviant behavior. In *Theories of Deviance*. 4th ed. ed. Stuart Traub and Craig Little. Itasca, IL: F. E. Peacock Publishers.

Cole, George, and Christopher Smith. 2005. *Criminal Justice in America*. Tampa, FL: Thompson Publishing.

Culberson, William. 1990. *Vigilantism: Political History of Private Power in America. (Contributions in Criminology and Penology,* Vol. 28). Westport, CT: Greenwood/Praeger.

Dignan, J. 2005. *Understanding Victims and Restorative Justice*. New York: Open University Press/McGraw Hill.

Doerner, William, and Steven Lab. 2005. *Victimology*. 4th ed. Bethesda, MD: Lexis Nexis.

Educom Review Staff. 1996. Cyber-Cops: Angels on the Net. *Educom Review* http://www.educause.edu/pub/er/review/reviewArticles/31134.html/.

Escott, Paul. 1989. White Republicanism and Ku Klux Klan terror: The North Carolina Piedmont during reconstruction. In *Race, Class and Politics in Southern History: Essays in Honor of Robert Durden*, ed. Jeffrey Crow, Paul Escott, and Charles Flynn, 3–34. Baton Rouge, LA: Louisiana State University Press.

Fletcher, George. 1988. *A Crime of Self Defense: Bernhard Goetz and the Law on Trial*. New York: The Free Press.

French, P. 2001. *The Virtues of Vengeance*. Lawrence, KS: University Press of Kansas.

George-Kosh, David. 2006. Toronto: Broke Guardian Angels may quit streets. *National Post* September 7. http://www.canada.com/nationalpost/news/toronto/story.html?id=88d8e9e5-ae53-4ec9-b50c-ff6462274ca7/.

Guardian Angels: Keeping It Safe. The Alliance of the Guardian Angels. www.guardianangels.org/.

Hil, Richard. 1998. Juvenile crime and autonomous citizen action. *Youth Studies Australia* 17:35–41.

Horwitz, Allan. 1990. *The Logic of Social Control*. New York: Springer.

Johnson, Les. 2001. Crime, fear and civil policing. *Urban Studies* 38:5–6.

Johnson, Les. 1996. What is vigilantism. *The British Journal of Criminology* 36:220–221.

Kenney, Dennis. 1987. *Crime, Fear, and the New York City Subways: The Role of Citizen Action*. Oxford, UK: Praeger.

Karmen, Andrew. 2007. *Crime Victims: An Introduction to Victimology*. 6th ed. Belmont, CA: Thompson Wadsworth.

Kleck, Gary. 1991. *Point Blank: Guns and Violence in America*. New York: Aldine de Gruyter.

Kohn, A. 2005. Straight Shooting on Gun Control. *Reason* 37:20–25.

Lamborn, Leroy. 1987. Victim Participation in the Criminal Justice Process: The Proposals for a Constitutional Amendment. *Wayne Law Review* 34:125–220.

Largen, M. 1981. Grassroots Centers and National Task Forces: A History of Anti-Rape Movement. *Aegis* 32:46–52.

Lenz, Timothy. 2005. Conservatism in American crime films. *Journal of Criminal Justice and Popular Culture* 12(2): 116–134. http://www.albany.edu/scj/jcjpc/vol12is2/lenz.pdf/.

Lott, J. 1998. *More Guns, Less Crime: Understanding Crime and Gun Control Laws*. Chicago: University of Chicago Press.

Lunardini, Christine. 1995. *Women's Rights (Social Issues in American History Series)*. Phoenix, AZ: Oryx Press.

Marx, G., and D. Archer. 1976. Community police patrols and vigilantism. In *Vigilante Politics,* ed. J. Rosenbaum and P. Sederberg, 129–157. Philadelphia, PA: University of Pennsylvania Press.

McGrath, Roger. 1987. *Gunfighters, Highwaymen and Vigilantes: Violence on the Frontier*. Berkeley, CA: University of California Press.

Merriam-Webster. 2007. *Merriam-Webster's Collegiate Dictionary*. 11th ed. Springfield, MA: Merriam-Webster. http://www.m-w.com.

Messner, Steven, Eric Baurner, and Richard Rosenfeld. 2006. Distrust of government, the vigilante tradition, and support for capital punishment. *Law and Society Review* 40:559–590.

Newton, Michael. 2006. *The Ku Klux Klan: History, Organization, Language, Influence and Activities of America's Most Notorious Secret Society*. Jefferson, NC: McFarland and Company.

Pedahzur, Ami, and Arie Perliger. 2003. The causes of vigilante political violence: The case of Jewish settlers. *Civil Wars* 6:9–30.

Pennell, Susan, Christine Curtis, Joel Henderson, and Jeff Taxman. 1989. Guardian Angels: A unique approach to crime prevention. *Crime and Delinquency* 35:378–400.

Raney, Arthur, and Bryant Jennings. 2002. Moral judgment and crime drama: An integrated theory of enjoyment. *Journal of Communication* 52:402–415.

Roach, Kent. 1999. *Due Process and Victim's Rights: The New Law and Politics of Criminal Justice*. Toronto, Canada: University of Toronto Press.

Rosenbaum, Dennis. 1987. The theory and research behind Neighborhood Watch: Is it a sound fear and crime reduction strategy? *Crime and Delinquency* 33:103–124.

Royce, Josiah. 1948. *California, from the Conquest in 1846 to the Second Vigilance Committee in San Francisco: A Study of American Character*. Boston, MA: Houghton.

Savage, Kerry. 2004. At 25, the Guardian Angels are now on Global Patrol. Columbia News Service. http://www.jrn.columbia.edu/studentwork/cns/2004-02-16/392.asp/.

Sherman, Lawrence. 1991. From initial deterrence to long term escalation: Short custody arrest for poverty ghetto domestic violence. *Criminology* 29: 821–850.

Shotland, L. 1976. Spontaneous vigilantism: A bystander response to criminal behavior. In *Vigilante Politics,* ed. J. Rosenbaum and P. Sederberg, 30–44. Philadephia, PA: University of Pennsylvania Press.

Smalley, Suzanne. 2007. Guardian Angels launch city patrol, expand across U.S. *The Boston Globe,* March 31. http://www.boston.com/news/local/massachussetts/articles/2007/03/31/guardian_angels/.

Stokes, P. 1996. Organized against crime: The work of communities organised for a greater Bristol (COGB) 1990–1994. In *Preventing Crime and Disorder: Targeting Strategies and Responsibilities* (Cambridge Cropwood Series), ed. T. Bennett. Cambridge, UK: University of Cambridge, Institute of Criminology.

Stubbs, J. 1991. Battered women's syndrome: An advance for women or further evidence of the legal system's inability to comprehend women's experience? *Current Issues in Criminal Justice* 3:267–270.

Weisburd, David. 1988. Vigilantism as community social control: Developing a quantitative criminological model. *Journal of Quantitative Criminology* 4:137–153.

Wilde, James. 1979. In New York: The magnificent thirteen. *Time* May 7. http://www.time.com/time/magazine/article/0,9171,920294-1,00.html/.

Williams, Kate. 2005. Caught between a rock and a hard place: Police experiences with the legitimacy of street watch partnerships. *The Howard Journal* 44:527–537.

Young, Andrew. 1996. *An Easy Burden: The Civil Rights Movement and the Transformation of America.* Oxford, UK: HarperCollins Publishers.

AP Images/Paul Buck, Pool

Dr. Henry Lee: Leading Practitioner in Forensic Criminal Investigations

Janet E. McClellan

Dr. Henry Chang-Yu Lee, popularly known to crime investigation and forensic investigations aficionados as Dr. Henry Lee, rose to national and international attention when he was hired by the O. J. Simpson defense team to examine the forensic evidence in the brutal double murder investigation. Dr. Lee's unpretentious and unassuming pragmatic presentation of the blunders and misrepresentations committed by the Los Angeles California Police Department and crime scene technicians during the months-long media fascination with the details of the trial in 1995 became the cornerstone of the defense. However, Dr. Lee's involvement in and dedication to the examination of investigative practices combined with careful scientific examination of forensic evidence had a long history of professional commitment and enthusiasm for meticulousness decades before he was thrust into the spotlight of public attention.

Dr. Henry Lee began his odyssey to become a leading proponent of conscientiously applied best investigative practices and rigorous scientific examination of the physical evidence discoverable at crime scenes in the late 1950s as a young police officer in Taiwan, to 1998 with the dedication of the Henry Lee Institute of Forensic Science at the University of New Haven. Dr. Lee's consultations in cases from around the world and his tireless efforts to advance the use of scientific investigative practices guarantee his place among the iconic crime fighters of the twentieth century.

LIFE IN CHINA

Dr. Henry Lee was born Henry Chang-Yu Lee in the Chinese province of Jiangsu in the city of Rugao on November 22, 1938. Rugao, China, historically has enjoyed a reputation as a major seaport city located on the Yangtze River where the Shanghai metropolitan area has had a significant history of cultural and economic prominence.

Henry C. Lee was born in the middle of what became known as the Chinese Civil War, during which factions in China waged war among themselves while simultaneously waging the Sino-Japanese War during World War II. The Chinese Civil War, involving decades of fighting between rival governmental entities, was to shape the future of the Chinese people and play a significant role in life of Henry Lee.

The Chinese Civil War had erupted in 1927 between the Chinese Nationalist Party led by General Chaing Kai-shek and members of the Chinese Communist Party and ultimately fomented the civil war. The war continued throughout World War II as China fought against the Japanese military invasion and lasted until after the end of World War II in 1950. In 1950, the Chinese Communist Party and the Chinese Nationalist Party ceased hostilities, leaving the Chinese Communist Party and its regime in control of mainland China.

In the midst of the turmoil in 1942, six-year-old Henry Chang-Yu Lee, his twelve siblings, and their mother fled China by escaping to Taiwan. Lee's father had been killed by the communists prior to the family's flight from mainland China. The death of Lee's father appears to have provoked the flight to Taiwan, where his mother later worked to provide for and raise her children alone. The courage of his parents and the enormous work ethic and effort of his mother may well have had significant and lasting affects on the focus and exceptional motivation he would begin to reveal as a young police candidate and officer in Taiwan.

EDUCATION AND TRAINING

In Taiwan as a young man, Lee attended what became known as the Central Police University in Taoyuan, Taiwan. Originally, the Central Police University had been created through the combining of a police high school and advanced police officer training in 1936. The school, as then established, provided for standardization of training for law enforcement administrative ranked officers throughout the various provinces. Most significantly, in its earliest history, the school supplied the training of future supervisory ranked law enforcement officers by providing for high school and some college level programs. By the time Henry Lee entered the school at the age of eighteen, the college was renamed the Central Police College and had added a number of courses including some basic course work in the forensic sciences. The college traditionally offered a free education to those who passed its entrance criteria, which made it possible for Henry C. Lee, one of thirteen children, to advance professionally.

During a reformation in 1957, the school was renamed and became the Central Police University and additionally established two primary educational departments that focused on police administration and criminal investigation. Henry Lee graduated from the university with a degree in criminal investigation and spent the next several years as a lieutenant, rising to the rank of captain in 1960. In 2002, in an interview with John Miller of the American Broadcasting Company (ABC), Dr. Lee stated that his first homicide investigation as a police officer involved the dismembered body of a male victim that he found so disturbing that he almost became a confirmed vegetarian.

Lee and his wife, Margret Song, immigrated to the United States in 1965 to pursue his education. Upon arriving, Lee discovered that his college degree from Taiwan was not accepted by U.S. institutions, so his dream of pursuing a medical degree was postponed. From 1965 to 1968, Lee worked as a waiter, stock boy, and groundskeeper while earning his associate degree from the City College of New York (Hewitt and Harms 1996). In 1968, Lee found employment as a research technician in the biochemistry department at the New York Medical Center and served in that capacity until 1974. With his expanding interest in criminal investigation and forensic science and after receiving a small scholarship from John Jay College of Criminal Justice, he enrolled in the Forensic Science program and later received his B.S. in 1972. Lee continued his studies, earning a master's degree in science in 1974 and a Ph.D. in biochemistry in 1975 at New York University in New York City. During his master's and doctoral studies, Lee worked as a research scientist in the biochemistry department at the New York Medical Center, thereby enhancing his academic training with practical skills applications.

Upon completing the Ph.D. in biochemistry from New York University, Lee received his first academic appointment with the University of New Haven in West Haven, Connecticut, in 1975. Dr. Lee was hired as an assistant professor in the criminal justice division and additionally as the director of the university's forensic science laboratory. Dr. Lee taught a wide variety of courses during his tenure at the university. Although too numerous to list completely, the courses Dr. Lee taught at the University of New Haven and at a myriad of other academic institutions include criminal investigation, criminalistics, crime scene reconstruction, fingerprints, forensic analysis, forensic science in the administration of criminal justice, DNA applications in forensic science, homicide investigation, medicolegal death investigation, serology, and methods of teaching math and science.

At the University of New Haven, Dr. Lee quickly rose through the academic ranks, from associate professor in 1977 to full professor in 1978 and the distinguished chair in of the Forensic Science division in 2000. From 1990 to 2006, Lee received nine honorary doctorates from a variety of academic institutions in Connecticut and Maryland.

CRIMINAL AND FORENSIC INVESTIGATIONS: FROM HUMBLE BEGINNINGS

In 1978, while at the University of New Haven, Dr. Lee began work with the Connecticut Crime Laboratory, although at the time the lab was operating in the only space provided by the State Police and that was in the men's restroom in the State Police Troop barracks at Bethany, Connecticut. It amounted to "little more than a polygraph machine, a fingerprint kit, and a microscope in a stripped-down men's room" (Herszenhorn 2000).

Although the facilities and equipment were at best humble, the laboratory provided eight forensic services to the State Police and other law enforcement agencies, including fingerprints, firearms/toolmarks, polygraph, voiceprints, documents, serology, trace evidence, and photography. In 1979, the lab was renamed the Connecticut State Police Forensic Science Laboratory, and after working there for almost a year, Dr. Lee was appointed its first chief criminalist. With an expanded budget, Dr. Lee began purchasing state-of-the-art equipment and the techniques and forensic procedures. Eventually, as the value and the importance of the services provided by Dr. Lee and others gained recognition and stature from their work on criminal investigation cases, the lab expanded services and was moved to Meriden, Connecticut, in 1984. Their new home was the converted building of the Meriden School for Boys, a facility that once had housed male delinquents.

In 1994, Dr. Lee and his team were moved to a new 24,000 square foot facility that became the home of the Connecticut Division of Scientific Services. By 2007, the Division of Scientific Services facility was expanded an additional 50,000 square feet to house the variety of services for the state of Connecticut's investigation needs. The variety of investigative and forensic scientific applications and examinations offered through the units and divisions of the lab in 2007 included those in criminalistics (DNA, trace evidence, forensic biology, etc.), identification (fingerprints, documents, firearms and tools), controlled substance and toxicology lab, and the computer crimes and electronic evidence lab.

NOTORIETY AND NOTORIOUS CASES

Dr. Lee taught at the University of New Haven in Connecticut for twenty-five years, and was the director and chief criminalist for the Connecticut State Police for twenty-three of those years. With prodigious energy, Dr. Lee served as an educator of hundreds of students and forensic investigator in thousands of cases for the citizens of Connecticut. However, Dr. Lee's energies and enthusiasm for criminalistics in and out of the classroom expanded his reputation among criminal justice professionals and resulted in his involvement in notorious homicide cases within and beyond Connecticut. Three of the more significant notorious cases in which he was involved and his contributions to the findings of evidentiary facts follow.

Helen Crafts: The Wood Chipper Case 1986 (Connecticut)

In a 2005 interview in Great Britain with a show host, Dr. Lee discussed his involvement in a case in 1986 that pursued the possibility of a murder without the availability of the victim's body. In the beginning of the interview, Dr. Lee stated that criminal investigators use deductive and inductive logic while forensic scientists apply scientific techniques and facts to piece together the facts and implications of the available evidence. Dr. Lee acknowledged that both sets of skills are necessary in successful investigation conclusions. More than merely acknowledge the necessary combined skills of investigative practices and forensic facts assessments processes and techniques,

Dr. Lee practiced his habit of being involved intimately in the examination, identification, collection, and assessment of crime scene analysis and evidence assembly.

On the morning of November 19, 1986, in the midst of a heavy winter storm in Newton, Connecticut, long-time resident, wife, and mother Helen Crafts disappeared. The last person believed to have seen her alive was her husband, Richard Crafts. Richard told the family's au pair that Helen had decided to drive to her sister's, more than 120 miles away, during the near blizzard conditions. Under his directions, the au pair readied the Crafts's children and herself to be taken to Helen Crafts's sister's home in Newport, Rhode Island. Upon arriving in Newport the au pair learned that Helen had not yet arrived. Richard Crafts returned alone to his residence in Newton.

After interviewing the au pair in December, Newton, Connecticut, detectives requested that Richard Crafts take a polygraph. He agreed and on December 4, 1986, Richard Crafts passed the first of three polygraphs he would take over the next several weeks. The Newton Police Department was stymied. Although Richard had passed his polygraph examinations, he had given a variety of conflicting stories accounting for his wife's absence to friends, family members, and the police. However, suspicious though these stories were, they did not rise to the levels of proof needed to secure search warrants. The Newport police needed substantive proofs to move the case forward.

The regional newspapers discussed the mystery and the lack of information available to the local police. Based on the lack of results and through a request from Helen Crafts's relative in mid-December 1986, Connecticut State Police investigators became involved in the investigation. As part of their initial examination of the case, the detectives examined Richard Crafts's recent credit card purchases and discovered a number of interesting items that later became significant in the solution to the case. Richard Crafts's credit card purchases and rentals revealed that in November, he had purchased a large capacity freezer and a Stihl® chainsaw, and he had rented a U-Haul™ truck and a Model 150XP Brush Bandit® wood chipper. The wood chipper is equipped with three twelve-inch steel high-speed rotating grinders and has an opening capacity through which to feed materials and a thirty-five-inch feeder tray. The chipper was designed to reduce matter introduced into the feeder tray by pulling, compressing, and grinding material into minutely shredded particles. The U-Haul™ truck and the wood chipper had been rented the day Helen disappeared.

With an extensive list of conflicting stories provided by their chief suspect, sworn statements from persons who had heard additional conflicting accounts of the whereabouts of Helen Crafts from Richard Crafts, and on the basis of the investigator's experience in working violent crimes investigation, the detectives requested a search warrant from a local magistrate. The state investigators contended appropriately that in the commission of a violent offense against another person and in the course of that physical violence, detectable forensic evidence would have been distributed during a violent contact. The resulting violence would have resulted in the dispersal of blood, bodily fluids, tool or instrumentality marks, fibers, fingerprints, and a myriad of other evidence substances, indicating the likely commission of that violent encounter. They received the search warrant.

On December 25 of that year, while Richard Crafts was out of town on Christmas vacation, the Connecticut State Police investigators accompanied by Dr. Henry Lee entered the Crafts's home where Helen and Richard had lived since 1975. Of the hundreds of pieces and items of potential evidence located and seized that day, Dr. Lee and his staff discovered minute spots of blood on the mattress in marital bedroom. Once returned to the lab, the blood splatters tested proved positive for human blood and a later DNA test confirmed that blood had belonged to the missing Helen Crafts.

Another stroke of luck occurred for the investigators on December 30 when a Newport municipal worker came forward and provided information when his memory was spurred after reading one of the newspaper accounts of the circumstances and dates surrounding Helen Crafts's disappearance. The municipal service worker had been putting sand on the icy roads during the storm on November 19, 1986, when he observed a U-Haul truck towing a wood chipper at 3:30 A.M. The worker was incredulous that anyone would be out at that hour in an ice storm chipping wood. The municipal worker also was able to tell investigators that he saw the vehicle and chipper heading toward a road that would take it to Lake Zoar near Newton, Connecticut. Most importantly, the municipal service worker took the investigators to the area near Lake Zoar where he had last seen the U-Haul and wood chipper.

The investigators combed the region and found a large area containing a variety of shredded materials and intact items. The shredded materials consisted of paper substances, wood chips, cloth, and matter that would later be revealed to be flesh, bone, and other human remains. From the materials on the banks of Lake Zoar, crime scene technicians and Dr. Lee searched through the debris to collect fifty bone chips, more than 2,600 pieces of hair, one tooth, a part of a fingernail, one-half a toe, and bone from the inner skull region of a human head. The bits and pieces of recovered crime scene evidence were identified through exhaustive examination and DNA analysis as the total of the remains of Helen Crafts.

During the next several days in early January 1987, divers searched the cold December waters of Lake Zoar for additional items of evidence and located a Stihl chainsaw with serial numbers that had been filed away. In his laboratory, Dr. Lee was able to restore the filed numbers to reveal that the saw was number E592626. Ultimately, Stihl was contacted and it was learned that E592626 had been purchased by Richard Crafts for $499.00. Back at the Connecticut State Police crime lab, Dr. Lee examined the muddied and befouled chainsaw, locating human flesh, clothing fabric, and bone chips on the chain links. Subsequent examination revealed that the flesh and bones were those of Helen Crafts. The items of forensic evidence, which were comprised of those minute items, provided additional definitive linkages in the violent death and disposal of Helen Crafts by her husband Richard.

On November 21, 1989, Richard Crafts was found guilty of murder and in January of the following year, the court sentenced him to 99 years in a Connecticut state prison.

Dr. Lee's habit of direct participation in and support of the investigative aspects of crime scene assessment, analysis, and evidence collection marked him as unique among his peers. His experience and training as a law enforcement officer, criminal investigator, and forensic scientist were part of his active practice. Not satisfied to wait for the arrival of evidence from the field, Dr. Lee engaged in actively supporting, conferring, and assessing crime scenes with the other state investigators.

The culmination of those skills and unique enthusiasms for discovering the facts surrounding a criminal event no doubt were tied to his ability to have provided significant key evidence in all of the more than 8,000 cases in which he had been involved and were why he was to become the recipient of more than 800 awards and honors from academia, law enforcement agencies, and professional associations in his lifetime.

O. J. Simpson Trial 1995 (California)

O. J. Simpson, a former football player who had gained media notoriety as an actor and entertainment personality, was arrested and charged with the June 12, 1994, brutal murders of Nicole Brown Simpson (his ex-wife) and her friend Ronald Goldman. The charges against Simpson accused him of being responsible for the homicides that had taken place near the entrance of the condominium on Bundy Drive in Los Angeles, California. As the attacker, O. J. Simpson stood accused of viciously slashing Nicole Brown Simpson with a sharp-edged weapon, resulting in her head being nearly severed her body, and stabbing Ronald Goldman in excess of thirty times with the same instrument.

In 1995, the American and world television-viewing public was able to witness the courtroom proceedings and testimony of the double-murder trial for the entirety of its 133 days of broadcast. Moreover, the forensic experts retained by the prosecution and defense presented to the viewing public the leading forensic science experts and authors in the United States in the person of such notables as forensic consultant Richard Saferstein, the published research works of James E. MacDonald, and testimony from Dr. Henry Lee.

During the lengthy trial, as part of the presentation and examination of physical evidence collected and scientifically scrutinized from the crime scenes of the attack and other locations, prosecution and defense attorneys examined, reexamined, and cross-examined the forensic expert witnesses retained by the state and the defense. Days and frequently weeks of testimony involving the intricacies of crime scene procedures, detectives, criminalistics technicians, the coroner, and forensic experts were probed by both sides. The minute examination of the processes and procedures followed, and errors committed by the Los Angeles law enforcement and investigative officials were revealed.

Through the presentation of evidence and procedural best practices as presented through the testimony and discussions of researchers and practitioners like forensic consultant Richard Saferstein, the published research works of James E. MacDonald, and testimony from Dr. Henry Lee, the viewing public became novice students in the processes and applications of forensic science applications and consideration in criminal investigations. Additionally, the emerging refinements of standards of practices associated with crime scene investigation procedures to include evidence recognition, collection, and handling by law enforcement agencies and forensic laboratory examinations would emerge henceforth as central and critical considerations in future criminal cases. As Dr. Lee stated during his testimony during the O. J. Simpson trial,

> Any investigation involves four important elements. One is the scene; the crime scene itself has to be in fact preserved. Anytime have a crime, have a victim, so victim itself become a crime scene. For example, a hit and run case involving a pedestrian, the pedestrian's body becomes a crime scene... Of course the suspect who person or persons commit the crime become a crime scene itself. In addition, physical evidence such as guns, shoeprint, hair, sometime earring can become a piece of physical evidence, tire track...To link you need the four-way linkage. You can link the suspect to the scene if you find certain crucial physical evidence. In addition, you can link the physical evidence back to the suspect or suspects. Also, you can link the physical evidence to the victim. So this four-way linkage is rather important (CourtTV.com 2007).

In a broadcast by the CCTV in 2005 wherein Dr. Lee discussed his involvement in the O. J. Simpson trial, he stated,

> You don't need a doctor degree, you need logic. Devotion is so important. What we do is not a job, it is a profession...we do not make up things—the physical evidence tells us everything (CCTV 2005).

Dr. Lee was hired by the team of defense attorneys representing O. J. Simpson and was questioned extensively by the state's prosecutor Hank Goldberg regarding several points of evidentiary contention that had been raised by the defense. In his five days of testimony during the trial, Dr. Lee testified that he had examined the official records and reports submitted by the investigative personnel, photographs of the crime scene, and the state's evidentiary forensic reports. He specifically testified regarding impression evidence on the belongings of victim Goldman, footprints and impression on the sidewalk where the murders took place, blood splatters from the scene and Nicole Brown Simpson residence, and other trace evidence and compression bloodstains on a sock belonging to O. J. Simpson taken by police from Mr. Simpson's residence.

Key elements of his testimony included a discussion of the proper procedures for cloth or similar materials containing probable biological fluids, the transfer of biological evidentiary artifacts on objects, the difference between swipes and compression of liquid substances onto the surfaces of materials, and the results of improper handling of biological evidence as it might cause or create degradation of DNA. Dr. Lee patiently and carefully replied to all of the prosecutor's questions, refusing to be lead, make assumptions, or waver from the precision of his presentation of facts as he knew them as based on his examination of the evidence.

One of the more interesting exchanges between prosecuting attorney Goldberg and Dr. Lee occurred when Goldberg attempted to use a text written by Dr. Richard Saferstein, a renowned forensic scientist, as the definitive explanation of the complications associated with the drying of crime scene materials containing biological substances, particularly blood. During the exchange, Goldberg appeared to attempt to maneuver Dr. Lee into either accepting in total the explanation of processes and complications of drying wet crime scene artifacts or contradicting the testimony previously offered by Dr. Richard Saferstein. Dr. Lee resisted both efforts and instead explained that as he had not written or contributed to the Saferstein text that the generalities discussed by Dr. Saferstein were precisely that, generalities and not specific to the case under examination. Additionally, when the prosecution attempted to suggest that a forensic laboratory manual developed by Labor and Epstein (1983) contained the definitive analysis of the complications associated with the drying of biological fluids as based on their controlled experiments with blood and other biological fluids, Dr. Lee countered that controlled experiments are not comparable to field or actual lab conditions. Furthermore, Dr. Lee pointed out that the assessments made in the manual and tables representing drying times were presented as general guidelines rather than the pronouncements of strict rules associated with the conduct of forensic processes. Throughout the examination and cross-examination by prosecution and defense attorney maneuverings, Dr. Lee presented the very picture of steady, thought-out, and considered scientific opinion, seemingly unassailable by even the most skilled attempts to set him to counter his considered findings and opinions.

However, although his testimony was impregnable and without apparent bias or prejudice, he disclosed many of his concerns regarding the integrity of the investigation and the procedural errors committed by the Los Angeles investigators and the state's forensic examinations during an interview on a Chinese talk show that subsequently was broadcast by the CCTV program *English Channel Close Up* in 2005. During the broadcast video interview, Dr. Lee revealed that although he did not believe the Los Angeles police had attempted to railroad O. J. Simpson, that a number of evidentiary artifacts could not be explained without considering that they had been planted by persons involved in the investigation to assist in the establishing of O. J. Simpson's guilt in the death of Nicole Brown Simpson and Ronald Goldman.

Dr. Lee specifically stated during the interview that he believed that the Los Angeles police investigators, crime scene, and forensic personnel had committed numerous errors associated with the recognition, identification, recovery, and examination of evidence associated with the case. He particularly cited an instance in which a technician who had collected a vial of blood from the scene had placed the vial in his pocket and forgot it was there for several days; the amount of preservative in vials of blood collected from the scene, which complicated the analysis and identification of the blood; that two cubic centimeters of blood mysteriously disappeared from a vial; and the compression of blood on the sock belonging to O. J. Simpson, which would have required its placement and pressing into the material rather than as a result of splatters from an attack.

Although criticized by some for his unflattering critique of the Los Angeles Police Department, the department's crime scene technicians, and subsequent laboratory examinations of evidence presented at the O. J. Simpson trial, Dr. Lee remained convinced that the failure to follow procedure, lack of protocol, and apparent attempts to cover those errors are a violation of principled law enforcement practices. Those convictions and respect for the considerations of due process are underscored by his statement that, "Our job is not to please someone; only the facts are pleasing" (CCTV 2005).

JonBenet Ramsey Homicide Investigation 1996 (Colorado)

In an interview in 2005, Dr. Lee was asked what lessons he would want law enforcement managers to learn regarding the investigations, practices, and procedures required in contemporary criminal justice. Dr. Lee replied there were a number of crucial issues that could not be ignored to secure the facts and arrive at the truth in investigations, specifically,

> Every year departments should look at how to train forensic scientists and crime scene investigators…Education is important…crime scene experts in the

field and the forensic lab experts should work together...[I]nstead of living in an ivory tower [forensic experts] should understand the crime scene and realize that searching a crime scene is not an easy job. The two groups should have total cooperation and communication...[B]adge or no badge [they] should work as a team instead of having a traditional turf war (Kanable 2005).

Strong opinions arising from years of experience, training, and observations as a law enforcement officer and forensic scientist combined with his involvement in controversial and noncontroversial cases has led Dr. Lee to his conclusions that

> The integrity and security of the crime scene are crucial. We absolutely have to meet the scientific and legal requirements...You cannot just do whatever you as an individual please (CourtTV.com 2001).

The importance of Dr. Lee's contentions regarding the integrity and security of the crime scene were particularly relevant to the investigation of the sexual assault and murder of a six-year-old Colorado girl named JonBenet Ramsey in 1996. The circumstances, processes, errors, and mismanagement of the investigation should serve as a reminder to law enforcement investigators everywhere that process and procedural errors are fatal flaws that ultimately prevent the successful closure of homicide investigations.

Dr. Lee joined the special prosecutor's team to aid the state of Colorado in the ongoing investigation of the murder and sexual violation of JonBenet Ramsey in 1999, three years after the child's death. Subsequently Dr. Lee wrote in his book *Cracking More Cases* (2004), a lengthy assessment and analysis of the investigation of the murder and sexual assault committed against the six-year-old victim, JonBenet Ramsey. Dr. Lee's book is an unapologetic analysis of a myriad of fatal flaws and missteps in the investigation into the murder of JonBenet Ramsey that culminated in the inability of law enforcement and prosecutors to identify the perpetrator or perpetrators of the child's murder.

The story of the sexual assault and homicide of JonBenet Ramsey began the morning of December 25, 1996, with the Boulder, Colorado, police department receiving a call from a frantic woman stating that her child had been kidnapped. What followed in the investigation processes conducted, ignored, or mismanaged by the Boulder Colorado Police department during the first twenty-four hours after the call from Patsy Ramsey could be described only as an instance in which "everything serves, if only as a bad example." A proliferation of missteps, miscalculations, lack of procedure, failure to follow procedure as it existed, resistive support from commanding law enforcement officials, and the abandonment or willful discounting of investigative officer's needs by command personnel hampered the preliminary investigation. The loss of control of the scene to potential suspect interference, deference to wealthy and political connected suspects, and the conflagration of media attention combined to render the case unsolvable.

After a patrol officer arrived at the Ramsey house and read the purported ransom note that Patsy Ramsey said had been left by persons claiming to have kidnapped JonBenet, he called for backup. During the next two hours while the initial responding patrol officers searched the exterior of the premises, several of Patsy Ramsey's friends whom she had called began arriving at the house and wandering through it without being challenged by the patrol officers. By the time two detectives arrived, two hours had passed, while the Ramseys, their son, and seven other persons meandered throughout the unsecured crime scene.

Other police officers arrived, including FBI agents who were attempting to set up telephone line taps and traps to record any phone calls from the kidnappers, who had communicated through the note found by Patsy Ramsey that they wanted $118,000 for the safe return of her daughter. A detective decided that there were too many people in the house and ordered all nonessential personnel to leave. After giving the order, he and the other law enforcement officials left the Ramsey residence, leaving one detective to ride herd over the remaining Ramsey family members, their friends and pastor, and the city victims' advocates who had arrived at Patsy Ramsey's urgings. The uncontrolled crime scene was reduced to the responsibility of a lone detective, while the investigator and other officers went to the police department to confer about additional investigative processes during the two hours that followed.

The detective called for assistance, but the requests were refused by senior personnel. A friend of the family, Stanford Lucas, and John Ramsey, father of JonBenet, searched the basement of the large fifteen-bedroom house. At approximately 12:55 P.M., nearly seven hours after Patsy Ramsey called the police informing them that her daughter had been kidnapped, John Ramsey discovered JonBenet's body in one of the several basement rooms in the house. John Ramsey covered his daughter's body in a blanket that had been on the floor of the basement and carried his daughter by her waist up the stairs and into the living room of the house.

On the main floor of the house, after placing the child's body in the front hallway, Mrs. Ramsey threw herself over the body. The child's body was removed from the front hallway and carried into the living room, placed near the family's Christmas tree, and covered again with a large jacket believed to have been worn by John Ramsey. Between approximately 1:15 P.M. and 1:30 P.M., two additional uniformed officers, Stanford Lucas, an FBI agent, and two Boulder, Colorado, detectives entered the basement at the Ramsey house and reportedly looked around the basement and examined the room in which JonBenet's body was found. It was not until 1:50 P.M. that investigators secured the house, sequestered the persons present, and began preparing information by which to obtain a search warrant. The search warrant was executed on the morning of December 26, 1996, and was concluded ten days later.

The coroners report concluded that JonBenet had been sexually assaulted, strangled, and bludgeoned. Manner of death was listed as strangulation, and cause of death was determined to be murder.

Throughout the course of the next several months, Patsy and John Ramsey refused to talk to police or provide samples for DNA swap analysis, although Patsy Ramsey did provide handwriting samples for comparisons of her writing with the ransom note she had found. The writing comparison was deemed inconclusive.

In June of 1997, the remaining Ramsey family moved from Boulder, Colorado, to Atlanta, Georgia. A grand jury investigation in Colorado into the death of the child beauty pageant winner ended without charges in 1999.

Patsy Ramsey died of ovarian cancer June 24, 2004. As of late 2007, John Ramsey was residing in Atlanta, Georgia. The murder of JonBenet Ramsey has remained unsolved.

In *Crime Scene Handbook*, authors Dr. Lee, Timothy Palmback, and Margaret Miller point out the central crucial theme of sound investigative practices, particularly,

> The foundation of all investigative practices is based on the ability of the crime scene investigator to recognize the potential importance of physical evidence, large and small, at the crime scene. The subsequent identification of the physical evidence…source or origin…[and] individualization, are the next steps in investigation…[P]roper crime scene investigation is the initiation of crime scene reconstruction…[C]areful processing, documentation, and collection of physical evidence are integral parts to…crime scene investigation (Lee, Palmbeck, and Miller 2001, 1–2).

Although the recitation of the investigation of the JonBenet Ramsey murder case is exceptionally brief, a majority of persons in 2007 would likely recognize or suspect many of the process and investigative errors and missteps that occurred early in the investigation. A brief recitation of investigative failures and missteps could include the fact that

1. The bare-handed handling of the ransom note by the initial responding officer would have complicated what opportunities may have existed to lift potential suspect fingerprints from the document.
2. While waiting for backup, the officer failed to control the premises and persons residing in the house.
3. The Ramseys were left alone while the officers searched the exterior of the house.

4. The searching officers failed to search the immediate premises for items of evidence and the then-presumed-missing child.

5. The Boulder Police Department policy precluded the ability of the responding detectives to arrive on the scene equipped with investigative equipment until after they had obtained their vehicles from the department lot, thereby delaying the arrival of the detectives.

6. While waiting for detectives to arrive, the first responding patrol officers allowed the friends of Patsy Ramsey to arrive unchallenged and to wander freely throughout the crime scene.

7. Other police officers arrived and began wandering throughout the premises without plan or purpose.

8. After detectives arrived, one of the detectives ordered all nonessential personnel to be removed from the crime scene and left one detective to manage seven civilians who continued to meander about the house.

9. The detective who remained at the Ramsey residence was rebuffed when she requested assistance to secure and control the crime scene.

10. The remaining detective used civilian personnel, including a potential suspect, to search the premises.

11. When JonBenet's father found her body and moved it from where it was found, he contaminated the evidence in the room and on the body.

12. The contamination of evidence continued when the body was placed on the hallway floor and then subsequently was moved to the living room.

13. The body was held, moved, and touched by several persons.

14. The body was wrapped and rewrapped in blankets and jackets worn by other persons in the household.

15. Numerous law enforcement officials entered and exited areas of the residence after the body was found, potentially destroying evidence where the body had been discovered.

If, as Dr. Lee indicates, the first and most significant activity of investigation is the ability of officers to recognize the probable importance of physical evidence, regardless of its size, then that essential element was absent throughout the investigation into the murder of JonBenet Ramsey. The most telling aspect of Dr. Lee's admonishments is the fact that without that primary recognition of the potentiality of evidence, there is little opportunity to recover from those mistakes. Although the investigation into the murder of JonBenet Ramsey was replete with substantive processing and procedural errors, it became a contest of wills between competing investigative agencies (Boulder Police, FBI, county district attorney's office, and Colorado Bureau of Investigation), further reducing the opportunities for success.

Dr. Lee's comments over the course of his career regarding the professional practices of criminal investigators and forensic scientist require, as he stated,

We always work as a team (investigators and forensic scientists)…Movies have to have their hero but in real life we don't…[A] team, including the first officers to arrive, are responsible for the outcome of an investigation…[T]he whole team gets the credit or blame (CCTV 2005).

To his great credit, it should be noted that the fees for consultation received by Dr. Lee in the various cases arising outside his former Connecticut jurisdiction were donated to various charities. Therefore, regardless which side of the trial system hired Dr. Lee, the profits that he might have pocketed were given to worthy causes.

Regarding the notoriety of the cases and resultant near-celebrity status he was accorded following his involvement in those cases and his generally successful involvement in more than 8,000 investigations, Dr. Lee remarked,

I don't want to be famous…[W]hat I like to do is to talk to young people because some will become judges, prosecutors, defense attorneys, scientists, and other professionals…[T]hey are the future of criminal investigation and forensic science (CCTV 2005).

ADVANCING SCIENTIFIC FORENSIC INVESTIGATION METHODOLOGIES

The list of articles coauthored by Dr. Lee beginning in 1976 and continuing through 1987 reflect his many interests in the use of scientific analysis as an investigative aid. A quick read of the titles of the articles clearly indicates Dr. Lee's significant and timely research in the emergent fields of bloodstain pattern analysis. The articles listed below are reflective of his contributions to the field of forensic science and criminal investigation practices and were obtained from Dr. Lee's 2006 *curriculum vitae* as available through the *Crime Laboratory Digest* of that same year:

Lee, H. C., and P. DeForest. 1976. Precipitin-inhibition test for determination of the human origin of the denatured bloodstain. *Journal of Forensic Science* 21(4):804–809.

Lee, H. C., and P. DeForest. 1977. The use of anti-human HB serum for bloodstain identification. *AAFS Abstract* 67.

Lee, H. C., and P. DeForest. 1978. Determination of age of bloodstains by G/A ratio. *IAFS Abstract* 184.

DeForest, P., H. C. Lee, and V. Crispino. 1978. Considerations and recommendations regarding the collection and handling of fresh bloodstains. *IAFS Abstract* 154.

Lee, H. C., R. E. Gaensslen, and P. DeForest. 1979. Estimation of age of bloodstains by G/A ratio. *AAFS Abstract*.

Lee, H. C., and P. DeForest. 1979. Identification of human bloodstains by anti-human HB serum. *Police Science* 9(34): 110 (Trans. by M. H. Lin).

Lee, H. C. et al. 1982. Various methods of concentrating dilute blood evidence for subsequent analysis. *AAFS Abstract* B9.

Lee, H. C. 1984. A review of bloodstain pattern interpretation. *Journal of Forensic Science*, January 29(1).

Lee, H. C., and R. E. Gaensslen. 1984. Multiple analysis of bloodstains. *IAFS Abstract*, September.

Gaensslen, Desio, and H. C. Lee. 1986. Genetic marker system for the individualization of blood and body fluids in forensic serology. In G. Davies, ed., *Forensic Science*, 2nd ed., Washington, DC: American Chemical Society.

Lee, H. C. et al. 1985. Multiple analysis of bloodstains. *AAFS Abstract*, February: 130–149.

Lee, H. C. et al. 1985. Forensic serology and genetic markers. Proceedings of the Symposium on Forensic Evidence. Peking, China.

Lee, H. C., R. E. Gaensslen, E. M. Pagliaro, and M. B. Guman. 1986. Effects of reagents for presumptive blood and body fluid testing, latent fingerprint enhancement and histological stains on subsequent serological tests. *AAFS Abstract*, New Orleans, Louisiana.

Lee, H. C. 1986. Estimation of original volume of bloodstains. *Identification News*, July.

Lee, H. C. 1986. Identification and grouping of bloodstains. *Forensic Science* (China) 21:34.

Lee, H. C. et al. 1987. Estimation of original volume of bloodstains. *International Association of Blood Pattern Analysis News*.

Bloodstain patterns and pattern analysis is an essential investigation process in any criminal investigation response to violent interactions between the victim(s) and the offender(s). Bloodstain pattern analysis provides an opportunity for the trained and experienced investigator to determine within the crime scene the location and classification of the bloodstains, blood impact angles, points of origin of blood splatters, positioning of the victim and the attacker during the assault, and the probable sequence of events. Furthermore, the research articles indicate Dr. Lee's interest in and discovery of techniques and applications of bloodstain and blood splatter investigative processes for law enforcement officials.

The dual concerns expressed in Dr. Lee's formidable research publications consistently reflected his scientific interests and pragmatic investigative applications of evidence-based research in criminal investigations. Because of his dual interests, Dr. Lee was able not only to advance and contribute to the growing field of forensic science, but he also contributed to the improvement in the application of processes and techniques by investigative personnel.

Although the history of DNA research rightfully includes the works of Gregor Mendel (1866) and the groundbreaking studies of Dr. Barbara McClintock (1983), DNA testing (also known as typing or profiling) was first described by Dr. Alec Jeffreys in 1989, who coined the term DNA testing and based his discovery on the fact that certain regions of DNA contained sequences (repeating sets) of markers and that those sequences varied from individual to individual. On the basis of his discovery, Dr. Jeffreys developed early techniques to examine the length variations of the repeated DNA sequences and therefore the ability to perform tests to determine human identity through those tests. Of significance are two articles of research results in which Dr. Lee was involved in the late 1980s that clearly demonstrate his involvement on the *leading edge* of the early scientific relevance for criminal investigative processes (DNA Genetic Topics 2007):

> Gaensslen, R. E., S. C. Bell, and H. C. Lee. 1987. Distribution of genetic markers in United States population: I. Blood group and secretor system. *Journal of Forensic Science* 32 (4, July).
>
> Gaensslen, R. E., S. C. Bell, and H. C. Lee. 1987. Distribution of genetic markers in United States population: II. Isoenzyme system. *Journal of Forensic Science* 32 (5, September).

ADVANCING CRIMINAL INVESTIGATION METHODOLOGIES

Not content simply to research issues central to forensic criminal investigative practices and publish in leading juried journals in the United States and internationally, Dr. Lee also dedicated his career to the furtherance of investigative practices and the improvements in the reliability of those practices. The following partial list of articles, manuals, and texts developed for the consideration and application by law enforcement investigative professionals provides substantive verification of career dual interests in forensic science and criminal investigation procedure:

> Lee, H. C., et al. 1981. Scientific evidence and homicide investigation. *AAFS Abstract*.
>
> Lee, H. C., et al. 1982. Trace evidence and arson investigation. *AAFS Abstract* B42.
>
> Lee, H. C., et al. 1983. The role of physical evidence in homicide investigation. *AAFS Abstract* B50.
>
> Lee, H. C., and R. E. Gaensslen. 1984. Analytical techniques used in homicide investigation. *Eastern Analytical Symposium* Abstract.
>
> DeForest, P. R., R. E. Gaensslen, and H. C. Lee. 1983. *Forensic Science—An Introduction to Criminalistics*. New York: McGraw-Hill.

Lee, H. C., S. Kelley, and E. Pagliaro. 1983. *Physical Evidence and Crime Scene Investigation*. Connecticut Police Training Academy.

Lee, H. C., et al. 1985. *Physical Evidence and Forensic Science*. Connecticut State Police Forensic Science Laboratory Connecticut Insurance Placement Facility, Hartford, Connecticut.

Lee, H. C., P. J. Desio, and R. E. Gaensslen. 1986. Methods for the recovery of accelerants from arson debris. In *Forensic Science*. 2nd ed., ed. G. Davies. Washington, D.C.: American Chemical Society.

Lee, H. C., R. E. Gaensslen, E. M. Pagliaro, R. J. Mills, and K. B. Zercie. 1991. *Physical Evidence in Criminal Investigation*. Westbrook, CT: Narcotic Officers Association.

Gaensslen, R. E., and H. C. Lee. 1996. *Sexual Assault Evidence: National Assessment and Guidebook*. Washington, D.C.: National Institute of Justice, U.S. Department of Justice, March 1996.

Lee, H. C., T. Palmbach, and M. T. Miller. 2001. *Henry Lee's Crime Scene Handbook*. London: Academic Press.

ADDITIONAL TEACHING POSTS (PARTIAL LIST)

Not one to sit on his laurels or engage in the narrowed sharing of his time, interests, and passions, Dr. Lee actively participated in a wide-ranging series of opportunities to share his knowledge with others. The list of academic posts that he held simultaneously while teaching at the University of New Haven include the following:

Adjunct Professor, Department of Sociology, Central Connecticut State University, 1993
Adjunct Professor, University of Connecticut Law School, 1992
Adjunct Professor, Forensic Science Program, John Jay College of Criminal Justice, New York
Visiting Professor, School of Law, People's University, Peking, China, Summer 1985
Adjunct Professor, Biology Department, Biology Program, Graduate Program, Bridgeport University, Bridgeport, Connecticut
Adjunct Professor, Department of Administration of Justice, Western Connecticut State University, Danbury, Connecticut, 1984

CONTINUING EDUCATION ATTENDED (PARTIAL LIST)

While pursuing his teaching career, forensic science investigations research, and duties as the chief forensic scientists with the Connecticut Crime Laboratory, Dr. Lee pursued the continuing advancement and understanding within the areas of his interests through participation in a wide-ranging series of continuing education and training opportunities. Some of the hundreds of seminars he attended included the following:

> Forensic Medicine and Science, Post Graduate Medical School, New York University
> Environmental Pathology Seminar, American Academy of Forensic Science
> Gas Chromatography School, Perkin-Elmer Company
> Forensic Microscopy Workshop, University of Connecticut
> Bloodstain Pattern Workshop, Northeastern Association of Forensic Scientists
> Analysis of Sexual Assault Evidence Symposium, FBI Academy
> Forensic Applications of Electrophoresis Symposium, FBI Academy
> Forensic Examination of Hair Evidence Symposium, FBI Academy
> Crime Scene Photography Workshop, Eastman Kodak Company
> Infrared Analysis School, Perkin-Elmer Company
> Infrared Spectroscopy Applications, Bowdoin College, Maine
> Infrared Data Station Analysis Course, Perkin-Elmer Company
> Advanced Laser Latent Fingerprint Symposium, FBI Academy

PROFESSIONAL MEMBERSHIPS (PARTIAL LIST)

A person of prodigious energies, awareness of responsibilities, recognizing the necessity for membership in the community of scientists, and possessing a keen sense of collegiality, Dr. Lee throughout his career has met the rigorous criteria of professional associations and has maintained those memberships to participate and learn. It would appear that Dr. Lee recognized that membership in professional societies and organizations provides an opportunity to meet with other persons of like minds, influence future inquiries, and participate in the conversations and controversies affecting the fields of his interest and occupations.

The various organizations listed below ensured that throughout his career he would come into contact with law enforcement officials, criminal investigators, academicians representing a wide range of criminological and criminal justice interests, researchers engaged in significant applied research efforts, theoretical implications of investigation and court decisions, and students focusing on their own emerging careers in criminal justice, criminology, and forensic science:

> American Academy of Forensic Science, Distinguished Fellow, 1990
> The Forensic Science Society, England, Member, 1978
> American Academy of Criminal Justice, Member, 1978
> New York Academy of Science, Member, 1979
> American Association for the Advancement of Science, Member, 1979
> American Society for Testing and Materials, Member, 1980
> International Association of Forensic Science, Member, 1980
> Association of Official Analytical Chemists, Member, Referee, 1980

The Fingerprint Society, England, Fellow, 1984

International Association of Bloodpattern Analysis, Regional Vice President, 1987

CHANCE FAVORS THE PREPARED

Dr. Henry Lee has been favored in his life by a combination of personal, professional, occupational, opportunistic, and historic alignments. In reality the events and what transpires in life are not merely our simple understanding of *luck*. Louis Pasteur (1822–1895), the famous French biologist/chemist who is best known for discovering the pasteurization process for milk and other food stuffs because he was convinced that the causes of most medical illness and death in the nineteenth century were related to germs (microscopic organisms detrimental the to health of healthy organisms, particularly humans), once remarked about his view regarding human luck, fate, or chance. Louis Pasteur believed as Seneca (5 B.C.-65 B.C.), the Roman philosopher, who stated, "Luck is where opportunity and preparation meet" (Holland 1920). If Seneca and Pasteur are correct, then surely, when one reviews the early education and training received by Dr. Henry Lee, his impressive energies and endeavors in teaching, forensic research, publications, and associations prepared him to meet the challenges of and involvement in the notorious cases that brought him to the public's attention. Moreover, by 1998 Dr. Henry parlayed his reputation, energies, and skills into the creation and development of educational and training institutes that would secure not only his legacy but continue to contribute to the advancement of evidence-based investigative practices and support new generations of investigators and forensic scientists.

THE LEGACY

Dr. Henry Lee was the founder of the Henry C. Lee College of Criminal Justice and Forensic Science (affiliated with the University of New Haven) in 1998. The Henry C. Lee Institute of Forensic Science marks the state of Connecticut as a world leader in the arena of public safety and forensic science. The institute specializes in interdisciplinary research, training, testing, consulting, and education in forensic science.

The goal of the Henry C. Lee College of Criminal Justice and Forensic Science is to provide an atmosphere in which scholars, students, forensic scientists, and others in the criminal justice community are linked for the purpose of addressing the scientific and social issues challenging forensic science and the criminal justice system nationally and internationally. The institute, through its various agencies offering training, consultation, and research, endeavors to make the various arenas of systems within the

Becoming a Forensic Scientist

Qualifications for a Career in Forensic Science

Introduction

Forensic science plays a crucial role in the criminal justice system. As an applied science, it requires a strong foundation in the natural sciences and the development of practical skills in the application of these sciences to a particular discipline. A forensic scientist must be capable of integrating knowledge and skills in the examination, analysis, interpretation, reporting, and testimonial support of physical evidence. A properly designed forensic science program should address these needs and strengthen the student's knowledge, skills, and abilities in these areas. A combination of education and practical training can prepare an individual for a career in forensic science.

Most of the nation's practicing forensic scientists are employed in *crime laboratories* associated with law enforcement or other government agencies. Forensic scientists come to the profession with diverse undergraduate science degrees. They also may go on to earn graduate degrees. This document contains suggestions for model programs in forensic science at both the undergraduate and graduate levels. A combination of personal, professional, and academic criteria will influence a prospective forensic science examiner's suitability for employment.

Government entities' hiring processes are driven by civil service regulations or collective bargaining agreements that are specific to the branch of government, state, or locality. Private laboratories have their own hiring processes. The hiring process may include written and practical tests, phone interviews, and one-on-one personal interviews or interviews conducted by a panel. New employees may be hired provisionally or go through a probationary period. *Provisional employment* offers may be revoked either before or after reporting for duty.

Model Candidate

A model candidate for all forensic science practices possesses personal integrity, holds a baccalaureate degree (at a minimum) in the natural sciences, and has additional KSAs that fulfill the recommendations set forth in this *Guide.*

Personal characteristics

Because forensic science is part of the criminal justice system, personal honesty, integrity, and scientific objectivity are paramount. Those seeking careers in this field should be aware that background checks similar to those required for law enforcement officers are likely to be a condition of employment. The following may be conducted and/or reviewed before an employment offer is made and may remain as ongoing conditions of employment (this list is not all-inclusive):

- Drug tests.
- History of drug use.
- Criminal history.
- Personal associations.
- Polygraph examination.
- Driving record.
- Past work performance.
- Credit history.
- Medical or physical examination.

Personal candor in these areas is critical. An individual's history of community service and outside activities may also be considered.

Academic qualifications

Forensic scientists need to have a strong fundamental background in the natural sciences. For example, new hires who analyze drugs, DNA, trace, and toxicological evidence in forensic science laboratories typically have a degree in chemistry, biochemistry, biology, or forensic science from an accredited institution. Although forensic scientists involved in the recognition and comparison of patterns (such as latent prints, firearms, and questioned documents) historically may not have been required to have a degree, the trend in the field is to strengthen the academic requirements for these disciplines and require a baccalaureate degree, preferably in a science. The academic qualifications required for some of the emerging disciplines, such as digital evidence, currently are being defined and will be published by the appropriate groups.

Copies of diplomas and formal academic transcripts generally are required as proof of academic qualification. Awards, publications, internships, and student activities may be used to differentiate applicants.

Claims in this regard are subject to verification through the background investigation process.

Professional skills

A variety of skills are essential to an individual's effectiveness as a forensic science professional, including:

(continued)

- Critical thinking (quantitative reasoning and problem solving).
- Decision-making.
- Good laboratory practices.
- Awareness of laboratory safety.
- Observation and attention to detail.
- Computer proficiency.
- Interpersonal skills.
- Public speaking.
- Oral and written communication.
- Time management.
- Prioritization of tasks.

For some of these skills, systematic tools are available that may be used to measure skill or proficiency at or after the time of hire.

Model Curriculum: Undergraduate Degree in Forensic Science

[Below are] minimum recommendations for a model undergraduate degree in forensic science. Such a degree provides an educational foundation that meets the current hiring requirements of forensic science laboratories. This curriculum emphasizes the strong natural science foundation that is essential to prepare a student for a successful career in forensic science.

This curriculum is not designed to produce case-ready forensic scientists. Laboratory managers, educators, and students may realize that prior to beginning casework, additional on-the-job training, and possible postgraduate studies may be necessary to meet the specific needs of the individual employer.

University general education

General education courses are courses that the university requires the student to take. They may include language, humanities, social sciences, mathematics, technical writing, computer science, and public speaking. The actual number of credit hours required may vary from university to university but generally ranges from 36 to 40. Some forensic degree coursework may count toward fulfilling this requirement. Carefully selected general education courses can complement the student's main program of study.

Natural science core

Certain natural science courses are required for any student in forensic science. Unlike other criminal justice professionals, a forensic scientist requires a foundation in chemistry, biology, physics, and mathematics.

The minimum general core requirements recommended for undergraduate forensic science programs (34–38 total credit hours) include:

- General chemistry I and II and lab for science majors (8 credit hours).
- Organic chemistry I and II and lab (8 credit hours).
- Biology I and II for science majors (4–8 credit hours).
- Physics I and II for science majors and lab (8 credit hours).
- Calculus (3 credit hours).
- Statistics for science majors (3 credit hours).

Specialized science courses

An undergraduate degree in forensic science is expected to be an interdisciplinary degree that includes substantial laboratory work and an emphasis on advanced (i.e., upper level) coursework in chemistry or biology. Students can use these additional courses to begin to specialize along a forensic science discipline track, such as forensic biology or forensic chemistry.

Specialized science courses may be selected from any of the following (minimum 12 credit hours and minimum of 2 laboratory courses):

- Biochemistry.
- Molecular biology.
- Genetics.
- Population genetics.
- Inorganic chemistry.
- Analytical/quantitative chemistry.
- Physical chemistry.
- Instrumental analysis.
- Cell biology.
- Pharmacology.
- Calculus II.
- Microbiology.

Forensic science core

It is essential to cover certain forensic science topics in specific courses or as portions of courses that combine several topics. Include the following topics as *core elements* in the forensic science curriculum:

(continued)

- Introduction to law/justice system.
- Ethics/professional practice.
- Forensic science specialty overview (survey course).

Total Credit Hours

- 36–40 hours of general university requirements.
- 46–50 hours of natural and specified science courses.
- 15 hours of forensic science courses (nine of which should include laboratory work).
- 19 hours of additional courses.

Total: 120 credit hours
  [Also] . . .

- Evidence identification, collection, and processing.
- Quality assurance.
- Courtroom testimony.
- Technical or scientific writing.

Forensic science laboratory courses

In addition to a strong foundation in the natural sciences, forensic science professionals are expected to recognize concepts integral to forensic science, such as individualization, reconstruction, association, and chain of custody of evidence. Because the work product of a forensic scientist is used by the justice system, it is expected to meet legal as well as scientific standards. The following courses are designed to give the student an understanding of the application of scientific analysis to the legal system (a minimum of 15 credit hours, for which a minimum of nine credit hours are expected to be laboratory science courses):

- Forensic chemistry and lab (3).
- Forensic biology and lab (3).
- Physical methods in forensic science and lab (3).
- Internship (up to 6) or independent study/research (up to 6).
- Microscopy and lab (3).

Source: U.S. Department of Justice, National Institute of Justice Report of Forensic Science Training and Careers. June 2004. http://www.aafs.org/pdf/NIJReport.pdf.

criminal justice system more effective through more rigorous, cost-efficient investigation applications and through its research to increase the effectiveness of crime prevention programs and activities.

Henry C. Lee College of Criminal Justice and Forensic Sciences is housed at the University of New Haven, a private comprehensive university with an eighty-seven-year history of strong professional programs. The Henry C. Lee College offers Bachelor of Science degrees in criminal justice, fire science, fire protection engineering, forensic science, and legal studies and Masters of Science degrees in criminal justice, fire science, forensic science, and national security and public safety. Plans for a Ph.D. program were under development in 2007. The Henry C. Lee College of Criminal Justice and Forensic Sciences boasted more than thirty full-time faculty serving more than 1,300 undergraduate majors and more than 350 graduate students in 2007.

FURTHER READING

ABC.com. April 2, 2002. 20/20: *Forensic scientist Henry Lee talks about his work in crime scene investigations* (transcript) http://www.lexisnexis.com. ezproxy.canton.edu:2048/us/lnacademic/results/docview/docview.do?risb=21_ T2119451411&format=GNBFI&sort=RELEVANCE&startDocNo=1&results UrlKey=29_T2119451415&cisb=22_T2119451414&treeMax=true&treeWidth= 275&selRCNodeID=54&nodeStateId=411en_US,1,53,7&docsInCategory=5&csi= 8277&docNo=2 (accessed September 21, 2007).

Brush Bandit Industries. 2007. *Model 150XP* (Brush Bandit). http://www.banditchippers. com/index.php?option=com_models&task=view&itemId=15&lineId=2&modelId= 2 (accessed September 15, 2007).

CCTV. English Channel Close Up. 2005. *Dr. Henry Lee: Modern Sherlock Holmes* (video transcript). http://www.cctv.com/program/UpClose/20050422/101645. shtml (accessed September 20, 2007).

Central Police University. 2007. *History of School*. http://cpuweb.cpu.edu.tw/ e-index.asp (accessed August 15, 2007).

Connecticut Department of Public Safety. 2007. *Scientific Services: Division History*. http://www.ct.gov/dps/cwp/view.asp?a=2155&q=317236 (accessed August 15, 2007).

CourtTV.com. http://www.courttv.com/onair/shows/trace_evidence/who_is_lee.html (accessed September 15, 2007).

CourtTV.com. 2001. In-Depth Specials: The JonBenet Ramsey Case. http://courttv. com/trials/caruuth/lee2.html (accessed September 15, 2007).

CourtTV.com. 2007. Los Angeles County Court. OJ Simpson Trial Transcript: Dr. Lee Testimony. http://www.courttv.com/casefiles/simpson/new_docs/lee_testimony. html (accessed August 15, 2007).

CNN.com 2007. http://www.cnn.com/US/9703/ramsey.case/index.html (accessed September 12, 2007).

Debre, P. 1994. Louis Pasteur. Baltimore, MD: John Hopkins University Press.

DNA Genetic Topics. 2007. http://www.d230.org/stagg/LiskaLinks/dna.htm (accessed September 12, 2007).

Encyclopedia Britannica Online. *China: The Sino-Japanese War.* http://www.britannica.com/eb/article-71823/China (accessed September 22, 2007).

Gado, M. 2007. *The Wood Chipper Murder Case.* Crime Library.com. http://www.crimelibrary.com/notorious_murders/family/woodchipper_murder/html (accessed September 15, 2007).

Henry C. Lee College of Criminal Justice and Forensic Science. 2007. http://www.newhaven.edu/show.asp?durki=9 (accessed August 15, 2007).

Henry Lee Institute. 2007. Institute website. http://www.henryleeinstitute.com/about/ (accessed August 15, 2007).

Herszenhorn, D. 2000. Dr. Lee, the man with all the clues. *New York Times, Connecticut Weekly Desk.* April 23. Lexis-Nexus Academic database (accessed August 15, 2007).

Hewitt, B., and J. Harmes. 1996. *Post Mortem* 45 (3, January 22): 38–42

Holland, F. C. 1969. *Seneca* (reprint of the 1920 edition). Manchester, NH: Ayer Company Publishers.

Kanable, R. 2005. Modern forensic science today and tomorrow: An interview with Dr. Henry Lee. *Law Enforcement Technology* 32(7), 8–18.

Laber, T. L., and B. P. Epstein. 1983. *Experiments and Practical Exercises in Blood Stain Pattern Analysis: Laboratory Manual.* Minneapolis, MN: Callin Publishing.

Ladd, C., M. S. Adamowicz, M. T. Bourke, C. A. Scherczinger, and H. C. Lee. 1999. A systematic analysis of secondary DNA transfer. *Journal of Forensic Science* 44 (6): 1270–1272.

Lee, H. C., T. Palmback, and M. T. Miller. 2001. *Henry Lee's Crime Scene Handbook.* San Diego, CA: Academic Press.

Lee, H. C. 2004. *Cracking More Cases.* Amherst, NY: Prometheus Books.

Lee, H. C. 2006. *Curriculum Vitae: Henry C. Lee (PhD). Crime Laboratory Digest,* from Federal Bureau of Investigation Laboratory in cooperation with The American Society of Crime Laboratory Directors Web site. http://www.drhenrylee.com/about/dr_lee_cv_resume.pdf (accessed August 15, 2007).

Linder, D. 2007. *The Trial of O. J. Simpson.* http://www.law.umkc.edu/faculty/projects/ftrials/Simpson/simpson.htm (accessed August 16, 2007).

Wikipedia. 2007. Chiang Kai-shek. http://en.wikipedia.org/wiki/Chiang_Kai-shek (accessed August 15, 2007).

Wikipedia. 2007. *Chinese Civil War.* http://en.wikipedia.org/wiki/Chinese_Civil_War (accessed August 15, 2007).

Wikipedia. 2007. *Henry Lee (forensic scientist).* http://en.wikipedia.org/wiki/Henry_Lee_(forensic_scientist) (accessed August 15, 2007).

Courtesy of the University of Tennessee

Dr. Bill Bass

Cécile Van de Voorde

I can't give people back their loved ones. I can't restore their happiness or innocence, can't give back their lives the way they were. But I can give them the truth. Then they will be free to grieve for the dead, and then free to start living again. Truth like that can be a humbling and sacred gift for a scientist to give.

—Bill Bass

Dr. William M. Bass III (Bill Bass) is one of the foremost scientists in the history of forensic anthropology. His revolutionary work on human decomposition and human osteology has left an invaluable legacy to the world of forensic science. A dedicated (now retired) professor of forensic anthropology and a passionate researcher, Dr. Bass has been a Diplomate of the American Board of Forensic Anthropology (ABFA) since 1977 (when he became the sixth certified Diplomate in the history of the ABFA). He has assisted local, state, federal, and international law enforcement agencies with hundreds of death investigations and helped solve many baffling cases, from historic burials to homicides to natural or human-made disasters. He has also gained worldwide fame by founding the Forensic Anthropology Facility at the University of Tennessee, otherwise known as the Body Farm. As such, he has become a truly iconic figure of crime fighting.

UNIVERSITY AND EARLY CAREER YEARS

A student of Clifford Evans at the University of Virginia, Bill Bass initially majored in psychology. As he explained in his 2003 memoir, "Virginia didn't actually have an anthropology department—just one lone professor, Clifford Evans, who was lumped into the Sociology Department. But Evans was an adventurous field researcher and an inspiring teacher…I took every class [he] taught" (Bass and Jefferson 2003, 18). In 1954, after a stint in the military, Bill Bass joined the master's program within the Department of Anthropology at the University of Kentucky. In April 1955, under the direction of his mentor, Dr. Charles E. Snow, he became involved in his first forensic case. The investigation into the case of a missing Kentucky woman led to the exhumation of a woman's "burned, rotten, and waterlogged" body that remains seared in Bass's memory. More importantly, the experience convinced Bass he had found his calling. He earned his master's degree in 1956 and proceeded to work with Clifford Evans, by then a curator of archaeology at the Smithsonian Institute, to study massive amounts of Native American skeletal remains from the Great Plains. The "old bones hidden in the earth" quickly taught him many valuable lessons. As he later emphasized, "[e]very one of these lessons would serve me well in the years ahead as I began applying the secrets I learned from the long-dead to understanding the stories of the recently murdered" (21). His first summer of intensive bone cataloging was followed in 1957 by extensive fieldwork in archeological digs in South Dakota. In 1961, Bass earned his Ph.D. in Anthropology from the University of Pennsylvania, where he had studied under the illustrious William M. Krogan, popularly known as the "bone detective." Dr. Bass later referred to him as "the Socrates of 'bone men'" (279).

At the University of Kansas in the sixties, Bass was "known throughout the university as a wonderful teacher" who inspired future forensic experts such as Douglas Ubelaker. The consensus today is that he belongs to a "generation of giants," along with famed forensic anthropologists Ellis Kerley, William R. Maples, and Clyde Snow. He has since worked on many high-profile cases that have contributed to his status as a living legend of forensic science.

Summary of Three Major Cases from *Death's Acre*

Among the cases depicted by Dr. Bass in *Death's Acre* (2003) are the following:

A Mass Murder in Mississippi

In December of 1993, "Big Mike" Rubenstein called 911 to report the deaths of his relatives in a cabin. Investigators responded and found the decomposing bodies of a man, a woman, and a four-year-old child. Rubenstein claimed to have visited the cabin in mid- and late-November, but found it empty. Then he'd come again in December and saw the bodies. It appeared to be the case of a shocked relative stumbling by accident into a crime scene, but when Rubenstein quickly applied to collect the insurance money, investigators grew suspicious. The accumulated mail and spoiled food also put Rubenstein's tale into doubt, so Bass was asked to help construct a timeline for when the deaths actually had occurred. Based on knowledge of insect development cycles and rate of decomposition in certain temperatures, he and his staff placed the deaths in mid-November—exactly when Rubenstein had admitted visiting the cabin. Ultimately he was convicted.

Serial Killer in Knox County, Tennessee

The 1999 murder trial of 38-year-old Thomas D. Huskey, accused killer of four women, was the first for a documented serial killer in Knox County, Tennessee, and prosecutors were seeking the death penalty. The two sides focused not only on the issue of his mental state at the time of the offenses, but also used insect analysis to evaluate the time since the deaths of two of the victims. Prostitutes had dubbed Huskey the "Zoo Man" because he once had worked at the Knoxville Zoo and he liked to take women close by for rough sex. Bass was called in after three of the victims had been discovered

(continued)

in a wooded area. His job was not only to estimate time since death but to determine if the victims had been killed where they lay or if the death scene was in fact elsewhere. He used his knowledge about what happens to bodies in the woods—specifically, the biomarkers in the vegetation and soil—to make the all-important determinations.

Tri-State Crematory Scandal

In 2002 more than three hundred decaying human bodies sent to the Tri-State Crematory for cremation were discovered left out in the open, buried in shallow pits, or crowded into vaults. Countless families were horrified to learn that the "ashes" of their loved ones were not human remains but possibly cardboard or wood ashes and that the deceased could be among those left in an undignified position. Tri-State's operator, Ray Brent Marsh, was arrested and charged with multiple counts of fraud and abuse of a body. The long process of identifying the remains began, and in many cases relatives filed lawsuits against Marsh and his business. Bill Bass assisted by analyzing the remains and letting people know exactly what they had.

Source: K. Ramsland. 2007b. Profile of Dr. Bill Bass, Founder of the Body Farm. http://www.crimelibrary.com/criminal_mind/forensics/bill_bass/.

DEVELOPMENT OF FORENSIC ANTHROPOLOGY AND OSTEOLOGY

Forensic anthropology is the discipline that applies the scientific knowledge of physical anthropology and archaeology to the collection and analysis of legal evidence. Although it was originally a subfield of physical anthropology, forensic anthropology has now grown into a distinct body of knowledge sharing common characteristics with other fields, most notably anthropology, biology, and the physical sciences.

"The science of forensic anthropology includes archeological excavation; examination of hair, insects, plant materials and footprints, determination of elapsed time since death; facial reproduction; photographic superimposition; detection of anatomical variants; and analysis of past injury and medical treatment" (Genge 2001). According to William R. Maples, "[T]he science of forensic anthropology, properly wielded, can resolve historical riddles and chase away bugbears that have bedeviled scholars for centuries" (Maples 1994, 3). Forensic anthropology is a young discipline with a long developmental history over the past 150 years. Thomas Dwight, the author of a seminal 1878 essay on human skeleton identification, may be credited as the "Father of Forensic Anthropology in the United States." (Burns 2007, 4).

On the other hand, Wilton M. Krogan, whom Bill Bass studied under as a doctoral student, is often described as "the founder of modern forensic anthropology since most of his research and writing were directed towards assisting medicolegal personnel" (Nafte 2000, 25). The evolution of forensic anthropology into a recognizable discipline dates back to the 1970s and the work of T. Dale Stewart and Bill Bass. In 1971, Bass's landmark publication, *Human Osteology: A Laboratory and Field Manual of the Human Skeleton*, was the first practical textbook for physical anthropologists. The first textbook to explicitly include the phrase "forensic anthropology" in its title was Stewart's *Essentials of Forensic Anthropology*. Moreover, although "'Forensic Anthropology' degree titles are a phenomenon of the late 1980s and 1990s...today, forensic anthropologists are employed by state, national, and international agencies around the world" (Burns 2007, 5).

"Recovery, description, and identification of human skeletal remains are the standard work of forensic anthropologists. The condition of the evidence varies greatly, including decomposing, burned, cremated, fragmented, or disarticulated remains" (5). According to Dr. Bass himself, "the ultimate goal [of a forensic investigation] is to make a positive identification" (Bass and Jefferson 2003, 35). If possible, one may also determine the cause of death (medical determination of the condition(s) that led or contributed to death) or the manner of death (legal determination based on evidence and opinion). Indeed,

> [T]he objectives of anthropological investigation are the same as those of a medical-legal investigation of a recently deceased person: identification, determination of cause and manner of death, estimation of time of death, and collection of any physical evidence supporting the conclusions or leading to further information (Burns 2007, 6).

However, "before you can tell who someone was and how they died—and you won't always be able to tell—you start with the Big Four: sex, race, age, and stature" (Bass and Jefferson 2003, 35).

Osteology is the study of bones. More specifically, human osteology is the scientific study of the physical growth, development, structure, function, and variation of the human skeleton. Most of the extant research is based on "information gathered from human skeletal populations of the past and present" (Nafte 2000, 25). Studies in human osteology focus on the effects of genetic origin, age, sex, diet, trauma, pathologies, anomalies, cultural influences, and decomposition.

> Within the human body are 206 bones...Together, they form a remarkable and, to the trained eye, informative framework of the body they once supported. They can show how the person lived; any debilitating illnesses the person had, such as rickets or polio; healed fractures; whether the person was right- or left-handed; and even possible clues as to occupation (Evans 2007, 144).

Hence, studying skeletal remains has important practical application inasmuch as it enables osteologists not only to describe a living person and identify a deceased person, but also evaluate the health of the person, recognize their habitual activities, determine the approximate time since death, and provide information about postmortem events. As Bass himself explains,

> [A]s a forensic anthropologist, I tend to see bodies that are long past their prime—bodies that are bloated, blasted, burned, buggy, rotted, sawed, gnawed, liquefied, mummified, or dismembered. Some are even skeletonized, reduced to bare bones—bare but brimming with data.
>
> Flesh decays; bone endures. Flesh forgets and forgives ancient injuries; bone heals, but it always remembers: a childhood fall, a barroom brawl; the smash of a pistol butt to the temple, the quick sting of a blade between the ribs. The bones capture such moments, preserve a record of them, and reveal them to anyone with eyes trained to see the rich visual record, to hear the faint whispers rising from the dead (Bass and Jefferson 2003, 34).

THE BODY FARM

The Forensic Anthropology facility at the University of Tennessee, otherwise known as the Body Farm, was founded by Dr. Bass in the early 1980s in order to study the decomposition of human bodies. Located a few miles away from downtown Knoxville, off of Alcoa Highway, it is nestled behind the University of Tennessee Medical Center. "The three-acre site, surrounded by chain-link fence topped with razor-edged concertina wire, is an outdoor forensic research laboratory designed to foster knowledge of what happens to a body once life expires" (Ricciuti 2007, 78). It was originally called the Anthropological Research Facility (ARF) and was developed concurrently with the Forensic Anthropology program, the focus of which "is the application of skeletal biological techniques to the identification of decomposing and skeletal remains for law enforcement and medicolegal agencies and investigations" (Genge 2002, 285).

> Research at the facility focuses on decomposition of the human body, such as how fast it decays under different conditions and the processes involved, such as amino-acid breakdown, and levels of gas in the tissue. Researchers study both how the natural processes of the body itself impact its rate of decomposition and how external agents, such as weather or insect activity, affect it (Ricciuti 2007, 79).

In 1981, Corpse 1-81 became the first resident of the Body Farm. Dr. Bass was at that time working with Bill Rodriguez, whose research on flies was about to "help spur a revolution in forensic science" (Bass and Jefferson 2003, 98). As Ramsland explains,

Bass laid out the first body, an unclaimed cadaver. He meticulously documented the conditions for its decomposition, and as he acquired more specimens, he placed them in other contexts: submerged in water, buried in earth, left inside buildings, locked in the trunks of cars.... From insect analysis to the nuances in odor at different points during the death process to death-related bacteriology, there seemed to be no end to the types of experiments that could be done to assist law enforcement. These researchers expanded in number and specialization, and the Body Farm became a center for training and consultation in difficult cases, including for the FBI (Ramsland 2007a, 238–39).

Although he had seen about 5,000 bodies before he even moved to Knoxville in 1971, Dr. Bass quickly realized that he had "a lot yet to learn about bodies and bugs" (Bass and Jefferson 2003, 99). Flies and maggots became part of his daily routine and helped him conduct landmark studies that truly revolutionized forensic science. In fact, "no other insect has aided more in determining the time of death than the blowfly or, more precisely, the maggots that hatch from the eggs that blowflies lay on dead bodies" (Ricciuti 2007, 79). Thus, Dr. Bass's research on human decomposition has made remarkable contributions to forensic entomology, which requires analyzing insect activity on human remains in order to estimate time and location of death. Ironically, Dr. Bass has an aversion for flies. Indeed, he once wrote,

I've had a strange, symbiotic relationship with flies ever since I was a small child. Shortly after my father's death, my mother and I moved in with her parents. We lived on a farm, and where there are farm animals, there are flies. My mother, who hated flies, made me a business proposition: for every ten dead flies I brought her, she'd pay me a bounty of one cent...The fly carcasses piled up, and so did my pennies. Ever since, tough—and as a scientist, I'm embarrassed to admit this—I have despised flies. I hate rattlesnakes more, but rattlesnakes are a lot less common, a lot more shy, and a lot easier to kill (Bass and Jefferson 2003, 99–100).

Dr. Bass's efforts to create a facility specifically designed for forensic anthropology research were spurred by the lack of opportunities for controlled research experiments on human decomposition. He viewed such experiments as necessary for more accurate recording and a deeper, more reliable understanding of what happens to a decaying body after death.

The earliest experimental work in this field was done on arthropods, mainly fly larvae, observing the patterns associated with their feeding on dead pigs, which were either buried or placed above the ground in various situations. The insects that came to feed on the pig flesh were monitored carefully, and a documentary record was kept of the order in which they arrived, how long they stayed, what happened to them while they were there, and the stages they went through. These patterns were then applied to observations of arthropod and insect activity on human remains; as a result, inferences could be made on how long the bodies had been where they were found and sometimes what had happened to them during and since death.

The problem with those experiments was that pigs were pigs; the need persisted for controlled observations of these same patterns in humans. Bill Bass had recognized this need for a long time, and after his transfer to the University of Tennessee he began to work on it in earnest. In the late 1970s he organized the Anthropological Research Facility (ARF) at Knoxville and commenced studies of decay rates under carefully monitored conditions with bodies donated from the Medical Examiner's Office that were either unidentified or unclaimed at the time of death. The skeletons later became part of a reference collection for the future recovery of data as the need arose.

Thus, ARF was essentially a decay rate facility or, as Ubelaker and Scammell called it, an "al fresco mortuary" (when local lawyers and forensic specialists added Bass's name to the facility acronym, it quickly became referred to as BARF). The facility still processes up to fifty bodies per year in its open-air morgue, as well as numerous dogs obtained from the city pound; more than 300 bodies have been donated by members of the general public. Remains are typically placed on concrete slabs or on the ground, or they may be wrapped in plastic or buried in shallow pits. They are "in their natural condition, usually without embalming. The only artificial aspect of the environment is its security; the fence precludes carnivore activity" (Ubelaker and Scammell 2006, 108).

Often described as "the mayor of the Body Farm," Dr. Bass has relentlessly battled to reconstruct identities, unravel mysterious deaths, and provide welcome answers for the ones who stay behind. "Uncertainty and dread are almost always harder to bear than the finality of certain loss" (Bass and Jefferson 2003, 275). Dr. Bass candidly explains that he used to believe in an afterlife. Following his father's suicide and the deaths of his first two wives, however, he shifted away from religion as he realized, "[w]e're organisms; we're conceived, we're born, we live, we die, and we decay. But as we decay we feed the world of the living: plants and bugs and bacteria" (279). He subsequently began to concentrate his fieldwork and intellectual efforts on the legacy each of us leaves behind when we die. Today, the Forensic Anthropology Center (FAC) within the Department of Anthropology at the University of Tennessee-Knoxville (UTK) officially represents the culmination of Dr. Bass's work since the early 1970s, both on and beyond the UTK campus. Dr. Bass has created a facility where scientists and law enforcement officials can "educate themselves in the science beyond the art of investigation" (Evans 2006, x). He has inspired and continues to rouse scores of budding or accomplished researchers and the legacy of his Body Farm is inestimable. In his memoir, he poignantly wrote,

> I still beam with pride, after all these years, when I spot something Krogman might have overlooked if he had been on the case. And so it will be, perhaps,

with my students. For some of them, I hope, I will always be looking over their shoulder at the shattered skull, the burned bones, the telltale insects; always questioning them, always challenging them, sometimes even inspiring them. There's a part of me that will live on, too, at the Body Farm, my proudest scientific creation. Looking back over the past quarter century, I'm amazed at the wealth of pioneering research that has emerged from such humble beginnings—it began in an abandoned sow barn—and even today the Anthropology Research Facility remains a simple metal shed and a patch of trees and honeysuckle vines, tucked behind a high wooden fence (recently enlarged and rebuilt with the help of Patricia Cornwell). That, plus a generation of bright, inquisitive minds eager to unlock the secrets of death. I certainly didn't set out to create something famous there. I just set out to find some answers to questions that were nagging me. As in life, so in science: One thing leads to another, and before you know it, you find yourself someplace you never imagined going" (Bass and Jefferson 2003, 279–80).

POSTMORTEM INTERVAL AND FORENSIC TAPHONOMY

When a body is found in unexpected circumstances, one of the first questions is, "How long has this person been dead?" This is called the postmortem interval or time since death. The information is important to both the identification process and the death investigation itself.

Forensic taphonomy can be defined as the multidisciplinary study of the postmortem interval. Forensic scientists specifically use the term taphonomy to refer to the process of decomposition. Thus, "taphonomy is the study of the fate of the remains of organisms after they die" (Burns 2007, 49). Taphonomic research for forensic purposes initially used case studies and comparative animal studies, mostly using pigs as models for human decomposition.

The forensic community initially was appalled by Dr. Bass's avant-garde, anticonformist research on human decomposition. However, they eventually acknowledged the significance of his work. "By the 1980s, research articles were appearing regularly in scientific publications. Forensic taphonomy is now a standard subject in the forensic sciences...Specialists include anthropologists, entomologists, botanists, and a variety of other experts, including soil scientists and preservation specialists" (49).

The work pioneered by Dr. Bass has shed light on the process of decomposition as well as the environmental and cultural factors that affect the decomposition rate and consequently the estimation of time since death. Dr. Bass's research has provided a deeper understanding of the overall process of decomposition. "From a biological perspective, death is not a definitive event but a continuous process that occurs over a period of time" (Nafte 2000, 39). Following somatic death, the process of death is characterized by cellular death or autolysis ("self-digestion"), whereby metabolism ceases and enzymes destroy cells from within and tissues break down and soften. Dr. Bass has studied the various stages of decomposition, from initial decay (stemming from internal microorganism activity) to putrefaction (bloating due to metabolic gas buildup and subsequent collapse through fluid purge) to butyric fermentation (flesh fermentation and molding), dry decay (flesh hardening), and finally skeletonization. "Immediate postmortem change may be viewed essentially as a competition between decomposition (decay and putrefaction) and desiccation" (Burns 2007, 250). Immediate postmortem changes have been scrutinized carefully at the Body Farm, including algor mortis (the cooling of the body within the first two hours after death), livor mortis (the purple skin coloration that develops under the body as blood gravitates one to four hours after death), and rigor mortis (stiffening of the muscles caused by chemical changes in the tissue two to four hours after death).

In addition, ARF research has focused on environmental factors in order to assess the impact of climate on human decomposition. Warm humid climates are typically good for decomposition, whereas cool and dry climates are favorable to preservation. Bass conducted a study on decomposition rates in different climates and seasons, including the moist, warm conditions of a Knoxville summer. His research, although later complemented by other studies on different conditions, does not offer standards to rely on because "decomposition is multifactorial and continuous, grave types differ, and investigators tend to define and delineate the stages of decomposition slightly differently" (250). Nevertheless, Dr. Bass's Tennessee summer decomposition information has been used as a model for the study of environmental conditions incorporating variations based on local conditions and grave type. The model shows that "[a]s long as moisture and temperature are constant, the decomposition rate can be relatively constant" (251). In addition, "the early decomposition of a body in a warm, arid environment is about the same as that of a body in a warm, moist environment" and "[r]apid desiccation results in mummification," while "[s]low desiccation results in more thorough decomposition" (251). The Bass study used remains that were fully exposed (i.e., naked bodies and surface burials). In order for it to be applicable to other conditions, one must take into consideration shade, clothing, protective covering or burial technique, which can all result in an increase or decrease of the decomposition rate depending on moisture, temperature, and predatory activity. Subsequent studies have established for instance that exposed remains decompose faster than shaded ones or that temperature differential is the primary factor of decomposition or that maggots are typically more active in warmer places and will slow down in the shade. Rodriguez and Bass studied the level of protection provided by burial. They buried six unembalmed cadavers one, two, and four feet deep. "The cadavers were exhumed and examined at intervals up to one year. It was demonstrated that the rate of decomposition is much slower in buried remains [because of the] lack (or reduction) of carrion-eating insects and lower temperatures" (252).

Dr. Bass's work additionally has highlighted the significant role carrion (dead-flesh-eating) insects play in the decomposition process. These insects will scavenge and reproduce in many of the soft tissues and natural body openings, as well as in areas of flesh exposed by cuts or wounds. Insect activity accelerates decomposition and in certain environments, notably hot and humid ones, can reduce a body to bones within weeks. The major carrion feeders are flies and beetles. Other arthropods, such as spiders, mites, centipedes, and scorpions, are attracted to carrion for the mere opportunity it presents for them to prey on the carrion-feeding insects. The information provided by these feeders goes beyond the postmortem interval: they can be used "to test for drugs and poisons ingested with the tissues of the dead body" (252). Larger carrion feeders can be classified as either specialists (e.g., vultures) or opportunists (e.g., raccoons). It is particularly important to study bone damage, so as to determine what type of scavengers have preyed on the remains. "Bird scavengers usually do little to damage bone. Small mammals, such as rodents, carry small bones off and gnaw on them long after the flesh is gone. Larger mammals, such as dogs, disarticulate the body, carry parts to different locations, and break or pulverize the bones" (252).

Research at the Body Farm continually improves our understanding of the interaction between body decomposition and plants. A dead body will release volatile fatty acids at the beginning of the decomposition process. As a result, plants in the surrounding area are destroyed, but they return as the acids dissipate. The body then serves as a natural fertilizing source, which may cause an abnormal plant growth. As Burns points out, "[I]t is a lot easier to use this plant growth to locate a grave than to estimate postmortem interval, but professional forensic botanists can squeeze a lot of information out of the plants" (252). Such specialists focus on plant variety, as well as analyses of roots, stems, leaves, branches, and flowers (including pollen).

Cultural factors can also have an effect on the rate of decomposition and may therefore adversely impact postmortem interval estimates. Dr. Bass's extensive work with Native American skeletal remains has made him especially sensitive to the significance of cultural dynamics. In particular, funerary practices have been studied meticulously over the past three decades in order to determine how they can slow down or even stop the progress of decomposition. For instance, embalming, which is designed to preserve anatomical specimens in dead bodies, has become a widespread practice across the globe. The fluid used for embalming purposes is a powerful antibacterial agent that is injected into a body through the vascular system while blood is drained out, injected into organs, and pumped into the body cavity. "The main ingredient of embalming fluid is formalin, an aqueous solution of the gas formaldehyde. Other ingredients may include alcohol, silicone, lanolin, coloring, fragrances, and more" (253).

Regardless of the formula, all of its ingredients must be accounted for when studying decomposition, especially since "different components decay at different rates" and "the residual is difficult to identify in skeletal remains unless it contains a detectable ingredient such as a heavy metal" (253). Heavy metals, such as arsenic, lead or mercury, are poisonous; they are therefore regulated by federal agencies and their use for embalming purposes is now illegal. The way a body is encased is also important to consider. Decomposition will differ depending on whether a burial shroud was used versus a wooden or metal casket or depending on the presence of a grave liner or concrete vault. Other preservation factors come into play, such as nontoxic methods (preservation by ice, smoke, salt, etc.), as does further evidence of funerary practices (e.g., plastic eye caps, metal jaw nails, wax, and clay).

THE BASS LEGACY BEYOND THE BODY FARM

Dr. Bass's facility is used as a teaching center where scientists not only conduct cutting-edge research but also offer demonstrations to law enforcement officials. For instance, the FBI has had agents take courses on clandestine grave discovery and excavation. Several technological advances that have now become key investigative tools were made by researchers who have worked with Dr. Bass at the Body Farm. This includes the concept of degree-days, whereby temperatures and decomposition rate are measured over several days in order to compare various geographical areas and climatic conditions. "Through a chemical analysis of soil samples from beneath a decomposing corpse, scientists can estimate how many degree days the found body has accumulated. Combining that with weather data from the geographic area over the course of the estimated decomposition, they can better determine time since death" (Ramsland 2007b).

In addition, the collection of bones from cadavers that have decomposed fully has proven a major and fruitful enterprise: Dr. Bass has gathered a collection of more than 400 twentieth-century skeletons—the largest in the United States, and he has made them available to anthropologists for analyses of skeletal dimensions. Tests with ground-penetrating radars have also been instrumental in the development of forensic death investigation in recent years. "One project [places] bodies under different thicknesses of concrete, buried at different depths. The researchers can then assess, from what they know about those bodies, the kinds of patterns the machine registers when it hits on one of them" (Ramsland 2007b). This method has been used to find remains of victims killed by political violence in Bosnia, Croatia, and Panama, especially where mass graves had to be located.

One of the significant tools recently developed at the Body Farm is "a large and ever-expanding Forensic Data Bank, which helps determine the racial or ethnic origin of an unknown victim by allowing comparisons with measurements from thousands of other, known skeletons from around the world" (Bass and Jefferson 2007, 253). Additionally, Dr. Richard Jantz has developed an innovative, sophisticated computer program known as forensic discrimination software, or ForDisc, which is "based on measurements from various areas of the bones, along with information about the person's race, height, age, and illnesses" (Ramsland 2007b). ForDisc essentially "automates the tedious, time-consuming comparison of skeletal measurements" (Bass and Jefferson 2007, 253) by making estimates "from a skeleton of unknown identity the gender, race, and stature, and the database is continually updated. This software also can be utilized by international tribunals for war crime and human rights investigations." (Ramsland 2007b). Moreover, Dr. Arpad Vass is developing a detector that will respond to the same scents that attract cadaver dogs (dogs will detect airborne decomposition biomarkers). The "artificial nose...pulls air through a tube into a spectrometer chamber" and "will isolate the specific chemicals...to pinpoint single molecules and make the unit portable for police use" (Ramsland 2007b). Finally, another area of investigation that has produced important results is what happens to a body in a fire, whether as a result of house fire, arson, or murder or as a means of faking a death.

However invaluable his work may have been, Dr. Bass is well aware that his observations are still a long way from setting a universal standard for the patterns followed by all human remains after death. "So many forces influence decomposition that even the most careful calculations estimating the time of death may be off target. Information gleaned from those bodies scattered about the Tennessee countryside are helping refine those techniques. And the success of William M. Bass's groundbreaking farm may spawn similar research centers in other parts of the United States" (Ricciuti 2007, 79).

As Ubelaker and Scammell point out, "[B]ecause of the success of his work...Bass's pioneering efforts contributed in large measure to the development of other research facilities for that same purpose in the Southwest, including California and Texas, and other areas. Through all of these programs, anthropologists continue to build up our understanding of the processes of decay, disarticulation, and disintegration, and how it works in different environments" (Ubelaker and Scammell 2006, 113). Indeed, forensic anthropologists increasingly have been endeavoring to develop facilities similar to the Body Farm. For instance, the Forensic Anthropology Center at Texas State (FACTS) in San Marcos, founded in 2007, provides "exceptional graduate level training in all facets of forensic anthropology, including methods and applications of forensic techniques, advanced human osteology, innovative decomposition research, and the opportunity for students to assist with actual forensic casework." Furthermore, FACTS provides "forensic anthropological recovery and identification services to Texas law enforcement agencies, and [hosts] yearly workshops and short courses designed for law enforcement members to better understand the role of forensic anthropology in medicolegal investigations" (FACTS). Likewise, in 2006, the Forensic Anthropology program at Western Carolina University created the Western Carolina Human Identification Laboratory (WCHIL), "a fully equipped facility dedicated to the recovery, storage, and analysis of human remains. The main WCHIL facility covers 1,100 square feet. This laboratory has a single body morgue refrigerator and freezer for the handling and maintenance of fresh and decomposing human remains." The WCHIL director, John Williams, is a board-certified forensic anthropologist and a Fellow of the American of Forensic Sciences with more than twenty-five years of experience working with the human skeleton and human remains. There have also been talks regarding the opening of a comparable facility in India.

Dr. Bass's work has had a substantial impact on popular culture, too, and the legacy of his work can be felt in forensics fiction today, from trendy crime novels to overly popular television crime dramas. Most notably, award-winning crime author Patricia Cornwell has published several bestsellers detailing the forensic sleuthing of fictional chief medical examiner Dr. Kay Scarpetta. Cornwell based *The Body Farm* on the legendary forensics research facility, thus contributing to its worldwide fame. Dr. Bass credits Cornwell for coining the "body farm" phrase that has since been used to describe his forensic lab, whereas she claims to have overheard it at a seminar in the 1980s. *Salon* columnist Mary Roach visited the Body Farm and wrote about the experience in a chapter of her nonfiction book about the use and handling of corpses, *Stiff: The Curious Lives of Human Cadavers*. The facility also was featured in various television shows, including *The Dead Zone* and *CSI: Crime Scene Investigation*, while a similar forensic research center has appeared in *Law & Order: Special Victims Unit*. Dr. Bass himself has produced both forensic fiction and nonfictional work. He first teamed up with Jon Jefferson, a documentary filmmaker and veteran journalist, in 2002 when, in association with the National Geographic Society, Jefferson wrote and produced a two-part documentary, *Death's Acre*, with sections titled "Biography of a Corpse" and "Anatomy of a Corpse."

In part one, he shows what happens to a single body from the moment it arrives at the facility to the final boxing of the bones. Then in "Anatomy of a Corpse," he features several professionals who have studied with Bass or have used the Body Farm's facilities for carrying on their own area of expertise. Steve Symes, for example, was an anthropologist on staff for the Memphis, Tennessee, Medical Examiner's Office at the time of the filming, who received his training under Bass's direction. A top bone trauma specialist, he can tell from a "signature" left on bone what kind of sharp-bladed implement might have been used, from knives to tree saws to chainsaws.

Dr. Bass cowrote his memoir with Jefferson, titled *Death's Acre: Inside the Legendary Forensic Lab, the Body Farm, Where the Dead Do Tell Tales*. In late 2006, under the pen name Jefferson Bass, they published *Carved in Bone: A Body Farm Novel*, a particularly realistic and thorough fictional account featuring forensic expert Dr. Bill Brockton, a palpable portrayal of Dr. Bass; a year later, they published *Flesh and Bone: A Body Farm Novel*. In 2007, they also published *Beyond the Body Farm: A Legendary Bone Detective Explores Murders, Mysteries, and the Revolution in Forensic Science*. Dr. Bass additionally contributed to *Bodies We've Buried: Inside the National Forensic Academy, the World's Top CSI Training School*, which could be criticized—along, in fact, with his fictional work—as an obvious marketing ploy devoid of scientific value and aimed at capitalizing on the general public's fixation with television shows such as *CSI: Crime Scene Investigation, Cold Case*, or *Forensic Files*.

According to crime author Patricia Cornwell, "[Y]ears come and go, as do the dead who have been reduced to ashes and bone, and all of Dr. Bass's patient translation adds to the fluency of a secret language that helps condemn the wicked and free those who have done no wrong" (Bass and Jefferson 2007, xii). Over the past four decades, Dr. Bass's influential work has shaped forensic anthropology and helped mold it into the acclaimed scientific field it is today. His contributions to our understanding of both human decomposition and osteology are invaluable. By devising efficient scientific tools to help solve crimes and constantly striving to refine forensic investigative techniques, Dr. Bass initiated a radical transformation of the forensic world—a revolution whose legacy he believes will be carried on after he is gone "by the research and the scientists emerging from a small, smelly, but forensically fertile patch of East Tennessee woods known as the Body Farm" (Bass and Jefferson 2007, 254). Viewed by many as a paragon in his field, Dr. Bass is a driven yet humble man who does not fail to notice his own limitations, a symbol of virtue, professional ethics, and integrity whose passion shall hopefully continue to inspire generations of forensic anthropologists, crime analysts, and amateur sleuths alike.

FURTHER READING

Bass, B., and J. Jefferson. 2003. *Death's Acre: Inside the Legendary Forensic Lab, the Body Farm, Where the Dead Do Tell Tales*. New York: G. P. Putnam's Sons.

Bass, B., and J. Jefferson. 2007. *Beyond the Body Farm: A Legendary Bone Detective Explores Murders, Mysteries, and the Revolution in Forensic Science*. New York: William Morrow.

Bass, J. 2006. *Carved in Bone: A Body Farm Novel*. New York: HarperCollins.

Bass, J. 2007. *Flesh and Bone: A Body Farm Novel*. New York: HarperCollins.

Bass, W. M. 1971. *Human Osteology: A Laboratory and Field Manual of the Human Skeleton*. Columbia, MO: Missouri Archaeological Society.

Bass, W. M. 1995. *Human Osteology: A Laboratory and Field Manual of the Human Skeleton.* 4th ed. Columbia, MO: Missouri Archaeological Society.

Bass, W. M. 1997. Outdoor decomposition rates in Tennessee. In *Forensic Taphonomy: The Postmortem Fate of Human Remains,* ed. W. D. Haglund and M. H. Sorg, 181–186. Boca Raton, FL: CRC Press.

Bass, W. M. 2005. *Human osteology: A Laboratory and field Manual* (5th edition). Columbia, MO: Missouri Archaeological Society.

Bass, W. M., and W. H. Birkby. 1978. Exhumation: The method could make the difference. *FBI Law Enforcement Bulletin* 47 (7): 6–11.

Burns, K. R. 2007. *The forensic anthropology training Manual* (2nd edition). New York: Prentice Hall.

Cornwell, P. 1994. *The Body Farm.* New York: Berkley Books.

El-Najjar, M. Y., and K. R. McWilliams. 1978. *Forensic Anthropology: The Structure, Morphology and Variation of Human Bone and Dentition.* Springfield, IL: Charles C. Thomas.

Evans, C. 2006. *The Father of Forensics: The Groundbreaking Cases of Sir Bernard Spilsbury, and the Beginnings of Modern CSI.* New York: Berkley Books.

Evans, C. 2007. *The Casebook of Forensic Detection: How Science Solved 100 of the World's Most Baffling Crimes.* 2nd ed. New York: Berkley Books.

Genge, N. E. 2002. *The Forensic Casebook.* New York: Ballantine Books.

Haglund, W. D., A. Galloway, and T. Simmons. 1999. *Practical Forensic Anthropology of Human Skeletal Remains: Recovery, Analysis, and Resolution.* Boca Raton, FL: CRC Press.

Hallcox, J., A. Welch, and B. Bass. 2006. *Bodies We've Buried: Inside the National Forensic Academy, the World's Top CSI Training School.* New York: Berkley Books.

Innes, B. 2000. *Bodies of Evidence: The Fascinating World of Forensic Science and How It Helped Solve more than 100 True Crimes.* London: Amber Books.

Jackson, D. M. 2001. *The Bone Detectives: How Forensic Anthropologists Solve Crimes and Uncover Mysteries of the Dead.* Boston: Little & Brown.

Mann, R. W., W. M. Bass, and L. Meadows. 1990. Time since death and decomposition of the human body: Variables and observations in case and experimental field studies. *Journal of Forensic Sciences* 35:103–111.

Maples, W. R. 1994. *Dead Men Do Tell Tales: The Strange and Fascinating Cases of a Forensic Anthropologist.* New York: Broadway Books.

Moore, P. 2004. *The Forensics Handbook: The Secrets of Crime Scene Investigation.* New York: Barnes & Noble.

Nafte, M. 2000. *Flesh and Bone: An Introduction to Forensic Anthropology.* Durham, NC: Carolina Academic Press.

Owen, D. 2000. *Hidden Evidence: Forty True Crimes and How Forensic Science Helped Solve Them.* Willowdale, Ontario: Firefly Books.

Ramsland, K. 2007a. *Beating the Devil's Game: A History of Forensic Science and Criminal Investigation.* New York: Berkley Books.

Ramsland, K. 2007b. *Profile of Dr. Bill Bass, Founder of the Body Farm.* http://www.crimelibrary.com/criminal_mind/forensics/bill_bass/ (accessed August 15, 2007).

Reichs, K. J., and W. M. Bass. 1998. *Forensic Osteology: Advances in the Identification of Human Remains.* Springfield, IL: Charles C. Thomas.

Ricciuti, E. 2007. *Forensics.* New York: Collins.

Roach, M. 2003. *Stiff: The Curious Lives of Human Cadavers.* New York: W. W. Norton & Company.

Rodriguez, W. C., and W. M. Bass. 1983. Insect activity and its relationship to decay rates of human cadavers in East Tennessee. *Journal of Forensic Sciences* 28:423–32.

Rodriguez, W. C., and W. M. Bass. 1985. Decomposition of buried bodies and methods that may aid in their location. *Journal of Forensic Sciences* 30:836–852.

Shean, B. S., L. Messinger, and M. Papworth. 1993. Observations of differential decomposition on sun exposed vs. shaded pig carrion in coastal Washington State. *Journal of Forensic Sciences* 38:938–949.

Stewart, T. D. 1979. *Essentials of Forensic Anthropology.* Springfield, IL: Charles C. Thomas.

Texas State University. 2007. *Forensic Anthropology Center at Texas State (FACTS).* http://www.txstate.edu/anthropology/facts/ (accessed September 23, 2007).

Thomas, P. 1995. *Talking Bones: The Science of Forensic Anthropology.* New York: Facts on File.

Ubelaker, D., and H. Scammell. 2006. *Bones: A Forensic Detective's Casebook.* Lanham, MD: M. Evans.

Western Carolina University. 2007. *Western Carolina Human Identification Laboratory (WCHIL).* http://www.wcu.edu/ (accessed September 23, 2007).

Selected Bibliography

Abrahams, Ray. *Vigilant Citizens: Vigilantism and the State*. Oxford: Polity Press, 1998.

Adler, Margot. *Organized Crime in the 21st Century*, Radio Transcript, "Justice Talking," National Public Radio, January 1, 2007.

All Politics: CNN Time. "Serious or 'Just Politics'?" Gallup Poll: Public Perceptions of Watergate. 1997. http://www.cnn.com/ALLPOLITICS/1997/gen/resources/watergate/poll/.

Anderson, Elijah. *Code of the Street: Decency, Violence, and the Moral Life of the Inner City*. New York: W. W. Norton, 2000.

Anonymous. "Guardian Angels Partnering With New York State to Keep Kids Safe on the Internet." Associated Press. 2006. http://222.wcbs880.com/pages/101038.php?contentType=4&contentID=219665.

Armao, Joseph P., and Leslie U. Cornefeld. "Why Good Cops Turn Rotten, *New York Times*, November 1, 1993, A-12. (The authors are chief counsel and deputy chief counsel to the Mollen Commission).

Arpaio, Joe, and Len Sherman. *America's Toughest Sheriff: How to Win the War Against Crime*. Arlington, TX: Summit Publishing Group, 1996.

Austern, D. *The Crime Victim's Handbook*. New York: Penguin Publishing, 1987.

Baker, Peter, and Charles Babington. "Bush Addresses Uproar Over Spying." *The Washington Post*. December 20, 2005. http://www.washingtonpost.com/wp-dyn/content/article/2005/12/19/AR2005121900211.html.

Barker, Joshua. "Vigilantes and the State." *Social Analysis* 50 (2006): 203–207.

Barker, T., and Robert W. Wells. "Police Administrators: Attitudes toward the Definition and Control of Police Deviance." *Law Enforcement Bulletin* (1982): 11.

Barrett, Wayne. *Rudy! An Investigative Biography of Rudolph Giuliani*. New York: Basic Books, 2000.

Bass, B., and J. Jefferson. *Death's Acre: Inside the Legendary Forensic Lab, the Body Farm, Where the Dead Do Tell Tales*. New York: G. P. Putnam's Sons, 2003.

Bass, B., and J. Jefferson. *Beyond the Body Farm: A Legendary Bone Detective explores Murders, Mysteries, and the Revolution in Forensic Science*. New York: William Morrow, 2007.

Bass, J. *Carved in Bone: A Body Farm Novel*. New York: HarperCollins, 2006.

Bass, J. *Flesh and Bone: A Body Farm Novel.* New York: HarperCollins, 2007.

Bass, W. M. *Human Osteology: A Laboratory and Field Manual of the Human Skeleton.* Columbia, MO: Missouri Archaeological Society, 1971.

Bass, W. M. *Human Osteology: A Laboratory and Field Manual of the Human Skeleton.* 4th ed. Columbia, MO: Missouri Archaeological Society, 1995.

Bass, W. M. "Outdoor Decomposition Rates in Tennessee." In *Forensic Taphonomy: The Postmortem Fate of Human Remains,* edited by W. D. Haglund and M. H. Sorg, 181–186. Boca Raton, FL: CRC Press, 1997.

Bass, W. M. *Human Osteology: A Laboratory and Field Manual.* 5th ed. Columbia, MO: Missouri Archaeological Society, 2005.

Bass, W. M., and W. H. Birkby. "Exhumation: The Method Could Make the Difference." *FBI Law Enforcement Bulletin* 47, no. 7 (1978): 6–11.

Beck, Allen J., and Jennifer C. Karberg. Prison and Jail Inmates at Midyear 2000. U.S. Department of Justice, Bureau of Justice Statistics Bulletin. NCJ 185989. March (2001): 1.

Benekos, Peter J., and Alida V. Merlo. "Three Strikes and You're Out!: The Political Sentencing Game," *Federal Probation* 59, no. 1 (1995): 5.

Bernstein, Carl, and Bob Woodward. "Bug Suspect Got Campaign Funds." *The Washington Post.* August 1, 1972. http://www.washingtonpost.com/wp-dyn/content/article/2002/06/03/AR2005111001229.html.

Bernstein, Carl, and Bob Woodward. "Mitchell Controlled Secret GOP Fund." *The Washington Post.* September 29, 1972. http://www.washingtonpost.com/wp-dyn/content/article/2002/06/03/AR2005111001231.html.

Bernstein, Carl, and Bob Woodward. "FBI Finds Nixon Aides Sabotaged Democrats." *The Washington Post.* October 10, 1972. http://www.washingtonpost.com/wp-dyn/content/article/2002/06/03/AR2005111001232.html.

Bernstein, Carl, and Bob Woodward. "Still Secret—Who Hired Spies and Why." *The Washington Post.* January 31, 1973. http://www.washingtonpost.com/wp-dyn/content/article/2002/05/31/AR2005112200788.html.

Bernstein, Carl, and Bob Woodward. *All the President's Men.* New York: Simon & Schuster, 1974.

Bittner, E. *The Functions of the Police in Modern Society.* Washington, D.C.: U.S. Government Printing Office, 1971.

Blakey, G. Robert, Ronald Goldstock, and Charles Rogovin. *Racket Bureaus: Investigation and Prosecution of Organized Crime,* Washington, D.C.: National Institute of Law Enforcement, 1978.

Blumenthal, Ralph. *Last Days of the Sicilians At War With the Mafia: The F.B.I. Assault on the Pizza Connection.* New York: Times Books, 1988.

Bonavolonta, Jules, and Brian Duffy. *The Good Guys: How We Turned the FBI 'Round and Finally Broke the Mob.* New York: Simon & Schuster, 1996.

Branch, Taylor. *Parting the Waters: America in the King Years, 1954–1963.* New York: Simon & Schuster, 1988.

Brener, Milton, E. *The Garrison Case.* New York: Clarkson N. Potter, 1969.

Brown, M. K. *Working the Street: Police Discretion and the Dilemmas of Reform.* New York: Russell Sage Foundation Press, 1981.

Brown, R. *Strain of Violence.* New York: Oxford University Press, 1975.

Brown, Richard. *Strain of Violence: Historical Studies of American Violence and Vigilantism.* Oxford, UK: Oxford University Press, 2002.

Buckler K., and L. Travis. "Assessing the News-worthiness of Homicide Events. *Journal of Criminal Justice and Popular Culture* 12 (2005):1–25.

Buckley, William F., Jr. "Where does Fuhrman take us?" (Editorial) *National Review.* September 25, 1995.

Buenker, John D. "A Battle For The Soul of New York: Tammany Hall, Police Corruption, Vice, and Reverend Charles Parkhurst's Crusade Against Them, 1892–1895." *American Historical Review* 109, no. 4 (2004): 1246–1247.

Bugliosi, Vincent T. "Not Guilty and Innocent—The Problem Children of Reasonable Doubt." *Criminal Justice Journal* 4 (1981): 349–374.

Bugliosi, Vincent T., and Ken Hurwitz. *Shadow of Cain: A Novel.* New York: W. W. Norton, 1981.

Bugliosi, Vincent T., with William Stadiem. *Lullaby and Good Night: A Novel Inspired by the True Story of Vivian Gordon.* New York: NAL Books, 1987.

Bugliosi, Vincent T., with Bruce B. Henderson. *And the Sea Will Tell.* New York: Ballantine, 1991.

Bugliosi, Vincent T. *Drugs in America: The Case for Victory: A Citizen's Call to Action.* New York: Knightsbridge, 1991.

Bugliosi, Vincent T. "No Justice, No Peace." *Playboy* 40, no. 2 (1993): 66–68, 156–162.

Bugliosi, Vincent T. *Outrage: The Five Reasons Why O. J. Simpson Got Away With Murder.* New York: W. W. Norton, 1996.

Bugliosi, Vincent T. *The Phoenix Solution: Getting Serious about Winning America's Drug War.* Beverly Hills, CA: Dove Audio, 1996.

Bugliosi, Vincent T. *No Island of Sanity: Paula Jones v. Bill Clinton: The Supreme Court on Trial.* New York: Ballantine, 1998.

Bugliosi, Vincent T. "None Dare Call It Treason." *The Nation* February 5, 2001. http://www.thenation.com/doc/20010205/bugliosi/.

Bugliosi, Vincent T. *The Betrayal of America: How the Supreme Court Undermined the Constitution and Chose our President.* New York: Thunder's Mouth Press/ Nation Books, 2001.

Bugliosi, Vincent T. *Reclaiming History: The Assassination of President John F. Kennedy.* New York: W. W. Norton, 2007.

Bugliosi, Vincent T., with Curt Gentry. *Helter Skelter: The True Story of the Manson Murders.* New York: W. W. Norton, 1974.

Bugliosi, Vincent T., with Ken Hurwitz. *Till Death Us Do Part: A True Murder Mystery.* New York: W. W. Norton, 1978.

Bullock, J. A., G. D. Haddow, D. Coppola, E. Ergin, L. Westerman, and S. Yeletaysi. *Introduction to Homeland Security.* London, UK: Elsevier, 2005.

Burns, K. R. *The Forensic Anthropology Training Manual.* 2nd ed. New York: Prentice Hall, 2007.

Capeci, Jerry. "Junior Don Behind Curtis Sliwa Shooting," *Gangland News.* June 26, 2003. http://www.ganglandnews.com/column336.htm/.

Caplan, Gerald M., ed. *Abscam Ethics: Moral Issues and Deception in Law Enforcement.* Cambridge, MA: Ballinger, 1983.

Carte, Gene E., and Elaine H. Carte. *Police Reform in the United States: The Era of August Vollmer, 1905–1932.* Berkeley, CA: University of California Press, 1975.

Carrigan, William. *The Making of a Lynching Culture: Violence and Vigilantism in Central Texas, 1836–1916.* Urbana: University of Illinois Press, 2004.

CBS News. "48 Hours Mystery: Mark Fuhrman Biography." http://www.cbsnews.com/stories/2001/07/13/48hours/main301303.shtml/.

CBS News. "Murder, They Wrote: Murder in Spokane, A Serial Killer on the Loose." February 15, 2002. http://www.cbsnews.com/stories/2002/02/15/48hours/murder/main329534.shtml/.

Cheatwood, Derral. "The Life-without-Parole Sanction: Its Current Status and a Research Agenda." *Crime & Delinquency* 34, no. 1 (1998): 43.

Chua-Eoan, Howard, and Elizabeth Gleick. "Making the Case." *Time*. October 16, 1995. http://www.time.com/time/magazine/article/0,9171,983569,00.html/.

Cloward, Richard. "Illegitimate Means, Anomie, and Deviant Behavior." In *Theories of Deviance*. 4th ed., edited by Stuart Traub and Craig Little. Itasca, IL: F. E. Peacock Publishers, 1994.

Cohen, Hubert I. "Wyatt Earp at the O.K. Corral: Six Versions." *The Journal of American Culture* 26, no. 2 (2003): 204–223.

Cole, George, and Christopher Smith. *Criminal Justice in America*. Tampa, FL: Thompson Publishing, 2005.

Coleman, Stephen. "Conflict of Interest and Police: An Unavoidable Problem." *Criminal Justice Ethics* 24, no. 2 (2005): 3–11.

Conditt, John H., Jr. 2001. "Institutional Integrity." *FBI Law Enforcement Bulletin* 70, no. 11 (2001): 18–22.

Conlon, Edward. *Blue Blood*. New York: Riverhead Books, 2004.

Conti, Norman, and James Nolan III. "Policing the Platonic Cave: Ethics and Efficacy in Police Training." *Policing and Society* 15, no. 2 (2005): 166–186.

Cooley, Rita W. "The Office of United States Marshal." *The Western Political Quarterly* 12, no. 1 (1959): 123–40.

Cooper, Courtney Riley. *Ten Thousand Public Enemies*. New York: Blue Ribbon Books, 1935.

Cornwell, P. *The Body Farm*. New York: Berkley Books, 1994.

Cox, Mike. "Filmology." In *Texas Ranger Tales II*, 265–279. Plano, TX: Republic of Texas Press, 1999.

Crank, J., Dan Flaherty, and Andrew D. Giacomazzi. "The Noble Cause: An Empirical Assessment." *Journal of Criminal Justice* 35, no. 1 (2007): 103–116.

Croke, Bill. "Lone Rangers: When Texas was Really Texas." *The Weekly Standard* 7, no. 43 (2002): 31–33.

Culberson, William. *Vigilantism: Political History of Private Power in America (Contributions in Criminology and Penology,* Vol. 28). Westport, CT: Greenwood/Praeger, 1990.

Dalberg, John E. E. "Lord Acton, Letter to Mandell Creighton, April 5, 1887." *Acton, Essays on Freedom and Power,* edited by Gertrude Himmelfarb, 335–336, 1972.

Daley, Robert. *Prince of the City: The True Story of a Cop Who Knew Too Much*. Boston: Houghton, Mifflin Company, 1971.

Daley, Robert. *Target Blue: An Insider's View of the N.Y.P.D.* New York: Dell Publishers, 1971.

Davis, M. "Rank Has No Privilege." *Criminal Justice Ethics* 22, (2003): 2.

Davy, William. *Let Justice Be Done: New Light on the Jim Garrison Investigation*. Reston, VA: Jordan Publishing, 1999.

Dear, Pamela S., ed. "Bugliosi, Vincent (T.) 1934–." In *Contemporary Authors: New Revision Series,* vol. 46, 50–52. Detroit, MI: Gale Research, 1995.

DeArment, Robert K. *Bat Masterson: The Man and the Legend.* Norman: University of Oklahoma Press, 1979.

Decker, S., and Allen Wagner. *Critical Issues in Policing: Contemporary Readings,* edited by Roger G. Dunham and Geoffrey P. Alpert. Prospect Heights, IL: Waverland Press, 1989.

Del Pozo, B. 2005. One Dogma of Police Ethics: Gratuities and the 'Democratic Ethos' of Policing. *Criminal Justice Ethics* 24, no. 2, Summer/Fall.

Demaris, Ovid. *The Director: An Oral Biography of J. Edgar Hoover.* New York: Harper's Magazine Press, 1975.

DeNevi, D., and J. E. Campbell. *Into the Minds of Madmen.* Amherst, NY: Prometheus Books, 2004.

Dewey, Thomas E. *Twenty against the Underworld. An Autobiography of a District Attorney and His Fight against Organized Crime,* edited by Rodney Campbell. New York: Doubleday, 1974.

Diehl, Christine S. "*WP* has a 'Sit-Down' With Joe Pistone/Donnie Brasco," *WP, The Magazine of William Paterson University* Winter (2006): 16–20.

Dignan, J. *Understanding Victims and Restorative Justice.* New York: Open University Press/McGraw Hill, 2005.

Dionne, E. J., Jr. *Why Americans Hate Politics.* New York: Simon & Schuster, 2004.

Doerner, William, and Steven Lab. *Victimology.* 4th ed. Bethesda, MD: Lexis Nexis, 2005.

Dombrink, John, and James W. Meeker. "Beyond 'Buy and Bust': Nontraditional Sanctions in Federal Drug Law Enforcement." *Contemporary Drug Problems: A Law Quarterly* 13, no. 4, (1986): 711–740.

Dombrink, John, and James W. Meeker. "Organized Crime in the 'Twilight of the Mob': Groups, Enterprise, and Legal Innovation from 1967–1992." In *The President's Crime Commission: 25 Years Later,* edited by John A. Conley, Cincinnati: Anderson Publishing Company, 1993.

Dombrink, John, and John Huey-Long Song. "Of Twilights and Dawns: The Challenges of Policing Emerging Organized Crime." In *Handbook of Organized Crime in the United States,* edited by Robert J. Kelly, et al., 415–430. Westport, CT: Greenwood Publishing Group, 1994.

Douglas, J. E., and A. E. Burgess. "Criminal profiling: A viable investigative tool against violent crime." *FBI Law Enforcement Bulletin* 9 (1986): 32–36.

Douglas, J. E., A. W. Burgess, A. G. Burgess, and R.K Ressler. *Crime Classification Manual.* San Francisco, CA: Jossey-Bass, 2006.

Douglas, J. E., A. W. Burgess, and R.K Ressler. "Rape and Rape Murder: One Offender and Twelve Victims." *American Journal of Psychiatry* 140 (1983): 36–40.

Douglas, J. E., and R. Hazelwood. "The Lust Murderer." *FBI Law Enforcement Bulletin* 49 (1980):8–12.

Douglas, J. E., and C. Munn. "Violent Crime Scene Analysis: Modus Operandi, Signature and Staging." *FBI Law Enforcement Bulletin* 61 (1992): 1–10.

Douglas, J. E., R.K Ressler, A. W. Burgess, and C. R. Hartman. "Criminal Profiling from Crime Scene Analysis." *Behavioral Sciences & the Law* 4 (1986): 401–421.

Douglas, J. E., and M. Olshaker, *Mindhunter.* New York: Scribner, 1995.

Douthit, Nathan. "August Vollmer, Berkeley's First Chief of Police, and the Emergence of Police Professionalism." *California Historical Quarterly* 54 (1975): 101–124.

Doyle, A. C. *The Original Illustrated Sherlock Holmes*. Secaucus, NJ: Castle, 1891.

Drago, Harry S. *The Legend Makers: Tales of the Old-time Peacemakers and Desperadoes of the Frontier*. New York: Dodd and Mead, 1975.

Draper, Robert. "The Twilight of the Texas Rangers." *Texas Monthly* 22, no. 2 (1994): 76–118.

Eckhart, Jerry. "Texas Ranger's Badge." *True West* 40, no. 9 (1993): 46–49.

Educon Review Staff. 1996. "Cyber-Cops: Angels on the Net," *Educom Review* http://www.educause.edu/pub/er/review/reviewArticles/31134.html/.

Egger, S. A. *The Killers among Us: An Examination of Serial Murder and Its Investigation*. Upper Saddle River, NJ: Prentice Hall, 1998.

El-Najjar, M. Y., and K. R. McWilliams. *Forensic Anthropology: The Structure, Morphology and Variation of Human Bone and dentition*. Springfield, IL: Charles C. Thomas, 1978.

Escott, Paul. "White Republicanism and Ku Klux Klan Terror: The North Carolina Piedmont During Reconstruction," In *Race, Class and Politics in Southern History: Essays in Honor of Robert Durden*, edited by Jeffrey Crow, Paul Escott, and Charles Flynn, 3–34. Baton Rouge: LA: Louisiana State University Press, 1989.

Evans, C. *The Father of Forensics: The Groundbreaking Cases of Sir Bernard Spilsbury, and the Beginnings of Modern CSI*. New York: Berkley Books, 2006.

Evans, C. *The Casebook of Forensic Detection: How Science Solved 100 of the World's Most Baffling Crimes*. 2nd ed. New York: Berkley Books, 2007.

Fay, Paul B. *The Pleasure of His Company*. New York: Harper & Row, 1966.

Fedburg, M. "Gratuities, Corruption, and the Democratic Ethos of Policing: The Case of the Free Cup of Coffee." In *Moral Issues in Police Work*, edited by F. Elliston and M. Feldberg, 267–276. Totowa, NJ: Rowman & Littlefield, 1985.

Federal Bureau of Investigation. "Frequently Asked Questions." 2007. http://www.Fbi.gov/faq/.

Fisher, A. J. *Techniques of Crime Scene Investigation*. 5th ed. New York: Elsevier, 1993.

Fletcher, George. *A Crime of Self Defense: Bernhard Goetz and the Law on Trial*. New York: The Free Press, 1988.

Fogelson, Robert M. *Big-city Police*. Cambridge, MA: Harvard University Press, 1977.

Fox, J. F., Jr. "Unique unto itself: The Records of the Federal Bureau of Investigation 1908 to 1945." *Journal of Government Information* 30 (2004): 470–481.

Freeh, Louis J. *My FBI: Bringing Down the Mafia, Investigating Bill Clinton, and Fighting the War on Terror*. New York: St. Martin's Press, 2005.

Fremont, Eleanor. *America's Mayor: Rudy W. Giuliani*. New York: Aladdin Paperbacks, 2002.

French, P. *The Virtues of Vengeance*. Lawrence: University Press of Kansas, 2001.

Fritsch, Eric J., Tory J. Caeti, and C. Hemmens. "Spare the Needle But Not the Punishment: The Incarceration of Waived Youth in Texas Prisons." *Crime & Delinquency* 42, no. 4 (1996): 593–609.

Fuhrman, Mark. *Murder in Brentwood*. New York: Regnery, 1997.

Fuhrman, Mark. *Murder in Greenwich: Who Killed Martha Moxley?* New York: HarperCollins, 1998.

Fuhrman, Mark. *Murder in Spokane: Catching a Serial Killer*. New York: Avon, 2001.

Fuhrman, Mark. *Death and Justice: An Expose of Oklahoma's Death Row Machine.* New York: HarperCollins, 2003.

Fuhrman, Mark. *Silent Witness: The Untold Story of Terri Schiavo's Death.* New York: HarperCollins, 2005.

Fuhrman, Mark. *A Simple Act of Murder: November 22, 1963.* New York: Harper-Collins, 2006.

Gado, M. "The Wood Chipper Murder Case." 2007. Crime Library.com. http://www.crimelibrary.com/notorious_murders/family/woodchipper_murder/html/.

Garrison, Jim. *On the Trail of the Assassins.* New York: Warner Books, 1988.

Gathman, Roger. "They Didn't Ride Off Into the Sunset." *Austin American-Statesman* March 25, 2007: J05.

Gelbspan, Ross. "Undercover Work: A Necessary Evil?" *Boston Globe.* November 26, 1988.

Geller, William A., and Norval Morris. "Relations between Federal and Local Police." In *Modern Policing. Crime and Justice,* vol. 15, edited by Michael Tonry and Norval Morris. Chicago: University of Chicago Press, 1992.

General Accounting Office. *War on Organized Crime Faltering—Federal Strike Forces Not Getting the Job Done.* Washington, D.C.: United States General Accounting Office, GGD-77-17, March 17, 1977.

General Accounting Office. *Stronger Federal Effort Needed in Fight Against Organized Crime,* Washington, D.C.: United States General Accounting Office, GGD-82-2, December 7, 1981.

General Accounting Office. *Issue Regarding Strikes Forces.* Washington, D.C.: United States General Accounting Office, GGD-89-67, April 3, 1989.

Genge, N. E. *The Forensic Casebook.* New York: Ballantine Books, 2002.

Genovese, Michael A. *The Nixon Presidency: Power and Politics in Turbulent Times.* Westport, CT: Greenwood Press, 1990.

Genovese, Michael A. *The Watergate Crisis.* Westport, CT: Greenwood Press, 1999.

Genovese, Michael A. *The Power of the American Presidency, 1789–2000.* New York: Oxford University Press, 2003.

Gentry, Curt. *J. Edgar Hoover: The Man and the Secrets.* New York: W. W. Norton & Company, 1991.

George-Kosh, David. 2006. "Toronto: Broke Guardian Angels May Quit Streets," *National Post.* September 7, 2006. http://www.canada.com/nationalpost/news/toronto/story.html?id=88d8e9e5-ae53-4ec9-b50c-ff6462274ca7/.

Geringer, Joseph. "The Martha Moxley Murder." http://www.crimelibrary.com/notorious_murders/famous/moxley/index_1.html/.

Gilliard, Darrell K., and Allen J. Beck, Prison and Jail Inmates at Midyear. 1996 U.S. Department of Justice, Bureau of Justice Statistics Bulletin. NCJ 162843. January (1997): 1.

Giuliani, Rudolph. *The Mayor of America in His Own Words: The Quotable Giuliani,* edited by Bill Adler and Bill Adler, Jr. New York: Pocket Books, 2002.

Gleick, Elizabeth. 1995. "Headliners." *Time.* December 25, 1995. http://www.time.com/time/magazine/article/0,9171,983884,00.html/.

Gleick, Elizabeth. "A Simpson Remake." *Time.* September 23, 1996. http://www.time.com/time/magazine/article/0,9171,985192,00.html/.

Goldfarb, Ronald. "Politics at the Justice Department." In *Conspiracy,* edited by John C. Raines. New York: Harper & Row, 1974.

Goldfarb, Ronald. *Perfect Villains, Imperfect Heroes: Robert F. Kennedy's War against Organized Crime*. Sterling, VA: Capital Books, 1995.

Goldstein, H. *Police Corruption: A Perspective on Its Nature and Control*, Washington, D.C.: Police Foundation, 1975.

Goldstock, Ronald. 1988. Testimony of Director, State of New York Organized Crime Task Force, United States Senate, Permanent Subcommittee on Investigations, Committee on Governmental Affairs, 100th Congress, April 21. Printed in committee report, S. HRG. 100–906, Organized Crime: 25 Years After Valachi.

Goode, James. *Wiretap: Listening In on America's Mafia*. New York: Simon & Schuster, 1988.

Goska, Danusha. "Mark Fuhrman." http://www.codypublishing.com/goska/furman.html/.

Grant, J. Kevin. "Ethics in Law Enforcement." *FBI Law Enforcement Bulletin* 71, no. 12 (2002): 11–14.

Griffith, James D., Matthew L. Hiller, Kevin Knight, and Donald D. Simpson. "A cost-effective analysis of in-prison therapeutic community treatment and risk classification." *Prison Journal* 79, no. 3 (1999): 352.

Grigg, William Norman. *One Man Against the Mob: A Legend in the Mold of Davy Crockett, Sheriff Buford Pusser Reclaimed Tennessee's McNairy County from the Murdeous "State Line Mob."* Appleton, WI. 2004. *The New American* 20, no. 14 (2004): 35.

Grosso, Sonny, and John Devaney. *Murder at the Harlem Mosque*. New York: Crown Publishers, 1977.

Guthman, Edwin O. *We Band of Brothers*. New York: Harper & Row, 1971.

Guthman, Edwin O., and Richard C. Allen, eds. *RFK: Collected Speeches*. New York: Viking, 1993.

Hack, Richard. *Puppetmaster: the Secret Life of J. Edgar Hoover*. Beverly Hills: New Millennium Press, 2004.

Haglund, W. D., A. Galloway, and T. Simmons. *Practical Forensic Anthropology of Human Skeletal Remains: Recovery, Analysis, and Resolution*. Boca Raton, FL: CRC Press, 1999.

Hallcox, J., A. Welch, and B. Bass. *Bodies We've Buried: Inside the National Forensic Academy, the World's Top CSI Training School*. New York: Berkley Books, 2006.

Haney, Craig and Philip Zimbardo. "The Past and Future of U.S. Prison Policy: Twenty-five years after the Stanford Prison Experiment," *American Psychologist* 53, no. 7 (1998): 709–727.

Hardin, Stephen L. *The Texas Rangers*. New York: Osprey, 1991.

Harris, R. N. *The Police Academy: An Inside View*. New York: John Wiley & Sons, 1973.

Harris, T. *The Red Dragon*. New York: Heineman, 1985.

Harris, T. *The Silence of the Lambs*. New York: Heineman, 1986.

Harris, T. *Hannibal*. New York: Heineman, 1999.

Harrison, Bob. "Noble Cause Corruption and the Police Ethic." *FBI Law Enforcement Bulletin* 68, no. 8 (1999).

Harry Ransom Center. "The Woodward and Bernstein Watergate Papers." University of Texas. http://www.hrc.utexas.edu/exhibitions/online/woodstein/.

Havill, Adrian. 1993. *Deep Truth: The Unauthorized Biography of Bob Woodward and Carl Bernstein.* New York: Carol Publishing Group.

Hazelwood, R. R., and S. Michaud. *The Evil That Men Do.* New York: St. Martin Press, 1999.

Hazelwood, R. R., and J. Warren. "The Serial Rapist: His Characteristics and Victims (Part I)." *FBI Law Enforcement Bulletin* 57 (1989): 11–17.

Herbert, Steve. *Policing Space: Territoriality and the Los Angeles Police Department.* Minneapolis, MN: University of Minnesota Press, 1997.

Herszenhorn, David M. "Edward R. Egan, Police Officer Who Inspired Movie, Dies at 65." *The New York Times* June 11, 1995.

Herszenhorn, D. "Dr. Lee, the Man with All the Clues." *New York Times, Connecticut Weekly Desk.* April 23, 2000.

Hibbing, John R., and John R. Alford. "Accepting Authoritative Decisions: Humans as Wary Cooperators." *American Journal of Political Science* 48 (January, 2004): 62–76.

Hibbing, John R., and Elizabeth Theiss-Morse. *Congress as Public Enemy: Public Attitudes toward American Political Institutions.* Cambridge, MA: Cambridge University Press, 1995.

Hill, Richard. "Juvenile Crime and Autonomous Citizen Action," *Youth Studies Australia* 17 (1998): 35–41.

Hilty, James W. *Robert Kennedy: Brother Protector.* Philadelphia: Temple University Press, 1997.

Horton, David M. and Ryan Kellus Turner. *Lone Star Justice.* Austin, TX: Eakin Press, 1999.

Horwitz, Allan. *The Logic of Social Control.* New York: Springer, 1990.

Howlett, J. B., K. A. Hanfland, and R. K. Ressler. "The violent criminal apprehension program—ViCAP: A progress report." *FBI Law Enforcement Bulletin* 14 (1986): 9–11.

Huberts, Leo W. J. C., Terry Lamboo, and Maurice Punch. "Police Integrity in the Netherlands and the United States: Awareness and Alertness." *Police Practice and Research* 4, no. 3 (2003).

Hurt, Henry. *Reasonable Doubt.* New York: Henry Holt and Co., 1985.

Ianni, Francis J., and Elizabeth Reuss-Ianni. *A Family Business: Kinship and Social Control in Organized Crime.* New York: Russell Sage Foundation, 1972.

Icove, D. J., and J. H. Estepp. "Motive based offender profiles of arson and fire-related crimes." *FBI Law Enforcement Bulletin* 17 (1987): 28–31.

Innes, B. *Bodies of Evidence: The Fascinating World of Forensic Science and How It Helped Solve More Than 100 True Crimes.* London: Amber Books, 2000.

Innes, B. *Profile of a Criminal Mind: How Psychological Profiling Helps Solve True Crimes.* Leicester, UK: Silverdale Books, 2003.

Ivkovic, Sanja Kutnjak. "To Serve and Collect: Measuring Police Corruption." *Journal of Criminal Law and Criminology* 93, no. 2/3 (2003): 593–649.

Ivkovic, Sanja Kutnjak. "Evaluating the Seriousness of Police Misconduct: A Cross-Cultural Comparison of Police Officer and Citizen Views." *International Criminal Justice Review* (Georgia State University) 14 (2004): 25–48.

Jacobs, James B. *Mobsters, Unions, and Feds: The Mafia and the American Labor Movement.* New York: New York University Press, 2006.

Jacobs, James B., and Lauryn P. Gouldin. "Cosa Nostra: The Final Chapter?" In *Crime and Justice*, vol. 25, 129–189, edited by Michael Tonry. Chicago: University of Chicago Press. 1999.

Jacobs, James B., with Christopher Panarella and Jay Worthington. *Busting the Mob: United States v. Cosa Nostra*. New York: New York University Press, 1994.

Jacobs, James B., with Coleen Friel and Robert Radick. *Gotham Unbound: How New York City Was Liberated From the Grip of Organized Crime*. New York: New York University Press, 1999.

Jacobs, Lawrence R. "The Presidency and the Press: The Paradox of the White House Communications War." In *The Presidency and the Political System*, edited by Michael Nelson. Washington, D.C.: CQ Press, 2006.

Jackson, D. M. *The Bone Detectives: How Forensic Anthropologists Solve Crimes and Uncover Mysteries of the Dead*. Boston: Little Brown, and Co., 2001.

Jeffers, H. P. *Profiles in Evil*. London: Warner Bros., 1992.

Johnson, Les. "What is Vigilantism?" *The British Journal of Criminology* 36 (1996): 220–221.

Johnson, Les. "Crime, Fear and Civil Policing," *Urban Studies* 38, no. 5–6 (2001).

Johnson, Roberta A. "Whistle Blowing and the Police." *Rutgers Journal of Law and Urban Policy* 3 (2005).

Johnson, Terrance A., and Raymond W. Cox III. "Police Ethics: Organizational Implications." *Public Integrity* 7, no. 1 (2004/05).

Jones, Mark. *Criminal Justice Pioneers in U.S. History*. New York: Pearson Education, 2005.

Jones, Thomas L. "Notorious Murders. Most Famous. OJ Simpson." http://www.crimelibrary.com/notorious_murders/famous/simpson/index_1.html/.

Jost, Kenneth. "Presidential Power: Is Bush Overstepping His Executive Authority?" *The CQ Researcher* 16 (February 24, 2006): 169–192.

Judiciary Act of 1789, 1 Stat. 73.

Kadish, Sanford H., Stephen J. Schulhofer, and Monrad G. Paulsen. *Criminal Law and Its Processes: Cases and Materials*. 3rd ed. Boston: Little, Brown Publishers, 1983.

Kahan, D. M. "Reciprocity, Collective Action, and Community Policing." *California Law Review* 90, no. 5 (2005): 1513.

Kahn, Jeremy. "The Story of a Snitch," *The Atlantic* April (2007): 79–92.

Kallstrom, James K. 1997. "Statement of FBI Assistant Director James K. Kallstrom Concerning the 'Second Notice of Capacity,'" Washington, D.C.: Federal Bureau of Investigation, FBI National Press Office, January 14.

Kanable, R. "Modern Forensic Science Today and Tomorrow: An Interview with Dr. Henry Lee." *Law Enforcement Technology* 32, no. 7 (2005): 8–18.

Kane, R. "The Social Ecology of Police Misconduct." *Criminology*, 40, no. 4 (November 2002).

Kania, Richard. "Should We Tell the Police to Say 'Yes' to Gratuities?" *Criminal Justice Ethics* 7, no. 2 (1982): 37–49.

Kappeler, V. K., R. D. Sluder, and G. P. Alpert. *Forces of Deviance: Understanding the Dark Side of Policing*. Prospect Heights, IL: Waveland Press, 1998.

Karmen, Andrew. *Crime Victims: An Introduction to Victimology*. 6th ed. Belmont, CA: Thompson Wadsworth, 2007.

Kelling, G. L., and R. B. Kliesmet. "Resistance to the Professionalization of the Police." *The Law Officer* (1972): 16–22.

Kelly, Robert J. *The Upperworld and the Underworld: Case Studies of Racketeering and Business Infiltrations in the United States.* New York: Kluwer Academic/ Plenum, 1999.

Kennedy, Robert. *The Enemy Within.* New York: Harper and Brothers, 1960.

Kennedy, Rose. *Times to Remember.* Garden City, NY: Doubleday, 1974.

Kenney, Dennis. *Crime, Fear, and the New York City Subways: The Role of Citizen Action.* Oxford, UK: Praeger, 1987.

Kinder, Donald R., Mark D. Peters, Robert P. Abelson, and Susan T. Fiske. "Presidential Prototypes." *Political Behavior* 2 (1980): 315–337.

Kingshott, Brian F., Kathleen Bailey, and Suzanne E. Wolfe. "Police Culture, Ethics, and Entitlement Theory." *Criminal Justice Studies* 17, no. 2 (2004): 187–202.

Kirtzman, Andrew. *Rudy Giuliani: Emperor of the City.* New York: Perennial, 2001.

Kleck, Gary. *Point Blank: Guns and Violence in America.* New York: Aldine de Gruyter, 1991.

Kleinig, John. *The Ethics of Policing.* New York: Cambridge University Press, 1996.

Klockars, C., S. K. Ivkovich, Willam E. Harver, and Maria R. Haberfeld. "The Measure of Police Integrity." *National Institute of Justice Research in Brief* May (2000).

Knapp Commission. *Knapp Commission Report of Police Corruption.* New York: George Braziller Publishers, 1973.

Koch, Edward. *Giuliani: Nasty Man.* New York: Barricade Books, 1999.

Kocsis, R. N. *Criminal Profiling: Principles and Practice.* Totowa, NJ: Humana Press, 2006.

Kohn, A. "Straight Shooting on Gun Control." *Reason* 37 (2005): 20–25.

Laber, T. L. and B. P. Epstein. *Experiments and Practical Exercises in Blood Stain Pattern Analysis: Laboratory Manual.* Minneapolis, MN: Callin Publishing, 1983.

Lafferty, Elaine. "Glove Story II." *Time.* October 21, 1996. http://www.time.com/ time/magazine/article/0,9171,985336,00.html/.

Lambert, Patricia. *False Witness: The Real Story of Jim Garrison's Investigation and Oliver Stone's Film JFK.* New York: M. Evans and Co., 1998.

Lamborn, Leroy. "Victim Participation in the Criminal Justice Process: The Proposals for a Constitutional Amendment." *Wayne Law Review* 34 (1987): 125–220.

Lane, Mark. *Fact or Fiction? The Movie-Goer's Guide to the Film JFK. Rush to Judgment.* New York: Thunder's Mouth, 1992.

Langer, W. *The Mind of Adolf Hitler.* New York: New American Library, 1972.

Largen, M. "Grassroots Centers and National Task Forces: A History of Anti-Rape Movement," *Aegis* 32 (1981): 46–52.

Lavine, Sigmund A. *Allan Pinkerton—America's First Private Eye.* New York: Dodd, Mead and Company, 1963.

Lazer, D., ed. *DNA and the Criminal Justice System: The Technology of Justice.* Boston: MIT Press, 2004.

'Lectric Law Library. "Mark Fuhrman's 10/2/96 Plea Agreement to Felony Perjury at OJ Simpson's Criminal Trial." http://www.lectlaw.com/files/case63.htm/. http://www.law.umkc.edu/faculty/projects/ftrials/Simpson/Fuhrman.htm/.

Lee, H. C. *Cracking More Cases.* Amherst, NY: Prometheus Books, 2004.

Lee, H. C., T. Palmback, and M. T. Miller. *Henry Lee's Crime Scene Handbook.* San Diego, CA: Academic Press, 2001.

Lehmann-Haupt, Christopher. "Corralling the Brutes and Boobs of the Mob," Review of Jules Bonavolonta and Brian Duffy, *The Good Guys. The New York Times.* February 8, 1996.

Lenz, Timothy. "Conservatism in American Crime Films," *Journal of Criminal Justice and Popular Culture* 12, no. 2 (2005). http://www.albany.edu/scj/jcjpc/vol12is2/lenz.pdf/.

Leuci, Robert. *All the Centurions: A New York City Cop Remembers His Years on the Street, 1961–1981.* New York: HarperCollins, 2004.

Lexow Committee. Committee Report Official Title: Report of the Special Committee Appointed to Investigate the Police Department of the City of New York, January 18, 1895.

Liebovich, Louis W. *Richard Nixon, Watergate, and the Press.* Westport, CT: Praeger, 2003.

Linder, D. "The Trial of O. J. Simpson." 2007. http://www.law.umkc.edu/faculty/projects/ftrials/Simpson/simpson.htm/.

Lord, Walter. *The Past That Would Not Die.* New York: Harper & Row, 1965.

Los Angeles Police Department. Board of Inquiry into the Rampart Area Corruption Incident. Los Angeles: LAPD March. Executive Summary, p. 7, Chapter 10, "Police Integrity Systems," 2000.

Lott, J. *More Guns, Less Crime: Understanding Crime and Gun Control Laws.* Chicago: University of Chicago Press, 1998.

Lunardini, Christine. *Women's Rights (Social Issues in American History Series).* Phoenix, AZ: Oryx Press, 1995.

Lundman, R. J. *Police Behavior: A Sociological Perspective.* New York: Oxford University Press, 1980.

Lyman, M. D. *The Police: An Introduction.* Upper Saddle River, NJ: Prentice Hall, 1999.

Maas, Peter. *Serpico.* New York: Bantam Books, 1973.

Maas, Peter. *Underboss: Sammy the Bull Gravano's Story of Life in the Mafia.* New York: HarperCollins, 1997.

Mackay, James. *Allan Pinkerton: The First Private Eye.* Indianapolis, IN: Wiley Publishing, 1997.

Mann, R. W., W. M. Bass, and L. Meadows. "Time Since Death and Decomposition of the Human Body: Variables and Observations in Case and Experimental Field Studies." *Journal of Forensic Sciences* 35 (1990): 103–111.

Maples, W. R. *Dead Men Do Tell Tales: The Strange and Fascinating Cases of a Forensic Anthropologist.* New York: Broadway Books, 1994.

Maricopa County Sheriff's Office. Phoenix, Arizona. http://www.mcso.org/.

Marrs, Jim. *Crossfire: The Plot that Killed Kennedy.* New York: Carroll & Graf Publishers, 1989.

Martinson, Robert. "What Works: Questions and Answers about Prison Reform," *The Public Interest* 22 (1974).

Marx, G., and D. Archer. "Community Police Patrols and Vigilantism." In *Vigilante Politics,* edited by J. Rosenbaum and P. Sederberg, 129–157. Philadelphia, PA: University of Pennsylvania Press, 1976.

Marx, Gary T. *Undercover: Police Surveillance in America.* Berkeley: University of California Press, 1988.

Marx, Gary T. "Recent Developments in Undercover Policing." In *Punishment and Social Control: Essays in Honor of Sheldon Messinger*, edited by Thomas G. Blomberg and Stanley Cohen. New York: Aldyne de Gruyter, 1995.

Maslin, Janet. "Donnie Brasco: Al Pacino as Gangster, A Guy Who's Not Wise." *The New York Times*. February 28, 1997.

McCary, G., and K. Ramsland. *The Unknown Darkness*. New York: Morrow, 2003.

McCormack, R. "An Update." In *Managing Police Corruption: International Perspectives*, edited by R. H. Ward and R. McCormack. Chicago: Office of International Criminal Justice, 1987.

McGrath, Roger. *Gunfighters, Highwaymen and Vigilantes: Violence on the Frontier*. Berkeley, CA: University of California Press, 1987.

Mellen, Joan. *A Farewell to Justice: Jim Garrison, JFK's Assassination, and the Case That Should Have Changed History*. Dulles, VA: Potomac Books, 2005.

Messner, Steven, Eric Baurner, and Richard Rosenfeld. "Distrust of Government, the Vigilante Tradition, and Support for Capital Punishment." *Law and Society Review* 40 (2006): 559–590.

Miller, Eric J. "Role-Based Policing: Restraining Police Conduct Outside the Legitimate Investigative Sphere." *California Law Review* 94, no. 3 (2006).

Mollen Commission. *The City of New York Commission to Investigate Allegations of Corruption and the Anti-Corruption Procedures of the Police Department: Commission Report*. City of New York, New York, 1994.

Mollenhoff, Clark, R. *Tentacles of Power: The Story of Jimmy Hoffa*. Cleveland, OH: World Publishing, 1965.

Montaldo, Charles. "Profile of Michael Skakel." http://crime.about.com/od/murder/p/michael_skakel.htm/.

Moore, Mark. *Buy and Bust*. Lexington, MA: D.C. Heath, 1977.

Moore, P. *The Forensics Handbook: The Secrets of Crime Scene Investigation*. New York: Barnes & Noble, 2004.

Moore, Robin. *The French Connection: A True Account of Cops, Narcotics, and International Conspiracy*. Guilford, CT: Lyons Press, 2003 [1969], 309.

Morn, Frank. *The Eye That Never Sleeps: A History of the Pinkerton National Detective Agency*. Bloomington, IN: Indiana University Press, 1982.

Morn, Frank. *Academic Politics and the History of Criminal Justice Education*. Westport, CT: Greenwood Press, 1995.

Morris, W. R. *The Twelfth of August: The Story of Buford Pusser*. Nashville, TN: Aurora Publishing, 1971.

Morton, J. *Bent Coppers: A Survey of Police Corruption*. New York: London: Little Brown and Company, 1993.

Mountain State University: Nixon Era Center. "The Nixon Era Times." Mountain State University. http://www.watergate.com.

Mueller, Robert S. Testimony of FBI Director, United States Congress, House of Representatives, Committee on the Judiciary, July 26, 2007.

Murano, Vincent. *Cop Hunter*. New York: Simon & Schuster, 1990.

Murphy, Patrick V., and Thomas Gordon Plate. *Commissioner: A View from the Top of American Law Enforcement*. New York: Simon & Schuster, 1977.

Nafte, M. *Flesh and Bone: An Introduction to Forensic Anthropology*. Durham, NC: Academic Press, 2000.

Nash, Jay Robert. *Citizen Hoover.* Chicago: Nelson Hall, 1972.

Navasky, Victor S. *Kennedy Justice.* New York: Atheneum, 1971.

Nelson, Michael. "Evaluating the Presidency." In *The Presidency and the Political System*, edited by Michael Nelson. Washington, D.C.: CQ Press, 2006.

Neustadt, Richard E. *Presidential Power and the Modern Presidents: The Politics of Leadership from Roosevelt to Reagan.* New York: Free Press, 1991.

Newburn, T. *Understanding and Preventing Police Corruption: Lessons From the Literature.* Police Research Series Paper 110, Policing and Reducing Crime Unit; Research, Development and Statistics Directorate; London, 2003.

Newfield, Jack. *Robert Kennedy: A Memoir.* New York: Dutton, 1969.

Newfield, Jack. *The Full Rudy: The Man, the Myth, the Mania.* New York: Thunder's Mouth Press/Nation Books, 2002.

NewsMax.Com. "Mark Fuhrman Probing Schiavo Case." http://www.newsmax.com/archives/ic/2005/5/6/230418.shtml/.

Newton, Michael. *The Ku Klux Klan: History, Organization, Language, Influence and Activities of America's Most Notorious Secret Society.* Jefferson, NC: McFarland and Company, 2006.

New York State Organized Crime Task Force. *Corruption and Racketeering in the New York City Construction Industry.* New York: New York University Press, 1990.

Norris, J. *Serial Killers.* London: Arrow Publications, 1988.

O'Brien, Lawrence F. *No Final Victories: A Life in Politics—from John F. Kennedy to Watergate.* Garden City, NY: Doubleday, 1974.

O'Conner, Richard. *Wild Bill Hickok.* New York: Doubleday and Company, 1959.

O'Donnell, Kenneth P., and David F. Powers, with Joseph McCarthy. *Johnny, We Hardly Knew Ye: Memories of John Fitzgerald Kennedy.* Boston: Little, Brown, and Co., 1972.

Oliver, Willard M., and James F. Hilgenberg, Jr. "A History of Crime and Justice in America." Boston, MA: Allyn & Bacon, 2006.

O'Malley, Timothy J. "Managing for Ethics." *FBI Law Enforcement Bulletin* 66, no. 4 (1997): 20–25.

One People's Project. "Mark Fuhrman." http://www.onepeoplesproject.com/index.php?option=content&task=view&id=83&Itemid=29/.

Opland, Stacey. 2000. *Pink Underwear Reveal Prison Escapee.* Coeur d'Alene, ID: The Backup Training Corporation. http://www.thebackup.com/archives_newsdetail.asp?id=753/.

Owen, D. *Hidden Evidence: Forty True Crimes and How Forensic Science Helped Solve Them.* Willowdale, Ontario, Canada: Firefly Books, 2000.

Palermo, G. B., and R. N. Kocsis. *Offender Profiling: An Introduction to the Socio-psychological Analysis of Violent Crime.* Springfield, IL: Charles C. Thomas, 2005.

Parker, Alfred E. *Crime Fighter: August Vollmer.* New York: The Macmillan Company, 1961.

Parker, Alfred E. *The Berkeley Police Story.* Springfield, IL: Charles C. Thomas Publisher, 1972.

Pedahzur, Ami, and Arie Perliger. "The Causes of Vigilante Political Violence: The Case of Jewish Settlers." *Civil Wars* 6 (2003): 9–30.

Pennell, Susan, Christine Curtis, Joel Henderson, and Jeff Taxman. "Guardian Angels: A Unique Approach to Crime Prevention." *Crime & Delinquency* 35 (1989): 378–400.

Perry, Frank L. "Repairing Broken Windows." *FBI Law Enforcement Bulletin* 70, no. 2 (2001): 23–26.

Peterson, Roger S. "Wyatt Earp." *American History* 29, no. 3 (1994): 54–62.

Pinizzotto, A. J. "Forensic Psychology: Criminal Personality Profiling." *Journal of Police Science and Administration* 12, no. 1 (1984): 32–40.

Pinizzotto, A. J., and N. J. Finkel. "Criminal Personality Profiling: An Outcome and Process Study." *Law and Human Behavior* 14 (1990): 215–233.

Pistone, Joseph. Testimony of Joseph D. Pistone, Former Special Agent, Federal Bureau of Investigation, before the U.S. Senate, Permanent Subcommittee on Investigations, Committee on Governmental Affairs, 100th Congress, April 21. Printed in committee report, S. HRG. 100–906, "Organized Crime: 25 Years After Valachi," 1988.

Pistone, Joseph D., and Charles Brandt. *The Way of the Wiseguy: True Stories from the FBI's Most Famous Undercover Agent.* Philadelphia: Running Press, 2004.

Pistone, Joe, and Charles Brandt. *Donnie Brasco: Unfinished Business.* Philadelphia: Running Press, 2007.

Pistone, Joseph D., with Richard Woodley. *Donnie Brasco: My Undercover Life in the Mafia.* New York: NAL Books, 1987.

Pollock, Joycelyn M. *Ethical Dilemmas and Decisions in Criminal Justice.* 5th ed. Belmont, CA: Thompson Wadsworth, 2007.

Polner, Robert, ed. *America's Mayor: The Hidden History of Rudy Giuliani's New York.* New York: Soft Skull Press, 2005.

President's Commission on Law Enforcement and Administration of Justice. Task Force on Organized Crime. *Task Force Report: Organized Crime.* Washington, D.C.: U.S. Government Printing Office, 1967.

Proctor, Ben. *Just One Riot: Texas Rangers in the 20th Century.* Austin, TX: Eakin Press, 1991.

Punch, M. *Conduct Unbecoming: The Social Construction of Police Deviance and Control.* New York: Methuen, 1985.

Raab, Selwyn. "Donnie Brasco: My Undercover Life in the Mafia. Book Reviews." *Washington Monthly.* June 1988.

Rachal, Patricia. *Federal Narcotics Enforcement: Reorganization and Reform.* Boston: Auburn House Publishing Company, 1982.

Ramsland, K. *Beating the Devil's Game: A History of Forensic Science and Criminal Investigation.* New York: Berkley Books, 2007.

Ramsland, K. "Profile of Dr. Bill Bass, Founder of the Body Farm." 2007. http://www.crimelibrary.com/criminal_mind/forensics/bill_bass/.

Raney, Arthur, and Bryant Jennings. "Moral Judgment and Crime Drama: An Integrated Theory of Enjoyment," *Journal of Communication* 52 (2002): 402–415.

Reaves, Jessica. "The Murder Case That Just Wouldn't Go Away." *Time.* January 19, 2000. http://www.time.com/time/nation/article/0,8599,37804,00.html/.

Reichs, K. J., and W. M. Bass. *Forensic Osteology: Advances in the Identification of Human Remains.* Springfield, IL: Charles C. Thomas, 1998.

Ressler, R. K., and A. W. Burgess. "Crime scene and profile characteristics of organized and disorganized murderers." *FBI Law Enforcement Bulletin* 18 (1985): 7–15.

Ressler, R. K., and A. W. Burgess. "Violent Crime: The Men Who Murdered." *FBI Law Enforcement Bulletin* 2 (1985): 32–39.

Ressler, R. K., and T. Shachtman. *Whoever Fights Monsters*. London: Simon & Schuster, 1992.

Reuss-Ianni, Elizabeth. *Two Cultures of Policing: Street Cops and Management Cops*. New Brunswick and London: Transaction Publishers, 1983.

Reuter, Peter H., Robert MacCoun, Patrick Murphy, Allan Abrahamse, and B. Simon. *Money From Crime: A Study of the Economics of Drug Dealing in Washington, D.C.* Santa Monica, CA: Rand Corporation, 1990.

Rhodes, Robert P. *Organized Crime: Crime Control vs. Civil Liberties*. New York: Random House, 1984.

Ricciuti, E. *Forensics*. New York: Collins, 2007.

Risinger, D. M., and J. L. Loop. "Three Card Monte, Monty Hall, Modus Operandi and 'Offender Profiling': Some Lessons of Modern Cognitive Science for the Law of Evidence." *Cardozo Law Review* 24 (2002): 193–185.

Roach, Kent. *Due Process and Victim's Rights: The New Law and Politics of Criminal Justice*. Toronto, Canada: University of Toronto Press, 1999.

Roach, M. *Stiff: The Curious Lives of Human Cadavers*. New York: W. W. Norton & Company, 2003.

Rodriguez, W. C., and W. M. Bass. "Insect Activity and Its Relationship to Decay Rates of Human Cadavers in East Tennessee." *Journal of Forensic Sciences* 28 (1983): 423–432.

Rodriguez, W. C., and W. M. Bass. "Decomposition of Buried Bodies and Methods That May Aid in Their Location." *Journal of Forensic Sciences* 30 (1985): 836–852.

Rosa, Joseph G. *The Gunfighter: Man or Myth?* Norman: University of Oklahoma Press, 1969.

Rosenbaum, Dennis. "The Theory and Research Behind Neighborhood Watch: Is It a Sound Fear and Crime Reduction Strategy?" *Crime & Delinquency* 33 (1987): 103–124.

Rosenberg, Philip, and Sonny Grosso. *Point Blank*. New York: Grosset & Dunlap, 1978.

Rosenbloom, David H., and Robert S. Kravchuck. *Public Administration: Understanding Management, Politics, and Law in the Public Sector*. New York: McGraw-Hill, 2005.

Rotella, Carlo. *Good with Their Hands: Boxers, Bluesmen, and Other Characters from the Rust Belt*. Berkeley, CA: University of California Press, 2002.

Roth, Mitchel P. *Crime and Punishment: A History of the Criminal Justice System*. Belmont, CA: Wadsworth, 2005.

Rothwell, Gary R., and Norman J. Baldwin. "Ethical Climate Theory, Whistleblowing, and the Code of Silence in Police Agencies in the State of Georgia." *Journal of Business Ethics* 70, no. 4 (2007).

Royce, Josiah. *California, from the Conquest in 1846 to the Second Vigilance Committee in San Francisco: A Study of American Character*. Boston, MA: Houghton, 1948.

Ruiz, Jim, and Christine Bono. "At What Price a 'Freebie'?" *Criminal Justice Ethics* 23, no. 1 (2004/2005): 44–54.

Rumbelow, D. *The Complete Jack the Ripper.* London: Penguin, 1988.

Savage, Kerry. "At 25, the Guardian Angels are Now on Global Patrol," Columbia News Service. 2004. http://www.jrn.columbia.edu/studentwork/cns/2004-02-16/392.asp/.

Schlesinger, Arthur M., Jr. *Robert Kennedy and His Times.* Boston: Houghton Mifflin Company, 1978.

Shean, B. S., L. Messinger, and M. Papworth. "Observations of Differential Decomposition on Sun Exposed vs. Shaded Pig Carrion in Coastal Washington State." *Journal of Forensic Sciences* 38 (1993):938–949.

Shelley, Louise. "The Nexus of Organized International Criminals and Terrorism." *International Annals of Criminology* 20, no. 1/2 (2002):85–92.

Shepard, Alicia C. *Woodward and Bernstein: Life in the Shadow of Watergate.* New York: John Wiley & Sons, 2007.

Sherman, L. W. "The Sociology and the Social Reform of the American Police: 1950–1973." *Journal of Police Science and Administration II* 2 (1974): 255–262.

Sherman, L. W. "Becoming Bent: Moral Careers of Corrupt Policemen." In *Moral Issues in Police Work*, edited by F. Elliston and M. Feldberg, 250–267. Totowa, NJ: Rowman & Littlefield, 1985.

Sherman, Lawrence. "From Initial Deterrence to Long Term Escalation: Short Custody Arrest for Poverty Ghetto Domestic Violence." *Criminology* 29 (1991): 821–850.

Shichor, David. "Three Strikes as Public Policy: The Convergence of the New Penology and the McDonaldization of Punishment." *Crime & Delinquency* 43, no. 4 (1997): 470–492.

Shotland, L. "Spontaneous Vigilantism: A Bystander Response to Criminal Behavior." In *Vigilante Politics,* edited by J. Rosenbaum and P. Sederberg, 30–44. Philadephia, PA: University of Pennsylvania Press, 1976.

Siegel, Fred. *The Prince of the City: Giuliani, New York and the Genius of American Life.* San Francisco: Encounter Books, 2005.

Sigler, Robert, and Timothy Dees. "Public Perception of Petty Corruption in Law Enforcement." *Journal of Police Science and Administration* 14 (1988).

Skolnick, Jerome H., and James J. Fyfe. *Above the Law: Police and the Excessive Use of Force.* New York: Free Press, 1993.

Smalley, Suzanne. "Guardian Angels Launch City Patrol, Expand Across U.S." *The Boston Globe.* March 31, 2007. http://www.boston.com/news/local/massachusetts/articles/2007/03/31/guardian_angels/.

Smith, Dwight C., Jr., and Ralph F. Salerno. "The Use of Strategies in Organized Crime Control." *The Journal of Criminal Law, Criminology, and Police Science* 61, no. 1 (1970): 101–111.

Smith, Kevin B., Christopher W. Larimer, Levente Littvay, and John R. Hibbing. "Evolutionary Theory and Political Leadership: Why Certain People Do Not Trust Decision-Makers." *Journal of Politics* 69, May (2007): 285–299.

Smith, Richard Norton. *Thomas E. Dewey and His Times. The First Full Scale Biography of the Maker of the Modern Republican Party.* New York: Simon and & Schuster, 1982.

Smothers, Ronald, and Jason George. "Former Officer In Newark Pleads Guilty To Corruption." *New York Times*, 154, no. 52982, p. B1-B2, Op. 1c, September 24, 2004.

Span, Paula. "The FBI's Veiled Threat: Joseph Pistone Spent Six Years Inside the Mafia and Lived to Tell the Tale." *Washington Post*, February 28, 1997.

Spitzer, Robert J. "Clinton's Impeachment Will Have Few Consequences for the Presidency." *PS: Political Science and Politics* 32 (1999): 541–545.

Steel, Ronald. *In Love with Night: The American Romance with Robert Kennedy.* New York: Simon & Schuster, 2000.

Stephens, Norman. "Ethics Do Not Begin When You Pin on the Badge." *FBI Law Enforcement Bulletin* 75, no. 11 (2006): 22–23.

Stewart, T. D. *Essentials of Forensic Anthropology.* Springfield, IL: Charles C. Thomas, 1979.

Stoddard, E. R. "The Informal 'Code' of Police Deviancy: A Group Approach to Blue-Coat Crime." *Journal of Criminal Law, Criminology and Police Science* 59 (1968): 210–213.

Stohlberg, Mary. *Fighting Organized Crime Politics: Justice and the Legacy of Thomas E. Dewey.* Boston: Northeastern University Press, 1995.

Stokes, P. "Organised Against Crime: The Work of Communities Organised for a Greater Bristol (COGB) 1990–1994." In *Preventing Crime and Disorder: Targeting Strategies and Responsibilities* (Cambridge Cropwood Series), edited by T. Bennett. Cambridge: University of Cambridge, Institute of Criminology, 1996.

Stubbs, J. "Battered Women's Syndrome: An Advance for Women or Further Evidence of the Legal System's Inability to Comprehend Women's Experience?" *Current Issues in Criminal Justice* 3 (1991): 267–270.

Summers, Anthony. *Conspiracy.* New York: Paragon House, 1989.

Summers, Anthony. *Official and Confidential: The Secret Life of J. Edgar Hoover.* New York: Pocket Books, 1993.

Sundt, Jody L., Francis T. Cullen, Brandon K. Applegate, and Michael G. Turner. "The Tenacity of the Rehabilitative Ideal Revisted: Have Attitudes toward Offender Treatment Changed?" *Criminal Justice and Behavior* 25, no. 4 (1998): 426–442.

Surette, R. *Media, Crime and Criminal Justice: Images and realities.* Pacific Grove, CA: Brooks/Cole Publishing Company, 1992.

Sykes, Gary. "The Functional Nature of Police Reform: The 'Myth' of Controlling the Police." *Justice Quarterly* 2 (1985):52–65.

Sykes, Gresham M., and David Matza. "Techniques of Neutralization: A Theory of Delinquency." *American Sociological Review* 22 (1957): 664–670.

Texas State University. "Forensic Anthropology Center at Texas State (FACTS)." February 12, 2008, http://www.txstate.edu/anthropology/facts/.

Theoharis, Athan. *Spying on Americans: Political Surveillance from Hoover to the Huston Plan.* Philadelphia: Temple University Press, 1978.

Theoharis, Athan, and John Stuart Cox. *The Boss: J. Edgar Hoover and the Great American Inquisition.* Philadelphia: Temple University Press, 1988.

Thomas, Evan. *Robert Kennedy: His Life.* New York: Simon & Schuster, 2000.

Thomas, P. *Talking Bones: The Science of Forensic Anthropology.* New York: Facts On File, 1995.

Thompson, D. "Above the Law?" *Law and Order* 49, January (2001): 1.

Toledano, Ralph de. 1973. *J. Edgar Hoover: the Man in his Time.* New Rochelle, NY: Arlington House.

Turco, R. N. "Psychological Profiling." *International Journal of Offender Therapy & Comparative Criminology* 34 (1990): 147–154.

Tyler, T. R., and C. J. Wakslak. "Profiling and Police Legitimacy: Procedural Justice Attributions of Motive and Acceptance of Police Authority." *Criminology* 42, no. 2 (2004): 253–281.

Ubelaker, D., and Scammell, H. *Bones: A Forensic Detective's Casebook.* Lanham, MD: M. Evans, 2006.

U.S. House of Representatives. *U.S.S. Iowa Tragedy: An Investigative Failure.* Report of the investigations subcommittee and the Defense Policy Panel of the Committee on Armed Services, House of Representatives, 101st Congress, 2nd Session, 1990.

United States Marshal Home Page. www:usmarshals.gov/.

Utley, Robert. *Lone Star Justice: The First Century of the Texas Rangers.* New York: Oxford University Press, 2002.

Utley, Robert M. "Tales of the Texas Rangers." *American Heritage* 53, no. 3 (2002): 40–47.

Van Biema, David. "A Crime in the Clan." *Time.* January 31, 2000. http://www.time.com/time/magazine/article/0,9171,995999,00.html/.

Van Wart, Montgomery. *Changing Public Sector Values.* New York: Garland Publishing, 1998.

Vartabedian, Ralph, Richard A Serrano, and Richard Marosi. "The Long, Crooked Line: Rise in Bribery Tests Integrity of U.S. Border." *Los Angeles Times,* Main News; National Desk; Part A. August 23, 2006.

The Village Voice. "Serpico: 'Nothing Has Changed,' Cops in Danger from Other Cops." 1999. www.villagevoice.com/news#CDD95/.

Vollmer, August. *The Police and Modern Society.* Berkeley, CA: University of California Press, 1936.

Vollmer, August. *The Criminal.* Brooklyn, NY: Foundation Press, 1949.

Vollmer, August, and Alfred E. Parker. *Crime, Crooks, & Cops.* New York: Funk & Wagnalls, 1937.

Vorpagel, R. E., and Harrington, J. *Profiles in Murder.* New York: Plenum, 1998.

Walker, Samuel. *A Critical History of Police Reform: The Emergence of Professionalism.* Lexington, MA: Lexington Books, 1977.

Wallance, Gregory. *Papa's Game.* New York: Rawson, Wade Publishers, 1981.

Walsh, James. "The Lessons of the Trial." *Time.* October 16, 1995. http://www.time.com/time/magazine/article/0,9171,983570,00.html/.

Walsh, John, with Philip Lerman. *No Mercy: The Host of America's Most Wanted Hunts the Worst Criminals in Our Time—in Shattering True Crime Cases.* New York: Pocket Books, 1998.

Walsh, John, with Philip Lerman. *Public Enemies: The Host of America's Most Wanted Targets the Nation's Most Notorious Criminals.* New York: Pocket Books, 2001.

Walsh, John, and Susan Schindehette. *Tears of Rage: From Grieving Father to Crusader for justice: the Untold Story of Adam Walsh.* New York: Pocket Books, 1997.

"Watergate Chronology." *The Washington Post.* http://www.washingtonpost.com/wp-srv/onpolitics/watergate/chronology.htm/.

Webb, Walter Prescott. *The Texas Rangers: A Century of Frontier Defense*. Boston: Houghton Mifflin Company, 1935.

Weisburd, David. "Vigilantism as Community Social Control: Developing a Quantitative Criminological Model." *Journal of Quantitative Criminology* 4 (1988): 137–153.

Weisburd, David, and Rosann Greenspan. *Police Attitudes Toward Abuse of Authority: Findings From a National Study*. Washington, D.C.: National Institute of Justice, 2000.

Weiss, Harold J., Jr. "The Texas Rangers Revisited: Old Themes and New Viewpoints." *Southwestern Historical Quarterly* 97, no. 4 (1994); 620–640.

Western Carolina University. "Western Carolina Human Identification Laboratory (WCHIL)." 2007. http://www.wcu.edu/.

Westley, W. *Violence and the Police*. Cambridge, MA: MIT Press, 1970.

Westmarland, Louis. "Police Ethics and Integrity: Breaking the Blue Code of Silence." *Policing and Society* 15, no. 2 (2005): 145–165.

Whittington-Egan, R. *A Casebook on Jack the Ripper*. London: Wiley, 1975.

Wildavsky, Aaron. *The Beleaguered Presidency*. New Brunswick, NJ: Transaction Publishers, 2001.

Wilde, James. "In New York: The Magnificent Thirteen." *Time*. May 7, 1979. http://www.time.com/time/magazine/article/0,9171,920294-1,00.html/.

Wilkins, Frederick. "The Texas Rangers: Birth and Legend." *Wild West* 11, no. 2 (1998): 42–48.

Williams, Kate. "Caught between a Rock and a Hard Place: Police Experiences with the Legitimacy of Street Watch Partnerships." *The Howard Journal* 44 (2005): 527–537.

Wilson, James Q. *The Investigators: Managing FBI and Narcotics Agents*. New York: Basic Books, 1978.

Wilson, James Q., and George Kelling. "Broken Windows: The Police and Neighborhood Safety." *Atlantic Monthly*. March 1982. http://www.theatlantic.com/doc/198203/broken-windows.

Wilson, O. W. "August Vollmer." *The Journal of Criminal Law, Criminology, and Police Science* 44, no. 1 (1953): 91–103.

Wolff, Craig. "Look Who's Talking: Defending Himself, Mark Fuhrman Returns to the Scene of the Crime." *The New York Times*. March 23, 1997. http://www.nytimes.com/books/97/03/23/reviews/970323.23wolfft.html/.

Wolfgang, M. E., and N. A. Weiner, eds. *Criminal Violence*. Thousand Oaks, CA: Sage, 1982.

Woodward, Bob. *Shadow: Five Presidents and the Legacy of Watergate*. New York: Touchstone, 1999.

Woodward, Bob. *Bush at War*. New York: Simon & Shuster, 2003.

Woodward, Bob. *Plan of Attack*. New York: Simon & Shuster, 2004.

Woodward, Bob. *The Secret Man: The Story of Watergate's Deep Throat*. New York: Simon & Shuster, 2005.

Woodward, Bob. *State of Denial: Bush at War, Part III*. New York: Simon & Shuster, 2006.

Woodward, Bob, and Carl Bernstein. "GOP Security Aide Among Five Arrested in Bugging Affair." *The Washington Post*. June 19, 1972. http://www.washingtonpost.com/wp-dyn/content/article/2002/05/31/AR2005111001228.html/.

Woodward, Bob, and Carl Bernstein. "Break-In Memo Sent to Ehrlichman." *The Washington Post*. June 13, 1973. http://www.washingtonpost.com/wp-dyn/content/article/2002/05/31/AR2005112200793.html/.

Woodward, Bob, and Carl Bernstein. "Nixon Debated Paying Blackmail, Clemency." *The Washington Post*. May 1, 1974. http://www.washingtonpost.com/wp-dyn/content/article/2002/05/31/AR2005112200804.html/.

Woodward, Bob, and Carl Bernstein. *The Final Days*. New York: Simon & Schuster, 1976.

Young, Andrew. *An Easy Burden: The Civil Rights Movement and the Transformation of America*. Oxford, UK: HarperCollins Publishers, 1996.

About the Editor and the Contributors

THE EDITOR

Jeffrey B. Bumgarner, PhD, is an associate professor of Political Science and Law Enforcement at Minnesota State University, Mankato, MN. He earned a BA in political science from the University of Illinois (Champaign-Urbana), an MAPA in public administration from Northern Illinois University, and a PhD in training and organization development from the University of Minnesota. Dr. Bumgarner has several years of experience in federal and local law enforcement, as well as in academe. He is the author of *Profiling and Criminal Justice in America* (2004), *Federal Agents: The Growth of Federal Law Enforcement in America* (2006), *Emergency Management: A Reference Handbook* (2008), and several articles and book chapters relating to public safety and homeland security.

CONTRIBUTORS

Amanda L. Belshaw is a co-owner of Belshaw & Associates Investigations in Houston, Texas. A native Texan, Amanda received her BA degree from University of Houston. Ms. Belshaw has extensive experience in the area of child abuse investigations and has consulted on numerous criminal and civil cases involving child physical and sexual abuse.

Scott H. Belshaw is currently a PhD student at Prairie View A&M University pursuing a PhD in Juvenile Justice (The only program of its kind in the country). Mr. Belshaw has served as a probation officer and gang intelligence officer for the Harris County Probation Department. For the past ten years, Mr. Belshaw has owned and operated Belshaw & Associates Investigations and Consulting, a private investigations firm specializing in criminal defense investigations. His research interests include juvenile delinquency and prevention, death penalty and sentencing related matters. Mr. Belshaw has published articles on juvenile mentoring and gender issues in various education and criminal justice journals.

Clairissa Breen earned her BA degree in political science from St. John Fisher College in Rochester, New York, and her Master's degree in criminal justice at Buffalo State College, New York. She is completing her PhD at Temple University, Philadelphia, Pennsylvania.

Ronald Burns is an Associate Professor and Director of the Criminal Justice Program at Texas Christian University. He is the author or editor of five books and over thirty-five journal articles and book chapters. His research interests include criminal case processing, corporate deviance, environmental crimes, and policing issues. Recent publications include articles in the *Journal of Criminal Justice Education*, the *Journal of Criminal Justice*, and *Crime and Delinquency*.

Elizabeth Quinn DeValve is an Assistant Professor in the Department of Criminal Justice at Fayetteville State University. Her research interests include crime victims and the criminal justice system, repeat victimization, and females and criminal justice. She has published articles and book chapters on victimization experiences, female wardens, drug-facilitated sexual assault, and police satisfaction with case handling. Her publications can be found in journals including *Applied Psychology in Criminal Justice* and *The Prison Journal*.

John Dombrink is a professor in the Department of Criminology, Law & Society in the School of Social Ecology at the University of California, Irvine. He has authored several articles on policing strategies and the use of RICO prosecution strategies against organized crime, as well as articles on nontraditional and global organized crime. He is the author of several articles on gambling in America and the co-author of a book about gambling legalization, *The Last Resort: Success and Failure in Campaigns for Casinos* (1990, with William N. Thompson). With Daniel Hillyard, he is the author of *Dying Right: The Death With Dignity Movement* (2001) and *Sin No More: From Abortion to Stem Cells--Crime, Law, and Morality in America*. (NYU Press, 2007).

Camille Gibson is a nationally certified psychotherapist. She has been a faculty member at Prairie View A & M University in the College of Juvenile Justice and Psychology since 2000. Her research interests include schools and delinquency, Jamaican organized crime, juvenile sex offending, child abuse, law enforcement and juvenile interactions. She is the author of the book *Being Real: Student-Teacher Interactions and African American Male Delinquency* (2002) and co-author of a soon to be released book with Donna Vandiver, *Juvenile Sex Offenders: What the Public Needs to Know.* Dr. Gibson is a recent past president of the Southwestern Association of Criminal Justice in which capacity she represented several criminal justice educators and researchers in Texas, Oklahoma, Arizona, Arkansas, New Mexico, and Colorado. She worked and studied in New York City during the Giuliani years at City University of New York's John Jay College of Criminal Justice from 1994 to 2000.

J. Scott Granberg-Rademacker is an Assistant Professor of Political Science at Minnesota State University, Mankato. He holds a PhD in Political Science from the University of Nebraska-Lincoln. His research interests include Bayesian methodology, missing data problems, and neural network theory. His recently published articles have appeared in *Political Research Quarterly, State Politics and Policy Quarterly, The Philippine Statistician,* and *The Southwest Journal of Criminal Justice.*

Richard N. Kocsis, PhD, is a forensic psychologist and the author, co-author, or editor of dozens of books, articles, and book chapters relating to criminal profiling, serial violent offenders, and the criminal investigation of serial violent crime. He has also held numerous academic positions in the areas of forensic psychology and criminology. In 2000, he was awarded the Australian Museum's *Eureka* prize for critical thinking in recognition of his scholarly research in the area of criminal profiling.

Christopher Larimer is Assistant Professor of Political Science at the University of Northern Iowa. He teaches and researches in the areas of public administration, state politics, and political behavior.

Ellen Leichtman is an Asstistant Professor of Criminal Justice at Eastern Kentucky University. She has a PhD from Brown University in Music (Ethnomusicology), and is ABD and has an MA from Temple University in Criminal Justice. She has published in *Critical Criminology, Postmodern Criminology, The Critical Criminologist,* and *The Latin American Music Review.* She is the editor of and contributor to *To the Four Corners: A Festschrift in Honor of Rose Brandel.*

Janet E. McClellan received her PhD from Northcentral University, in Prescott, AZ. She received her Master's Degree in Public Administration from the University of Dayton (OH) and her Bachelors Degree from Park University, Parkville, MO. Her research focuses on sexualized violence, in particular lust murder. Among her publications are the following: "Sexual (Lust) Homicide: Definitional Constructs, Dynamics, and Investigative

Considerations" in *Serial Murder and the Psychology of Violent Crimes* (Chapter 13); "Delivery Drivers and Long-Haul Truckers: Traveling Serial Murderers" in the *Journal of Applied Security Research*; "Childhood Animal Abuse and Future Interpersonal Violence: A Review of Linkages" in the *Journal of Applied Security Research*; and "Urban Homicide: An Analysis of Verbal Models and Current Research" in *Transactions*. McClellan has over 20 years of criminal justice agency experience and joined the University of Alaska—Fairbanks (UAF) Justice Department faculty in the fall of 2007.

Willard M. Oliver is an associate professor of Criminal Justice at Sam Houston State University, Huntsville, Texas. He is currently working on a biography of August Vollmer.

Kilby Raptopoulos is a former probation officer who is now a graduate assistant in the Criminal Justice Department at the University of Arkansas, Little Rock. She has since taught Introduction to Criminal Justice at the undergraduate level and presented several professional presentations at the meetings of the Academy of Criminal Justice Sciences. She also recently served on the Student Affairs Committee of ACJS. Following her graduate assistantship, Kilby will be taking over as Project Coordinator for a joint Juvenile Justice Center/Arkansas Division of Youth Services Grant that provides serious and violent juvenile offenders with college mentors. Publications include a forthcoming article in *Journal of Criminal Justice Education* (with Jeff Walker) and a book review in *Criminal Justice Review*.

Jacob Rodriguez is an assistant professor with the Department of Criminology and Criminal Justice. He received his PhD in Juvenile Justice from Prairie View A&M University in 2007. John's research interests include transnationalism, gangs, and Latinos in the criminal justice system.

Brion Sever is an associate professor of criminal justice at Monmouth University, West Long Branch, New Jersey. He earned his Master's and PhD in criminology and criminal justice from Florida State University. His research interests include criminal justice public policy, race and the criminal justice system, and criminal justice ethics.

Edward J. Schauer was instrumental in the recent development of the Texas Juvenile Crime Prevention Center, the College of Juvenile Justice and Psychology, and the first doctoral program in juvenile justice, all at Prairie View A&M University. His research interests lie in the areas of homicide investigation, sex trafficking and prostitution, minority student academic success, and applied theatre. He received his PhD from Sam Houston State University and teaches criminology, ethics, women and criminal justice, and critical thinking.

Kelli Stevens has a Bachelor's degree in Psychology and a Master's in Criminology and Criminal Justice. She has thirteen years experience in the field of criminal justice, ten of those serving as an adult probation officer in Texas. Mrs. Stevens has been a Court Officer, Specialized Substance Abuse Officer, Academy Training Officer, and a Specialized Sex Offender Officer. She is now the supervisor for the Tarrant County CSCD Training Academy and formerly the supervisor over the Sex Offender Unit. She is a member of the Tarrant County CSCD Search & Seizure team and serves as a Team Leader. Mrs. Stevens also has seven years experience teaching at the University level and has several publications including numerous on-line articles and a Criminal Investigations Interactive CD-ROM. She is a member of the Tarrant County Council Sexual Abuse Advisory Council and has served as site coordinator for the Council on Sex Offender Treatment in the state of Texas in collecting data for a legislative-mandated study to review the validity of risk levels in relation to community notification and sex offender registration.

Morris A. Taylor is an Associate Professor in the Department of Public Administration and Policy Analysis at Southern Illinois University, Edwardsville Illinois. He received his PhD in Public Policy Analysis from Saint Louis University. He currently teaches courses in Public Law, Policy Analysis, Public Safety Administration and Pro-seminar in Public Administration. His research focuses on social jurisprudence, police organizations, and ethics. During 2004-2005, he served as the *Ira Glasser Racial Justice Fellow* for the American Civil Liberties Union of Eastern Missouri investigating issues of racial profiling and police misconduct. He also served as a patrol officer with both the City of St. Louis, Missouri and St. Louis County Police departments.

Cécile Van De Voorde, LL.M., Ph.D. is an assistant professor of criminal justice at John Jay College, City University of New York. She holds a Master's in criminology from Indiana State University, a PhD in criminology from the University of South Florida, and an LL.M. from the Grenoble School of Law, Université Pierre Mendès France, Grenoble, France. She has conducted research and published extensively in the area of political violence—especially terrorism and genocide.

Jeffery T. Walker is a professor of Criminal Justice and Criminology in the Department of Criminal Justice at the University of Arkansas, Little Rock. Dr. Walker also holds joint appointments with the University of Arkansas, Fayetteville and the University of Arkansas Medical School. Dr. Walker has written six books, over thirty journal articles and book chapters, seventeen technical reports, and delivered over seventy professional papers and presentations. He has obtained over $9 million in grants from the Department of

Justice, National Institute of Drug Abuse, and others. His areas of interest are social/environmental factors of crime and the study of non-linear dynamics as they relate to crime. He is the immediate past president of the Academy of Criminal Justice Sciences. Editorial experience includes service as Editor of the *Journal of Criminal Justice Education*, Editor in Chief of *Journal of Critical Criminology*, and Editor of *Crime Patterns and Analysis*. Previous publications include articles in *Justice Quarterly, Journal of Quantitative Criminology*, and *Journal of Criminal Justice Education*, and the books *Leading Cases in Law Enforcement* (7th Edition), *Statistics in Criminal Justice and Criminology: Analysis and Interpretation* (3nd Edition) and *Myths in Crime and Justice*.

Elvira M White, JD/PhD, is an assistant professor in criminal justice at Fayetteville State University. She practiced criminal law for twenty years before entering university teaching full-time in 1999. White is the author of several book chapters including co-authoring "African American PhD women in criminal justice higher education: equal impact or the myth of equality," in *It's a Crime: Women & Justice*. She more recently authored Youth Gangs and The W. Haywood Burns Institute for the Encyclopedia of Race and Crime. White is currently the first and only person in the nation with a JD in conjunction with a PhD in juvenile justice. Her research includes juvenile justice issues, criminological theory, sentencing and dispositional outcome, ethical and theoretical orientations in sentencing, disproportionate minority confinement, and criminal justice education.

Tusty Zohra is a PhD student at the University of Nebraska at Omaha. She has a Bachelors of Arts in Criminal Justice and Philosophy from the University of Arkansas at Little Rock. She received Master's degree in Criminal justice also from the University of Arkansas at Little Rock. Her areas of interest consist of theory, statistics, drugs, gangs, and international studies. Zohra has been in involved in various research projects such as incarcerated parents and their children, hazing in universities, Weber's Rational-Formal Law, and Stigmata. Zohra plans to finish her education and become a professor, where her goal is to excel in her teaching and research abilities.

Index